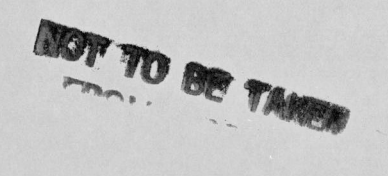

REFERENCE

OUTSTANDING AMERICAN ILLUSTRATORS TODAY
イラストレーションU.S.A.

Distributed in the U.S.A. and Canada by
G. K. Hall & Co.
70 Lincoln Street
Boston, MA 02111
ISBN in the U.S.A. and Canada 0-8161-8749-5

Coordinator	Satoru Fujii & Marshall Arisman
Editor	Satoru Fujii
Publisher	Graphic-sha Publishing Co., Ltd.
Responsible in publication	Toshiro Kuze
Production Manager	Yoshimasa Okamoto
Editorial Assistant	Rico Samejima
Layout & Design	Kenichi Yanagawa
Cover & title page illustration	Ikuo Takeda
Typesetting	Hagiwara Printing Co., Ltd. HIPAL
Printing & Binding	Toppan Printing Co., Ltd.

First Publishing, 1984
© copyright 1984 by
Graphic-sha Publishing Co., Ltd.
1-9-12, Kudan-Kita, Chiyoda-Ku,
Tokyo 102, Japan
Tel: (03) 263-4318

Printed in Japan
ISBN 0-8161-8749-5

All rights reserved. No part of this publication may be reproduced
or used in any form or by any means — graphic, electronic, or
mechanical, including photocopying, recording, taping, or information
storage and retrieval systems — without written permission of the
publisher.

OUTSTANDING AMERICAN ILLUSTRATORS TODAY
★
イラストレーションU.S.A.

グラフィック社

目次

凡例 — 8	トム・デイリー — 61	ラファエル・ゴウテルス — 113
★ ジュリアン・アレン — 10	★ アラン・ダニエルズ — 62	★ ペネロープ・ゴットリーブ — 114
★ マーシャル・アリスマン — 11	★ ボー・ダニエルズ — 64	★ ジェームス・グラカ — 115
★ トム・バレンジャー — 14	★ ビル・デイヴィス — 65	★ アレッサ・グレース — 116
★ ミッシェル・バーンズ — 15	★ ポール・デイヴィス — 66	★ デーリック・グロス — 117
★ ジェームス・バークレイ — 16	★ マイケル・J・ディーズ — 69	★ ボブ・グラハム — 118
★ バスコーヴ — 17	★ チャールズ・D・ドゥマール — 70	★ デイヴィッド・グローヴ — 120
★ レオナード・バスキン — 18	★ ハーベイ・ディナースタイン — 71	★ スティーヴン・ガルナーシア — 122
★ ドン・バウム — 19	★ ジョン・テイラー・ディズミュークス — 72	★ ヘレン・ゲータリー — 123
★ ルー・ビーチ — 20	★ デニス・ディートリッヒ — 73	★ クニオ・ハギオ — 124
★ デイヴィッド・M・ベック — 22	★ パティ・ドライデン — 74	★ H・トム・ホール — 126
★ ロジャー・ビアワース — 24	★ アンドレイ・デュディンスキー — 75	★ エイブ・ガーヴィン — 128
★ デイヴ・バング — 25	★ アレックス・エベル — 76	★ ジョン・ハマガミ — 129
★ ブロート・ブローズ — 26	★ ジャック・エンデウォルト — 77	★ キャシー・ヘック — 130
★ マイケル・D・ブラウン — 29	★ ジョン・イーストマン — 78	★ ジョー・ハイナー, キャシー・ハイナー — 131
★ トレーシー・W・ブリット — 30	★ ジェームズ・R・エンディコット — 80	★ アルバート・ハーシュフェルド — 132
★ ルー・ブルックス — 31	★ アンカ・エンテ — 81	★ マーティン・ホフマン — 134
★ フィリップ・バーク — 32	★ ビル・アーズランド — 82	★ ジャミー・ホーガン — 135
★ スティーブン・バッツ — 33	★ ルイ・エスコベード — 83	★ ブラッド・ホランド — 136
★ キャサリン・コールダーウッド — 34	★ ジム・エヴァンス — 84	★ ホリー・ホリントン — 138
★ カーク・コールドウェル — 35	★ テレサ・ファソリーノ — 85	★ キャサリン・ホルト — 139
★ ジャスティン・キャロル — 36	★ アン・フィールド — 86	★ ロバート・ハント — 140
★ ロン・チャン — 37	★ ヴィヴィアン・フレッシャー — 87	★ ビル・イムホフ — 141
★ エリック・チャン — 38	★ ディック・フラッド — 88	★ グレン・イワサキ — 142
★ ジム・チェリー — 40	★ ロバート・フロアザーク — 89	★ バリー・ジャクソン — 143
★ スティーヴン・チョーニー — 41	★ パトリック・フロシェ — 90	★ キャシー・ヤコブ — 144
★ ジェームス・C・クリステンセン — 42	★ フィル・フランケ — 91	★ ジェイ — 145
★ シーモア・クワスト — 44	★ ダグマール・フリンタ — 92	★ ユージン・カーリン — 146
★ ケイ・クレイ — 48	★ ニコラス・ガエターノ — 93	★ ロニー・スー・ジョンソン — 148
★ フランソワ・クロトー — 50	★ バーナード・フックス — 94	★ ジョン・M・キルロイ — 149
★ ボビー・コクラン — 51	★ スタンレー・W・ガリ — 96	★ チョル・サ・キム — 150
★ アラン・E・コバー — 52	★ ニクソン・ギャロウェイ — 98	★ テア・クリロス — 151
★ シャーリーン・コリコット — 54	★ ジョン・ガマッシュ — 100	★ リチャード・M・クレグラー — 152
★ クリフォード・アラ・コンダック — 55	★ ジョン・ガンパート — 101	★ ジョン・A・カーツ — 153
★ クリス・コンサーニ — 56	★ ジョー・ガーネット — 102	★ ボブ・カーツ — 154
★ ホセ・クルーズ — 57	★ ジェリー・ガーステン — 103	★ デイヴ・ラフローア — 156
★ レイ・クルーズ — 58	★ ジョージ・ギュースティ — 104	★ ジム・ラム — 157
★ トム・カリー — 59	★ ロバート・ギュースティ — 107	★ ソール・ランバート — 158
★ ジェリー・ダッズ — 60	★ ミルトン・グレーサー — 108	★ ジョアン・ランディス — 159
	★ アレクサンダー・ニジコー — 112	★ バーニー・レティック — 160

- ★ ベット・リバイン —— 163
- ★ ティム・ルイス —— 164
- ★ エド・リンドロフ —— 165
- ★ スー・ルウェリン —— 166
- ★ ジョン・ライクス —— 167
- ★ ダニエル・マフィア —— 168
- ★ グレッグ・マンチェス —— 169
- ★ リチャード・マンテル —— 170
- ★ マーク・メレック —— 171
- ★ シンシア・マーシュ —— 172
- ★ ジョン・J・マルチネス —— 173
- ★ マーヴィン・マテルソン —— 174
- ★ ビル・メイヤー —— 175
- ★ デイヴッド・B・マッティングレー —— 176
- ★ ジェリー・マクドナルド —— 178
- ★ カレン・M・マクドナルド —— 179
- ★ ミック・マクギンティ —— 180
- ★ マーク・マクマホン —— 181
- ★ ウィルソン・マクリーン —— 182
- ★ ジェームズ・マクマラン —— 184
- ★ フランク・メディエイト —— 185
- ★ ポール・ミーゼル —— 186
- ★ ゲーリー・メール —— 187
- ★ ポール・メリア —— 188
- ★ リック・マイヤーウィッツ —— 189
- ★ ゲーリー・メイヤー —— 190
- ★ ウェンデル・マイナー —— 192
- ★ ポール・モック —— 193
- ★ マリリン・モンゴメリー —— 194
- ★ デイヴィッド・モンティエール —— 195
- ★ ジャッキー・モーガン —— 196
- ★ フランク・K・モリス —— 197
- ★ デニス・ムカイ —— 198
- ★ タク・ムラカミ —— 199
- ★ ビル・ネルソン —— 200
- ★ ウィル・ネルソン —— 201
- ★ メレディス・ネミロフ —— 202
- ★ バーバラ・ネッシム —— 203
- ★ スーザン・ナザレー —— 204
- ★ メル・オドム —— 205
- ★ J・ラファル・オルビンスキー —— 206
- ★ ジム・オーエンス —— 207
- ★ ジャック・パルデュー —— 208
- ★ アル・パーカー —— 209
- ★ ゲーリー・パターソン —— 212
- ★ ボブ・ピーク —— 214
- ★ ジム・ピアソン —— 218
- ★ エヴァレット・ペック —— 219
- ★ ジュディ・ペダーソン —— 220
- ★ ロバート・ペルース —— 221
- ★ ジュリー・ピーターソン —— 222
- ★ クライヴ・ピアーシー —— 223
- ★ ジェリー・ピンクニー —— 224
- ★ パオラ・ピグリア —— 226
- ★ スコット・ポラック —— 227
- ★ アイバン・パウエル —— 228
- ★ ドン・アイバン・パンチャッツ —— 230
- ★ ビル・プロクノー —— 232
- ★ ダン・クウォンストローム —— 233
- ★ マイク・クウォン —— 234
- ★ スコット・レイノルズ —— 236
- ★ ウィリアム・レイノルズ —— 237
- ★ ウィリアム・リーサー —— 238
- ★ フランク・ライリー —— 239
- ★ ロバート・リスコー —— 240
- ★ スタンレー・ロバーツ —— 241
- ★ ブライアン・ロブレー —— 242
- ★ ロバート・ロドリゲス —— 243
- ★ マリオ・ロセッティ —— 244
- ★ ジョン・ラッシュ —— 245
- ★ トレーシー・サビン —— 246
- ★ ジム・サルバティ —— 247
- ★ エマニュエル・ションゲット —— 248
- ★ ダニエル・シュワルツ —— 249
- ★ ジェフェリー・シーバー —— 250
- ★ イサドア・セルツァー —— 251
- ★ R・J・シェイ —— 252
- ★ マモル・シモコウチ —— 253
- ★ ウィリアム・A・スローン —— 254
- ★ ダグ・スミス —— 255
- ★ ジェス・スミスバック —— 256
- ★ グレッグ・スパレンカ —— 257
- ★ ランディ・スピア —— 258
- ★ バロン・ストアリー —— 259
- ★ ジョージ・スタヴリノス —— 260
- ★ デュガルド・スターマー —— 262
- ★ スーザン・スミックラスト —— 264
- ★ ジョージ・スエオカ —— 265
- ★ ブロック・スワンソン —— 266
- ★ ニック・タガート —— 267
- ★ ユリコ・タカタ —— 268
- ★ ロバート・ターネンバウム —— 269
- ★ C・ウィンストン・テイラー —— 270
- ★ アキ・トミタ —— 272
- ★ トム・T・トミタ —— 273
- ★ デール・C・ヴァゼール —— 274
- ★ フラン・ヴクサノヴィッチ —— 275
- ★ ウィリアム・ヴクサノヴィッチ —— 276
- ★ ジェフ・ワック —— 278
- ★ ロバート・L・ウェード —— 279
- ★ リチャード・ウォルドレップ —— 280
- ★ スタン・ワッツ —— 281
- ★ ロバート・ウィーバー —— 284
- ★ ドン・ウェラー —— 287
- ★ ジム・ホワイト —— 290
- ★ キム・ホワイトサイズ —— 292
- ★ テリー・ワイドナー —— 293
- ★ ラリー・C・ウィンボーグ —— 294
- ★ ロン・ウォーリン —— 295
- ★ ブルース・ウルフ —— 296
- ★ テレサ・ウッドワード —— 298
- ★ ゲーリー・ヤードホール —— 299
- ★ ジェームス・コートニー・ザール —— 300
- ★ ブライアン・ジック —— 301
- ★ ジョン・ジーリンスキー —— 302
- ★ アンディ・ジート —— 303

作家紹介 —— 306
あとがきに代えて —— 342

Contents

Acknowledgment — 8

★ ALLEN, Julien — 10
★ ARISMAN, Marshall — 11
★ BALLENGER, Tom — 14
★ BARNES, Michelle — 15
★ BARKLEY, James — 16
★ BASCOVE — 17
★ BASKIN, Leonard — 18
★ BAUM, Don — 19
★ BEACH, Lou — 20
★ BECK, David M. — 22
★ BEERWORTH, Roger — 24
★ BHANG, Dave — 25
★ BRALDS, Braldt — 26
★ BROWN, Michael D. — 29
★ BRITT, Tracy W. — 30
★ BROOKS, Lou — 31
★ BURKE, Philip — 32
★ BUTZ, Steven — 33
★ CALDERWOOD, Kathleen — 34
★ CALDWELL, Kirk — 35
★ CARROLL, Justin — 36
★ CHAN, Ron — 37
★ CHAN, Eric — 38
★ CHERRY, Jim — 40
★ CHORNEY, Steven — 41
★ CHRISTENSEN, James C. — 42
★ CHWAST, Seymour — 44
★ CLAY, Kay — 48
★ CLOTEAUX, Francois — 50
★ COCHRAN, Bobbye — 51
★ COBER, Alan E. — 52
★ COLLICOTT, Sharleen — 54
★ CONDAK, Clifford Ara — 55
★ CONSANI, Chris — 56
★ CRUZ, Jose — 57
★ CRUZ, Ray — 58
★ CURRY, Tom — 59
★ DADDS, Jerry — 60

★ DALY, Tom — 61
★ DANIELS, Alan — 62
★ DANIELS, Beau — 64
★ DAVIS, Bill — 65
★ DAVIS, Paul — 66
★ DEAS, Michael J. — 69
★ deMAR, Charles D. — 70
★ DINNERSTEIN, Harvey — 71
★ DISMUKES, John Taylor — 72
★ DITTRICH, Dennis — 73
★ DRYDEN, Patty — 74
★ DUDZINSKI, Andrzej — 75
★ EBEL, Alex — 76
★ ENDEWELT, Jack — 77
★ EASTMAN, John — 78
★ ENDICOTT, James R. — 80
★ ENTE, Anka — 81
★ ERSLAND, Bill — 82
★ ESCOBEDO, Louis — 83
★ EVANS, Jim — 84
★ FASOLINO, Teresa — 85
★ FIELD, Ann — 86
★ FLESHER, Vivienne — 87
★ FLOOD, Dick — 88
★ FLORCZAK, Robert — 89
★ FOURSHÉ, Patric — 90
★ FRANKÉ, Phil — 91
★ FRINTA, Dagmar — 92
★ GAETANO, Nicholas — 93
★ FUCHS, Bernard — 94
★ GALLI, Stanley W. — 96
★ GALLOWAY, Nixon — 98
★ GAMACHE, John — 100
★ GAMPERT, John — 101
★ GARNETT, Joe — 102
★ GERSTEN, Gerry — 103
★ GIUSTI, George — 104
★ GIUSTI, Robert — 107
★ GLASER, Milton — 108
★ GNIDZIEJKO, Alexander — 112

★ GOETHALS, Raphaelle — 113
★ GOTTLIEB, Penelope — 114
★ GRACA, James — 115
★ GRACE, Alexa — 116
★ GRÖSS, Daerick — 117
★ GRAHAM, Bob — 118
★ GROVE, David — 120
★ GUARNACCIA, Steven — 122
★ GUETARY, Helene — 123
★ HAGIO, Kunio — 124
★ HALL, H. Tom — 126
★ GURVIN, Abe — 128
★ HAMAGAMI, John — 129
★ HECK, Cathy — 130
★ HEINER, Joe & Kathy — 131
★ HIRSCHFELD, Albert — 132
★ HOFFMAN, Martin — 134
★ HOGAN, Jamie — 135
★ HOLLAND, Brad — 136
★ HOLLINGTON, Holly — 138
★ HOLT, Katheryn — 139
★ HUNT, Robert — 140
★ IMHOFF, Bill — 141
★ IWASAKI, Glen — 142
★ JACKSON, Barry — 143
★ JACOBI, Kathy — 144
★ Jay — 145
★ KARLIN, Eugene — 146
★ JOHNSON, Lonni Sue — 148
★ KILROY, John M. — 149
★ KIM, Choel Sa — 150
★ KLIROS, Thea — 151
★ KRIEGLER, Richard M. — 152
★ KURTZ, John A. — 153
★ KURTZ, Bob — 154
★ LaFLEUR, Dave — 156
★ LAMB, Jim — 157
★ LAMBERT, Saul — 158
★ LANDIS, Joan — 159
★ LETTICK, Birney — 160

★ LEVINE, Bette — 163	★ OLBINSKI, J. Rafal — 206	★ SMITHBACK, Jes — 256
★ LEWIS, Tim — 164	★ OWENS, Jim — 207	★ SPALENKA, Greg — 257
★ LINDLOF, Ed — 165	★ PARDUE, Jack — 208	★ SPEAR, Randy — 258
★ LLEWELLYN, Sue — 166	★ PARKER, Al — 209	★ STOREY, Barron — 259
★ LYKES, John — 167	★ PATTERSON, Gary — 212	★ STAVRINOS, George — 260
★ MAFFIA, Daniel — 168	★ PEAK, Bob — 214	★ STERMER, Dugald — 262
★ MANCHESS, Greg — 169	★ PEARSON, Jim — 218	★ SUMICHRAST, Susan — 264
★ MANTEL, Richard — 170	★ PECK, Everett — 219	★ SUYEOKA, George — 265
★ MAREK, Mark — 171	★ PEDERSON, Judy — 220	★ SWANSON, Brock — 266
★ MARSH, Cynthia — 172	★ PELUCE, Robert — 221	★ TAGGART, Nick — 267
★ MARTINEZ, John J. — 173	★ PETERSON, Julie — 222	★ TAKATA, Yuriko — 268
★ MATTELSON, Marvin — 174	★ PIERCY, Clive — 223	★ TANENBAUM, Robert — 269
★ MAYER, Bill — 175	★ PINKNEY, Jerry — 224	★ TAYLOR, C. Winston — 270
★ MATTINGLY, David B. — 176	★ PIGLIA, Paola — 226	★ TOMITA, Aki — 272
★ McDONALD, Jerry — 178	★ POLLACK, Scott — 227	★ TOMITA, Tom T. — 273
★ McDONALD, Karen Mercedes — 179	★ POWELL, Ivan — 228	★ VERZAAL, Dale C. — 274
★ McGINTY, Mick — 180	★ PUNCHATZ, Don Ivan — 230	★ VUKSANOVICH, Fran — 275
★ McMAHON, Mark — 181	★ PROCHNOW, Bill — 232	★ VUKSANOVICH, William — 276
★ McLEAN, Wilson — 182	★ QUARNSTROM, Dan — 233	★ WACK, Jeff — 278
★ McMULLAN, James — 184	★ QUON, Mike — 234	★ WADE, Robert L. — 279
★ MEDIATE, Frank — 185	★ REYNOLDS, Scott — 236	★ WALDREP, Richard — 280
★ MEISEL, Paul — 186	★ REYNOLDS, William — 237	★ WATTS, Stan — 281
★ MELE, Gary — 187	★ RIESER, William — 238	★ WEAVER, Robert — 284
★ MELIA, Paul — 188	★ RILEY, Frank — 239	★ WELLER, Don — 287
★ MEYEROWITZ, Rick — 189	★ RISKO, Robert — 240	★ WHITE, Jim — 290
★ MEYER, Gary — 190	★ ROBERTS, Stanley — 241	★ WHITESIDES, Kim — 292
★ MINOR, Wendell — 192	★ ROBLEY, Bryan — 242	★ WIDENER, Terry — 293
★ MOCH, Paul — 193	★ RODORIGUEZ, Robert — 243	★ WINBORG, Larry C. — 294
★ MONTGOMERY, Marilyn — 194	★ ROSSETTI, Mario — 244	★ WOLIN, Ron — 295
★ MONTIEL, David — 195	★ RUSH, John — 245	★ WOLFE, Bruce — 296
★ MORGAN, Jacqui — 196	★ SABIN, Tracy — 246	★ WOODWARD, Teresa — 298
★ MORRIS, Frank K. — 197	★ SALVATI, Jim — 247	★ YEALDHALL, Gary — 299
★ MUKAI, Dennis — 198	★ SCHONGUT, Emanuel — 248	★ ZAR, James Courtney — 300
★ MURAKAMI, Tak — 199	★ SCHWARTZ, Daniel B. — 249	★ ZICK, Brian — 301
★ NELSON, Bill — 200	★ SEAVER, Jeffery — 250	★ ZIELINSKI, John — 302
★ NELSON, Will — 201	★ SELTZER, Isadore — 251	★ ZITO, Andy — 303
★ NEMIROV, Meredith — 202	★ SHAY, R.J. — 252	
★ NESSIM, Barbara — 203	★ SHIMOKOCHI, Mamoru — 253	Artists profile — 305
★ NETHERY, Susan — 204	★ SLOAN, William A. — 254	
★ ODOM, Mel — 205	★ SMITH, Doug — 255	

Acknowledgment

OUTSTANDING AMERICAN ILLUSTRATORS TODAY is a collection of nearly 900 splendid illustrations done by 234 contemporary and outstanding illustrators from the East Coast as New York, New Jersey, Connecticut, the West Coast as Los Angeles, San Francisco, and Midstates and the South as Chicago, Atlanta, who are working actively in this field. The creativity of the selected artist is captured in this one volume. With this valuable reference record, you can get a full picture of how the contemporary American illustrators work and see how this book is convenient and enjoyable one, for not only designers and illustrators, but also the general people who love art.

All the artworks are presented by artists themselves or their representative agents. However, on editing I skipped the ones which were already introduced in "Illustrators Annual" by Hasting House, "Art Director's Index" by Roto Vision, "American Showcase" by American Showcase, and "Vision: American Artists Today" magazine I edited for Tokyo Designer's Gakuin College.

Each illustration has its own data like a. materials used and techniques, b. purpose of work, c. date of work indicated and described on 1-4 pages for each artist in alphabetical order. On the B/W pages, there appeared the profile of the artists. However, I digested the very long one, and the Japanese text for all of them.

On closing, I dedicated my special thanks to Mr. Marshall Arisman, Mrs. Dee Arisman, Mr. Akira Miyazaki & Mr. Yuzo Mizuno (N.Y.), Mr. Eric Chan & Mr. Minoru Furuta (Los Angeles), Mr. Kazuyuki Okutomi & Mrs. Jill Okutomi, Mr. Dan Sell (Chicago), Mr. Minoru Akita & Ms. Atsuko Konno of Tokyo Designer's Gakuin College, who gave me much favour and kind cooperations.

凡例：

1. 作品は作家ごとにまとめ、作家は原則としてアルファベット順に掲載いたしました。
2. 作品に付けたデータは、以下の順に並べてあります。
   a.——用具用材
   b.——使用目的
   c.——制作年

Works 作品

Julien Allen

1. JOHN GLENN RUNNING IN SPACE a. alkyd color b. illustration for Mother Jones magazine c. 1983
2. LOOKING FOR HEMMINGWAY a. alkyd oil paint b. illustration for Esquire for story about American writers in Paris in the '50's c. 1983
3. a. THE EMIGRE a. alkyd oil paint b. illustration for '50 years of Esquire, for story about the Emigres of the 1930's c. 1983

ジュリアン・アレン

1. a. アルキド絵具　b. 雑誌イラスト　c. 1983年
2. a. アルキド絵具　b. 雑誌イラスト　c. 1983年
3. a. アルキド絵具　b. 雑誌イラスト　c. 1983年

Represented by Artist

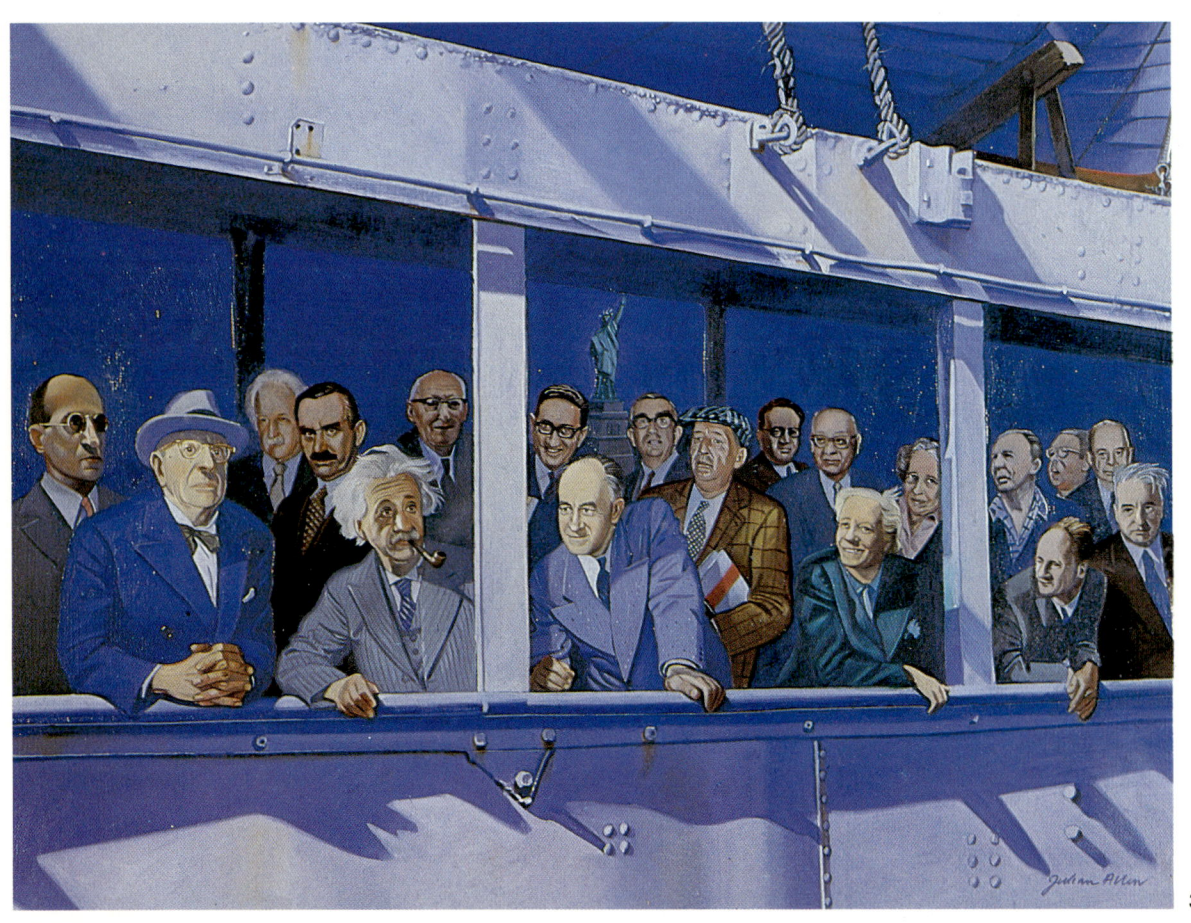

Marshall Arisman　マーシャル・アリスマン

1. a. oil on paper b. cover illustration for "Fitcher's Bird" children's book by Grimm c. 1983

1.a. 油彩絵具，紙　b. 絵本表紙　c. 1983年

Represented by Artist

2. a. oil on paper b. cover illustration for children's book c. 1983
3. a. oil on paper b. cover illustration for children's book c. 1983
4. a. oil on paper b. cover illustration for children's book c. 1983
5. a. oil on paper b. cover illustration for children's book c. 1983

2.a. 油彩絵具, 紙　b. 絵本表紙　c. 1983年
3.a. 油彩絵具, 紙　b. 絵本表紙　c. 1983年
4.a. 油彩絵具, 紙　b. 絵本表紙　c. 1983年
5.a. 油彩絵具, 紙　b. 絵本表紙　c. 1983年

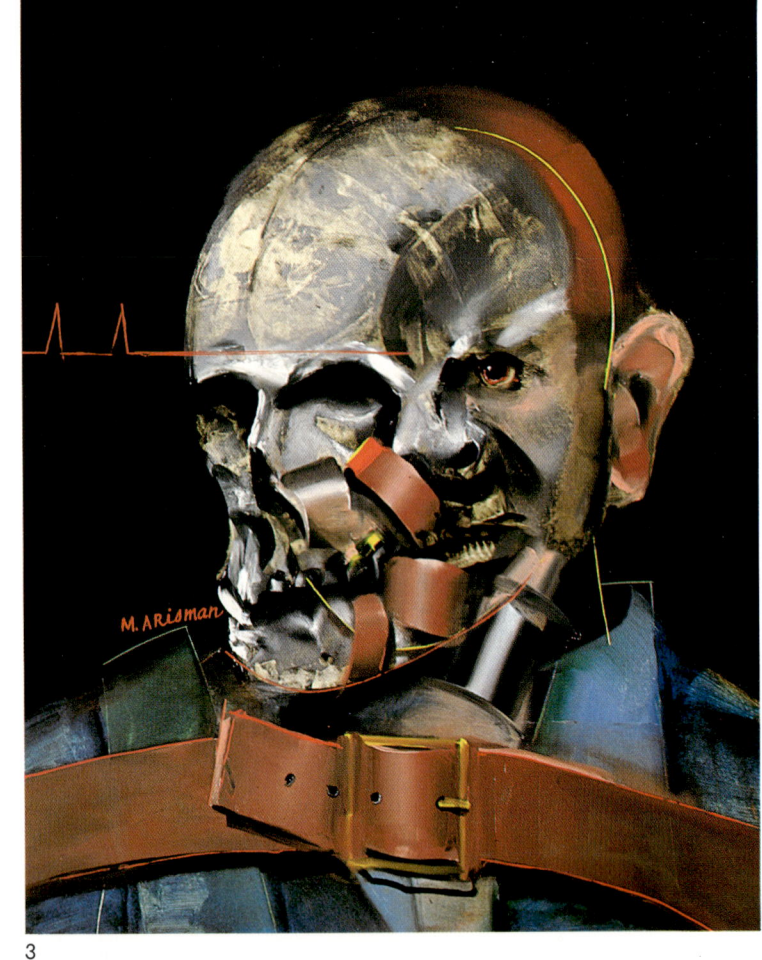

Represented by Artist

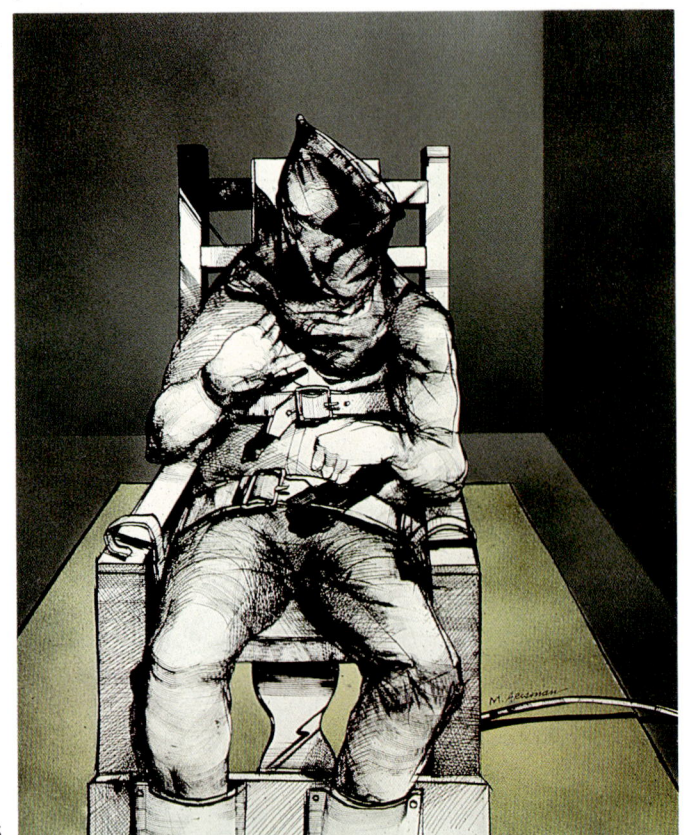

Michelle Barnes

1. a. pastel on paper b. article on "Avant-Garde L.A." c. 1983
2. a. pastel b. portrait of "Grace Jones" for illustration c. 1984
3. a. crayon on paper b. promotion piece for ice cream shop c. 1982

ミッシェル・バーンズ

1. a. パステル, 紙 b. 雑誌イラスト c. 1983年
2. a. パステル, 紙 b. グレイス・ジョーンズの肖像 c. 1982年
3. a. クレヨン b. 広告イラスト c. 1984年

Represented by Artist

James Barkley

ジェームス・バークレイ

16

1. a. dyes and acrylics b. limited edition print c. 1982
2. a. dyes and acrylics b. promotion poster for movie (The Island) c. 1982
3. a. dyes b. promotion poster for The Art Source new address

1.a. 染料, アクリル絵具　b. 限定版画　c.1982年
1.a. 染料, アクリル絵具　b. 映画ポスタ　c.1982年
3.a. 染料　b. ポスター

Represented by Artist

Bascove

1. a. woodcut, watercolor b. bookcover Viking Press c. 1982
2. a. woodcut, watercolor b. bookcover Clarkson & Potter c. 1983
3. a. linoleum cut, watercolor b. bookcover Random House c. 1983
4. a. woodcut, watercolor b. bookcover Random House c. 1983

バスコーヴ

1. a. 木版, 水彩絵具 b. 書籍表紙 c. 1982年
2. a. 木版, 水彩絵具 b. 書籍表紙 c. 1983年
3. a. リノリウムカット, 水彩絵具 b. 書籍表紙 c. 1983年
4. a. 木版, 水彩絵具 b. 書籍表紙 c. 1983年

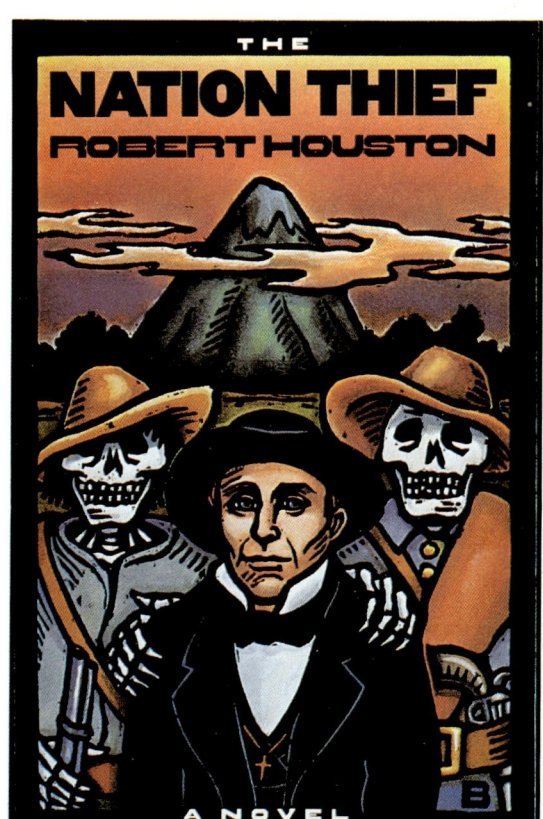

Represented by Artist

Leonard Baskin

レオナード・バスキン

1. PARTIAL CROW ON RED SKY a. watercolor on paper c. 1983
2. THE RAPTORS a. watercolor on paper c. 1983
3. THE MOTHERS: A SERIES II a. watercolor on paper c. 1983
4. FUMBLING MAN a. watercolor on paper c. 1983

1.a. 水彩絵具, 紙 c.1983年
2.a. 水彩絵具, 紙 c.1983年
3.a. 水彩絵具, 紙 c.1983年
4.a. 水彩絵具, 紙 c.1983年

Represented by Artist

Don Baum ドン・バウム

1. THE PARROT THAT MET PAPA a. sculpture b. Playboy Magazine c. 1972
2. a. sculpture b. Playboy Magazine. unpublished piece on John Holms
3. ORGANIZED CRIME a. sculpture b. Playboy Magazine c. 1974

1. a. 彫刻 b. 雑誌イラスト c. 1972年
2. a. 彫刻 b. 雑誌イラスト (未発表作品)
3. a. 彫刻 b. 雑誌イラスト c. 1974年

Represented by Artist

Lou Beach

1. a. color prints/collage b. record cover c. 1980
2. a. color paper collage b. magazine cover design c. 1983
3. a. color prints and magazine scrap/collage b. record cover c. 1980
4. a. color print/collage b. record cover c. 1982

ルー・ビーチ

1. a. カラープリントのコラージュ b. レコードジャケット c.1980年
2. a. カラーペーパーのコラージュ b. 雑誌表紙 c.1983年
3. a. カラープリントと雑誌切り抜きのコラージュ b. レコードジャケット c.1980年
4. a. カラープリントのコラージュ b. レコードジャケット c.1982年

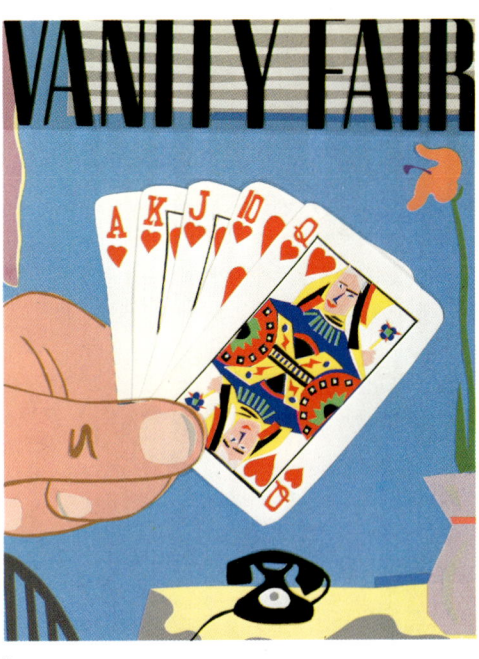

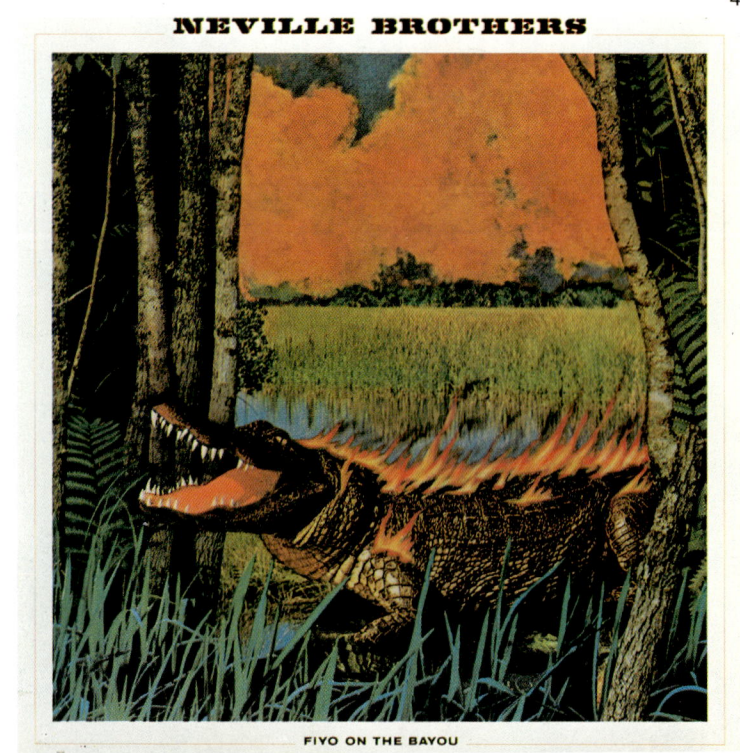

Represented by Artist

5. a. mixed media/multi-plane photo assemblage b. directory cover c. 1983

5.a. 各種画材と写真のアッサンブラージュ b. 住所録 表紙 c.1983年

Represented by Artist

David M. Beck ディヴィッド・M・ベック

1. a. mixed media on illustration board b. self-promotion piece c. 1983
2. a. mixed media on illustration board b. promotion piece c. 1982

1.a. 各種絵具, イラストレーションボード b. セルフプロモーション c.1983年
2.a. 各種絵具, イラストレーションボード b. セルフプロモーション c.1982年

Represented by Artist

4. TREFOIL a. oils on canvas. opaques + glazes. sable brushes b. illustration for advertisement + brochure for developing corporation in Connecticut depicting the animal life in this particular state. Title used in ad. "What Will the Neighbors Like" c. 1983

5. PELICAN a. oils on masonite. opaques + glazes. sable brushes b. conceptual piece for "RADIO EYES" lyrics set to art. double spread. illustrated lyric "SITTIN' AT THE DOCK OF THE BAY" by Otis Redding c. 1983

4. a. 油彩絵具，キャンバスボード，セーブル筆。グラッシ及びオペーク技法 b. パンフレット c. 1983年
5. a. 油彩絵具，メゾナイト，セーブル筆。グラッシ及びオペーク技法 b. 詩画集 c. 1983年

4

5

Represented by Artist

28

6. CONDOR FENCE a. oils on masonite. opaques + glazes. sable brushes b. editorial series for Atlantic Monthly Magazine. Story on the endangered "CALIFORNIAN CONDOR" c. 1983
7. CONDOR HEAD a. b. c. same as 6

6.a. 油彩絵具，メゾナイト，セーブル筆。グラッシ及びオペーク技法　b. 雑誌連載小説挿画　c. 1983年
7.a. 油彩絵具，メゾナイト，セーブル筆。グラッシ及びオペーク技法　b. 雑誌連載小説挿画　c. 1983年

6

7

Represented by Artist

Michael D. Brown　　　　　　　　　　　　　　　　　　マイケル・D・ブラウン　　　　　　　　　　29

1. UNDERSTANDING TAXES a. engravings, photography scraps, original illustrations, multiple collage b. poster for the Internal Revenue Service distributed to students in the U.S. c. 1983
2. a. film overlays b. National Archives 50th Anniversary Commemorative Postage Stamp c. 1984
3. EXPERIMENTS IN RELIGIOUS PERCEPTIONS a. pen & ink on board b. book jacket for "OUTLOOK REVIEW" series c. 1983

1.a. 彫刻，写真，オリジナルイラストのコラージュ　b. ポスター　c.1983年
2.a. オーバーレイ　b. 記念切手　c.1984年
3.a. ペン，インク，ボード　b. 書籍表紙　c.1983年

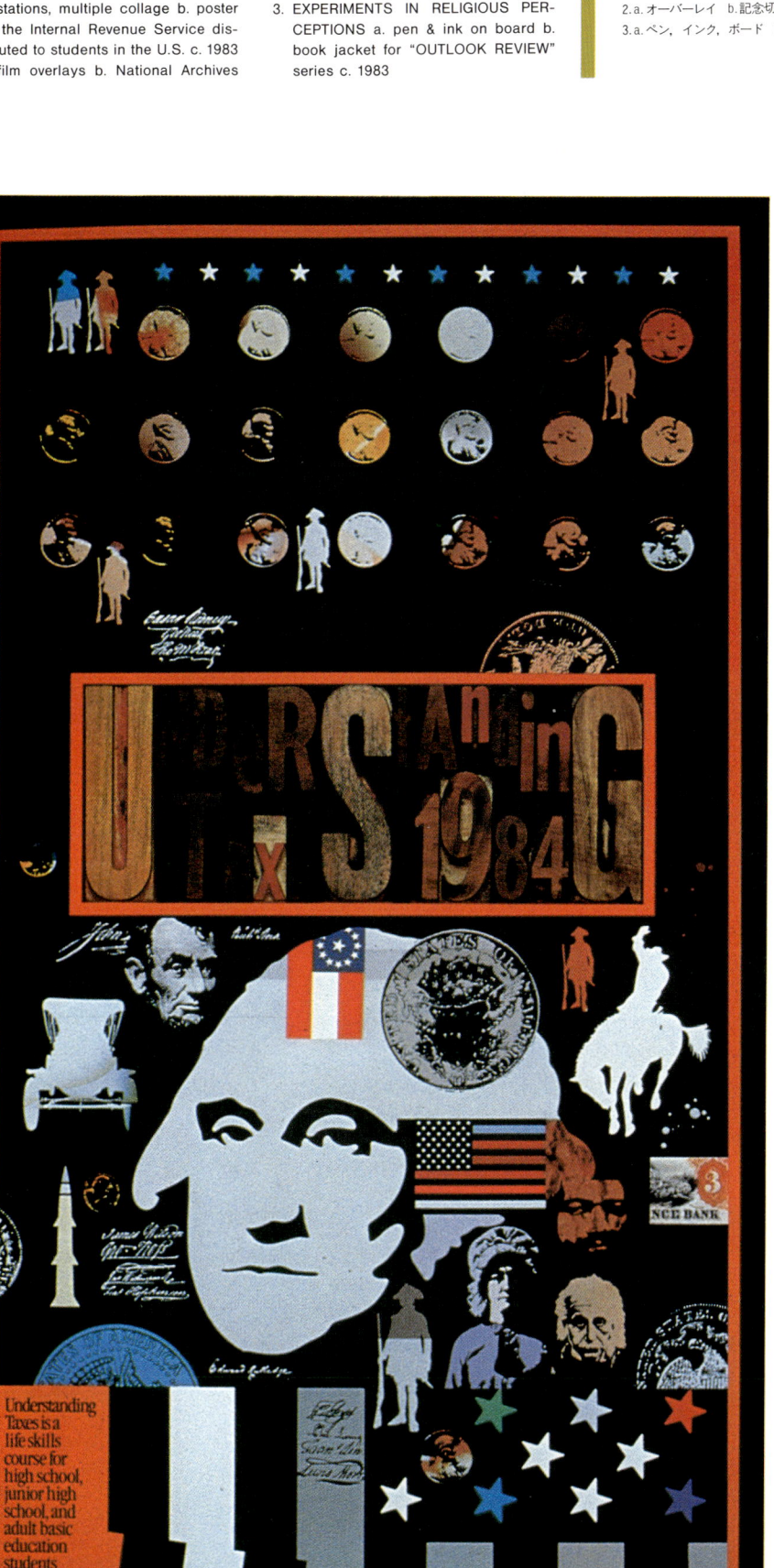

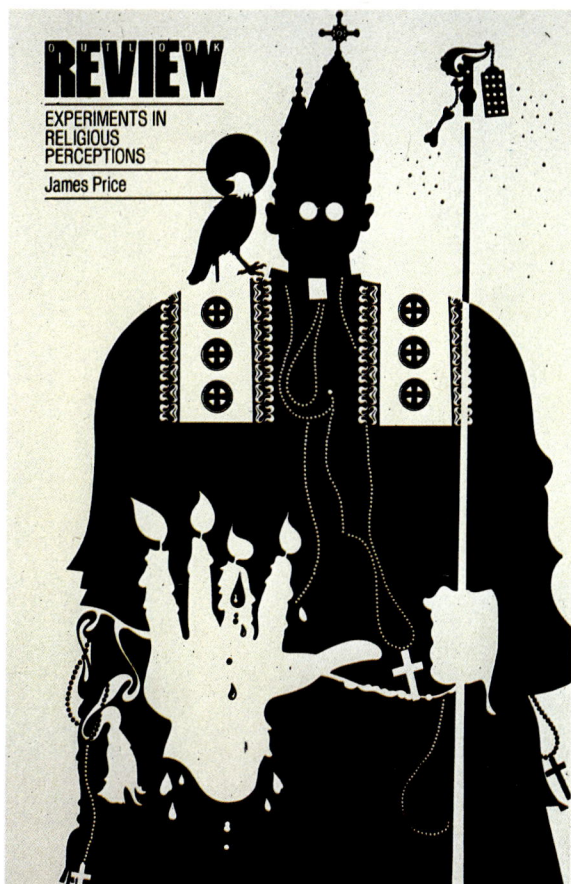

Represented by Artist

Tracy W. Britt

1. a. acrlylic, airbrush, illustration board
 b. album cover c. 1983
2. a. acrylic, airbrush, illustration board b. self-promotion c. 1982
3. a. acrylic, airbrush, illustration board b. bank promotion c. 1982

トレーシー・W・ブリット

1. a. アクリル絵具，エアブラシ，イラストレーションボード　b. レコードジャケット　c. 1983年
2. a. アクリル絵具，エアブラシ，イラストレーションボード　b. セルフプロモーション　c. 1982年
3. a. アクリル絵具，エアブラシ，イラストレーションボード　b. 広告イラスト　c. 1982年

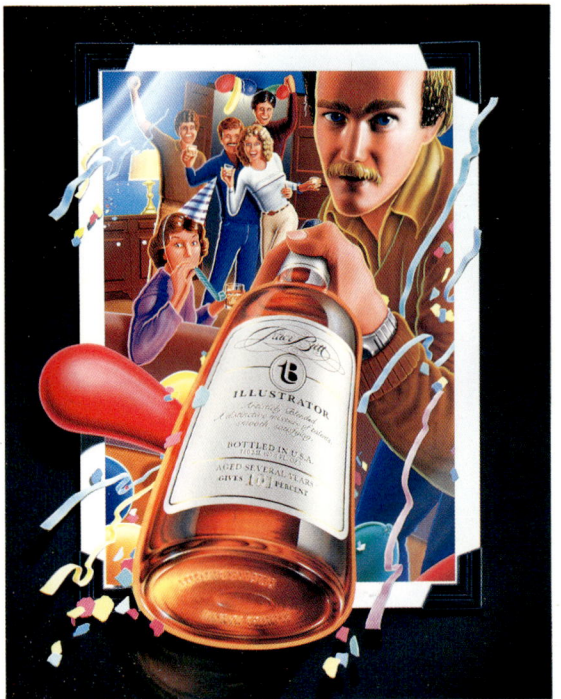

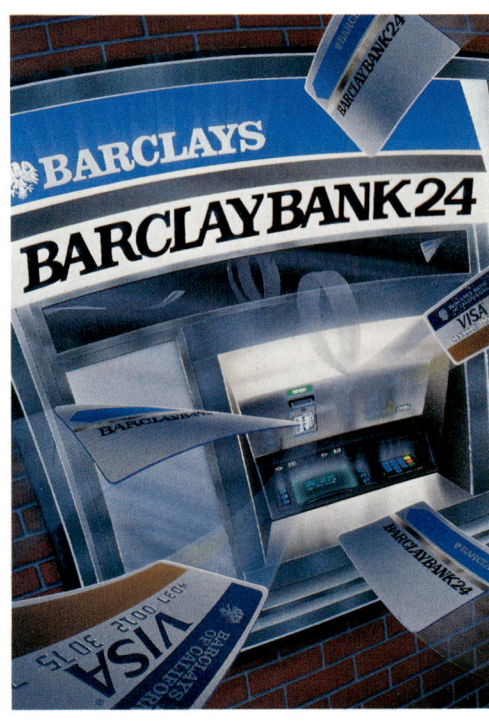

30

Represented by Artist

Lou Brooks

1. a. pen, ink, airbrush b. illustration for the April 1979 issue of Rolling Stone magazine c. 1979
2. a. pen, ink, airbrush b. cover illustration for the Nov. 1983 issue of Video Game Player magazine c. 1983
3. a. pen, ink, airbrush b. illustration for the Nov. 1983 issue of Vanity Fair magazie c. 1983
4. a. pen, ink, airbrush b. cover illustration for the Dec. 1983 issue of Executive magazine c. 1983

ルー・ブルックス

1. a. ペン，インク，エアブラシ b. 雑誌イラスト c. 1979年
2. a. ペン，インク，エアブラシ b. 雑誌表紙 c. 1983年
3. a. ペン，インク，エアブラシ b. 雑誌イラスト c. 1983年
4. a. ペン，インク，エアブラシ b. 雑誌表紙 c. 1983年

Represented by Artist

Philip Burke

1. MICHAEL JACKSON a. oil b. painting for Vanity Fair c. 1984
2. ANDY WARHOL a. oil b. painting for Vanity Fair c. 1984
3. NIXON a. oil on canvas b. VANITY FAIR feature c. 1984
4. MAGGIE THATCHER a. oil on canvas b. VANITY FAIR feature c. 1983

フィリップ・バーク

1. a. 油彩絵具　b. 雑誌イラスト（未発表）　c. 1984年
2. a. 油彩絵具　b. 雑誌イラスト　c. 1984年
3. a. 油彩絵具、キャンバスボード　b. 雑誌イラスト　c. 1983年
4. a. 油彩絵具、キャンバスボード　b. 雑誌イラスト　c. 1984年

Represented by Artist

Steven Butz

1. BEAR BRYANT a. mixed media acrylic, colored pencil, colored chalk, spray, on illustration board b. for movie "Bear Bryant"
2. ORCA a. acrylic, colored pencil on illustration board b. for movie "Orca"
3. a. acrylic on illustration board b. book of 20,000 Leagues Under The Sea, title page. Raintree Publishing
4. a. b. c. same as 3

1.a. アクリル絵具，色鉛筆，カラーチョーク，スプレー，イラストレーションボード b.映画ポスター
2.a. アクリル絵具，色鉛筆，イラストレーションボード b.映画ポスター
3.a. アクリル絵具，イラストレーションボード b.書籍扉絵
4.a. アクリル絵具，イラストレーションボード b.書籍扉絵

Represented by Artist

Kathleen Calderwood

1. a. acrylic on canvas, painted b. poster for Rochester Chamber of Commerce (Roch. N.Y.) c. 1983
2. a. acrylic on hardboard, painted with very small amount of airbrushing b. editorial illustration for article entitled "The Bomb and Beyond" Playboy Magazine c. 1982
3. a. acrylic on hardboard. paint applied with brushes b. editorial illustration for "The Pulitzer's of Palm Beach" in Playboy Magazine c. 1983

キャサリン・コールダーウッド

1. a.アクリル絵具，キャンバス b.ポスター c.1983年
2. a.アクリル絵具，ハードボード，エアブラシ b.雑誌イラスト c.1982年
3. a.アクリル絵具，ハードボード b.雑誌イラスト c.1983年

Represented by Artist

Ron Chan

1. a. pen & ink on Duralene with Zip-a-tone b. cover illustration for California Living on events in San Jose c. 1982
2. a. pen & ink on Duralene with overlay tints b. illustration for Oceans magazine on an article about schuba diving classes c. 1982
3. a. pen & ink on Duralene with Zip-a-tone b. package illustration for Electronic Art's game software c. 1983
4. a. pen & ink on Duralene with Zip-a-tone b. cover illustration for California Living on weekend outings c. 1983

ロン・チャン

1. a. ペン、インク、デュラレーン、ジップ・ア・トーン b. 雑誌表紙 c.1982年
2. a. ペン、インク、デュラレーン、ティントオーバーレイ b. 雑誌イラスト c.1982年
3. a. ペン、インク、デュラレーン、ジップ・ア・トーン b. ソフトウェアのパッケージ c.1983年
4. a. ペン、インク、デュラレーン、ジップ・ア・トーン b. 雑誌表紙 c.1983年

Represented by Artist

Eric Chan

1. CARAVELLE EXECUTIVE AIRLINER a. acrylic painting with airbrush on illustration board b. commissioned by Go Leasing, Inc. c. 1980
2. B-1 AT EDWARDS AIR FORCE BASE a. charcoal & acrylic on corrugated board b. owned by artist c. 1980

1.a. アクリル絵具, エアブラシ, イラストレーションボード b. 企業所蔵作品 c. 1980年
2.a. チャコール, アクリル絵具, コルゲートボード b. 未発表作品 c. 1980年

Represented by Artist

3. SEA FURY OVER KOREA a. acrylic on canvas b. owned by artist c. 1979
4. REFUELING F-15 EAGLES a. acrylic on board b. owened by artist c. 1981
5. PANTHERS OVER YODO ISLAND, KOREA a. acrylic on canvas b. owned by artist c. 1982

3. a. アクリル絵具, キャンバス b. 未発表作品 c. 1979年
4. a. アクリル絵具, ボード b. 未発表作品 c. 1981年
5. a. アクリル絵具, キャンバス b. 未発表作品 c. 1982年

Represented by Artist

Jim Cherry

1. a. gouache, dyes, acrylics on illustration board, with airbrush, sable brush and colored pencil b. record jacket for single "She's Got A Gun" (Group — "Yello") c. 1981
2. a. gouache, dyes, and acrylics on illustration board, with airbrush, sable brushes and colored pencil b. bookcover "Baby Driver". St. Martin's Publishers c. 1980
3. a. gouache, dyes, and acrylics on illustration board, done with airbrush, sable brush and colored pencil b. video game package — "Eggo Mania" game c. 1983
4. a. gouache, dyes, and acrylics on illustration board, with airbrush, sable brush and colored pencil b. video game package — "Scavenger Hunt" game c. 1983

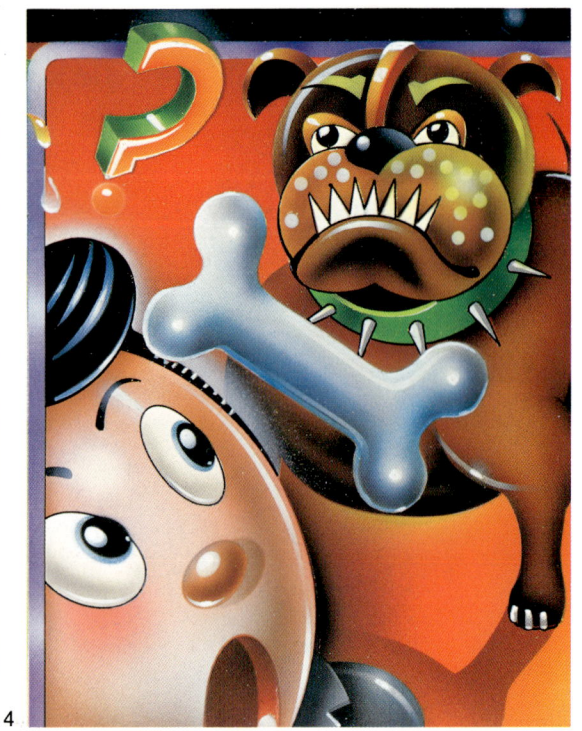

Represented by Artist

Steven Chorney

1. a. acrylics and Prismacolor on Lyntex board b. poster for motion picture campaign, Warner-Brothers c. 1983
2. a. gouache, airbrush b. title treatment for TV promotion, MCA-Universal Television c. 1983
3. a. acryics and Prismacolor on gesso board b. greeting card, Paper Moon c. 1980
4. a. colored inks with cel vinyl overlays b. software packaging, Texas Instruments c. 1982

スティーヴン・チョーニー

1. a. アクリル絵具, 色鉛筆, リンテックスボード b. 映画ポスター c. 1983年
2. a. ガッシュ, エアブラシ b. テレビ番組のプロモーション c. 1983年
3. a. アクリル絵具, 色鉛筆, ジェッソボード b. グリーティングカード c. 1980年
4. a. カラーインク, オーバーレイ b. ソフトウェアのパッケージ c. 1982年

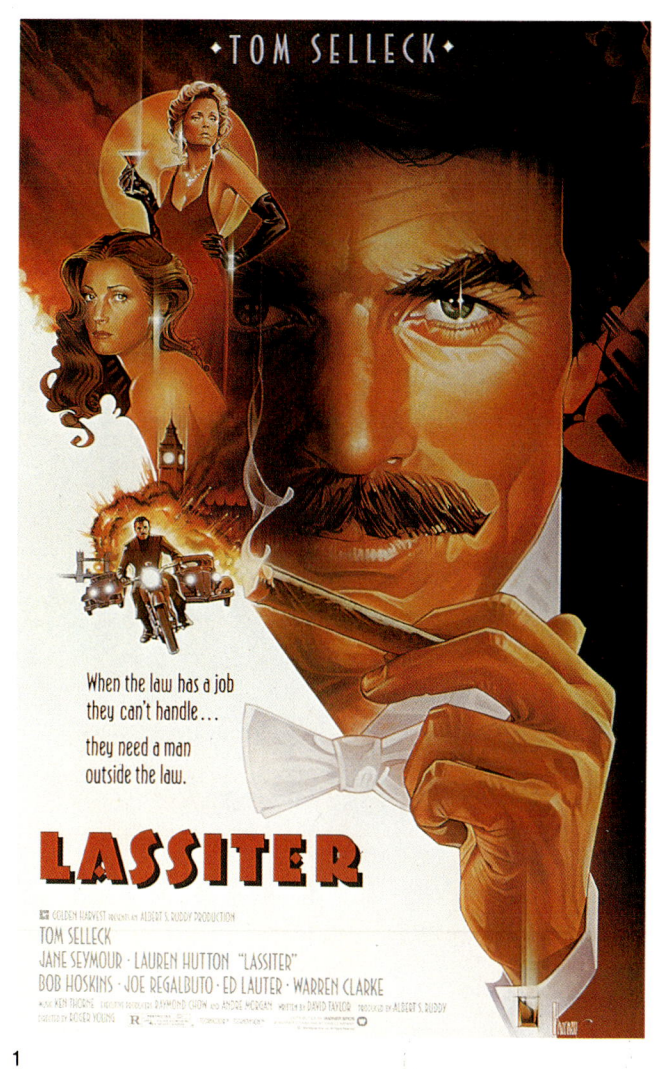

Represented by Artist

James C. Christensen

ジェームズ・C・クリステンセン

42

1. a. acrylic on panel with brush b. cover art for *The Best of Jack Vance*. Timescape Book. c. 1982
2. a. acrylic on panel with brush b. cover for "Dialogue" Magazine c. 1983
3. a. acrylic on panel with brush b. "Fine Kite" illustration in article on the artist in South-East Art Magazine c. 1982

1. a.アクリル絵具, 筆, パネル b.書籍表紙 c.1982年
2. a.アクリル絵具, 筆, パネル b.雑誌表紙 c.1983年
3. a.アクリル絵具, 筆, パネル b.雑誌イラスト c.1982年

Represented by Artist

43

4. a. acrylic on panel with brush b. "Card Game at LaTour's" published in brochure on the artist by Springville Museum of Art c. 1981
5. a. acrylic on panel with brush b. book illustration for Fairy Book (unpublished) c. 1983
6. a. acrylic on panel with brush b. illustration for Southwest Art Magazine Editors page c. 1982

4. a. アクリル絵具, 筆, パネル b. カタログ・イラスト c. 1981年
5. a. アクリル絵具, 筆, パネル b. 未発表作品 c. 1983年
6. a. アクリル絵具, 筆, パネル b. 雑誌イラスト c. 1982年

Represented by Artist

Seymour Chwast　シーモア・クワスト　44

1. CARTA DI PASTA a. pen & ink with plastic overlay for color b. poster to be sold c. 1982

1.a. ペン，インク，プラスチックオーバーレイ　b. ポスター　c. 1982年

Represented by Artist

2. a. pastel b. poster c. 1984

2. a. パステル b. ポスター c. 1984年

Represented by Artist

3. FORBES – GET YOU TO THE CORNER OFFICE a. pen & ink with plastic overlays for color b. poster promoting business magazine c. 1982
4. b. poster c. 1984
5. GRAPHIS POSTERS 83 a. pen & ink with plastic overlays for color b. book jacket for book on posters c. 1983

3. a. ペン，インク，プラスチックオーバーレイ b. ポスター c. 1982年
4. b. ポスター c. 1984年
5. a. ペン，インク，プラスチックオーバーレイ b. 書籍表紙 c. 1983年

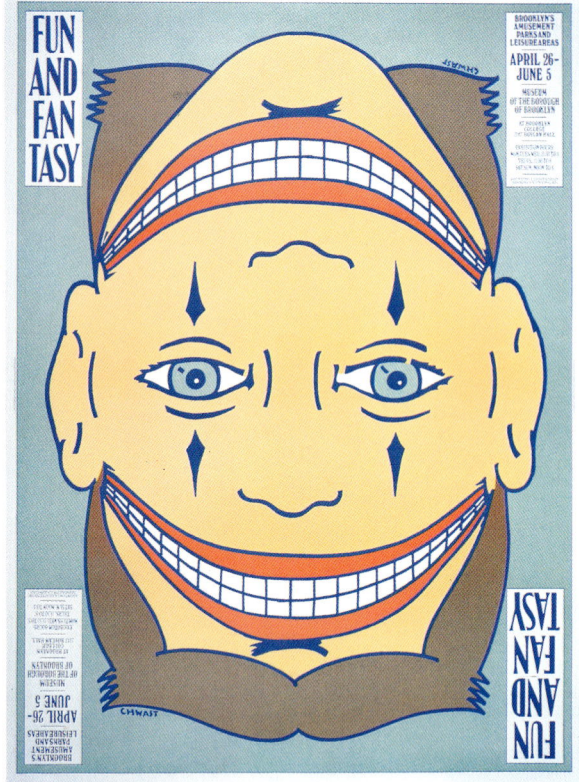

Represented by Artist

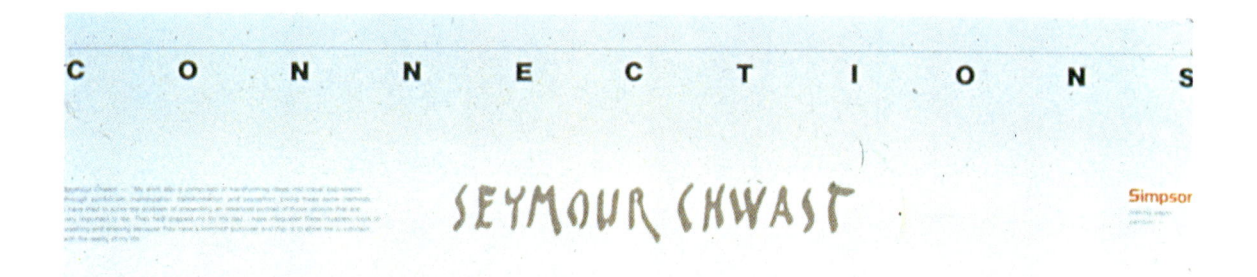

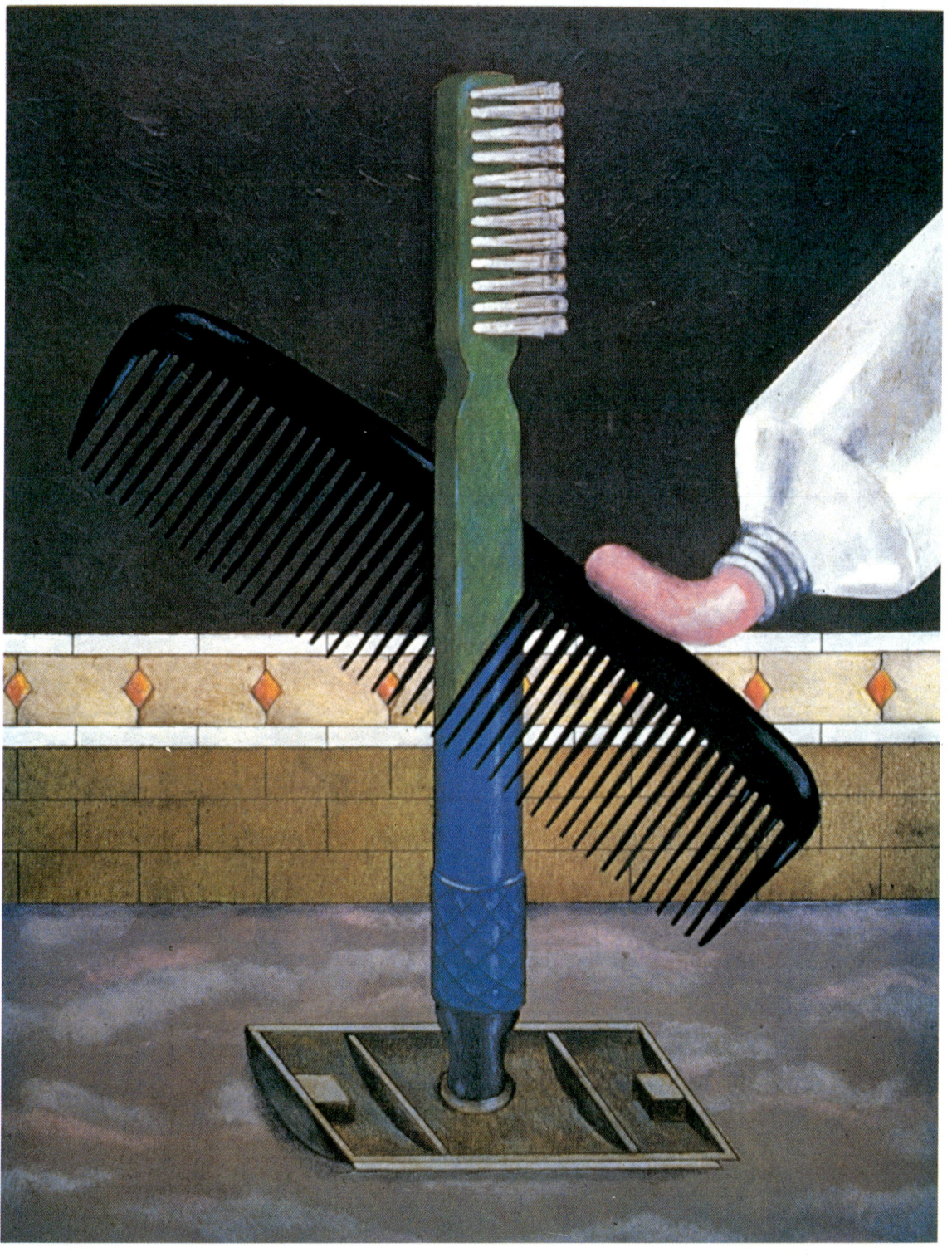

6. SIMPSON CONNECTIONS a. acrylic on chipboard b. promote paper company c. 1983

6.a.アクリル絵具，ボール紙 b.広告イラスト c.1983年

Kay Clay

1. DAHLIA BORDER a. watercolor b. currently at the Indianapolis Museum of Art c. 1984
2. VERMEER NEVER PAINTED FLOWERS a. watercolor b. collection of Mark Kriese, Indianapolis, Indiana c. 1984
3. a. watercolor b. painting from a series of Indiana Flowers c. 1983
4. BEGONIAS AND FANS a. watercolor b. for the artist's sister c. 1983

ケイ・クレイ

1. a. 水彩絵具 b. 美術館所蔵作品 c. 1984年
2. a. 水彩絵具 b. プライベートコレクション c. 1984年
3. a. 水彩絵具 b. インディアナ州花を描いた一連のシリーズ c. 1983年
4. a. 水彩絵具 b. 作家の身内のために描いた作品 c. 1983年

48

1

2

3

4

Represented by Artist

5. SQUARES RISING (LYNN IN A PENSIVE MOOD) a. watercolor b. this study from life was for a show at the Indianapolis Museum of Art c. 1983–1984

5.a. 水彩絵具　b. 美術館所蔵作品　c. 1983〜1984年

Represented by Artist

Francois Cloteaux フランソワ・クロトー

1. a. airbrush b. promotion piece c. 1982
2. a. airbrush b. editorial c. 1979
3. a. airbrush b. institutional c. 1979
4. a. airbrush b. poster c. 1981

1. a. エアブラシ b. セルフプロモーション c.1982年
2. a. エアブラシ b. エディトリアル c.1979年
3. a. エアブラシ b. ポスター c.1979年
4. a. エアブラシ b. ポスター c.1981年

50

Represented by Artist

Bobbye Cochran

1. a. zip-a-tone b. for McCarty Co. c. 1983
2. a. silkscreen b. for Agriculture Council of America c. 1981
3, 4 non data

ボビー・コクラン

1. a. オーバーレイ（ジップ・ア・トーン） b. 広告イラスト c. 1983年
2. a. シルクスクリーン b. 広告イラスト c. 1981年
3.4. データ不明

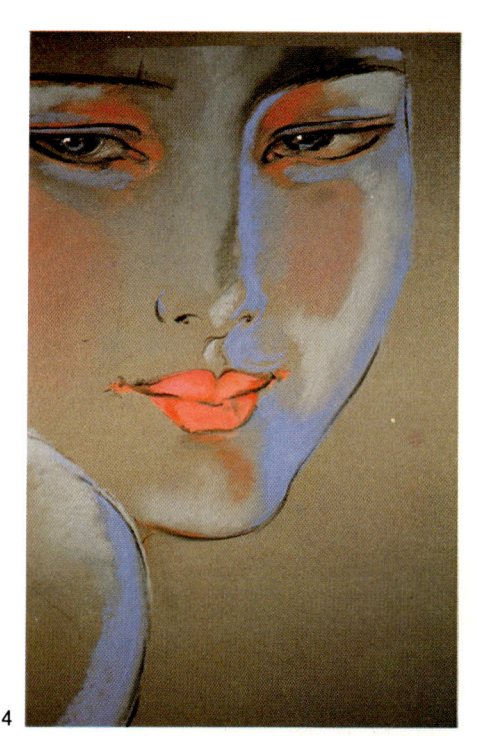

Represented by Artist

Alan E. Cober

アラン・E・コバー

1. a. ink, watercolor, and some color pencil on arches 140 cold press paper b. commissioned piece for the 250th Birthday of G. Washington c. 1981–82

1.a. ペン，インク，水彩絵具，色鉛筆，水彩画紙 b. G・ワシントン生誕250年記念作品 c. 1981〜1982年

2. a. pen & ink, watercolor on arches paper with toothbrush b. to illustrate word (concentration) c. 1978
3. a. pen & ink, water color on arches paper with brush b. lead illustration on 6 pages on the Assassination of Martin Luther King Jr. for Skeptic May c. 1977
4. a. pen & ink on arches paper b. for U.S. Navy to present new torpede. Honeywell Corp. c. 1979

2. a. ペン，インク，水彩絵具，水彩画紙，歯ブラシ b. 未発表作品 c. 1978年
3. a. ペン，インク，水彩絵具，水彩画紙，画筆 b. 雑誌イラスト c. 1977年
4. a. ペン，インク，水彩画紙 b. 合衆国海軍へのプレゼンテーション用新型魚雷イラスト c. 1979年

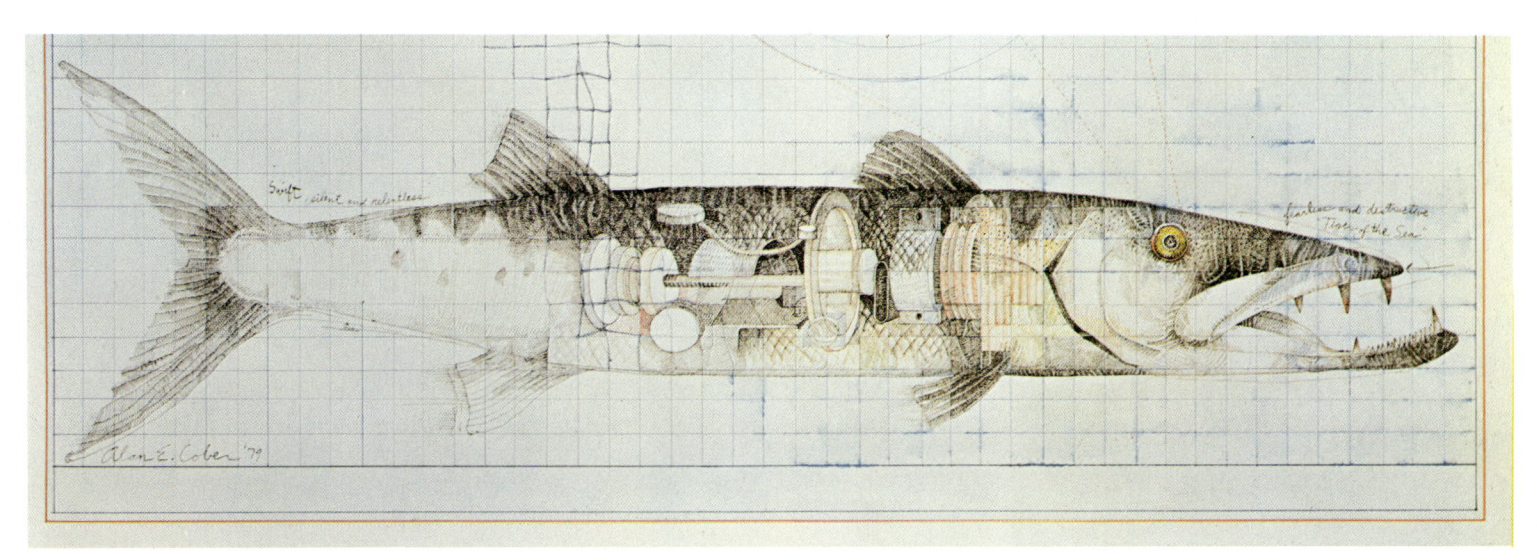

2

3

4

Represented by Artist

Sharleen Collicott

1. a. egg tempera, gesso b. poster c. 1981
2. THE WINDS OF WINTER a. gouache b. greeting card c. 1980
3. FROG PRINCE a. gouache b. greeting card c. 1980

シャーリーン・コリコット

1. a. テンペラ、ジェッソボード b. ポスター c. 1981年
2. a. ガッシュ b. グリーティングカード c. 1980年
3. a. ガッシュ b. グリーティングカード c. 1980年

Represented by Artist

Clifford Ara Condak

1. a. watercolor dyes, pen, brush b. album cover BILLIE HOLIDAY "God Bless the Child" Columbia Records c. 1976
2. a. black ink mixed with brown dyes and Reg. watercolor dyes, brush, on paper b. album cover "Stravinski" Conducts "Oedipusrex" Columbia Records c. 1975
3. a. watercolor dyes, pen, brush b. album cover "Ravel La Valse" conducted by Boulez. Columbia Records c. 1979

クリフォード・アラ・コンダック

1. a. カラーインク，ペン，画筆 b. レコードジャケット c.1976年
2. a. 茶色の染料を混ぜた黒インク，カラーインク，画筆，紙 b. レコードジャケット c.1975年
3. a. カラーインク，ペン，画筆 b. レコードジャケット c.1979年

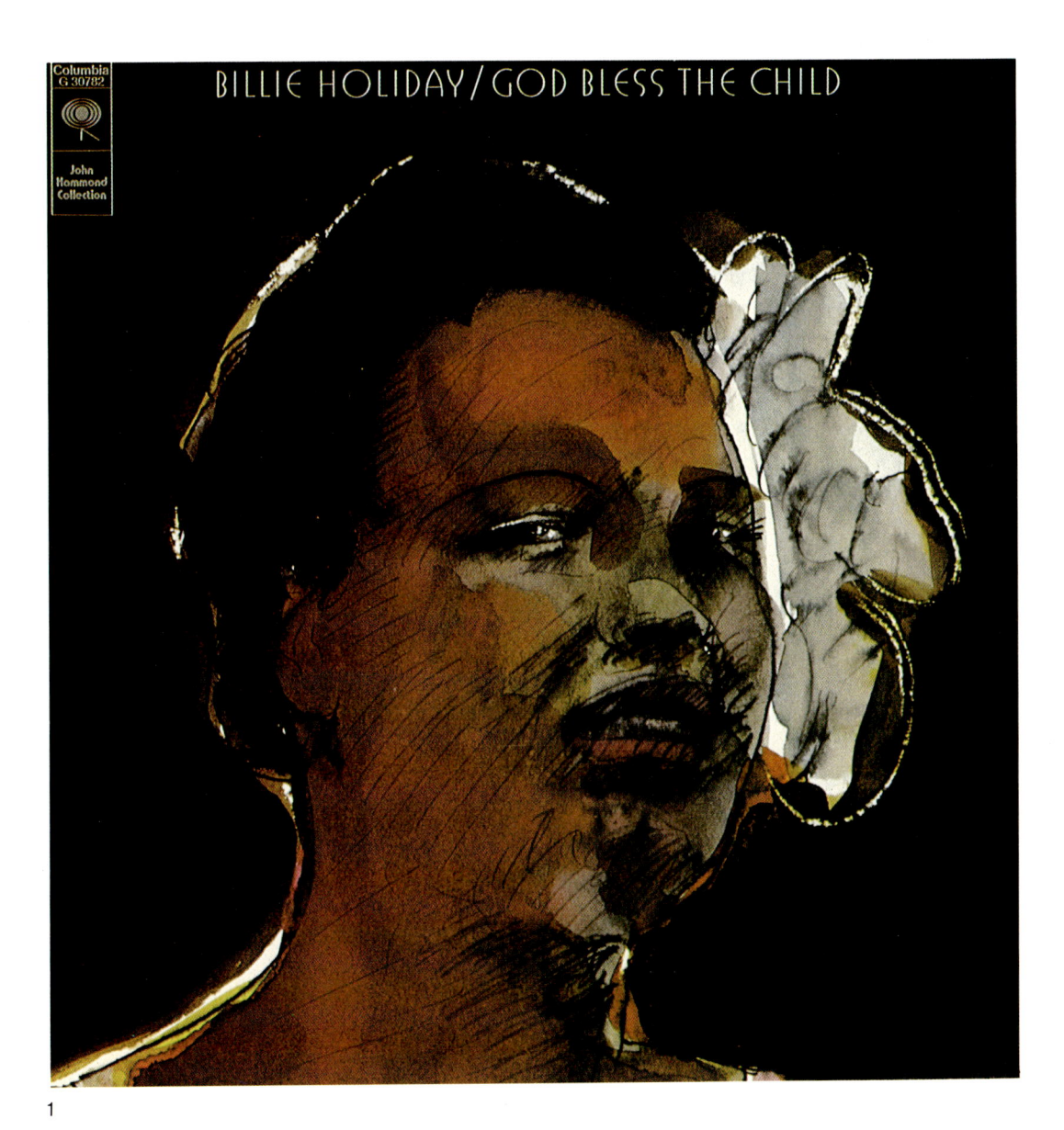

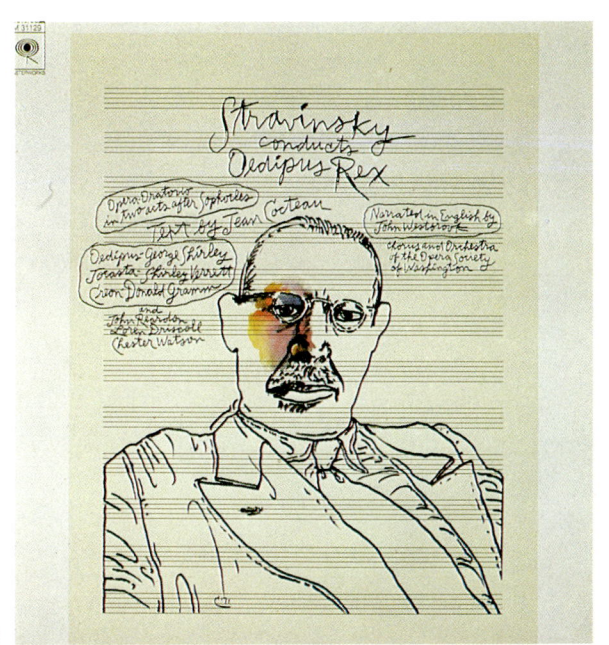

Represented by Artist

Chris Consani

1. IRVINE MEADOWS AMPHITHEATRE '83 a. acrylic on illustration board with airbrush b. cover for Irving Meadows Amphitheatre brouchure c. 1983
2. FRANK a. acrylic on illustration board with airbrush b. promotional c. 1982
3. NOIL a. acrylic on illustration board with airbrush b. promotional c. 1983
4. JUNE WEDDING a. acrylic on illustration board with airbrush b. calendar for Lamb Weston c. 1982

クリス・コンサーニ

1. a. アクリル絵具, イラストレーションボード, エアブラシ b. カタログの表紙 c. 1983年
2. a. アクリル絵具, イラストレーションボード, エアブラシ b. 広告 c. 1982年
3. a. アクリル絵具, イラストレーションボード, エアブラシ b. 広告 c. 1982年
4. a. アクリル絵具, イラストレーションボード, エアブラシ b. カレンダー c. 1982年

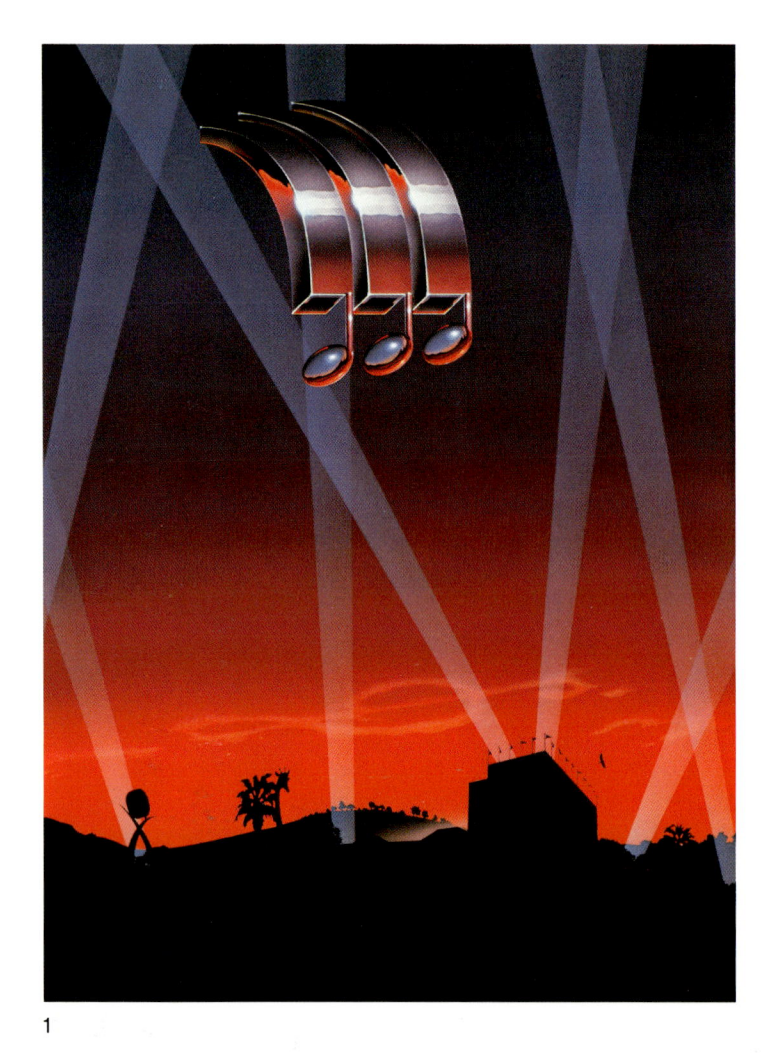

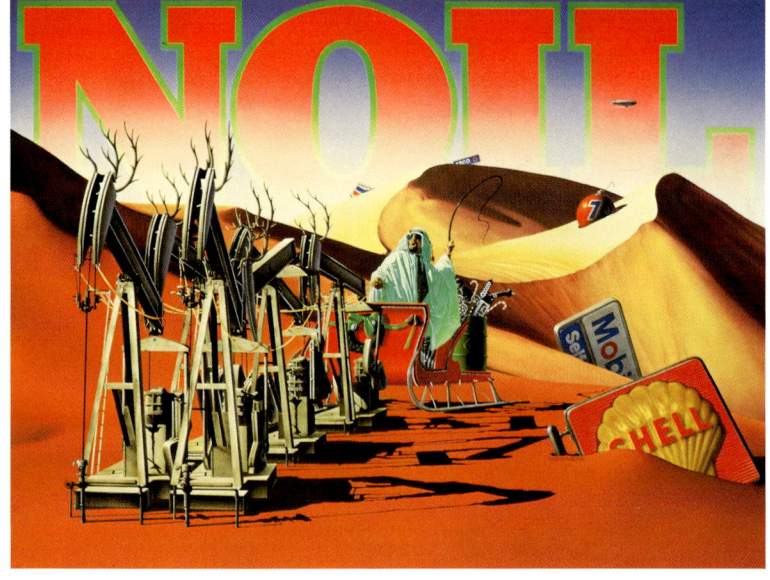

Represented by Artist

Jose Cruz

1. NU WAVE ROCK IN THE 80'S a. acrylic, ink, mixed media. airbrush collage, rubber stamping b. calendar c. 1983
2. LADY IN STRETCHPANTS CAUGHT ON FISHING LINES a. acrylic. airbrush, splatter b. self-promotional postcards c. 1983
3. THE ICE CRACKED... (WOMAN ABSTRACT) a. acrylic. plastic moving eyes, transfer letters. airbrush, splattering, collage b. self-promotional postcards c. 1983
4. NIPPON GOLDFISH a. airbrush b. calendar/datebook c. 1982

ホセ・クルーズ

1. a. アクリル絵具, インク, エアブラシ, コラージュ, ゴムスタンプ b. カレンダー c. 1983年
2. a. アクリル絵具, エアブラシ, スプラッタリング b. ポストカード c. 1983年
3. a. アクリル絵具, ムービングアイ, タイプ文字転写, エアブラシ, スプラッタリング b. ポストカード c. 1983年
4. a. エアブラシ b. カレンダー, スケジュール帳 c. 1982年

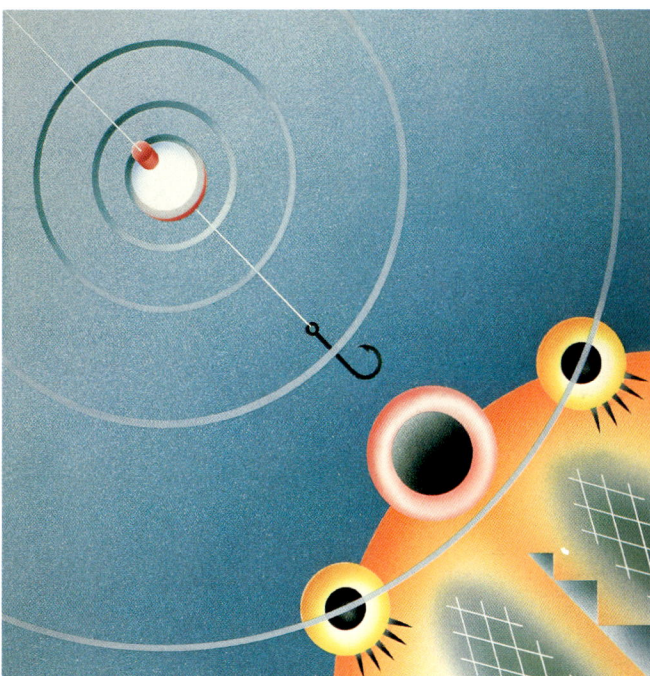

Represented by Artist

Ray Cruz

1. a. pen and ink and dyes
2. a. pen and ink, dyes, airbrush
3. a. pencil and watercolor

レイ・クルーズ

1. a. ペン, インク, カラーインク
2. a. ペン, インク, カラーインク, エアブラシ
3. a. 鉛筆, 水彩絵具

Represented by Artist

Tom Curry

1. CACTUS JACK a. acrylic on canvas. drybrush b. painting for Texas Monthly Magazine "Western Art" series c. 1983
2. COWBOY HORNED TOAD a. acrylic on canvas. drybrush b. promotion poster illustration for Clampitt Paper Company c. 1981
3. DOUBLE TALK a. acrylic on canvas. drybrush b. editorial illustration for the Cleveland Plain Dealer c. 1983
4. THE INEVITABILITY OF DEATH a. acrylic on canvas. drybrush b. editorial illustration for the Discipleship Journal c. 1984

トム・カリー

1. a. アクリル絵具, キャンバス。ドライブラッシュ技法 b. 雑誌イラスト c. 1983年
2. a. アクリル絵具, キャンバス。ドライブラッシュ技法 b. ポスター c. 1981年
3. a. アクリル絵具, キャンバス。ドライブラッシュ技法 b. 雑誌イラスト c. 1983年
4. a. アクリル絵具, キャンバス。ドライブラッシュ技法 b. 雑誌イラスト c. 1984年

Represented by Artist

Jerry Dadds

1. a. woodcut b. self-promotion c. 1979
2. a. colored pencil on colored paper b. calendar art for computer company c. 1982
3. a. wood engraving b. book jacket. University of Missouri Press c. 1981
4. a. colored pencil on colored paper b. calendar art for computer company c. 1982

ジェリー・ダッズ

1. a. 木版画　b. セルフプロモーション　c.1979年
2. a. 色鉛筆, カラーペーパー　b. カレンダー　c.1982年
3. a. 木版画　b. 書籍表紙　c.1981年
4. a. 色鉛筆, カラーペーパー　b. カレンダー　c.1982年

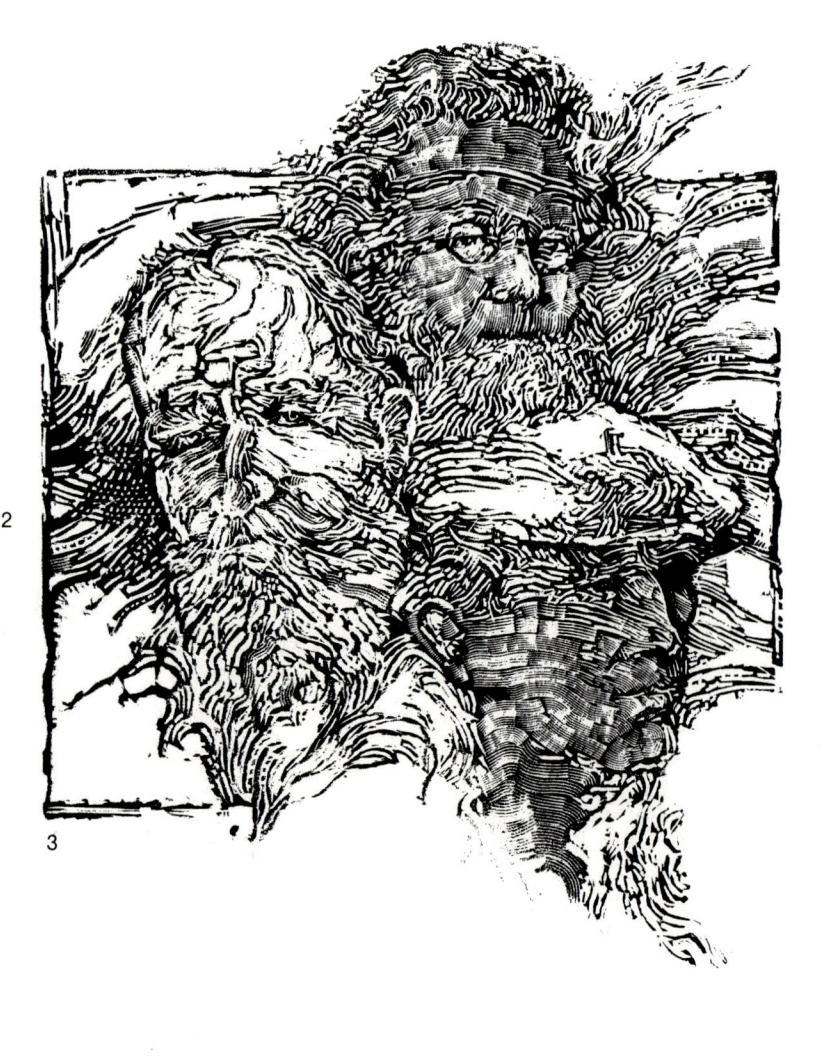

Represented by Artist

Tom Daly

1. a. ink and watercolor on illustration board with drawing pen and airbrush b. 3rd Anniversary announcement for "Cinemax"-Day. TV Cable c. 1983
2. a. designers gouache on illustration board with airbrush b. restaurant poster c. 1983
3. a. designers gouache on illustration board with airbrush b. student recruitment poster for "John Carroll Univ." c. 1983
4. a. designers gouache on illustration board with watercolor brush b. store poster, advertising New Variety of soups for children c. 1982

トム・デイリー

1. a. インク, 水彩絵具, イラストレーションボード, ドローイングペン, エアブラシ b. 広告イラスト c. 1983年
2. a. ガッシュ, イラストレーションボード, エアブラシ b. ポスター c. 1983年
3. a. ガッシュ, イラストレーションボード, エアブラシ b. ポスター c. 1983年
4. a. ガッシュ, イラストレーションボード, エアブラシ b. ポスター c. 1982年

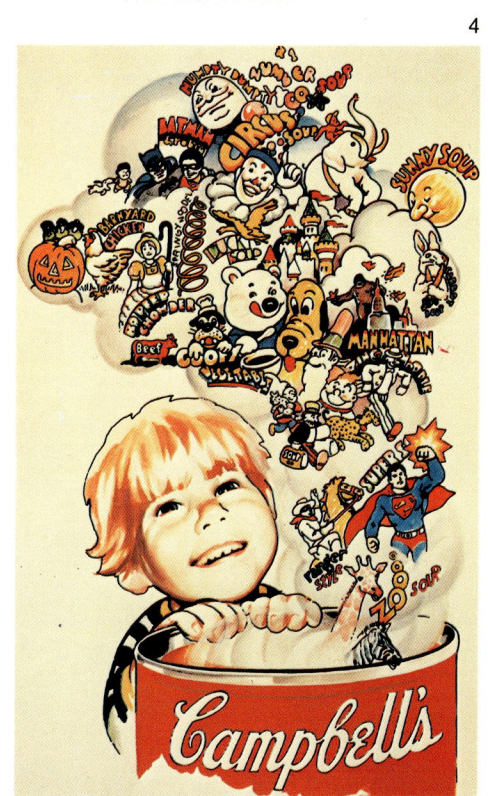

Represented by Artist

Alan Daniels

1. a. airbrush b. trade brochure. client 20th Century Fox c. 1983
2. a. airbrush b. editorial c. 1982
3. a. airbrush b. trade brochure "Sega" c. 1983
4. a. acrylic, airbrush, brush b. movie poster for BLADERUNNER c. 1982
5. a. ink, crayon, airbrush b. editorial c. 1982

アラン・ダニエルズ

1. a.エアブラシ b.カタログ・イラスト c.1983年
2. a.エアブラシ b.エディトリアル c.1982年
3. a.エアブラシ b.カタログ・イラスト c.1983年
4. a.アクリル絵具, エアブラシ, 画筆 b.映画ポスター c.1982年
5. a.インク, クレヨン, エアブラシ b.エディトリアル c.1982年

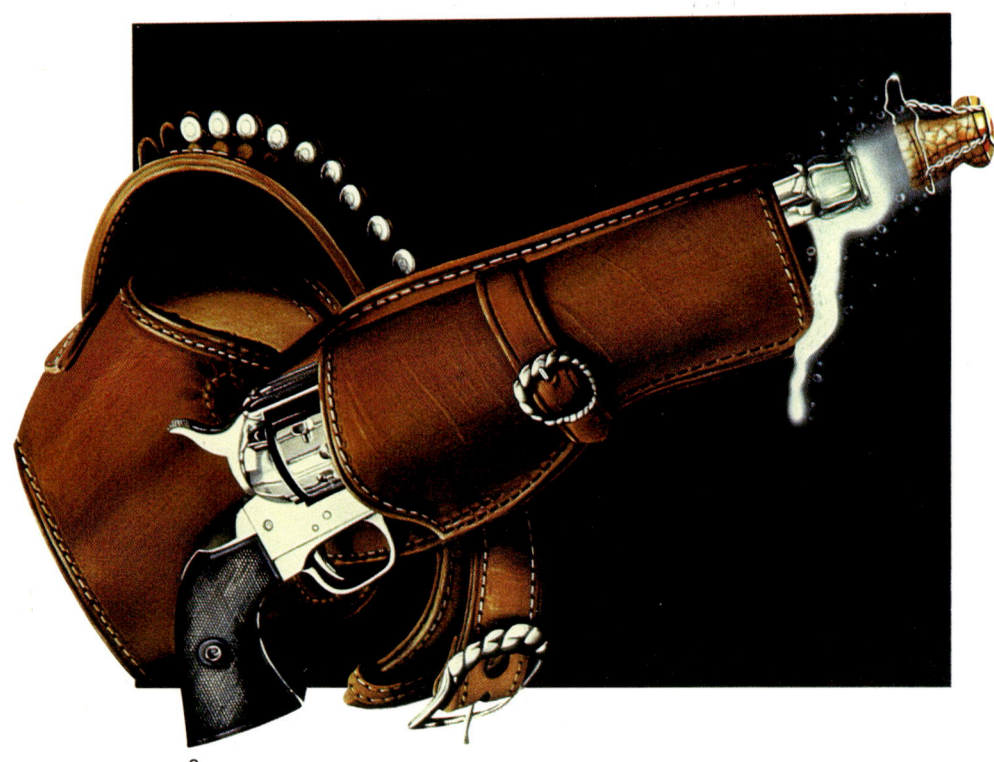

Represented by Artist

63

3

4  5

Represented by Artist

Beau Daniels　　　　ボー・ダニエルズ

1. a. dyes, airbrush b. advertisement for VIVITAR c. 1983
2. a. inks, airbrush b. advertisement for PLAYBOY c. 1982
3. a. airbrush dyes, airbrush b. advertising for HONDA c. 1983

1. a. 染料, エアブラシ b. 広告イラスト c. 1983年
2. a. インク, エアブラシ b. 広告イラスト c. 1982年
3. a. カラーインク, エアブラシ b. 広告イラスト c. 1983年

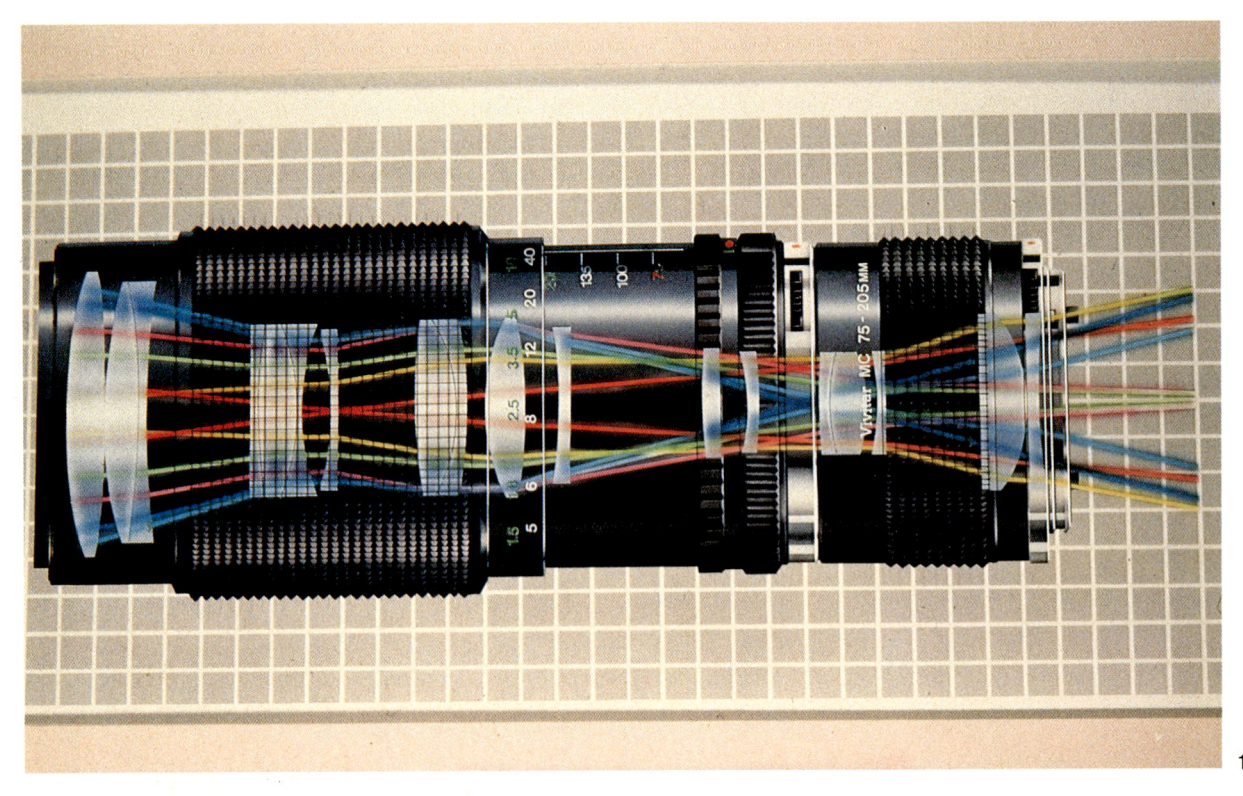

Represented by Artist

Bill Davis

1. JUGGLERS a. dyes and color charcoal pencil on board b. Sesame Street Magazine illustration c. 1982
2. DWEEDO a. ink & overlays b. Electric Company Magazine illustration c. 1983–1984
3. SHOGUN a. acrylic on canvas b. promotion poster c. 1981

ビル・デイヴィス

1. a. 染料, カラーチャコールペンシル, ボード b. 雑誌イラスト c. 1982年
2. a. インク, オーバーレイ b. 雑誌イラスト c. 1983~84年
3. a. アクリル絵具, キャンバス b. ポスター c. 1981年

65

Represented by Artist

Paul Davis

ポール・デイヴィス

66

1. KING LEAR a. acrylic on board b. advertisement for TV program c. 1983

1.a. アクリル絵具，ボード　b. TV番組宣伝用　c. 1983年

Represented by Artist

2. DISREALI a. acrylic on canvas b. advertisement for TV program c. 1979
3. REMEMBER NELSON a. acrylic on canvas b. advertisement for TV show c. 1981
4. DRINKS BEFORE DINNER a. acrylic on board b. advertisement for a play c. 1978

2. a. アクリル絵具, キャンバス b. TV番組宣伝用 c. 1979年
3. a. アクリル絵具, キャンバス b. TVショー番組宣伝用 c. 1981年
4. a. アクリル絵具, ボード b. 演劇の宣伝用 c. 1978年

Represented by Artist

5. ORWELL a. acrylic on board b. magazine cover illustration (Harper's) c. 1982
6. MONTH IN THE COUNTRY a. acrylic on board b. advertisement for a play c. 1979
7. a. acrylic on canvas b. poster c. 1979

5. a. アクリル絵具, ボード b. 雑誌表紙 c. 1982年
6. a. アクリル絵具, ボード b. 広告イラスト c. 1979年
7. a. アクリル絵具, キャンバス b. ポスター c. 1979年

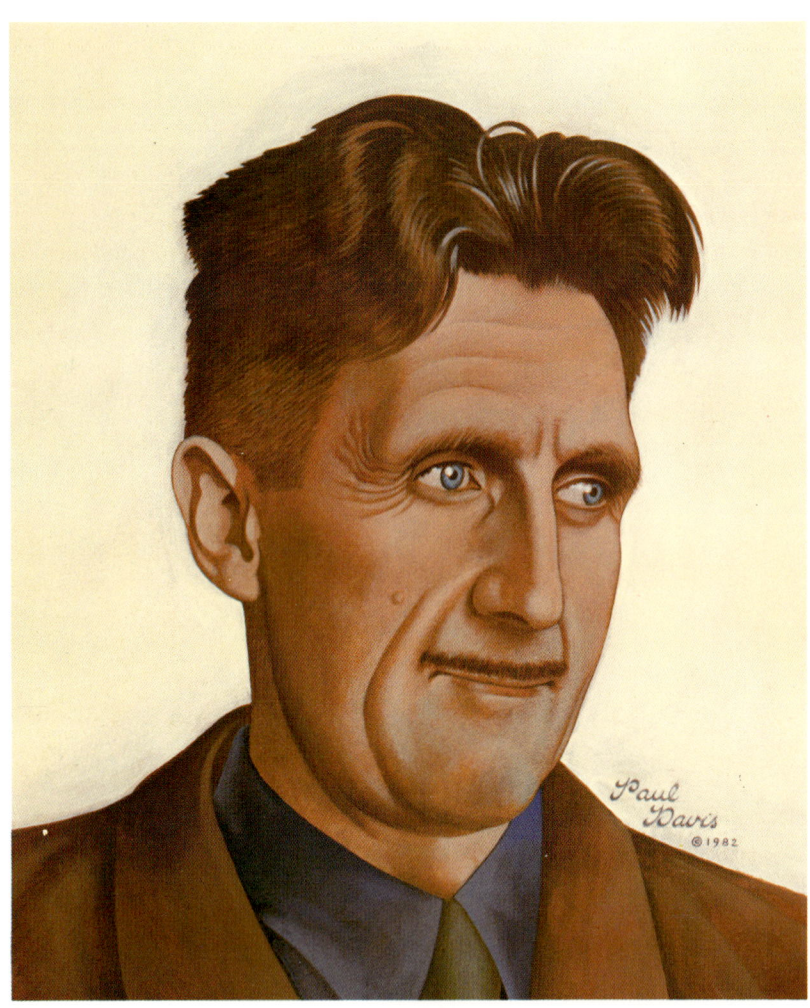

Represented by Artist

Michael J. Deas

1. a. egg tempera and oil on panel b. jacket illustration for Avon Books c. 1981
2. a. oil on panel b. jacket illustration for Avon Books c. 1982
3. a. egg tempera and oil on panel b. full page advertisement for pharmaceutical company c. 1983
4. a. oil on panel b. two-page illustration for a short story in Good Housekeeping magazine c. 1983

マイケル・J・ディーズ

1. a. エッグテンペラ，油彩絵具，パネル b. 書籍表紙 c. 1981年
2. a. 油彩絵具，パネル b. 書籍表紙 c. 1982年
3. a. エッグテンペラ，油彩絵具，パネル b. 広告イラスト c. 1983年
4. a. 油彩絵具，パネル b. 雑誌イラスト c. 1983年

Represented by Artist

Charles D. deMar

1. a. acrylics and gesso on masonite b. greeting card, Paper Moon c. 1982
2. a. Prismacolor and acrylics on colored board with airbrush b. poster for motion picture campaign, Warner Brothers c. 1981
3. a. acrylics on canvas b. poster for motion picture campaign, Warner Brothers c. 1982

チャールズ・D・ドゥマール

1. a. アクリル絵具, ジェッソ, メゾナイト b. グリーティングカード c. 1982年
2. a. 色鉛筆, アクリル絵具, カラーボード, エアブラシ b. 映画のキャンペーンポスター c. 1981年
3. a. アクリル絵具, キャンバス b. 映画のキャンペーンポスター c. 1982年

Represented by Artist

Harvey Dinnerstein ハーベイ・ディナースタイン

1-4 PARADE a. oil on canvas b. Esquire Magazine 50th Anniversary Issue "How We Lived" c. 1983 except #1 (1982)

1.-4. a. 油彩絵具, キャンバス b. 雑誌50周年記念号のイラスト c. 1983年(1のみ1982年)

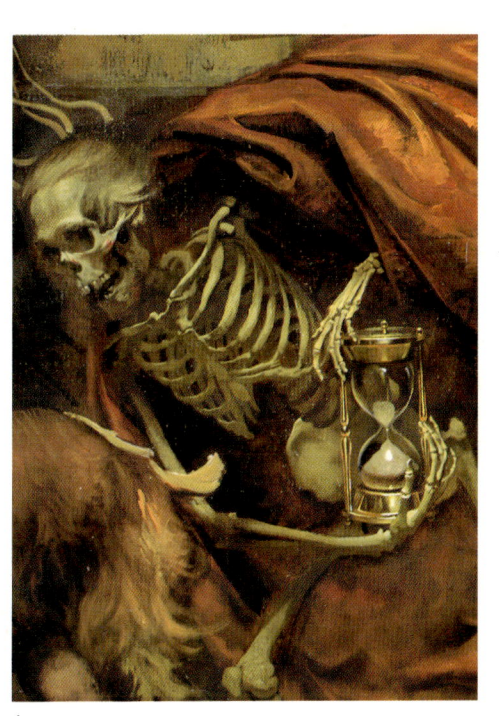

Represented by Artist

John Taylor Dismukes

1. DEMOLITION MAN a. acrylic and ink on board. airbrush and brush b. illustration featured in book RADIO EYES c. 1983
2. a. acrylic and ink on board. airbrush and brush. b. poster for exhibition. Design 81, Helsinki, Finland c. 1981
3. MEAN STREAK by Y.T. a. acrylic and ink on board. airbrush and brush b. album cover, A&M Records c. 1983
4. MODERN MEDICINE by Doc. Holiday a. acrylic and ink on board. airbrush and brush. b. album cover, A&M Records c. 1983

ジョン・テイラー・ディズミュークス

1.a.アクリル絵具、インク、ボード、エアブラシ、画筆 b.書籍イラスト c.1983年
2.a.アクリル絵具、インク、ボード、エアブラシ、画筆 b.ポスター c.1981年
3.a.アクリル絵具、インク、ボード、エアブラシ、画筆 b.レコードジャケット c.1983年
4.a.アクリル絵具、インク、ボード、エアブラシ、画筆、ペン b.レコードジャケット c.1983年

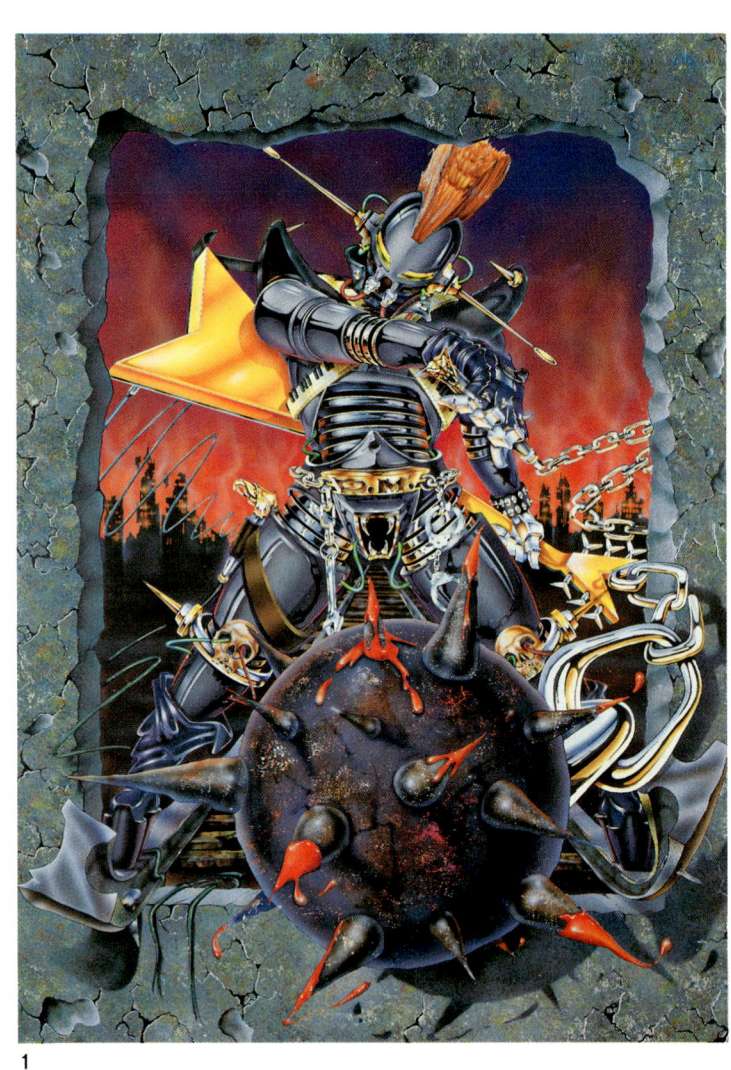

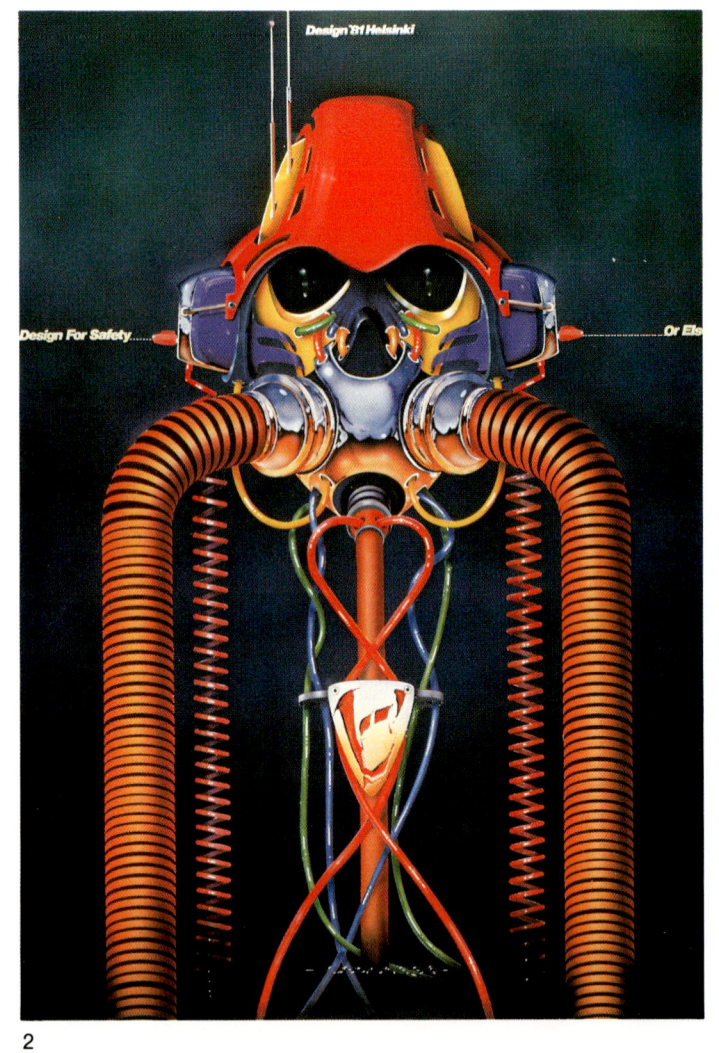

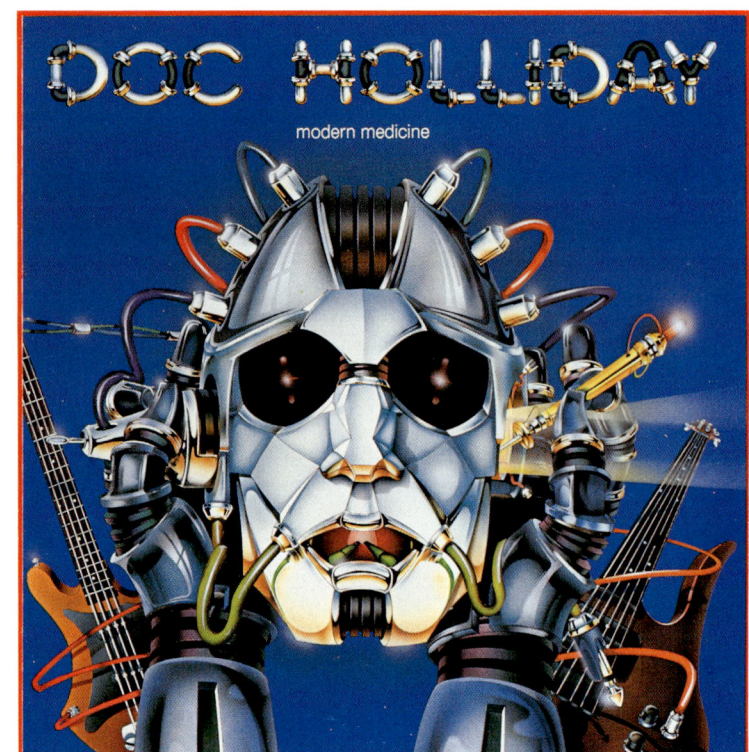

72

Represented by Artist

Dennis Dittrich

1. a. watercolor b. magazine cover for "Communications of the Acm" Magazine c. 1983
2. a. pen & ink/watercolor b. self-promotion
3. a. pen & ink/watercolor b. brochure cover for corporate productivity contest. client: Equitable Life
4. a. pen & ink/watercolor b. editorial illustration for "Outdoor Life" Magazine

デニス・ディートリッヒ

1. a. 水彩絵具 b. 雑誌表紙 c. 1983年
2. a. ペン，インク，水彩絵具 b. セルフプロモーション
3. a. ペン，インク，水彩絵具 b. 企業社内誌イラスト
4. a. ペン，インク，水彩絵具 b. 雑誌イラスト

Represented by Artist

Patty Dryden

1. GIRL IN BATHING SUIT a. pastel on paper b. part of a fashion series for New York Magazine c. 1983
2. PORTRAIT OF MAN HOLDING A DRINK a. oil on glass. finger painted b. commissioned portrait c. 1983
3. MAN WITH BEARD a. oil on glass. finger painted b. promotion piece c. 1983
4. YELLOW CHAIR a. pastel on paper b. promotion piece c. 1983

パティ・ドライデン

1. a.パステル、紙 b.雑誌イラスト c.1983年
2. a.油彩絵具、ガラス。フィンガーペインティング b.肖像画 c.1983年
3. a.油彩絵具、ガラス。フィンガーペインティング b.セルフプロモーション c.1983年
4. a.パステル、紙 b.セルフプロモーション c.1983年

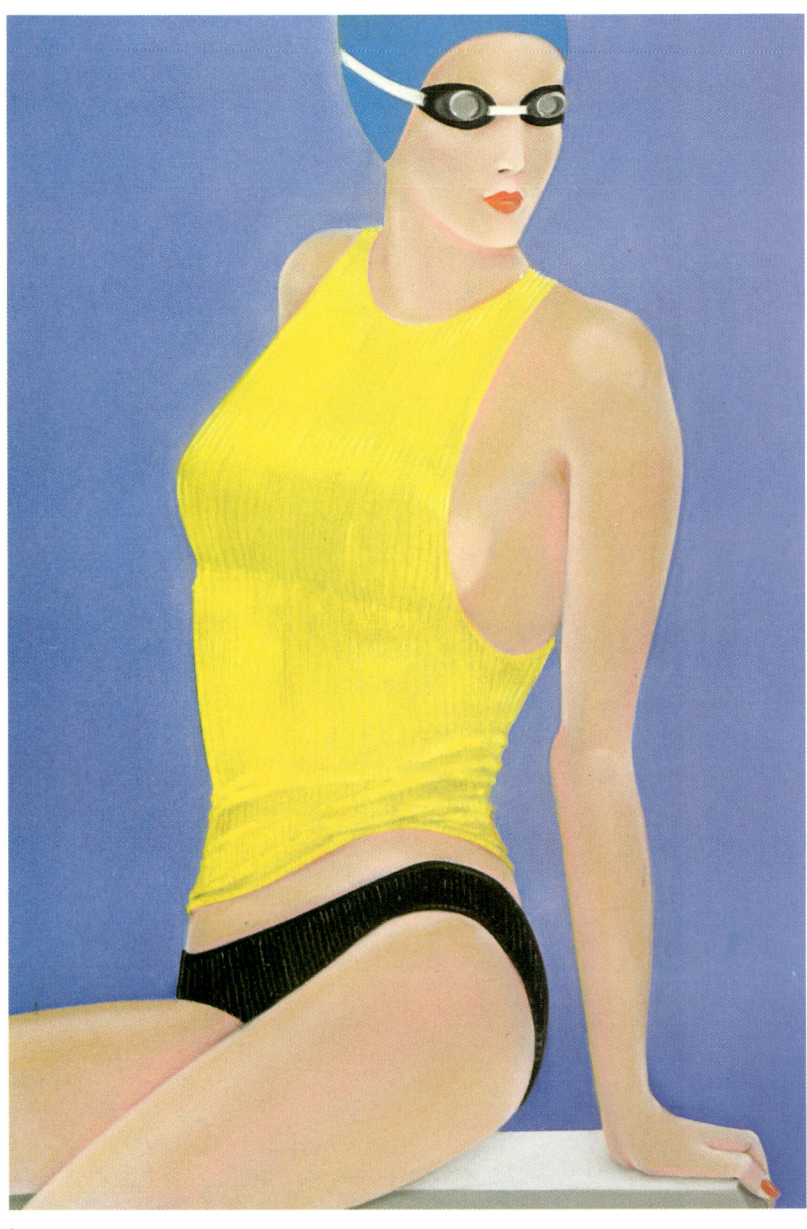

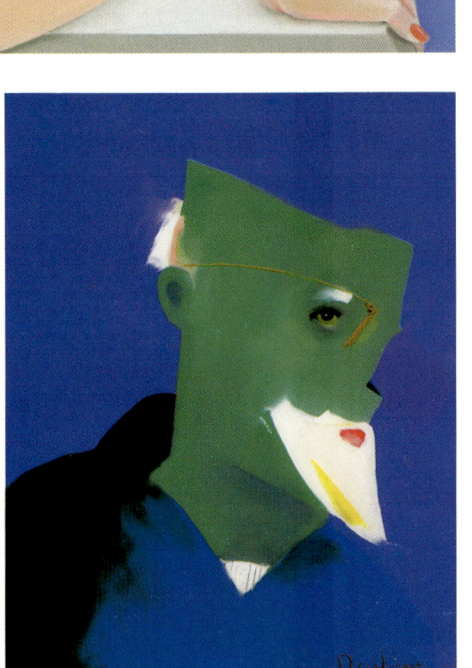

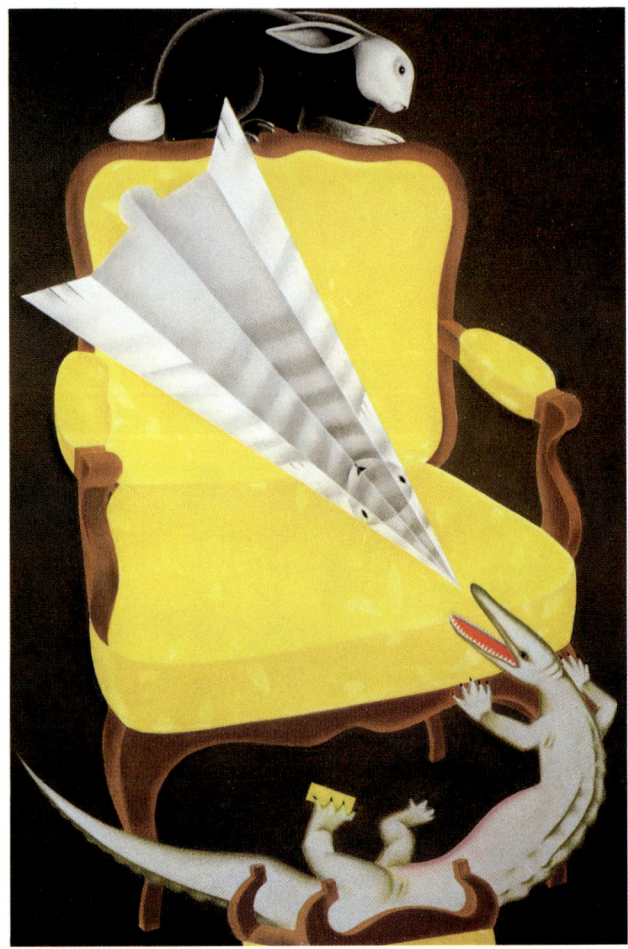

Represented by Artist

Andrzej Dudzinski

1. a. Neocolor (oil crayon) on paper b. illustration for Beauty in Vogue (London) c. 1983
2. a. Neocolor on paper b. illustration for Texas Monthly c. 1983
3. a. Neocolor on paper b. illustration for Boston Globe Magazine c. 1983
4. a. Neocolor on paper b. personal work from the Spectators' series published as a part of artist's portfolio in Racquet Quarterly c. 1984

アンドレイ・デュジンスキー

1. a. ネオカラー(油性クレヨン), 紙 b. 雑誌イラスト c.1983年
2. a. ネオカラー, 紙 b. 雑誌イラスト c.1983年
3. a. ネオカラー, 紙 b. 雑誌イラスト c.1983年
4. a. ネオカラー, 紙 b. ポートフォリオ c.1984年

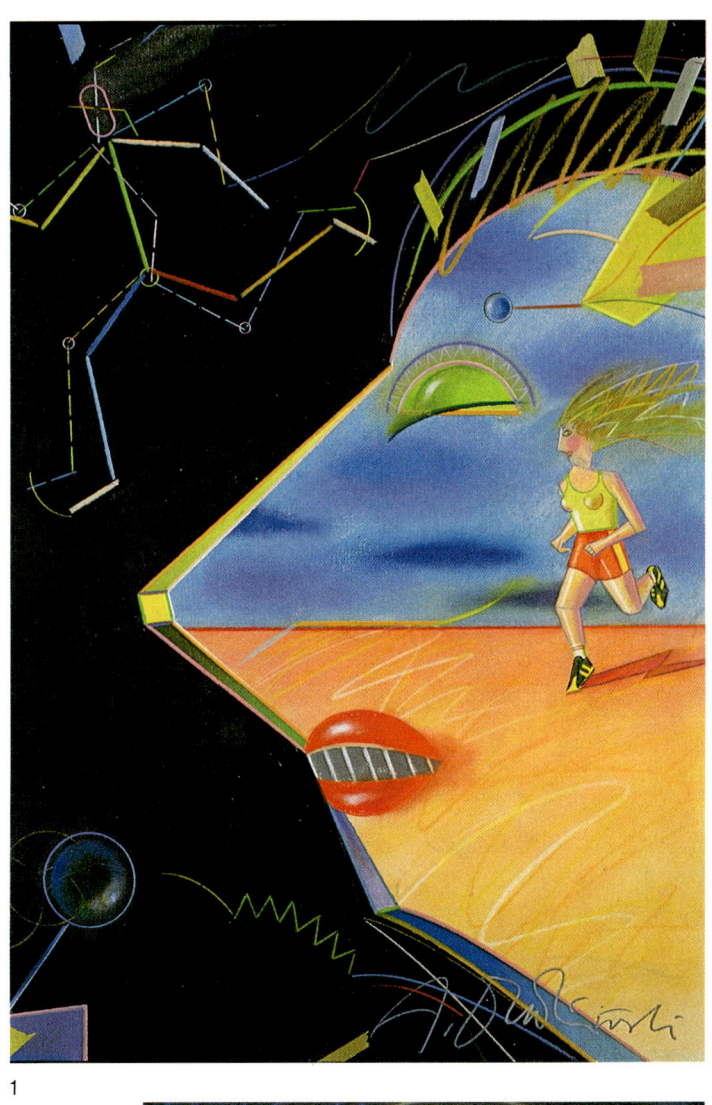

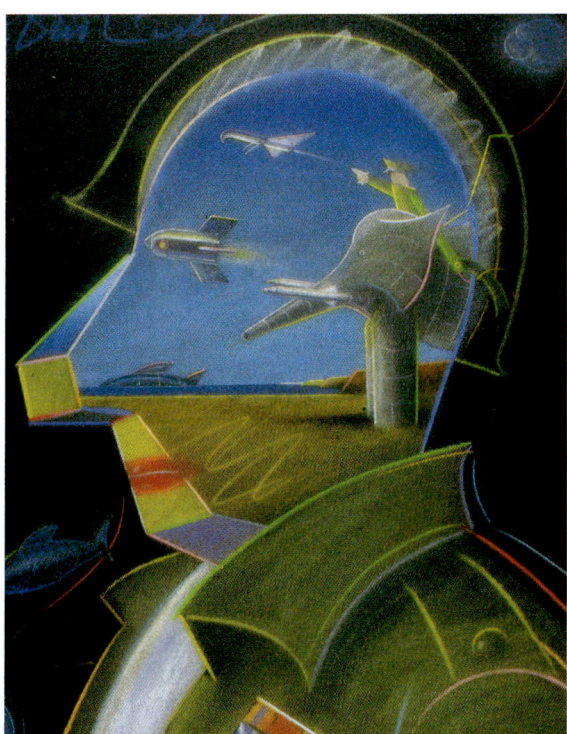

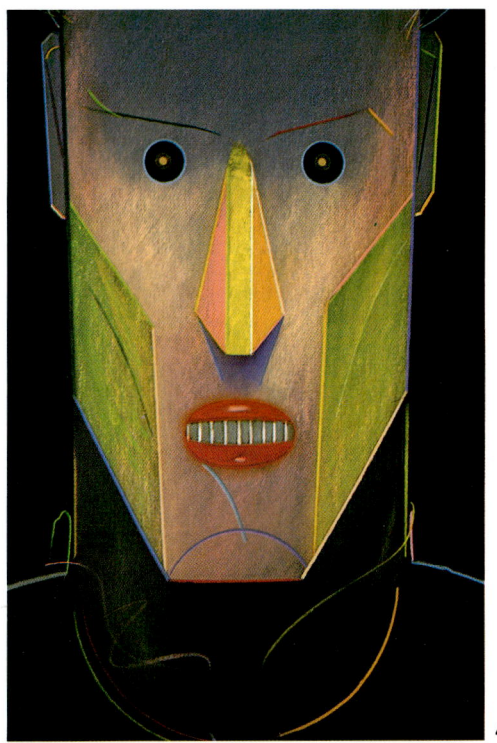

Represented by Artist

Alex Ebel

アレックス・エベル

76

1. a. dyes & inks. Ebel Technique b. magazine illustration c. 1983
2. a. dyes & inks. Ebel Technique b. Ballantine Books c. 1982
3. a. dyes & inks. Ebel Technique b. Chick magazine c. 1982

1. a. 染料, インク, エベル技法 b. 雑誌イラスト c. 1983年
2. a. 染料, インク, エベル技法 b. 書籍イラスト c. 1982年
3. a. 染料, インク, エベル技法 b. 雑誌イラスト c. 1982年

Represented by Artist

Jack Endewelt

1. a. watercolor
2. a. watercolor
3. a. watercolor

ジャック・エンデウォルト

1. a. 水彩絵具
2. a. 水彩絵具
3. a. 水彩絵具

77

Represented by Artist

John Eastman

1-6. a. lithograph
1-6. b. limited edition poster

ジョン・イーストマン

1-6.a.リトグラフ
1-6.b.限定版ポスター

1

2

Represented by Artist

Anka Ente

1. FRUITS a. pencil, transparent dyes on cold press board b. client: Chevron (Ortho Div.) c. 1982
2. MONEY WITH BOLT a. pencil on cold press board b. client: MCA Corporation c. 1983
3. LUCKY STRIKE a. transparent dyes, pencil on cold press board b. Portfolio self-promotion piece c. 1983

Represented by Artist

Bill Ersland

1. a. watercolor b. "Industry Week" magazine article entitled "Putting Your Act Together" c. 1982
2. a. watercolor b. "TV Guide" magazine article entitled "Cameras in the Courtroom" c. 1982
3. a. watercolor b. editorial c. 1983
4. a. watercolor and gouache b. N.F.L. magazine article about John Stallworth of the Pittsburgh Steelers c. 1983

ビル・アーズランド

1. a. 水彩絵具 b. 雑誌イラスト c. 1982年
2. a. 水彩絵具 b. 雑誌イラスト c. 1982年
3. a. 水彩絵具 b. エディトリアル c. 1983年
4. a. 水彩絵具 b. 雑誌イラスト c. 1983年

Represented by Artist

Louis Escobedo

1. WATERBABIES a. oil on canvas b. call for entries poster — Dallas Illustrators 3-84 c. 1984
2. COMING OF DAWN a. acrylic on illustration board b. self-promotion c. 1983
3. RISE & SHINE a. acrylic on illustration board with airbrush b. for Texas A&M University c. 1980

ルイ・エスコベード

1. a. 油彩絵具, キャンバス b. ポスター c. 1984年
2. a. アクリル絵具, イラストレーションボード b. セルフプロモーション c. 1983年
3. a. アクリル絵具, イラストレーションボード, エアブラシ b. 広告イラスト c. 1980年

Represented by Artist

Jim Evans

1. a. acrylic, dyes, and pencil on illustration board with airbrush b. ad and poster for Life Link Intl. c. 1983
2. a. acrylic, dyes, and pencil on illustration board with airbrush b. ad and poster for Life Link Intl. c. 1983
3. a. acrylic, dyes, and pencil on illustration board with airbrush b. poster for NASA Space Movie c. 1981
4. a. acrylic, dyes, and pencil on illustration board with airbrush b. album cover for Columbia Records c. 1980

ジム・エヴァンス

1. a.アクリル絵具，染料，鉛筆，イラストレーションボード，エアブラシ b.広告，ポスター c.1983年
2. a.アクリル絵具，染料，鉛筆，イラストレーションボード，エアブラシ b.広告，ポスター c.1983年
3. a.アクリル絵具，染料，鉛筆，イラストレーションボード，エアブラシ b.映画ポスター c.1981年
4. a.アクリル絵具，染料，鉛筆，イラストレーションボード，エアブラシ b.レコードジャケット c.1980年

Represented by Artist

Teresa Fasolino

1. a. acrylic on canvas b. illustration for cover of TV Guide, Christmas c. 1982
2. a. acrylic on canvas. b. poster for Grand Union Supermarkets c. 1983
3. a. acrylic on canvas b. illustration for poem by Emily Dickenson "There's A Certain Slant of Light" published by Macmillan Inc. c. 1983
4. a. acrylic on canvas b. illustration for poem by Emily Dickenson "A Funeral in My Mind" published by Macmillan Inc. c. 1983

テレサ・ファソリーノ

1. a. アクリル絵具，キャンバス b. TVガイド誌表紙 c.1982年
2. a. アクリル絵具，キャンバス b. ポスター c.1983年
3. a. アクリル絵具，キャンバス b. 詩集挿画 c.1983年
4. a. アクリル絵具，キャンバス b. 詩集挿画 c.1983年

Represented by Artist

Ann Field

1. SAILOR GIRL a. pastel and pencil crayon b. unpublished c. 1981
2. FASHION SHOW SKETCHES a. chalk and charcoal b. editorial illustration for London Evening Newspaper, on Chloe and Calvin Klein c. 1982
3. TORSO a. pastel drawing b. advertisement for Thierry Mugler Accessories, Paris c. 1982

アン・フィールド

1. a. パステル, クレヨン b. 未発表作品 c. 1981年
2. a. チョーク, チャコール b. 新聞イラスト c. 1982年
3. a. パステル b. 広告イラスト c. 1982年

Represented by Artist

Robert Florczak

1. THE LION & THE CROSS a. oil glazes on masonite b. Ballantine Bookcover c. 1980
2. HAREM a. oil glazes on masonite b. Ballantine bookcover c. 1981
3. BICYCLE BUILT FOR SPACE a. oil glazes on masonite b. Ace bookcover c. 1980
4. THE DUEL a. oil glazes on masonite b. Jove Press bookcover c. 1982

ロバート・フロアザーク

1. a. オイルグレイズ，メゾナイト b. 書籍表紙 c. 1980年
2. a. オイルグレイズ，メゾナイト b. 書籍表紙 c. 1981年
3. a. オイルグレイズ，メゾナイト b. 書籍表紙 c. 1980年
4. a. オイルグレイズ，メゾナイト b. 書籍表紙 c. 1982年

Represented by Artist

Patric Fourshé

1. THE EVENING NEWS a. alkyd on canvas b. book. painting illustrates article about the governing principles behind media reporting c. 1982
2. COOKOUT a. acrylic on canvas b. food oriented calendar c. 1979
3. SPRINGWALK a. casein & acrylic on watercolor board b. calendar depicting springtime scene c. 1977

パトリック・フロシェ

1. a. アルキド, キャンバス b. 書籍イラスト c.1982年
2. a. アクリル絵具, キャンバス b. カレンダー c.1979年
3. a. カゼイン, アクリル絵具, 水彩ボード b. カレンダー c.1977年

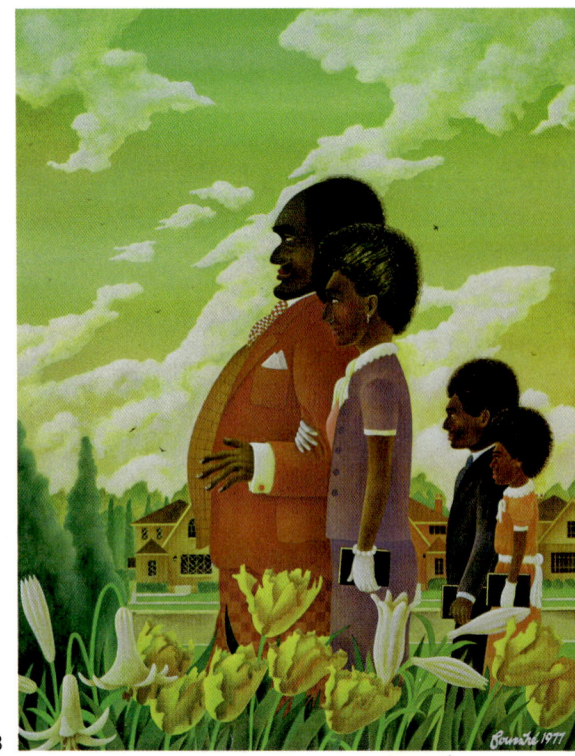

Represented by Artist

Phil Franké

1. TRUCK RUNNER a. pen & ink, watercolor, acrylic on illustration board b. promotional poster c. 1981
2. a. graphite and transparent dyes b. editorial c. 1982
3. a. pen, indian ink on illustration board b. movie poster c. 1981
4. GEORGE C. SCOTT a. graphite, watercolor, and designer's gouache on illustration board b. promotional poster c. 1979

フィル・フランケ

1. a. ペン，インク，水彩絵具，アクリル絵具，イラストレーションボード　b. ポスター　c. 1981年
2. a. グラファイト鉛筆，透明染料　b. エディトリアル　c. 1982年
3. a. ペン，墨汁，イラストレーションボード　b. 映画ポスター　c. 1981年
4. a. グラファイト鉛筆，水彩絵具，ガッシュ，イラストレーションボード　b. ポスター　c. 1979年

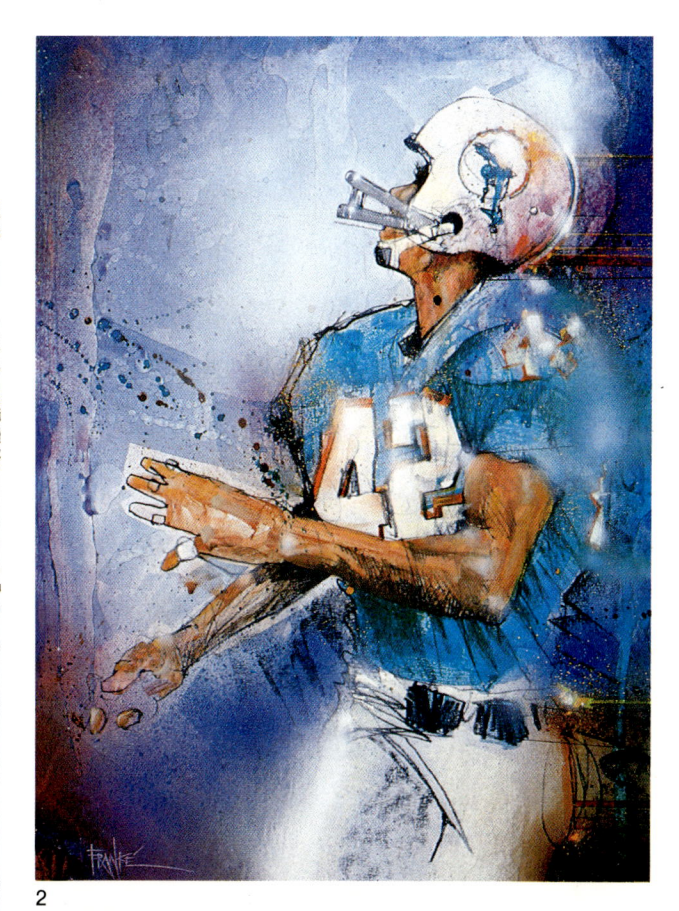

Represented by Artist

Dagmar Frinta ダグマール・フリンタ 92

1. a. pen, ink, watercolor b. The Franklin Library c. 1983
2. a. pen, ink, watercolor b. TWA Ambassador Magazine c. 1983
3. a. pen, ink, weatercolor b. Science 83 c. 1983

1. a.ペン，インク，水彩絵具 b.注文製作 c.1983年
2. a.ペン，インク，水彩絵具 b.雑誌イラスト c.1983年
3. a.ペン，インク，水彩絵具 b.雑誌イラスト c.1983年

Represented by Artist

Nicholas Gaetano

1. a. acrylic b. poster and ad for the "Workbook" portfolio c. 1984
2. a. acrylic b. poster sold at galleries c. 1983
3. a. acrylic b. ad for Frontier Airlines c. 1983

1. a.アクリル絵具 b.ポスター, 広告 c.1984年
2. a.アクリル絵具 b.ポスター c.1983年
3. a.アクリル絵具 b.広告 c.1983年

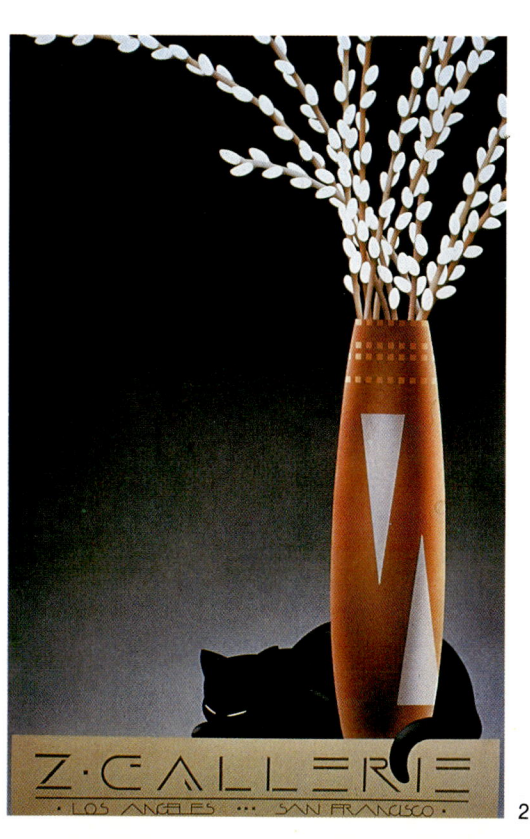

Represented by Artist

Bernard Fuchs

1. INDIANS b. painting for O'Grandy Galleries, Chicago Ill. and Scottsdale Ariz.
2. b. illustration of trucks for an advertisement for IU International, a shipping company
3. b. portrait of Le Corbusier — French Architect
4. b. illustration for Reader's Digest story, "Words by Heart" by Ouida Sebestyen.

バーナード・フックス

1. b. ギャラリー展示作品
2. b. 広告イラスト
3. b. 肖像画
4. b. 雑誌イラスト

Represented by Artist

2

3

4

Represented by Artist

Stanley W. Galli

1. SPANISH WALK a. oil on canvas b. museum and gallery exhibitions
2. FIGHTING COCK a. oil on canvas b. museum and gallery exhibitions
3. AMIGOS a. acrylic wash on canvas b. museum and gallery exhibitions
4. MOUNTAIN SHEEP a. acrylic wash on canvas b. museum and gallery exhibitions
5. MISSION HARVEST a. oil on canvas b. museum and gallery exhibitions
1–5. c. 1978–1984

スタンレー・W・ガリ

1. a. 油彩絵具, キャンバス b. ギャラリー展示品
2. a. 油彩絵具, キャンバス b. ギャラリー展示品
3. a. アクリル絵具, キャンバス b. ギャラリー展示品
4. a. アクリル絵具, キャンバス b. ギャラリー展示品
5. a. 油彩絵具, キャンバス b. ギャラリー展示品
1-5. c. 1978年-1984年

Represented by Artist

3

4

5

Represented by Artist

Nixon Galloway　ニクソン・ギャロウェイ

1. TORCHBEARER a. pencil and wash. The original drawing was done in soft graphite pencil on acrylic board, then, a photo was made onto which I added the color using dyes and spray mark. b. cover and dust jacket for the book "An Approved History of the Olimpic Games" by Bill Henry. c. 1983

1.a. 鉛筆, ウォッシュ技法。原画はアクリルボードにソフトグラファイト鉛筆で描き, それを紙焼きにした後, カラーインクで着色し, スプレイをかける
b. 書籍表紙　c. 1983年

Represented by Artist

2. 747 a. acrylic and Luma dyes b. for marketing campaign by United Airlines c. 1980
3. UNITED KINGDOM AT EPCOT a. acrylic and tempia, architectural blueprints. b. brochure for stockholders of WED Enterprises (Disney) c. 1982

2. a. アクリル絵具, カラーインク b. キャンペーン・イラスト c. 1980年
3. a. 建築写真の青焼きにアクリル絵具, テンピアで彩色 b. パンフレット・イラスト c. 1982年

Represented by Artist

John Gamache

1. a. gouache & dyes on illustration board with airbrush b. self-promotion c. 1983
2. a. dyes on illustration board with airbrush b. intended cover for Heavy Metal Magazine c. 1982
3. a. oils and gouache on illustration board with paint brush & airbrush b. intended movie poster c. 1983
4. a. gouache on illustration board with airbrush b. private collection c. 1982

ジョン・ガマッシュ

1. a. ガッシュ, 染料, イラストレーションボード, エアブラシ b. セルフプロモーション c. 1983年
2. a. 染料, イラストレーションボード, エアブラシ b. 雑誌表紙 c. 1982年
3. a. 油彩絵具, ガッシュ, イラストレーションボード, 画筆, エアブラシ b. 映画ポスター c. 1983年
4. a. ガッシュ, イラストレーションボード, エアブラシ b. 個人所蔵作品 c. 1982年

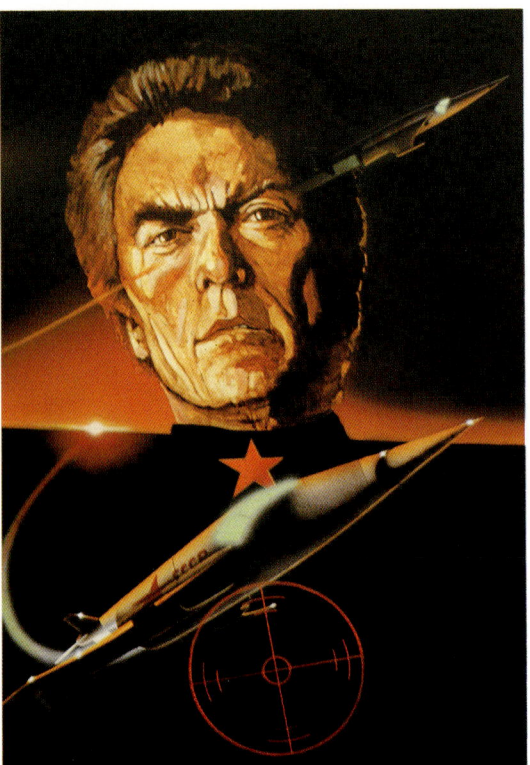

Represented by Artist

John Gampert　　　ジョン・ガンパート

1. EAGLE a. acrylic on WC paper b. book illustration. Vanishing Wildlife by Silver Burdette c. 1983
2. LOUIS a. acrylic and airbrush on board b. poster art-Fanta Graphics c. 1983
3. PREZ a. mixed media b. jazz calendar Fanta Graphics c. 1984

1. a. アクリル絵具，水彩画紙　b. 書籍イラスト　c. 1983年
2. a. アクリル絵具，エアブラシ，ボード　b. ポスター　c. 1983年
3. a. 各種画材　b. カレンダー　c. 1984年

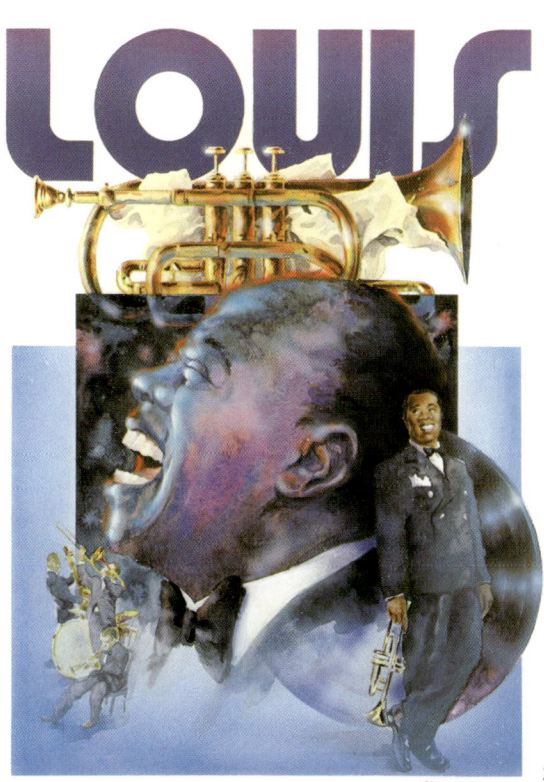

Represented by Artist

Joe Garnett

1. SWIMMER a. airbrush b. olympic poster
2. a. airbrush b. olympic poster, not used
3. DINER a. airbrush b. poster for movie "Diner"

ジョー・ガーネット

1. a. エアブラシ b. オリンピックのポスター
2. a. エアブラシ b. オリンピックのポスター（未発表作品）
3. a. エアブラシ b. 映画ポスター

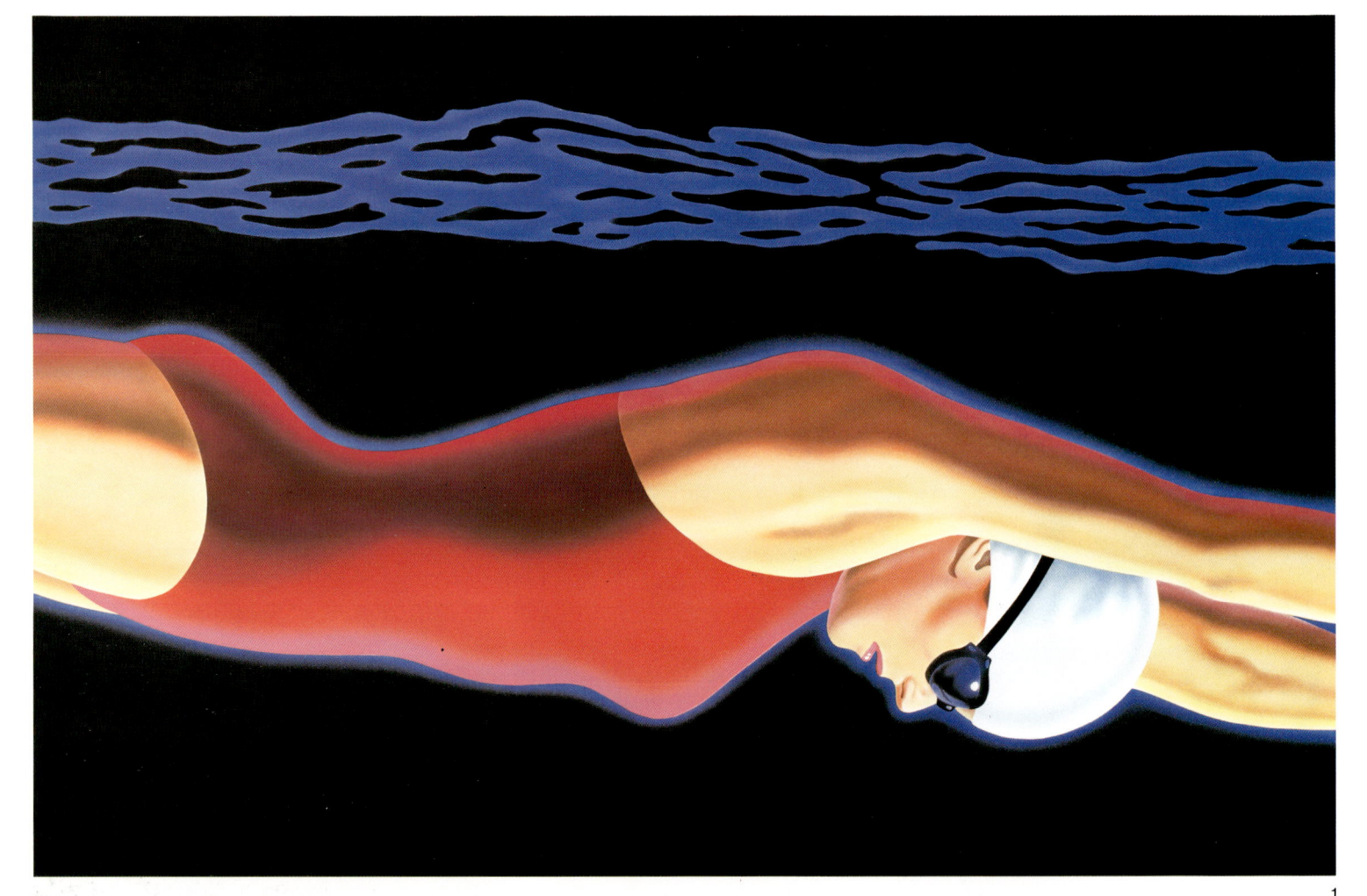

102

Represented by Artist

Gerry Gersten

1. WOODY ALLEN a. pencil on vellum b. one of a series of authors for "Book of the Month" book club c. 1983
2. CAPYBANA a. pen and ink with dyes b. Time/Life books. story about Rodents c. 1980
3. CASTRO & HOLMENI a. pen & ink with dyes b. mailing piece for "The Economist" magazine c. 1981
4. BASEBALL PITCHER a. pencil on vellum with dyes b. "New Times" magazine, story about strange behavior among athletes c. 1981

Represented by Artist

George Giusti

1. a. paper sculpture b. calendar page. The Million & Cocktail. Japan Barmen Association c. 1981
2. a. Indian ink and tempera b. "Tofranil" series. Antidipressant

1.a. 紙彫刻　b. カレンダー　c. 1981年
2.a. 墨, テンペラ　b. "トフラニル"シリーズ

1

2

Represented by Artist

3. a. champion paper insert b. paper for records labels c. 1980
4. a. acrylic b. project for Geigy-Pharma c. 1980

3. a. ペーパーインサート b. レコードラベル c. 1980年
4. a. アクリル絵具 b. 企業計画書イラスト c. 1980年

Represented by Artist

106

5. a. Böhringer, aluminum, stainless steel b. Alupent (Farmaceutical Lungs) c. 1979
6. a. stainless steel sculpture b. TV guide cover c. 1979

5. a. ステンレス彫刻　b. クライアント：アルーペント　c. 1979年
6. a. ステンレス彫刻　b. TVガイドの表紙　c. 1979年

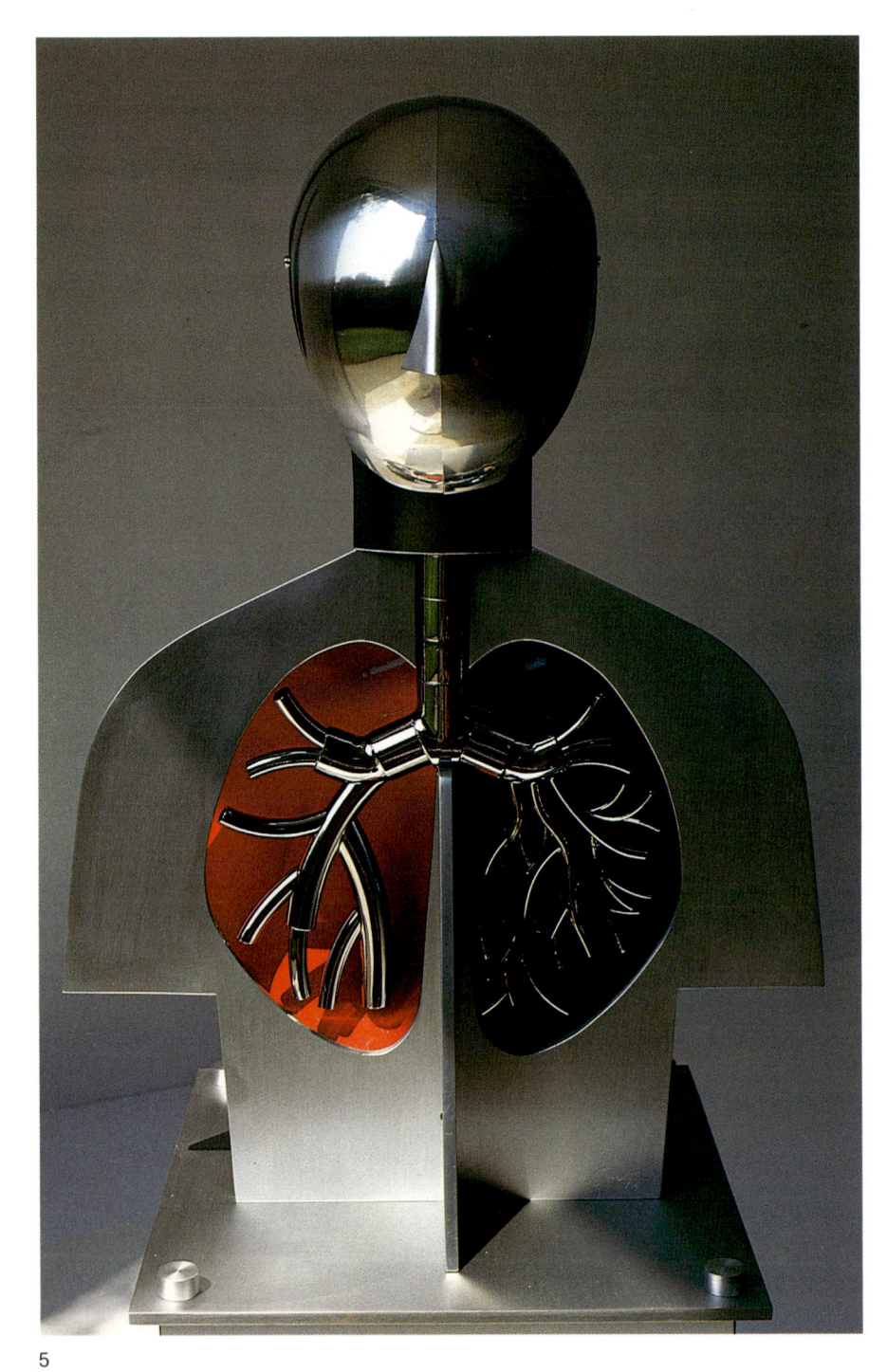

5

6

Represented by Artist

Robert Giusti

1. MFSB "MYSERIES OF THE WORLD" a. acrylic on canvas b. record cover (CBS) c. 1980
2. BLUE HIGHWAYS a. acrylic on canvas b. editorial magazine illustration c. 1982

1.a. アクリル絵具，キャンバス b. レコードジャケット c. 1980年
2.a. アクリル絵具，キャンバス b. 雑誌イラスト c. 1982年

Represented by Artist

Milton Glaser ミルトン・グレーサー 108

1. SONIA DELAUNAY a. colored inks and dyes b. Delaunay's portrait c. 1983

1.a. カラーインク，染料 b. 肖像画 c. 1983年

Represented by Artist

2. GOERGIA O'KEEFE a. colored pencil, torn paper b. O'Keefe's portrait c. 1983
3. EDWARD MUNCH a. colored inks and dyes, India ink, crayon b. Munch's portrait c. 1983

2. a. 色鉛筆, ちぎり紙 b. 肖像画 c. 1983年
3. a. カラーインク, 染料, 墨, クレヨン b. 肖像画 c. 1983年

2

3

Represented by Artist

4. ODILON REDON a. oil pastels, photostat b. Redon's portrait. the background is a reproduction of actual lithograph by Redon c. 1983
5. PIET MONDRIAN a. colored inks and dyes, colored pencil, crayon b. Mondrian's portrait c. 1983

4.a. 油性パステル，複写写真　b. 肖像画　c. 1983年
5.a. カラーインク，染料，色鉛筆，クレヨン　b. 肖像画　c. 1983年

4

5

Represented by Artist

6. GIORGIO DE CHIRICO a. colored inks and dyes, colored pencil, tempera paint b. Chirico's portrait c. 1983

6.a. カラーインク, 染料, 色鉛筆, テンペラ絵具 b. 肖像画 c.1983年

Represented by Artist

Alexander Gnidziejko　アレクサンダー・ニジコー

1. a. oil b. editorial for McCall's magazine c. 1975
2. OVER THE RAINBOW a. watercolor c. 1981
3. AMY ARTIST a. oil glazes on masonite b. student composition poster c. 1983

1. a. 油彩絵具　b. 雑誌イラスト　c. 1975年
2. a. 水彩絵具　c. 1981年
3. a. 油彩絵具, グラッシ技法, メゾナイト　b. ポスター　c. 1983年

Represented by Artist

Raphaelle Goethals ラファエル・ゴゥテルス 113

1. a. colored pencil on board b. "Christmas Gift" piece for the artist's portfolio c. 1982
2. a. pencil and acrylic on board b. self-promotion piece c. 1983
3. a. watercolor b. illustration for the artist's portfolio c. 1983

1. a. 色鉛筆, ボード b. ポートフォリオ c. 1982年
2. a. 色鉛筆, アクリル絵具, ボード b. セルフプロモーション c. 1983年
3. a. 水彩絵具 b. ポートフォリオ c. 1983年

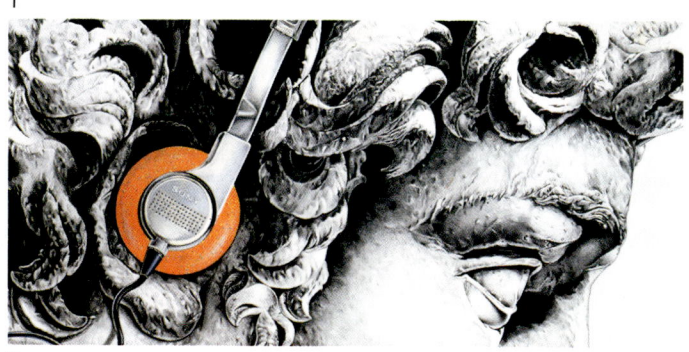

Represented by Artist

Penelope Gottlieb ペネローペ・ゴッドリーブ 114

1. a. watercolor
2. a. acrylic, airbrush
3. b. Editorial. Swank Magazine
4. a. acrylic, airbrush

1. a. 水彩絵具
2. a. アクリル絵具, エアブラシ
3. b. 雑誌イラスト
4. a. アクリル絵具, エアブラシ

Represented by Artist

James Graca

1. a. inks, Dr. Martin Dyes, Prisma pencil, photo collage, with airbrush b. movie poster, 20th Century Fox Studios c. 1982
2. a. acrylics, inks, Dr. Martin Dyes, Prisma pencil, white gouache, airbrush b. promotional piece c. 1982
3. a. pencil, inks, Dr. Martin Dyes, Prisma pencil, white opaque b. illustration for ad for television show "Candid Camera" for NBC c. 1980.

ジェームス・グラカ

1. a. インク，カラーインク，色鉛筆，写真のコラージュ，エアブラシ b. 映画ポスター c.1982年
2. a. アクリル絵具，インク，カラーインク，色鉛筆，ホワイトガッシュ，エアブラシ b. セルフプロモーション c.1982年
3. a. 鉛筆，インク，カラーインク，色鉛筆，ホワイトオペーク b. TVショーイラスト c.1980年

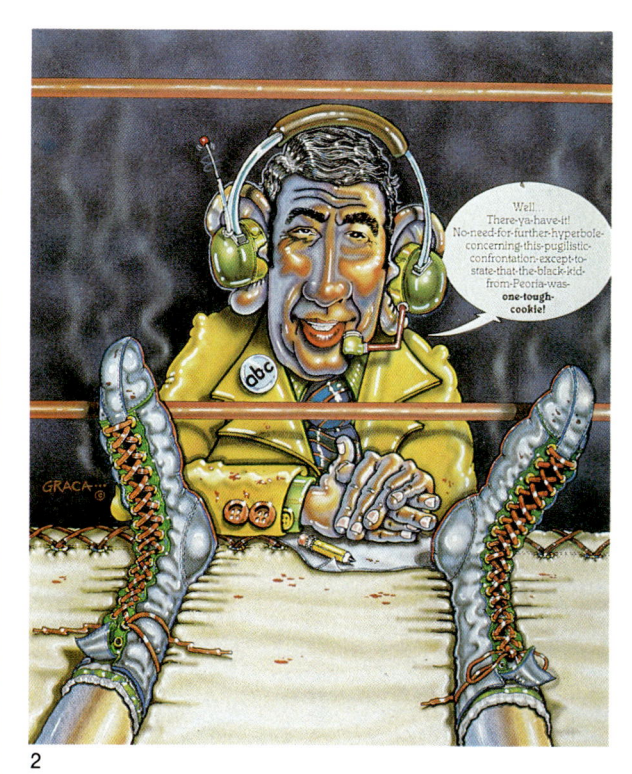

Represented by Artist

Alexa Grace

1. THE NURSES a. collage of wood and sandpaper b. personal work for an exhibition of the Graham Gallery c. 1981
2. WHAT'S MISSING HERE? OR MONKEY CHILDREN EAT LUNCH TOO. a. porcelain, paper, pastel b. personal work for exhibition c. 1981
3. PLEASE REMEMBER THIS. YOU WON'T FORGET, WILL YOU? a. wood, paper, paint b. personal work for exhibition c. 1981

アレッサ・グレース

1. a. 木とサンドペーパーのコラージュ b. 展示会出品作品 c. 1981年
2. a. 磁器, 紙, パステル b. 展示会出品作品 c. 1981年
3. a. 木, 紙, 絵具 b. 展示会出品作品 c. 1981年

Represented by Artist

Daerick Gröss

1. POPEYE/WILLIAMS a. colored pencils, full saturation b. gift, c. 1982
2. SCHWARZENAGER/COLUMBU a. colored pencils & dyes b. magazine feature c. 1983
3. MR. AMERICA a. acrylics, gouache, airbrush b. poster c. 1980

デーリック・グロス

1. a. 色鉛筆（水彩技法） b. ギフト c. 1982年
2. a. 色鉛筆, 染料 b. 雑誌イラスト c. 1983年
3. a. アクリル絵具, ガッシュ, エアブラシ b. ポスター c. 1980年

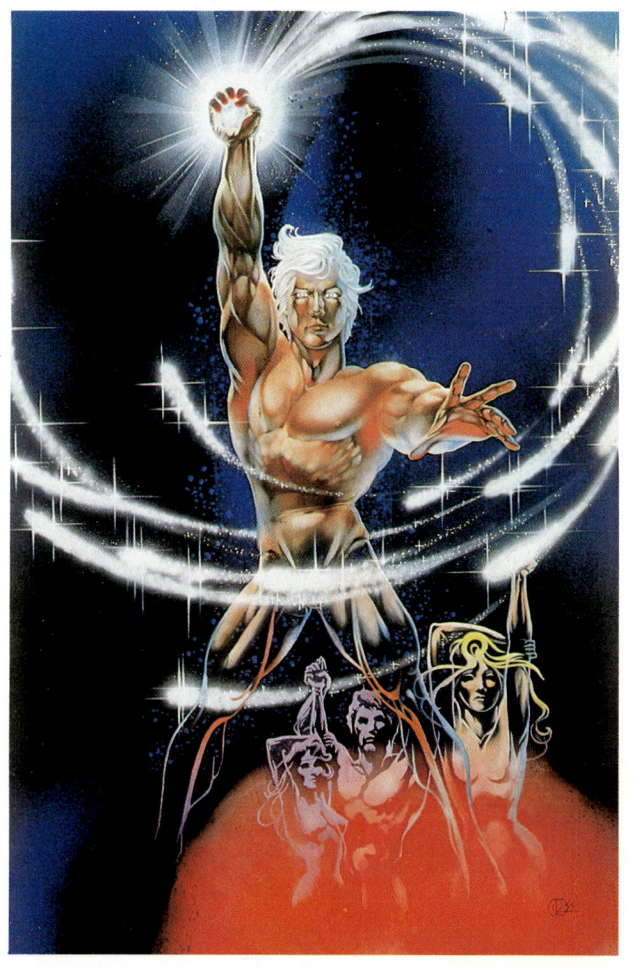

Represented by Artist

Bob Graham

ボブ・グラハム

118

1. THE PIPER a. oil on canvas b. cover of "Brown's Guide to Georgia" magazine c. 1975

1.a. 油彩絵具, キャンバス b. 雑誌表紙 c. 1975年

Represented by Artist

2. MAURICE a. pastel on paper b. portrait commissioned c. 1981
3. ATHENA a. pastel on paper b. portrait commissioned c. 1982
4. JOHN LENNON-SPIRIT IN THE SKY a. Alkyd painting on canvas b. artist's collection c. 1983

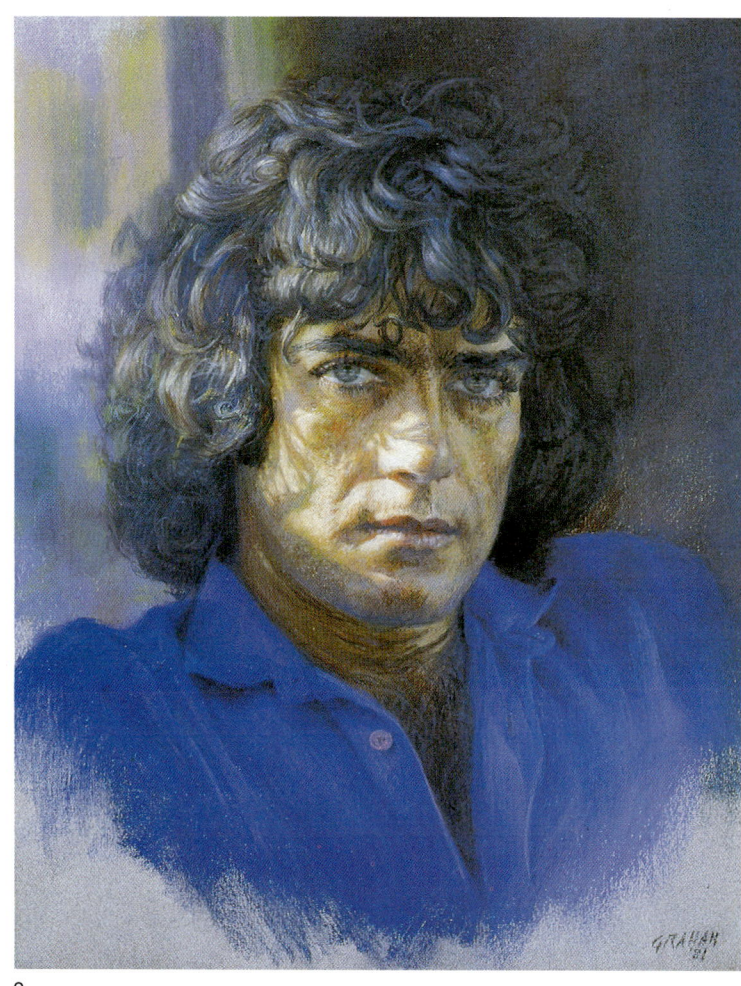

Represented by Artist

David Grove

デイヴィッド・グローヴ

1. TROPHY a. gouache and acrylic on gesso board b. the program cover, poster and collector's print of the 1983 Indianapolis 500 c. 1983

1.a. ガッシュ, アクリル絵具, ジェッソボード b. プログラム表紙, ポスター c.1983年

Represented by Artist

2. SWEATER a. gouache and acrylic on gesso board b. magazine ad for Pendleton Woolen Mills c. 1983
3. PINK DANCER a. gouache and acrylic on gesso board b. part of a ballet print series which has not yet been published c. 1982
4. WOLF a. gouache and acrylic on gesso board b. film poster for the Carroll Ballard film: "Never Cry Wolf" produced by Walt Disney Productions c. 1982

2. a. ガッシュ，アクリル絵具，ジェッソボード b.雑誌広告 c.1983年
3. a. ガッシュ，アクリル絵具，ジェッソボード b.未発表作品 c.1982年
4. a. ガッシュ，アクリル絵具，ジェッソボード b.映画ポスター c.1982年

Represented by Artist

Steven Guarnaccia

1. a. watercolor and ink on watercolor paper b. bookcover for Harper & Row "Free Agent" c. 1984
2. a. ink & watercolor on watercolor paper b. buying guide cover for Boston Globe Magazine c. 1981
3. a. watercolor on watercolor paper b. illustration for Boston Globe Magazine c. 1983
4. a. ink & watercolor on watercolor paper b. cover for Scarlett Letters Typography Catalog c. 1983

スティーヴン・ガルナーシア

1. a. 水彩絵具, インク, 水彩画紙 b. 書籍表紙 c.1984年
2. a. インク, 水彩絵具, 水彩画紙 b. 雑誌表紙 c.1981年
3. a. 水彩絵具, 水彩画紙 b. 雑誌イラスト c.1983年
4. a. インク, 水彩絵具, 水彩画紙 b. カタログの表紙 c.1983年

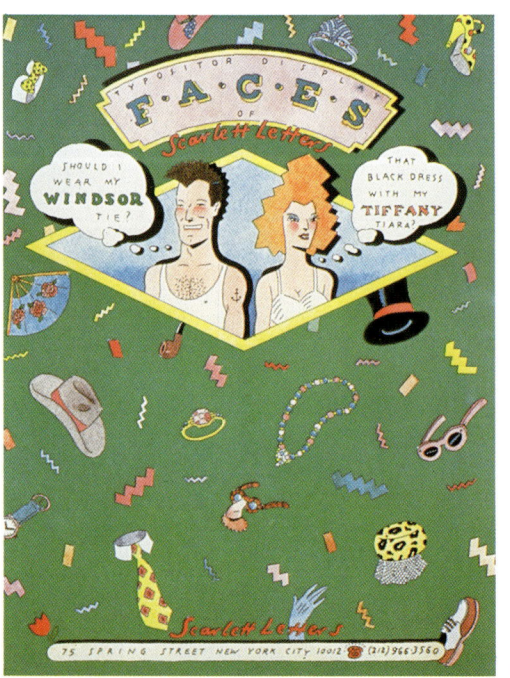

122

Represented by Artist

Helene Guetary

ヘレン・ゲータリー

123

1. a. color pencil b. editorial, Self magazine c. 1982
2. a. pencil & ink b. editorial c. 1982
3. a. pencil b. editorial c. 1982

1. a. 色鉛筆 b. 雑誌イラスト c. 1982年
2. a. 鉛筆, インク b. エディトリアル c. 1982年
3. a. 鉛筆 b. エディトリアル c. 1982年

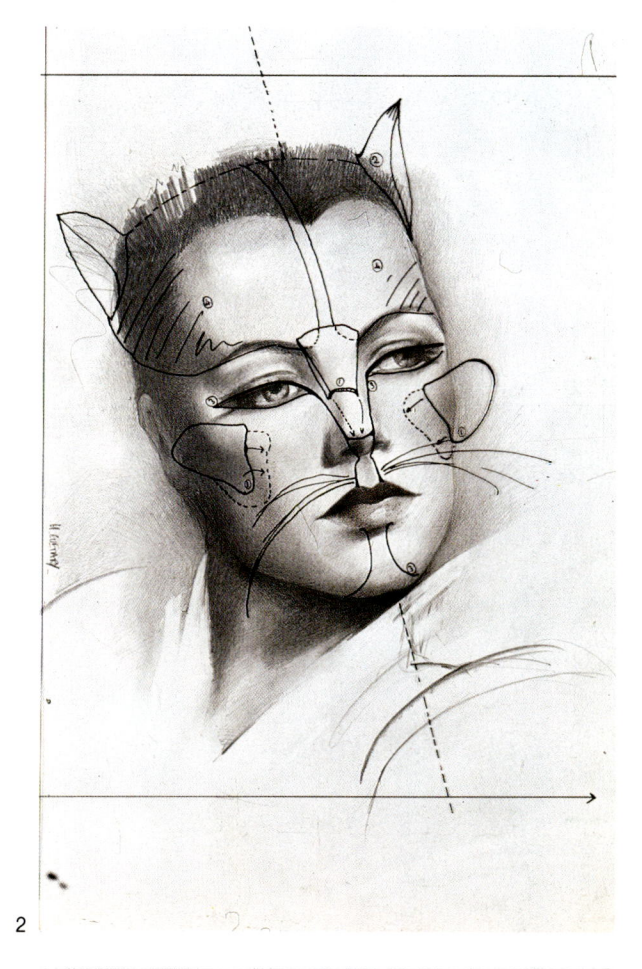

Represented by Artist

Kunio Hagio

1. YODA a. oils on gessoed masonite with brush b. article in Playboy Magazine c. 1982

クニオ・ハギオ

1. a. 油彩絵具, ジェッソメゾナイト, 画筆　b. 雑誌イラスト　c.1982年

124

Represented by Artist

125

2. CONAN THE BARBARIAN a. oil glazes and color pencils on cold press board with paint brush b. Universal Studios-promotion for movie c. 1982
3. JOHN BELUSHI a. watercolors and color pencils on cold press board with brush b. Tribune c. 1982
4. YOUNG BOY IN BEDROOM a. oil paint and color pencil on cold press board with brush b. promotion for Electronic Hardwares (knobs) c. 1981
5. JOHN LENNON a. watercolors, oils, and colored pencil on cold press board with brush b. article in Penthouse magazine c. 1983

2. a. 油彩絵具（グラッシ技法），色鉛筆，画筆，コールドプレスボード b. 映画のプロモーション c. 1982年
3. a. 水彩絵具，色鉛筆，画筆，コールドプレスボード b. 雑誌イラスト c. 1982年
4. a. 油彩絵具，色鉛筆，画筆，コールドプレスボード b. 広告 c. 1981年
5. a. 水彩絵具，油彩絵具，色鉛筆，画筆，コールドプレスボード b. 雑誌イラスト c. 1983年

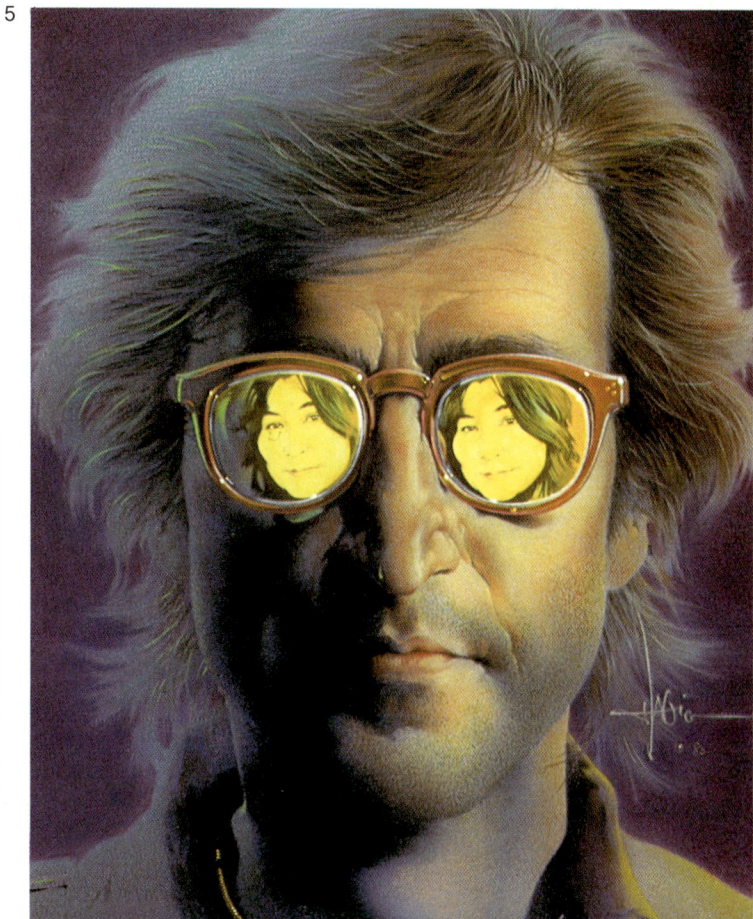

Represented by Artist

H. Tom Hall

1. A VALLEY CALLED DISAPPOINTMENT a. acrylic on gesso panel b. bookcover of Ballantine Books c. 1983
2. STRANGERS ON THE TRAIN a. acrylic on gesso panel b. title page of Reader's Digest Books c. 1981
3. MY LORD MONLEIGH a. acrylic on gesso board b. bookcover of Avon Books c. 1978
4. MOTHS a. acrylic on gesso panel b. Warner Books c. 1978

H・トム・ホール

1. a. アクリル絵具, ジェッソパネル b. 書籍表紙 c. 1983年
2. a. アクリル絵具, ジェッソパネル b. 書籍扉 c. 1981年
3. a. アクリル絵具, ジェッソパネル b. 書籍表紙 c. 1978年
4. a. アクリル絵具, ジェッソパネル b. 書籍表紙 c. 1978年

Represented by Artist

Represented by Artist

Abe Gurvin   エイブ・ガーヴィン

1. a. gouache with airbrush b. Sun Giant poster c. 1982
2. a. ink b. Taco Bell ad book c. 1980
3. a. ink with airbrush b. computer communication ad c. 1982

1. a. ガッシュ，エアブラシ b. ポスター c. 1982年
2. a. インク b. 広告イラスト c. 1980年
3. a. インク，エアブラシ b. 広告イラスト c. 1982年

Represented by Artist

John Hamagami

1. a. inks & acrylics with airbrush b. group show. "100 unpublished works by 100 published illustrators" c. 1983
2. a. inks & acrylics with airbrush b. L.A. Workbook (divider page) c. 1983
3. a. inks & acrylics with airbrush b. Seiniger & Associates (Universal Pictures) c. 1980

ジョン・ハマガミ

1. a. インク，アクリル絵具，エアブラシ b. グループ展出品作品 c. 1983年
2. a. インク，アクリル絵具，エアブラシ b. ワークブックのイラスト c. 1983年
3. a. インク，アクリル絵具，エアブラシ b. 広告 c. 1980年

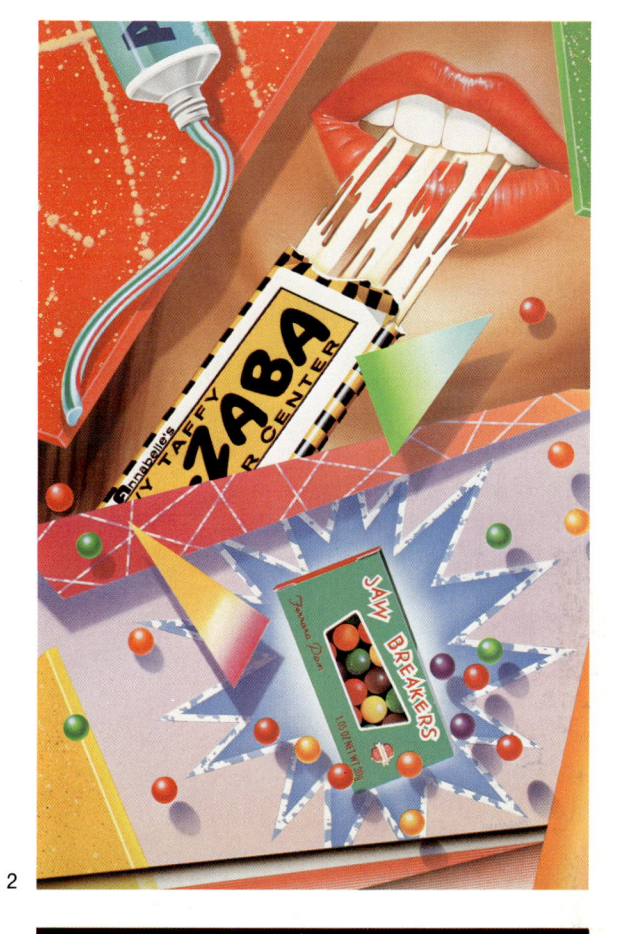

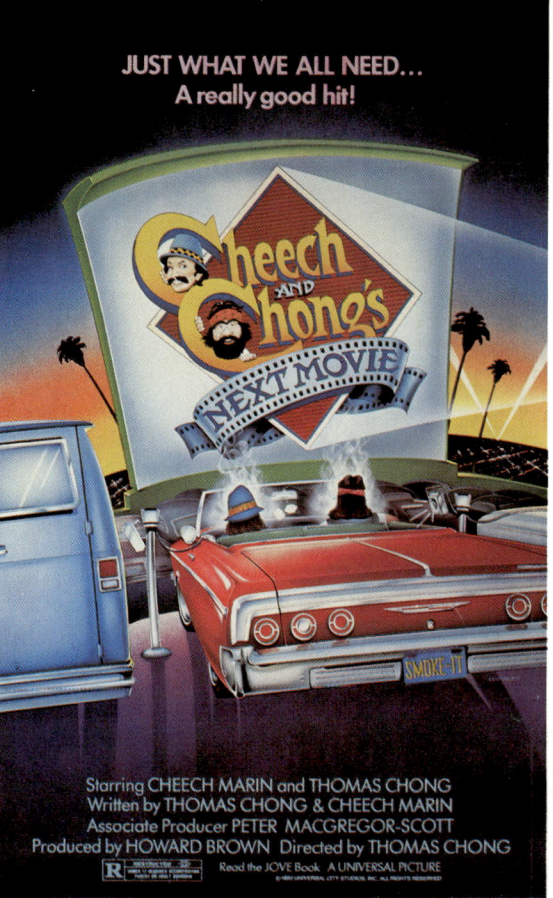

Represented by Artist

Cathy Heck

1. a. watercolor & ink b. advertisement c. 1983
2. a. watercolor & ink b. advertisement c. 1983
3. a. ink b. Young & Rubicam In-House-Poster c. 1982
4. a. acrylic b. book cover c. 1983

キャシー・ヘック

1. a. 水彩絵具, インク b. 広告イラスト c. 1983年
2. a. 水彩絵具, インク b. 広告イラスト c. 1983年
3. a. インク b. ポスター c. 1982年
4. a. アクリル絵具 b. 書籍表紙 c. 1983年

Represented by Artist

Joe & Kathy Heiner ジョー・ハイナー，キャシー・ハイナー 131

1. GOLD AHEAD '84 a. dyes & gouache on black & white photographic print with airbrush b. Adidas poster c. 1983
2. MAN IN SWAMP a. dyes & gouache on black & white photographic print with airbrush b. movie poster for "Southern Comfort" 20th Century Fox c. 1981
3. LEVIS 501 JEANS a. dyes & gouache on black & white photographic print with airbrush b. Levi billboard, poster etc. c. 1982

1.a. 白黒の紙焼きに彩色。染料，ガッシュ，エアブラシ　b. ポスター　c.1983年
2.a. 白黒の紙焼きに彩色。染料，ガッシュ，エアブラシ　b. 映画ポスター　c.1981年
3.a. 白黒の紙焼きに彩色。染料，ガッシュ，エアブラシ　b. ポスターなど　c.1982年

Represented by Artist

Albert Hirschfeld

1. BETTY COMDEN & ADOLPH GREEN 2. JOEL GREY & LIZA MINNELLI IN "CABARET" 3. JOSÉ IN "A LIFE IN THE THEATER" 4. BARBARA ERWIN, ROBERT FITCH, DOROTHY LOUDON 5. JAMES COCO IN "THE TRANSFIGURATION OF BENNO BLIMPIE" 6. LENORA NEMETZ IN "CHICAGO" 7. MARIA CALLAS 8. CHARLIE CHAPLIN a. pen & ink

アルバート・ハーシュフェルド

1.ベティ・コムデンとアドルフ・グリーン 2.ジョエル・グレイとライザ・ミネリ 3.ホセ・ファーラー 4.バーバラ・アーウィン、ロバート・フィッチ、ドロシー・ルードン 5.ジェームス・ココ 6.レノーラ・ネメツ 7.マリア・カラス 8.チャーリー・チャップリン

Represented by Artist

133

Represented by Artist

Martin Hoffman

1. a. acrylic on paper b. American Vogue presentation c. 1984
2. a. acrylic on paper b. American Vogue presentation c. 1984
3. a. acrylic on paper b. American Vogue presentation c. 1984
4. a. acrylic on paper b. American Vogue presentation c. 1984

1. a. アクリル絵具, 紙　b. 雑誌へのプレゼンテーション　c. 1984年
2. a. アクリル絵具, 紙　b. 雑誌へのプレゼンテーション　c. 1984年
3. a. アクリル絵具, 紙　b. 雑誌へのプレゼンテーション　c. 1984年
4. a. アクリル絵具, 紙　b. 雑誌へのプレゼンテーション　c. 1984年

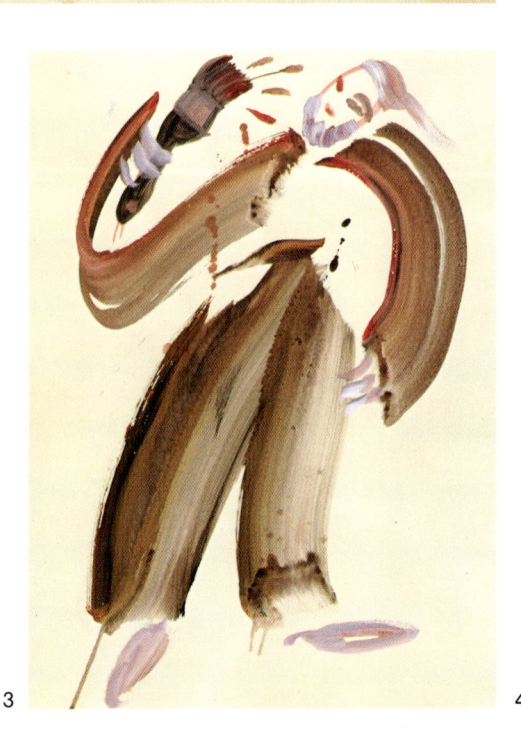

Represented by Artist

Jamie Hogan   ジャミー・ホーガン

1. a. charcoal, gouache, and collage b. self-promotion c. 1983
2. a. charcoal & pastel b. self-promotion c. 1983
3. a. charcoal, collage, & pastel b. Philadelphia Inquirer Magazine c. 1983

1. a. チャコール, ガッシュ, コラージュ b. セルフプロモーション c.1983年
2. a. チャコール, パステル b. セルフプロモーション c.1983年
3. a. チャコール, コラージュ, パステル b. 雑誌イラスト c.1983年

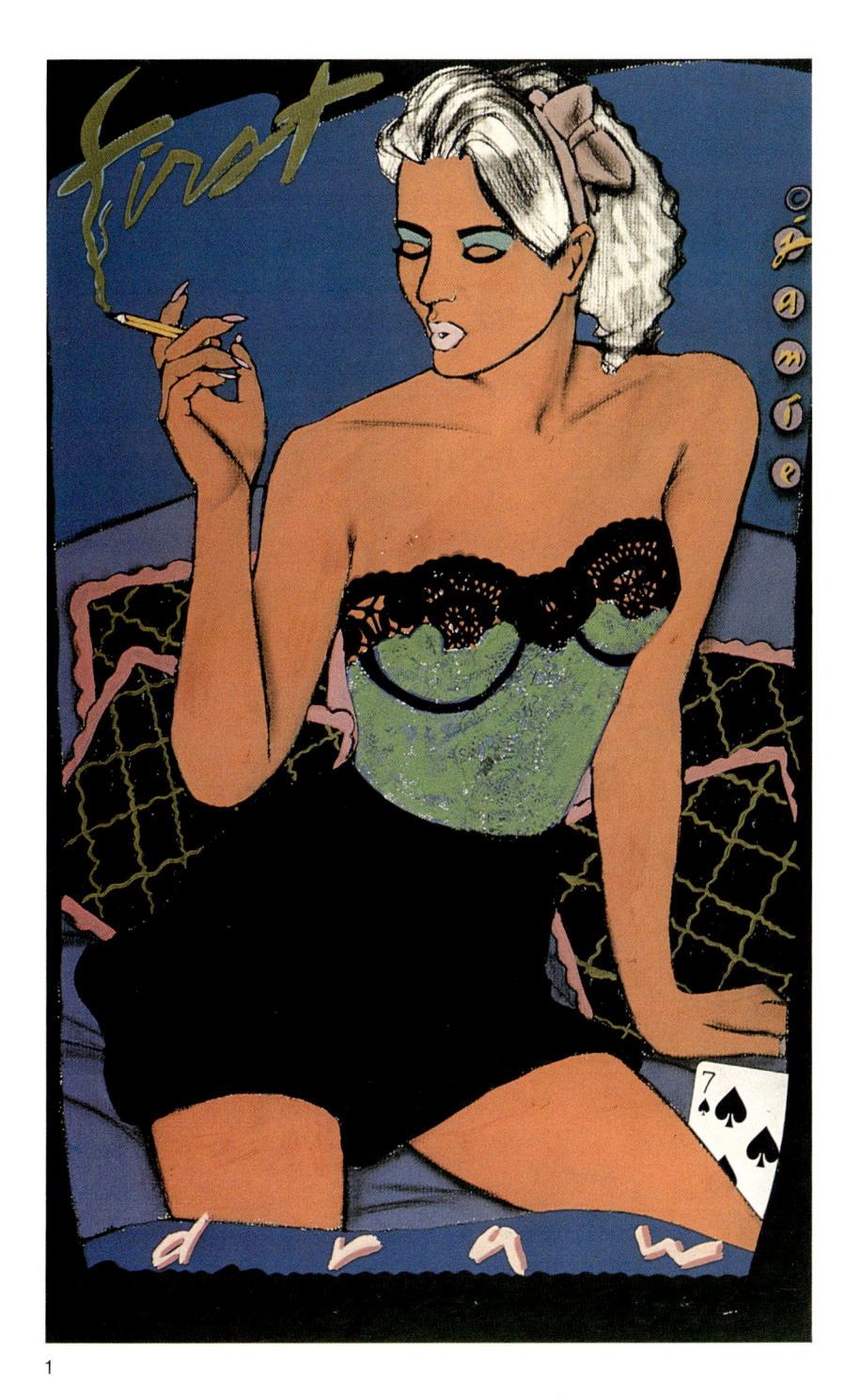

Represented by Artist

Brad Holland ブラッド・ホランド

1. a. acrylic b. cover of the New York Times magazine c. 1983

1.a.アクリル絵具 b.雑誌表紙 c.1983年

Represented by Artist

137

2. a. acrylic b. record album cover c. 1978
3. a. acrylic b. Playboy magazine c. 1982
4. a. acrylic b. Playboy magazine c. 1982

2.a. アクリル絵具　b. レコードジャケット　c.1978年
3.a. アクリル絵具　b. 雑誌イラスト　c.1982年
4.a. アクリル絵具　b. 雑誌イラスト　c.1982年

Represented by Artist

Holly Hollington

1. a. gouache, pastel, and pencil with airbrush b. portrait c. 1980
2. a. gouache, pencil, pastel with paint brush and airbrush b. illustration for jewelry bracelets. Tatler magazine c. 1980
3. a. gouache, ink, and pencil with airbrush b. hat illustration. Tatler magazine c. 1983

Represented by Artist

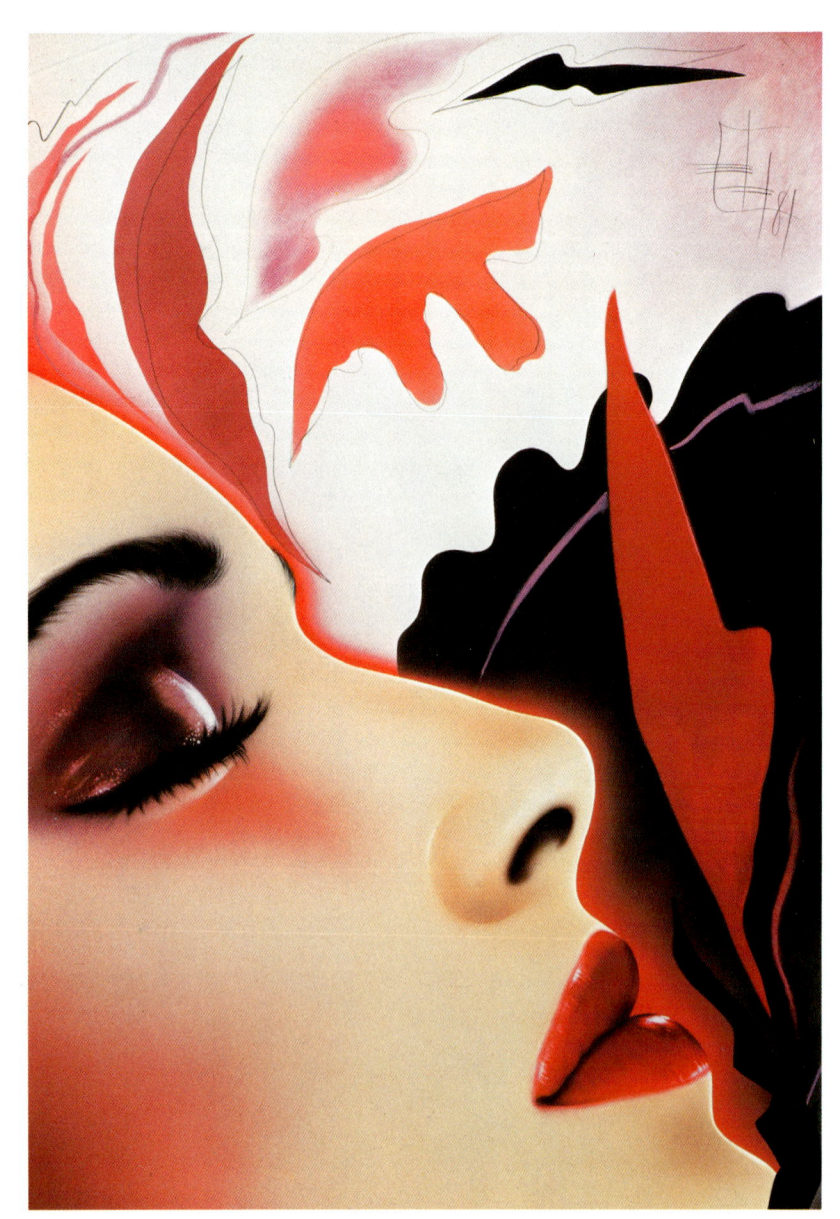

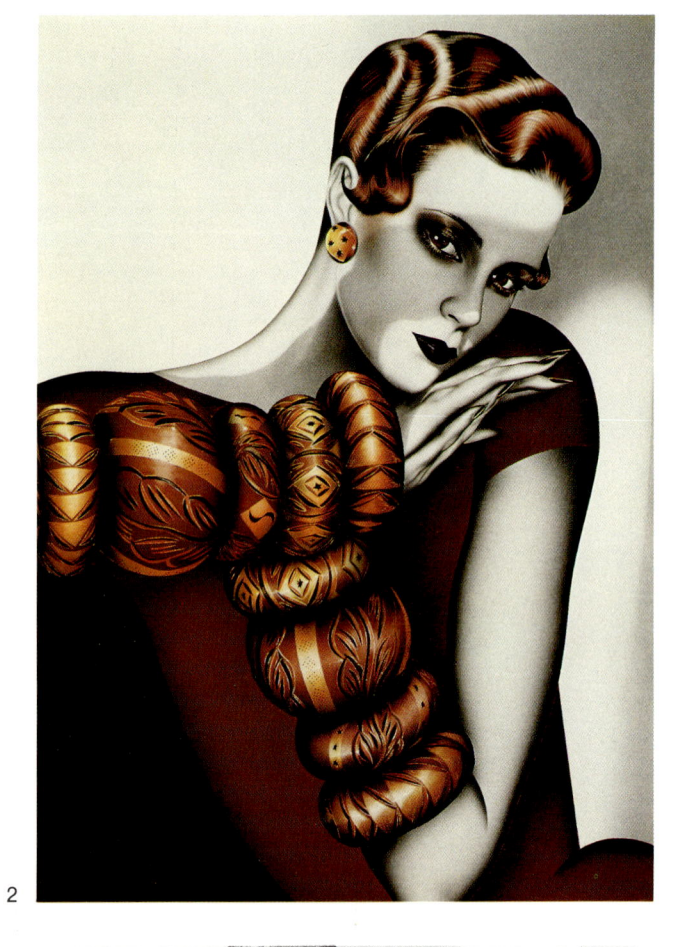

Katheryn Holt

1. a. mixed media b. editorial
2. a. mixed media b. editorial
3. a. mixed media b. editorial
4. a. mixed media b. editorial

1. a. 各種画材 b. エディトリアル
2. a. 各種画材 b. エディトリアル
3. a. 各種画材 b. エディトリアル
4. a. 各種画材 b. エディトリアル

Represented by Artist

Robert Hunt

1. a. oil on canvas over gouache underpainting b. advertising illustration for Levi Strauss Co. c. 1983
2. a. oil on gesso board b. book jacket. "The Walking Drum" by Louis L'Amour Bantam Books c. 1983
3. a. oil on canvas b. illustration for 1984 olympic calendar. Levi Strauss Co. c. 1983

ロバート・ハント

1. a. 油彩絵具, キャンバス（ガッシュを下塗り） b. 広告イラスト c. 1983年
2. a. 油彩絵具, ジェッソボード b. 書籍表紙 c. 1983年
3. a. 油彩絵具, キャンバス b. カレンダー c. 1983年

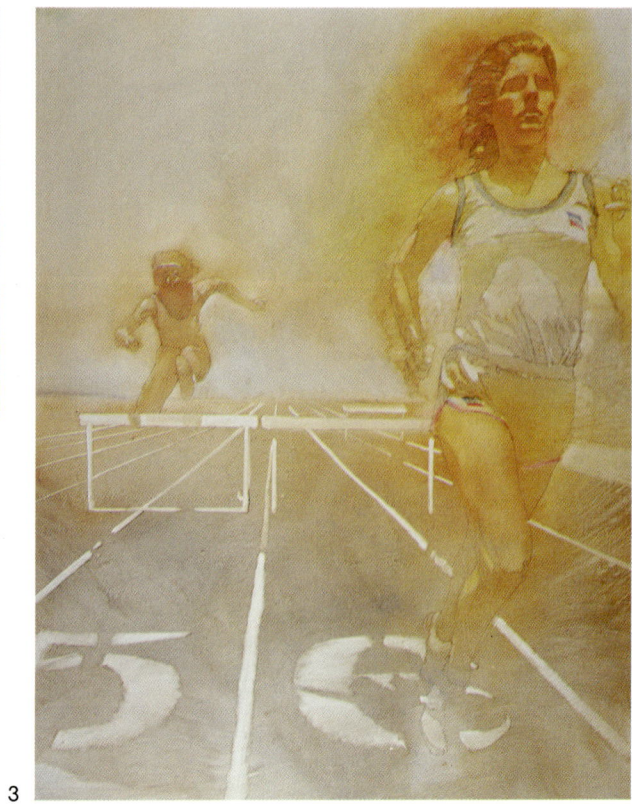

Represented by Artist

Bill Imhoff

1. a. dyes on illustration board with airbrush b. for Playgirl magazine c. 1981
2. a. dye on illustration board with airbrush b. studio art (Eros & Psyche) c. 1983
3. a. dye on illustration board with airbrush b. studio art (Eros & Psyche) c. 1983
4. a. dye on illustration board with airbrush b. book jacket (Avon Books) c. 1981

ビル・イムホフ

1. a. 染料，イラストレーションボード，エアブラシ b. 雑誌イラスト c.1981年
2. a. 染料，イラストレーションボード，エアブラシ b. 未発表作品 c.1983年
3. a. 染料，イラストレーションボード，エアブラシ b. 未発表作品 c.1983年
4. a. 染料，イラストレーションボード，エアブラシ b. 書籍表紙 c.1981年

Represented by Artist

Glen Iwasaki グレン・イワサキ

1-3. a. pen and ink, gouache, colored pencils b. series of experimental paintings based on the theme of Robots/Machines

1.a.ペン、インク、ガッシュ、色鉛筆 b.実験作品
2.a.ペン、インク、ガッシュ、色鉛筆 b.実験作品
3.a.ペン、インク、ガッシュ、色鉛筆 b.実験作品

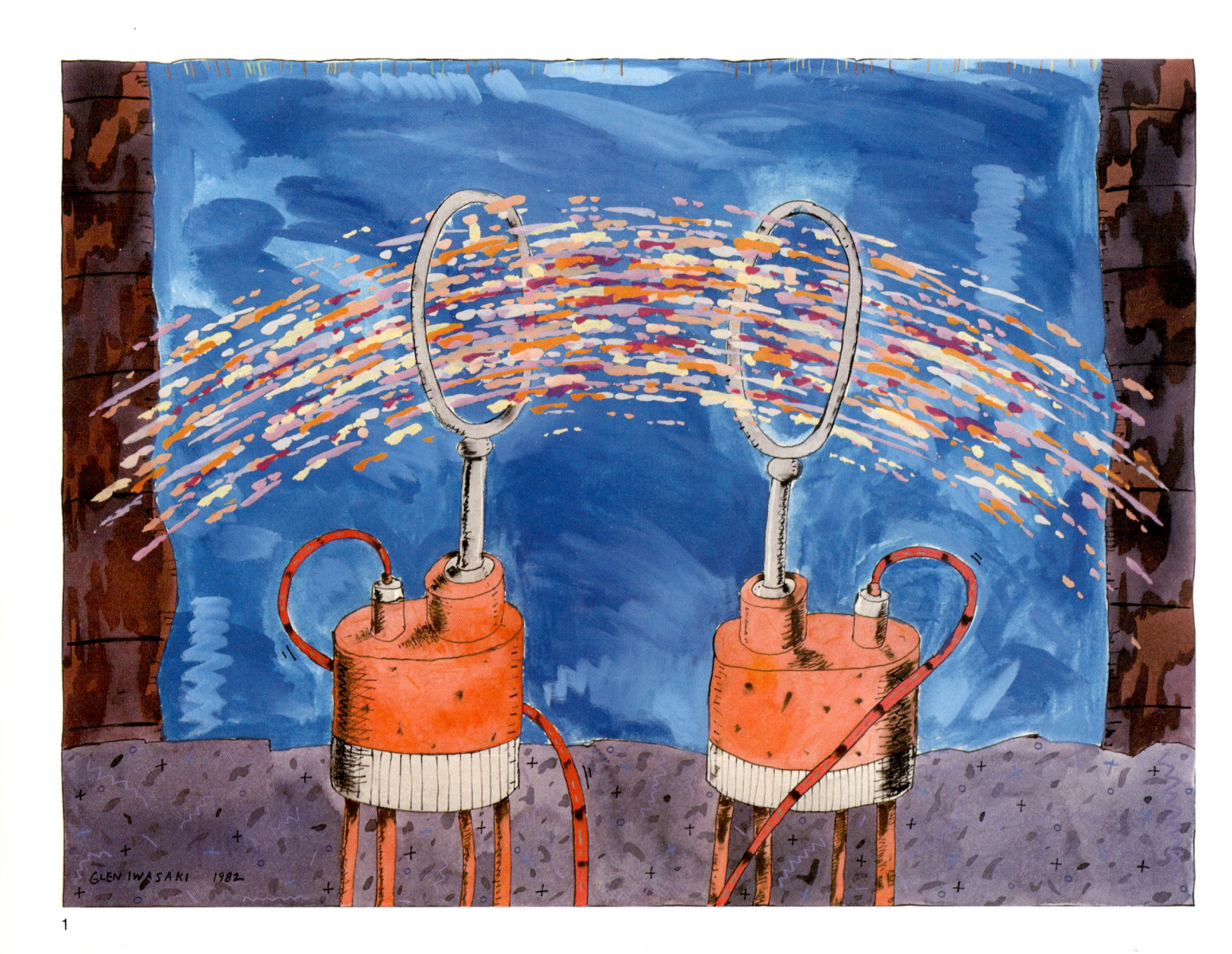

Represented by Artist

Barry Jackson

バリー・ジャクソン

143

1. a. acrylic paint b. self promotional calendar c. 1980
2. a. acrylic paint b. ad campaign for movie "American Pop" c. 1980
3. a. acrylic paint b. self promotional calendar c. 1984

1. a. アクリル絵具 b. カレンダー c. 1980年
2. a. アクリル絵具 b. 映画キャンペーン c. 1980年
3. a. アクリル絵具 b. カレンダー c. 1984年

Represented by Artist

Kathy Jacobi

1. THE PROCESSION a. mixed media b. book called A MORAL ENTERTAINMENT: COLLECTED POEMS OF R.H. DEUTSCH c. 1983
2. DOG ALONE a. watermedia and ink b. illustration for a book in progress called TOGETHER WITH DOG c. 1983
3. CECILIA C. a. intaglio (etching and aquatint, copperplate) b. a part of a suite of ten etchings in an edition of 40 illustrating the novel INVITATION TO A BEHEADING by Vladimir Nabokov c. 1978

キャシー・ヤコブ

1. a. 各種画材　b. 書籍イラスト　c.1983年
2. a. 水彩絵具, インク　b. 書籍イラスト　c.1983年
3. a. 沈み彫り（エッチング, アクアティント, 銅版彫刻）
   b. 書籍イラスト　c.1978年

Represented by Artist

Jay

1. a. watercolor and airbrush b. promotional piece c. 1983
2. a. line and wash b. promotional piece c. 1984
3. a. line and Dr. Martin's watercolor b. promotional piece c. 1984

1.a. 水彩絵具エアブラシ b. セルフプロモーション c. 1983年
2.a. ウォッシュ技法 b. セルフプロモーション c. 1984年
3.a. 水彩絵具 b. セルフプロモーション c. 1984年

Represented by Artist

Eugene Karlin ユージン・カーリン

1. a. pen and ink and watercolor b. illustration for book cover c. 1983

1.a. ペン, インク, 水彩絵具 b. 書籍表紙 c.1983年

Represented by Artist

147

2. a. crayon b. pharmaceutical illustration c. 1983
3. a. pen and ink b. greeting card c. 1983
4. a. pen and ink b. pharmaceutical booklet c. 1983

2. a. クレヨン b. エディトリアル c. 1983年
3. a. ペン，インク b. グリーティングカード c. 1983年
4. a. ペン，インク b. エディトリアル c. 1983年

Represented by Artist

Lonnie Sue Johnson

1. WINE BOTTLES a. watercolor and ink on paper b. New York Times magazine illustrated article on wine c. 1982
2. BASEBALL a. ink, watercolor on paper b. Channels magazine illustrated article on cable TV c. 1982
3. STILL LIFE a. watercolor and ink on paper b. poster for Weymouth Design annual party (Boston) c. 1983

ロニー・スー・ジョンソン

1. a. 水彩絵具, インク, 水彩画紙 b. 雑誌イラスト c. 1982年
2. a. インク, 水彩絵具, 水彩画紙 b. 雑誌イラスト c. 1982年
3. a. 水彩絵具, インク, 水彩画紙 b. ポスター c. 1983年

Represented by Artist

John M. Kilroy

1. a. acrylic and pencil on masonite b. Yankee magazine fiction piece "The White House Christmas Tree" c. 1983
2. a. pencil, acrylic and gouache b. Computerworld on Communication editorial piece "Morale and Management" c. 1984
3. a. acrylic on masonite b. self promotional mailer c. 1984

ジョン・M・キルロイ

1. a. アクリル絵具, 鉛筆, メゾナイト b. 雑誌イラスト c.1983年
2. a. 鉛筆, アクリル絵具, ガッシュ b. エディトリアル c.1984年
3. a. アクリル絵具, メゾナイト b. セルフプロモーション c.1984年

Represented by Artist

Choel Sa Kim

チョル・サ・キム

1. a. pencil & acrylic
2. a. pen & ink
3. a. charcoal pencil
4. a. charcoal pencil

1.a. 鉛筆, アクリル絵具
2.a. ペン, インク
3.a. チャコールペンシル
4.a. チャコールペンシル

Represented by Artist

Thea Kliros

1. a. pastel and gouache b. Treveria ad
2. a. pastel and fabric b. Treveria ad
3. a. watercolor, pastel, collage b. promotion piece

Represented by Artist

Richard M. Kriegler

1. RAIDERS OF THE LOST ARK a. acrylic on illustration board with brush and airbrush b. movie poster c. 1982
2. BELIEVE IT OR NOT a. acrylic on illustration board with brush and airbrush b. portrait of Jack Palance. poster for ABC Network and collateral promotional material c. 1983
3. OUTLANDER a. acrylic on illustration board with brush and airbrush b. cover of video game box c. 1983
4. STAR WARS a. acrylic on illustration board with brush and airbrush b. magazine cover c. 1983

リチャード・M・クレグラー

1. a. アクリル絵具, イラストレーションボード, 画筆, エアブラシ b. 映画ポスター c. 1982年
2. a. アクリル絵具, イラストレーションボード, 画筆, エアブラシ b. TV番組の宣伝ポスター c. 1983年
3. a. アクリル絵具, イラストレーションボード, 画筆, エアブラシ b. ビデオゲームのパッケージ c. 1983年
4. a. アクリル絵具, イラストレーションボード, 画筆, エアブラシ b. 雑誌表紙 c. 1983年

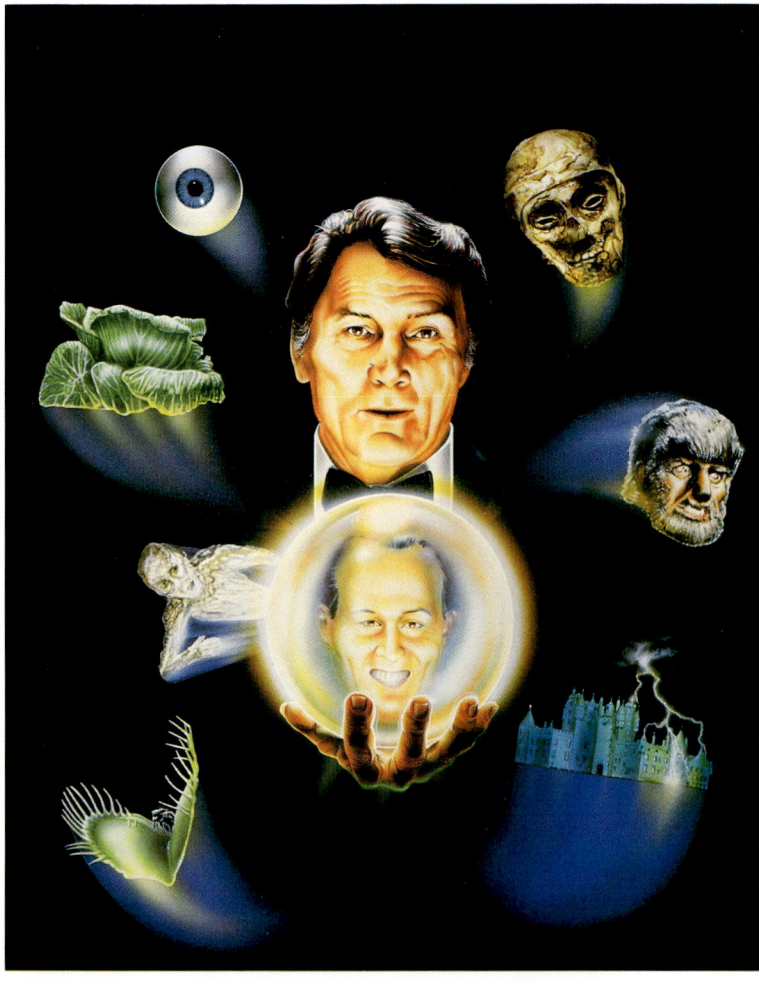

Represented by Artist

John A. Kurtz

1. a. acrylic on canvas b. Playboy magazine c. 1980
2. UNTITLED (PARAKEET) a. acrylic on canvas c. 1983
3. LEARNING TO LIVE ON ANOTHER PLANET a. acrylic on canvas c. 1982

ジョン・A・カーツ

1. a. アクリル絵具，キャンバス b. 雑誌イラスト c. 1980年
2. a. アフリル絵具，キャンバス c. 1983年
3. a. アクリル絵具，キャンバス c. 1982年

153

Represented by Artist

Bob Kurtz

1-5. a. drawings first done on paper. Next they are transferred onto acetate cel in ink, by hand. Each cel is then hand painted with water-soluble vinyl paint. Cels are filmed on 35mm film
1. ONE TO GROW ON b. artwork for beginning of the children's show. NBC TV Program c. 1984
2. FINGER BAR b. TV commercial for Good Humor Ice Cream comercial c. 1983
3. HANG TEN "HANG TEN" b. TV commercial for Hang Ten, advertising their full line of sportswear and sporting goods c. 1980
4. "TRADING PLACES" STARKIST JERKY TREATS b. TV commercial for dog food c. 1983
5. "LOUIE THE LIGHTNING BUG/HOME" b. TV commercial for a public utility. Alabama Power Company c. 1983

ボブ・カーツ

1-5.a.原画をインクでアセテートセルに描き写し水性ビニールペイントで着色する。35mmフィルムに写す。
1.b.TV子供番組 c.1984年
2.b.TVコマーシャル c.1983年
3.b.TVコマーシャル c.1980年
4.b.TVコマーシャル c.1983年
5.b.TVコマーシャル c.1983年

Represented by Artist

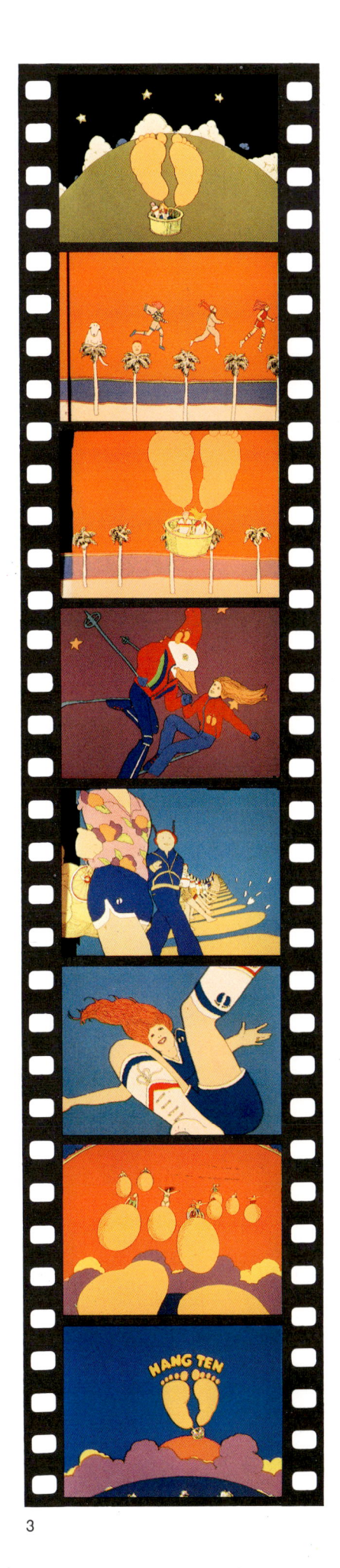

3

4

5

Represented by Artist

Dave LaFleur

1. a. watercolor, gouache, & colored pencils b. book cover describing various tribes & customs of the North American Indians c. 1983
2. a. watercolor, colored pencils & airbrush b. article in Cal Today magazine on the merchandising of television personality 'Mr. T'. c. 1983
3. a. watercolor, acrylics & gouache b. article in Cal Today magazine describing the behavior of obsessed personalities c. 1983
4. a. watercolor, colored pencils & airbrush b. article in Cal Today magazine describing the falsity & anxiety surrounding pseudo-male or macho attitudes c. 1983

デイヴ・ラフローア

1. a. 水彩絵具, ガッシュ, 色鉛筆 b. 書籍表紙 c. 1983年
2. a. 水彩絵具, 色鉛筆, エアブラシ b. 雑誌イラスト c. 1983年
3. a. 水彩絵具, アクリル絵具, ガッシュ b. 雑誌イラスト c. 1983年
4. a. 水彩絵具, 色鉛筆, エアブラシ b. 雑誌イラスト c. 1983年

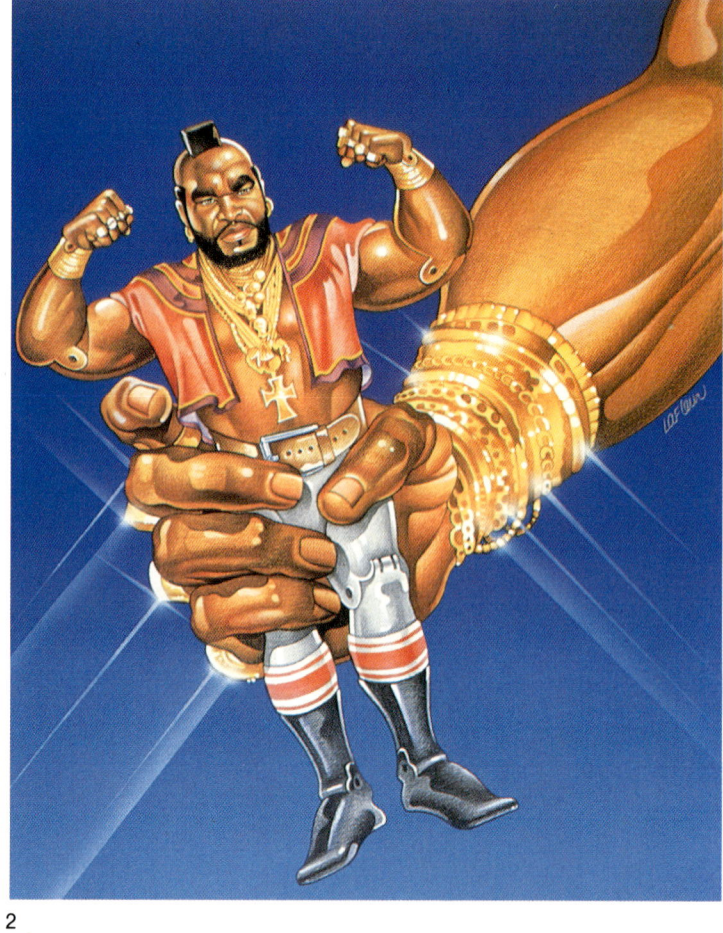

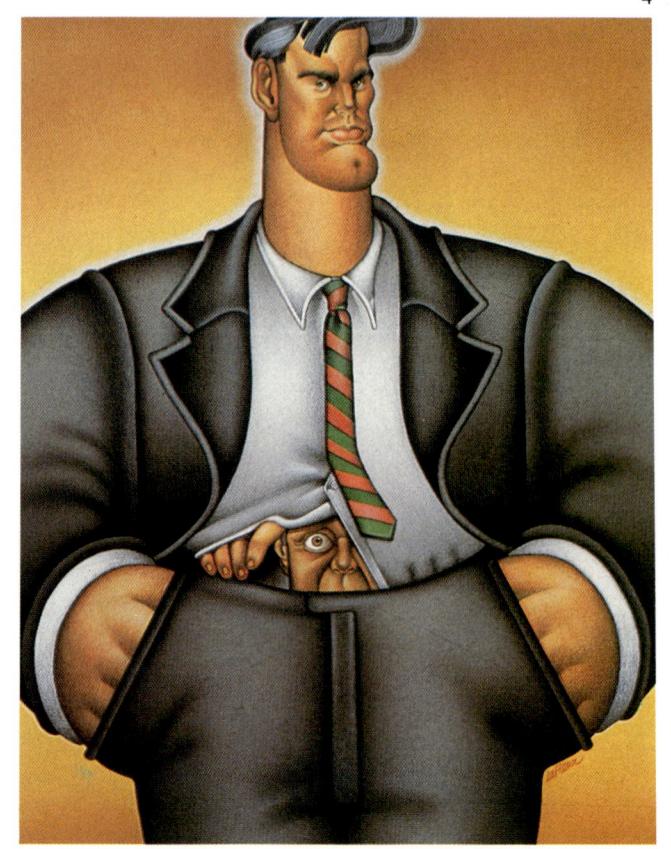

Represented by Artist

Jim Lamb

1. a. oil on board with brush b. poster, movie "Secret of Nimh" MGM/United Artists c. 1982
2. a. acrylic on board with brush b. calendar for Lamb & Weston Food Corp. c. 1982
3. a. oil on canvas board with brush b. Christmas card for Cask & Cleaver restaurant chain c. 1983

ジム・ラム

1. a. 油彩絵具，ボード，画筆 b. 映画ポスター c. 1982年
2. a. アクリル絵具，ボード，画筆 b. カレンダー c. 1982年
3. a. 油彩絵具，キャンバスボード，画筆 b. クリスマスカード c. 1983年

Represented by Artist

Saul Lambert

1. a. watercolor b. editorial, Sports Illustrated c. 1979
2. a. watercolor b. editorial c. 1979
3. a. watercolor b. advertisement c. 1979
4. a. watercolor b. newspaper, New York Times c. 1979

ソウル・ランバート

1. a. 水彩絵具 b. 雑誌イラスト c. 1979年
2. a. 水彩絵具 b. エディトリアル c. 1979年
3. a. 水彩絵具 b. 広告イラスト c. 1979年
4. a. 水彩絵具 b. 新聞イラスト c. 1979年

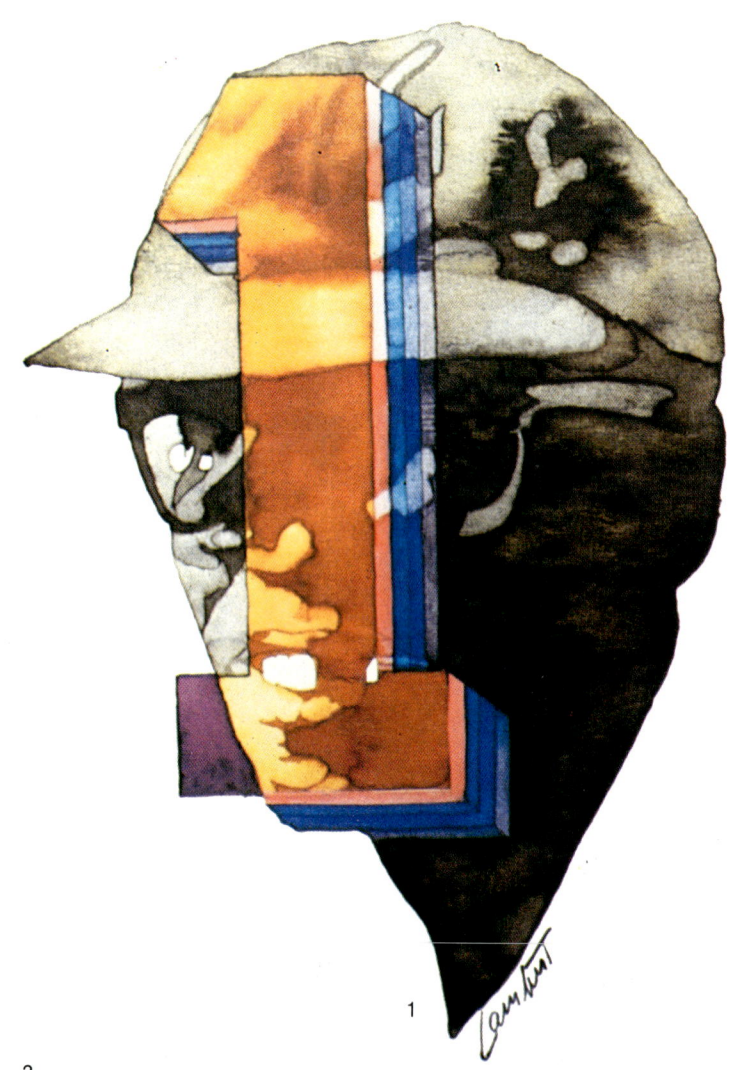

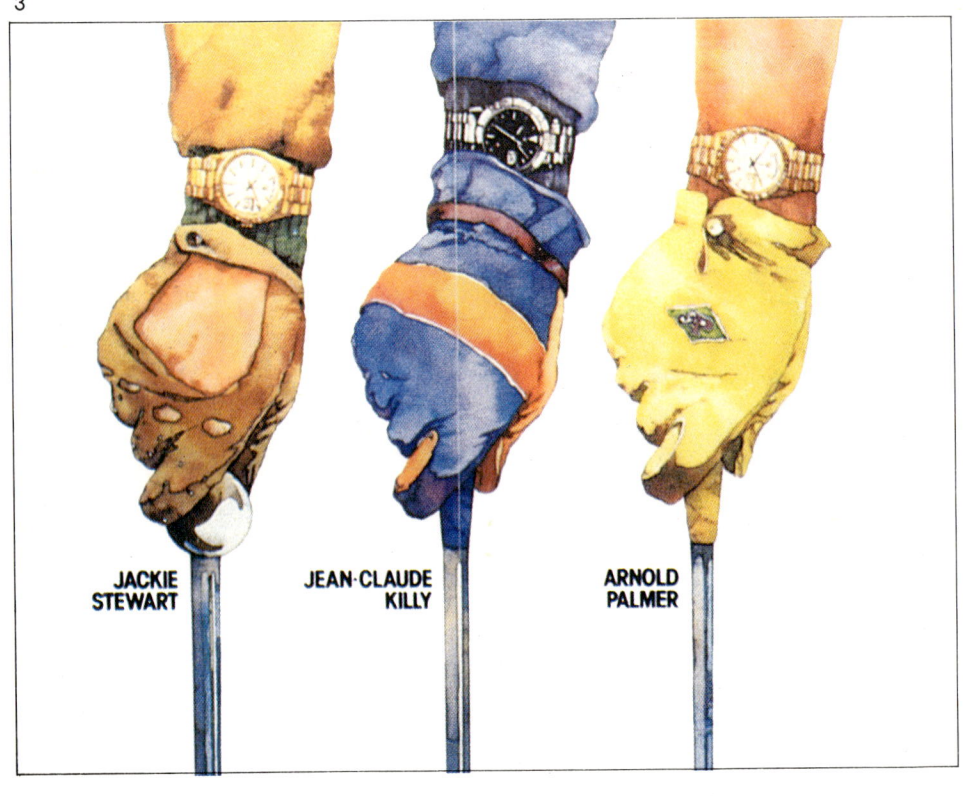

Represented by Artist

Joan Landis

1. a. acrylic b. TV commercial and poster for Vintage Cheese. Swift, Inc. c. 1983
2. a. acrylic b. Bus Shelter poster and postcard. client: Balducci's c. 1983
3. a. acrylic b. family history c. 1982

ジョアン・ランディス

1. a. アクリル絵具 b. TVコマーシャル, ポスタ c. 1983年
2. a. アクリル絵具 b. ポスター, ポストカード c. 1983年
3. a. アクリル絵具 b. 家族史イラスト c. 1982年

Represented by Artist

Birney Lettick　バーニー・レティック

1. HEAVEN CAN WAIT a. oil on crescent board with flat sable brush b. movie poster c. 1975

1.a. 油彩絵具, クレセントボード, セーブル平筆　b. 映画ポスター　c.1975年

Represented by Artist

2. a. oil on crescent board with flat sable brush b. for IBM. advertising two special shows for television
3. SERGEANT PEPPER LONELY HEART CLUB BAND- BEE GEES a. oil on crescent board with flat sable brush b. movie poster c. 1978
4. ESCAPE FROM ALCATRAZ a. oil on crescent board with flat sable brush b. movie poster c. 1980
5. COALMINER a. oil on crescent board with flat sable brush b. cover for Time magazine c. 1977

2. a. 油彩絵具, クレセントボード, セーブル筆 b. 広告イラスト
3. a. 油彩絵具, クレセントボード, セーブル筆 b. 映画ポスター c.1978年
4. a. 油彩絵具, クレセントボード, セーブル筆 b. 映画ポスター c.1980年
5. a. 油彩絵具, クレセントボード, セーブル筆 b. 広告イラスト c.1977年

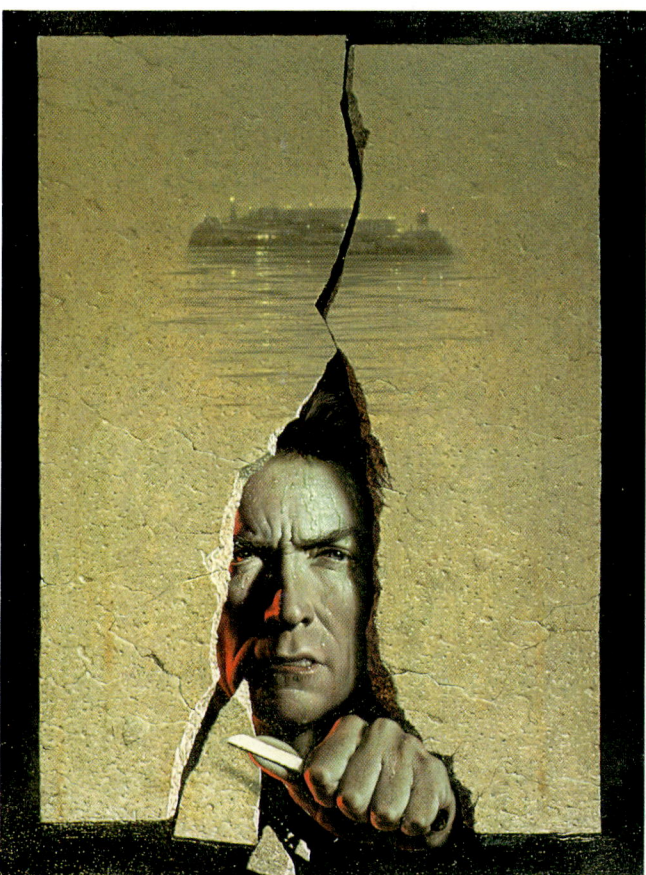

Represented by Artist

6. a. oil on crescent board with flat sable brush b. client: Herefords. advertisement c. 1975

6.a. 油彩絵具, クレセントボード, セーブル平筆 b. 広告イラスト c.1975年

Represented by Artist

Bette Levine

1. STOCKINGS (SHEER SENSATIONS) a. transparent dyes with airbrush b. Erotic Art Book c. 1983
2. LEATHER ANGEL (BABES IN TOYLAND) a. dyes with airbrush b. self-promotion c. 1982
3. GIRL WITH STRAWBERRY a. transparent dyes with airbrush b. Exhibition c. 1983

ベット・リバイン

1. a. 透明染料, エアブラシ b. 書籍イラスト c. 1983年
2. a. 染料, エアブラシ b. セルフプロモーション c. 1982年
3. a. 透明染料, エアブラシ b. 展示会出品作品 c. 1983年

Represented by Artist

Tim Lewis

1. a. collage (cut from an actual stock certificate, and rulers, scales, calipers, thermometer, etc.) b. AT & T's magazine, Long Lines. c. 1982
2. a. Dr. Martin Dyes on arches watercolor paper b. illustration for Crocker Bank's in-house magazine c. 1982
3. a. collage (marbleized paper, ink, watercolor, zip-a-tones, cut paper, ink on clear acetate, pre-existing print of capitol building) b. cover for AMTRAK'S magazine placed on their trains. c. 1984
4. a. Dr. Martin's dyes on tracing paper mounted on illustration board b. cover art commissioned for VANITY FAIR magazine (not used) for a summer month c. 1983

ティム・ルイス

1. a. コラージュ（株券，メジャー，定規など） b. 雑誌イラスト c. 1982年
2. a. カラーインク，水彩画紙 b. 企業社内誌イラスト c. 1982年
3. a. コラージュ（マーブル紙，インク，水彩絵具，切り紙，プリント，ジップ・ア・トーンなど） b. 鉄道車内誌 c. 1984年
4. a. カラーインク，トレーシングペーパーを貼ったイラストレーションボード b. 雑誌表紙 c. 1983年

Represented by Artist

Ed Lindlof

エド・リンドロフ

1. a. pen & ink with watercolor b. promotion in conjunction with GE exhibit at Epcot Center, Disney World c. 1983
2. a. acrylics b. self-promotion c. 1984
3. a. pen & ink with watercolor b. book cover c. 1983

1. a. ペン，インク，水彩絵具 b. 広告イラスト c. 1983年
2. a. アクリル絵具 b. セルフプロモーション c. 1984年
3. a. ペン，インク，水彩絵具 b. 書籍表紙 c. 1983年

Represented by Artist

Sue Llewellyn

1. a. acrylic b. a calendar sent out by Katz and Lee Printing Co., Dallas, Texas c. 1984
2. a. watercolor b. client "Science Digest" New York c. 1982
3. a. acrylic on D'Arches b. personal work shown at the Metro Gallery LA c. 1983

スー・ルウェリン

1. a. アクリル絵具 b. カレンダー c. 1984年
2. a. 水彩絵具 b. 雑誌イラスト c. 1982年
3. a. アクリル絵具，水彩画紙 b. 個展出品作品 c. 1983年

Represented by Artist

John Lykes

ジョン・ライクス

1. THE DESERT FOX a. oils in the old masters technique b. fine art c. 1982
2. BILLY CARTER a. oils b. for Chic magazine c. 1979
3. FLOWER GIRL a. oils b. fine art c. 1977

1. a. 油彩絵具　b. オリジナル作品　c. 1982年
2. a. 油彩絵具　b. 雑誌イラスト　c. 1979年
3. a. 油彩絵具　b. オリジナル作品　c. 1977年

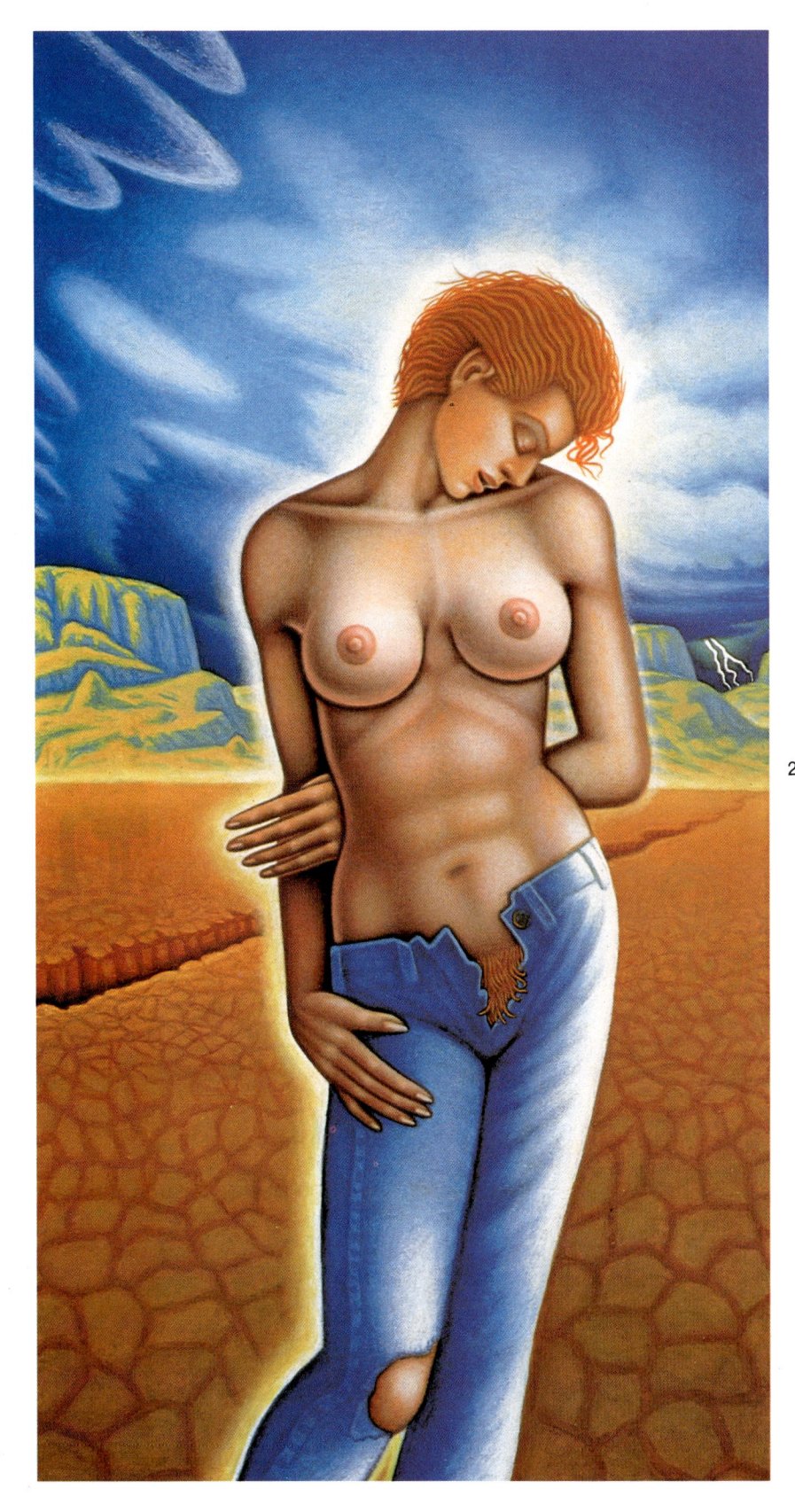

Represented by Artist

Daniel Maffia

1. a. oil on newsprint b. editorial for Cosmopolitan c. 1983
2. a. gouache and oil on newsprint b. editorial for Gallery c. 1982
3. a. oil on newsprint b. editorial for Psychology Today c. 1980
4. a. watercolor on newsprint b. editorial c. 1978

Represented by Artist

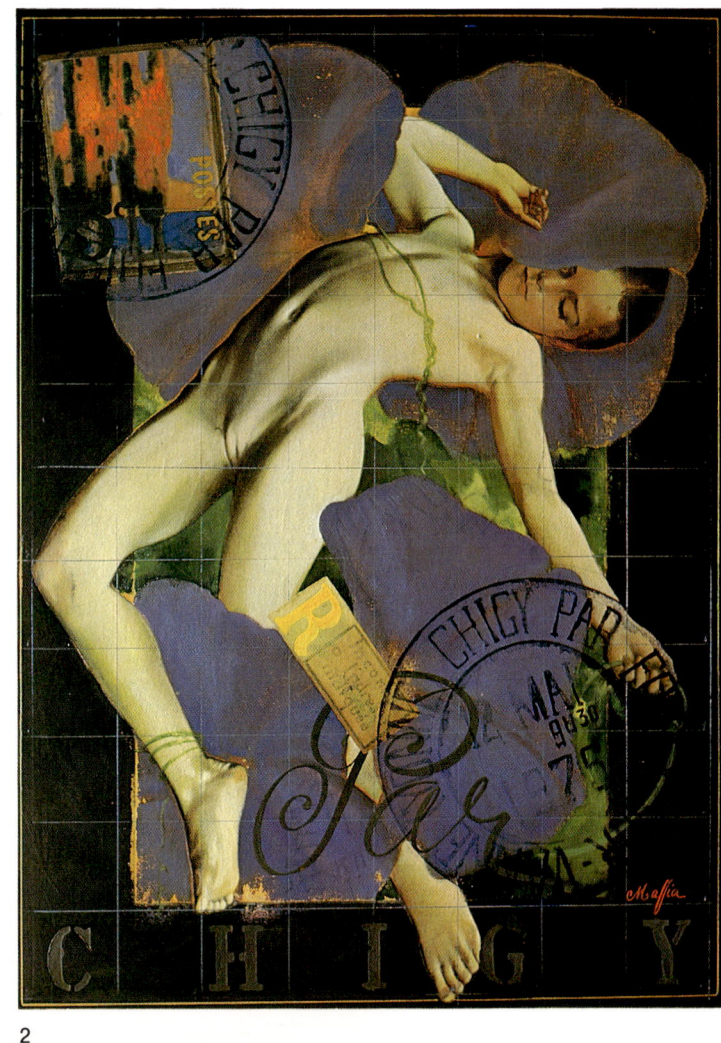

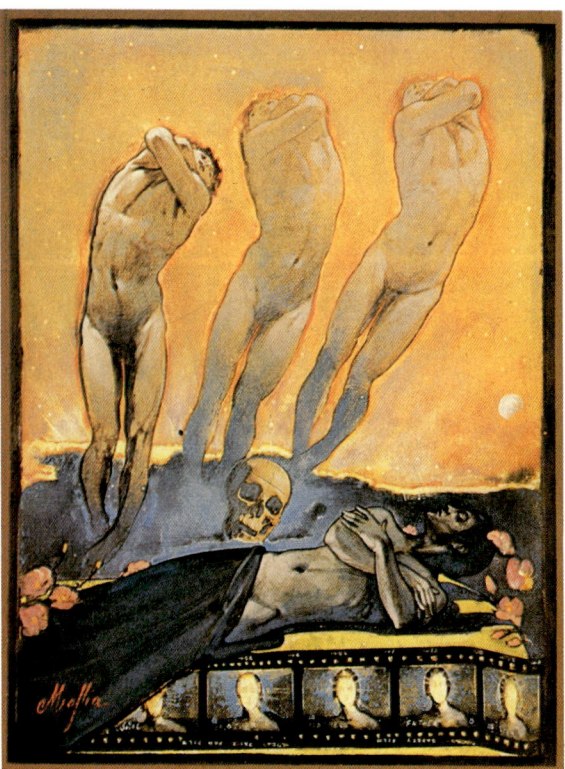

Greg Manchess

1. a. oil b. unpublished poster sample for film "Bladerunner" c. 1982
2. a. oils b. poster for movie version of book "Congo" by Michael Crichton c. 1983
3. a. oils b. for Doubleday Books, Literary Guild magazine for book "The Danger" by Dick Francis c. 1983

グレッグ・マンチェス

1. a. 油彩絵具 b. 映画ポスター（未発表） c. 1982年
2. a. 油彩絵具 b. ポスター c. 1983年
3. a. 油彩絵具 b. 書籍イラスト c. 1983年

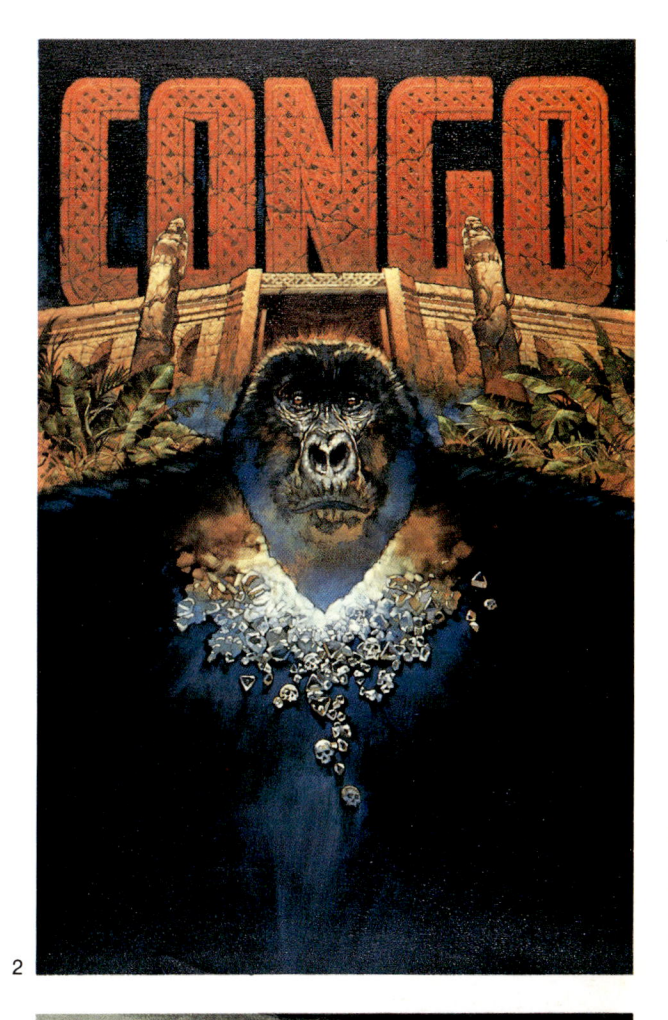

169

Represented by Artist

Richard Mantel　リチャード・マンテル

1. a. acrylic on old lithograph b. poster for U.S. Information Service c. 1983
2. a. acrylic on canvas b. illustration for The Push Pin Graphic c. 1981
3. a. acrylic on canvas b. book jacket for Random House c. 1983

1. a. アクリル絵具，古い石版画　b. ポスター　c. 1983年
2. a. アクリル絵具，キャンバス　b. "プッシュピン・グラフィック"　c. 1981年
3. a. アクリル絵具，キャンバス　b. 書籍表紙　c. 1983年

1 　　2　　3

Represented by Artist

Mark Marek

1. a. pentel and pantone on paper b. Manhattan Design's New Wave Comics, a collection of artist's strips c. 1983
2. a. black acrylic and pantone on paper b. movie magazine c. 1983
3. a. pentel and pantone b. Manhattan Design's Christmas rapping paper c. 1982
4. a. acrylic and felt marker on paper b. for artist's portfolio c. 1983

マーク・メレック

1. a. ペンテル・サインペン，パントン・カラートーン，紙 b. 続きマンガの1こま c.1983年
2. a. 黒アクリル絵具，パントン・カラートーン，紙 b. 映画雑誌イラスト c.1983年
3. a. ペンテル・サインペン，パントン・カラートーン b. 包装紙 c.1982年
4. a. アクリル絵具，フェルトマーカー，紙 b. ポートフォリオ c.1983年

Represented by Artist

Cynthia Marsh

1. THE BEACH BOYS: THE WALK OF FAME a. 7 color silkscreen collage b. from a portfolio of prints; The Walk of Fame c. 1981
2. JOHNNY CARSON: THE WALK OF FAME a. 7 color silkscreen collage b. from a portfolio of prints; The Walk of Fame c. 1981
3. THE GOGO'S BEAUTY AND THE BEAT a. photo illustration using airbrush, graphic arts photography, and various proofing methods b. record cover IRS Records c. 1981
4. LET'S SPEND THE NIGHT TOGETHER a. photo illustration using various camera techniques and proofing methods b. poster for Embassy Films c. 1983

シンシア・マーシュ

1. a. 7色シルクスクリーンのコラージュ b. ポートフォリオ c.1981年
2. a. 7色シルクスクリーンのコラージュ b. ポートフォリオ c.1981年
3. a. エアブラシを使った写真イラスト, グラフィックアート写真 b. レコードジャケット c.1981年
4. a. 写真イラスト b. ポスター c.1983年

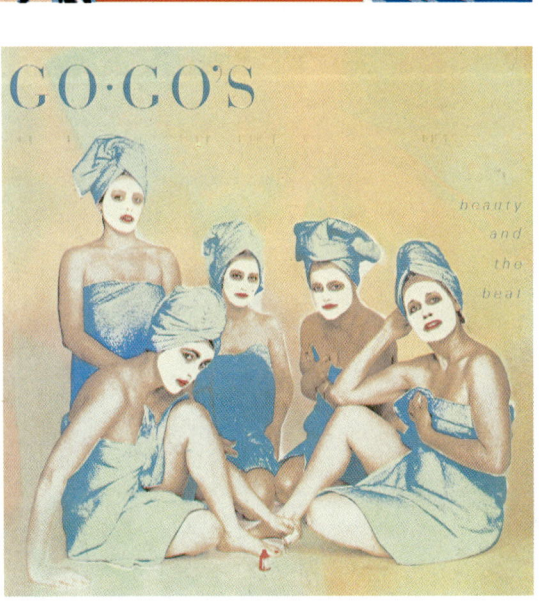

Represented by Artist

John J. Martinez

1. REFLECTIONS IN A PIANO a. silkscreen b. limited edition poster. client; Newport-New York Jazz Festival c. 1979
2. DEW DROP INN a. offset lithography b. mailer. client; New Orleans Downtown Development District c. 1980
3. UNTITLED a. offset lithography b. print advertising. client; Seagaram's/Boodles Gin c. 1984
4. RAINBOW BOX a. offset lithography b. book jacket client; Congdon Weed Publishing c. 1983
5. PIANO a. silkscreen b. limited edition poster. client; Mirage Galleries c. 1981

ジョン・J・マルチネス

1. a. シルクスクリーン　b. 限定版ポスター　c. 1979年
2. a. オフセットリトグラフ　b. ダイレクトメール　c. 1980年
3. a. オフセットリトグラフ　b. 広告イラスト　c. 1984年
4. a. オフセットリトグラフ　b. 書籍表紙　c. 1983年
5. a. シルクスクリーン　b. 限定版ポスター　c. 1981年

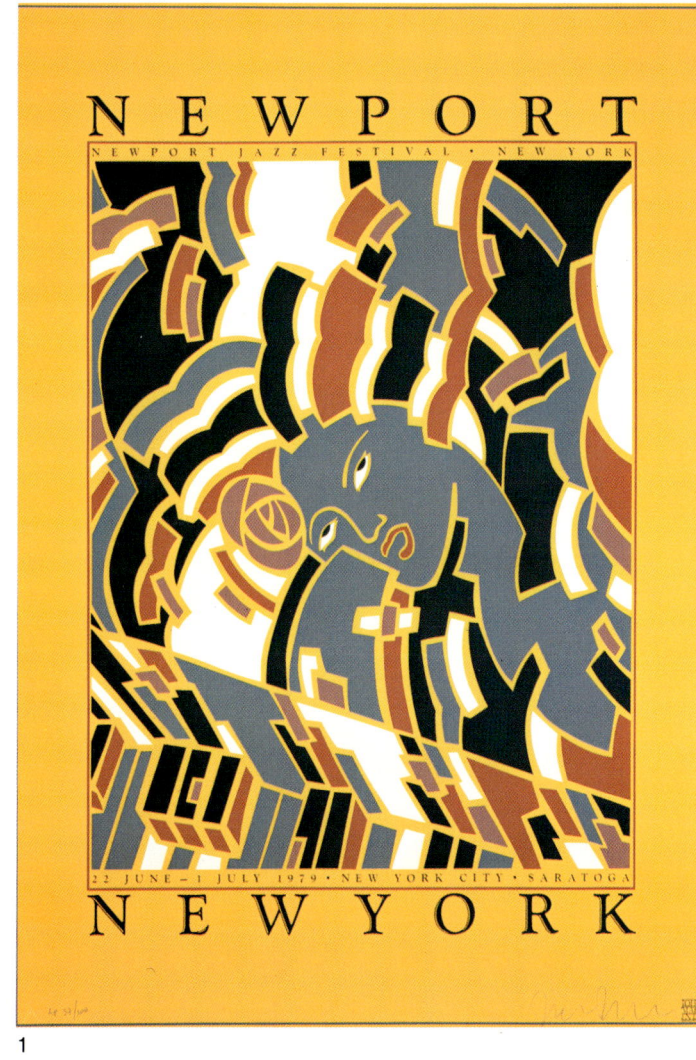

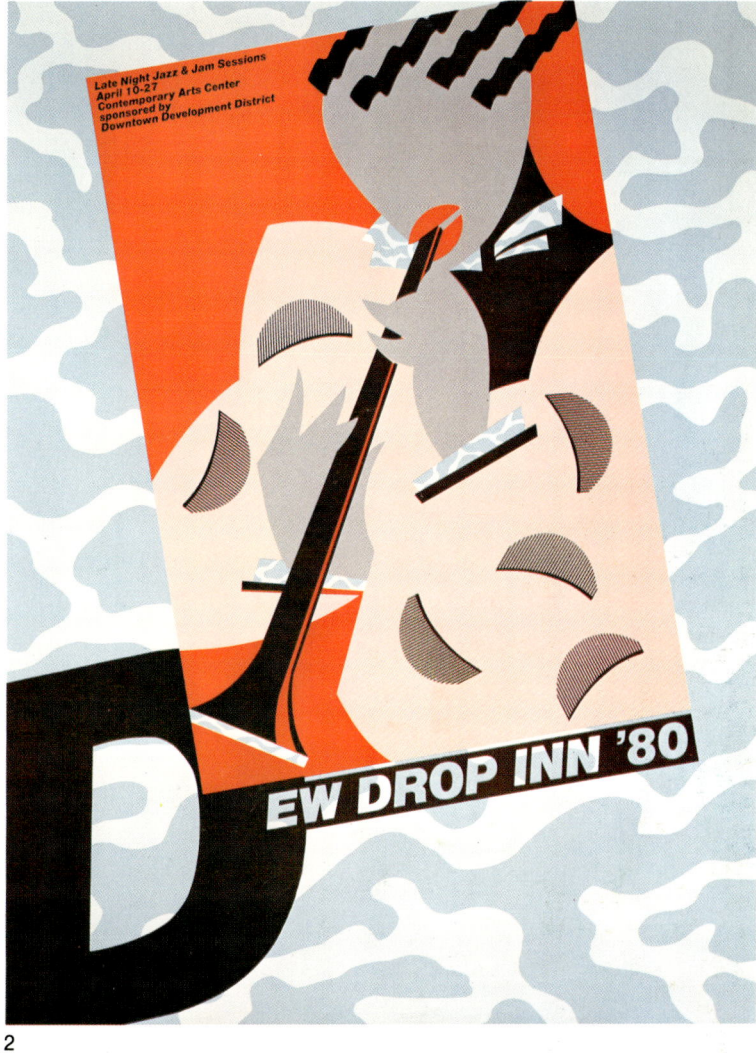

Represented by Artist

Marvin Mattelson

1. a. acrylic on canvas with brush b. Society of Illustrators poster #26 c. 1983
2. a. acrylic on canvas b. cover for Agatha Christie book entitled "The Mysterious Mr. Quinn" c. 1982
3. a. acrylic on canvas b. cover of Agatha Christie book "The Moving Finger" c. 1982

マーヴィン・マテルソン

1. a. アクリル絵具, キャンバス, 画筆 b. ポスター c. 1983年
2. a. アクリル絵具, キャンバス b. 書籍表紙 c. 1982年
3. a. アクリル絵具, キャンバス b. 書籍表紙 c. 1982年

174

Represented by Artist

Bill Mayer

1. a. pencil and watercolors b. self-promotion c. 1981
2. a. pencil and watercolors b. character for a children's book. presently in the works c. 1983
3. a. pencil and watercolors b. editorial illustration for article about Sun Care Products. Baby Forum magazine c. 1982

ビル・メイヤー

1. a. 鉛筆, 水彩絵具 b. セルフプロモーション c. 1981年
2. a. 鉛筆, 水彩絵具 b. 絵本のキャラクター c. 1983年
3. a. 鉛筆, 水彩絵具 b. 雑誌イラスト c. 1982年

Represented by Artist

David B. Mattingly

デイヴッド・B・マッティングレー

1. ORION a. acrylic on illustration board b. book cover. Tor Books c. 1983

1. a. アクリル絵具, イラストレーションボード b. 書籍表紙 c. 1983年

Represented by Artist

2. CHILDREN OF THE STARS a. acrylic on illustration board b. bookcover. Del Rey Books c. 1981

3. LIGHT CITY a. acrylic on illustration board b. bookcover. Del Rey Books c. 1979

4. FLYING HIGH a. acrylic on illustration board b. poster for New World Picture c. 1979

2. a. アクリル絵具，イラストレーションボード　b. 書籍表紙　c.1981年
3. a. アクリル絵具，イラストレーションボード　b. 書籍表紙　c.1979年
4. a. アクリル絵具，イラストレーションボード　b. 映画ポスター　c.1979年

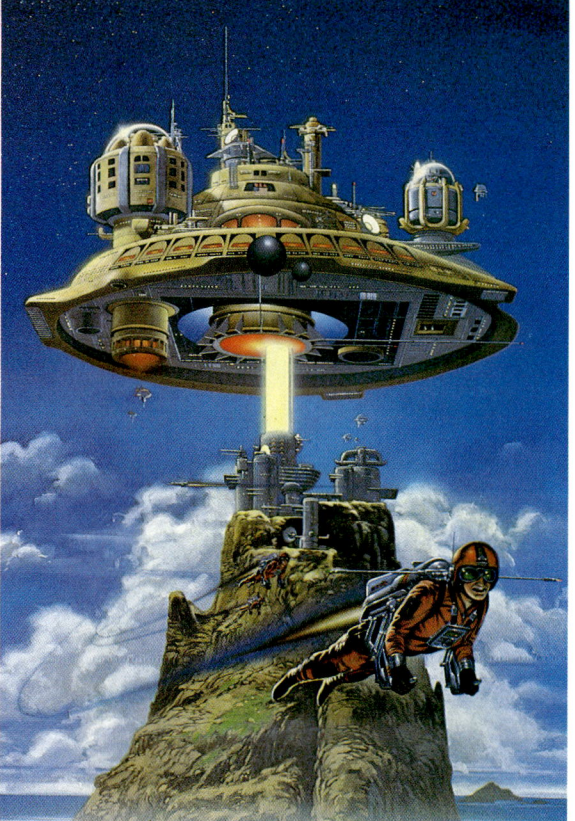

Represented by Artist

Jerry McDonald

1. a. pencil and watercolor on illustation board b. editorial illustration, CHORIZO magazine c. 1984
2. a. pencil and watercolor on illustration board b. editorial illustration, PC WORLD magazine c. 1983
3. a. pencil and watercolor on illustration board b. PORTABLE COMPUTER magazine c. 1983

ジェリー・マクドナルド

1. a. 鉛筆, 水彩絵具, イラストレーションボード b. 雑誌イラスト c.1984年
2. a. 鉛筆, 水彩絵具, イラストレーションボード b. 雑誌イラスト c.1983年
3. a. 鉛筆, 水彩絵具, イラストレーションボード b. 雑誌イラスト c.1983年

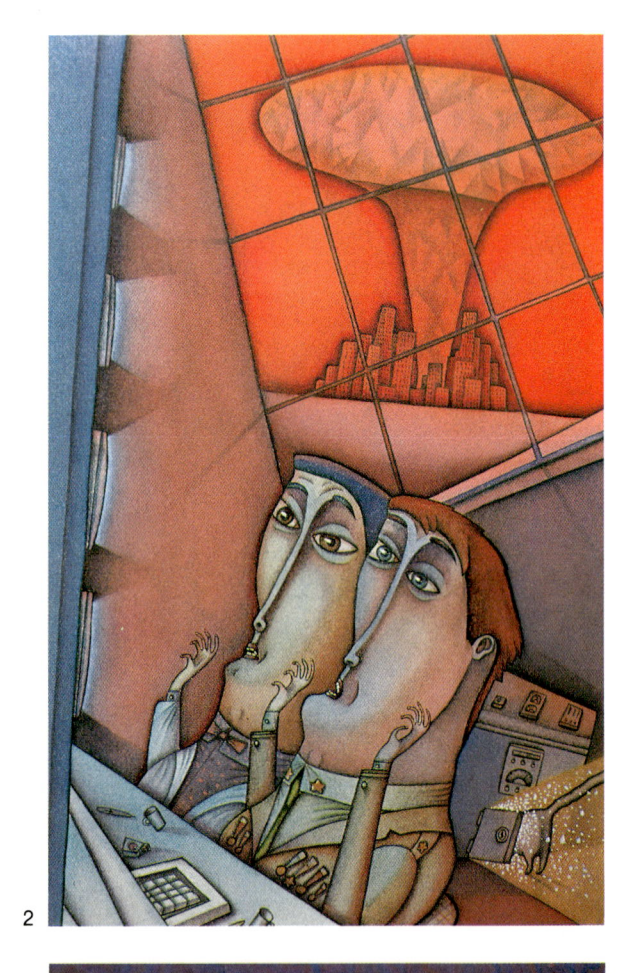

Represented by Artist

Karen M. McDonald

1. a. pastel b. personal work c. 1982
2. a. pastel b. personal work c. 1982
3. a. pastel b. illustration for TWA Ambassador Magazine c. 1983

カレン・M・マクドナルド

1. a. パステル b. 未発表作品 c.1982年
2. a. パステル b. 未発表作品 c.1982年
3. a. パステル b. 雑誌イラスト c.1983年

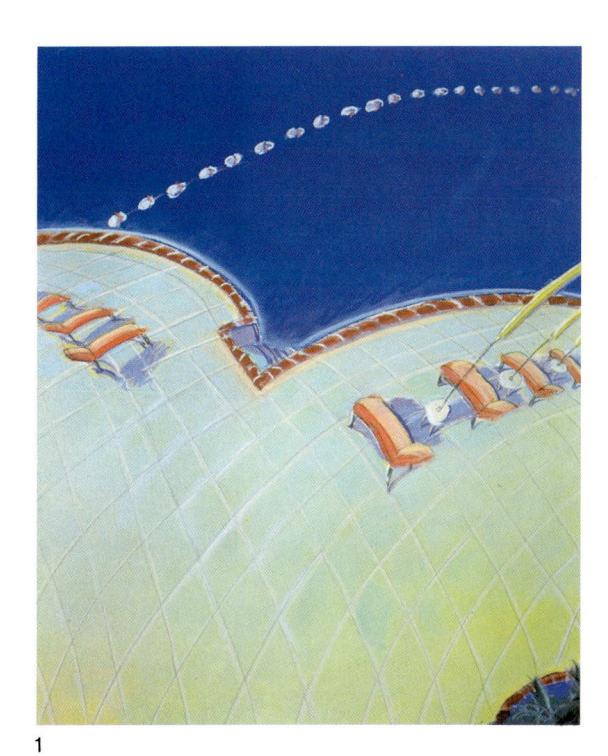

Represented by Artist

Mick McGinty

1. a. acrylics on cold press board, mixed media b. National Consumer ad, Heublein c. 1980
2. a. acrylics on cold press board with airbrush b. National Consumer ad, Levi Strauss c. 1983
3. a. acrylics on cold press board with airbrush b. display and consumer ad. California Raisin Advertising Board c. 1983
4. a. acrylics on cold press board with airbrush b. National Consumer ad, MTV c. 1982

Represented by Artist

Mark MacMahon

1. a. watercolor b. limited edition poster
2. a. watercolor b. greeting card
3. a. watercolor b. annual report for a company

マーク・マクマホン

1. a. 水彩絵具 b. 限定版ポスター
2. a. 水彩絵具 b. グリーティングカード
3. a. 水彩絵具 b. 企業年次報告書

181

Represented by Artist

Wilson McLean　　ウィルソン・マクリーン

1. WHITE EGRET & LANDSCAPE a. acrylic on canvas with brush b. Holland American Travel Poster c. 1983

1. a. アクリル絵具, キャンバス, 画筆　b. ポスター c. 1983年

Represented by Artist

2. INTERIOR OF ROOM WITH COMPUTER a. acrylic on canvas with brush b. Gatefold cover for "Citibank" annual report c. 1984
3. COW a. acrylic on canvas with brush b. Mother Jones magazine c. 1984
4. GLOBE PLUGS a. acrylic on canvas with brush b. "Citibank" annual report c. 1984
5. 2 TRIBAL HEAD. MIXED CULTURES a. oil on canvas with brush b. Psychology Today magazine c. non-published to date

2.a.アクリル絵具, キャンバス, 画筆 b.企業年次報告書の表紙 c.1984年
3.a.アクリル絵具, キャンバス, 画筆 b.雑誌イラスト c.1984年
4.a.アクリル絵具, キャンバス, 画筆 b.企業年次報告書のイラスト c.1984年
5.a.油彩絵具, キャンバス, 画筆 b.雑誌イラスト (未発表)

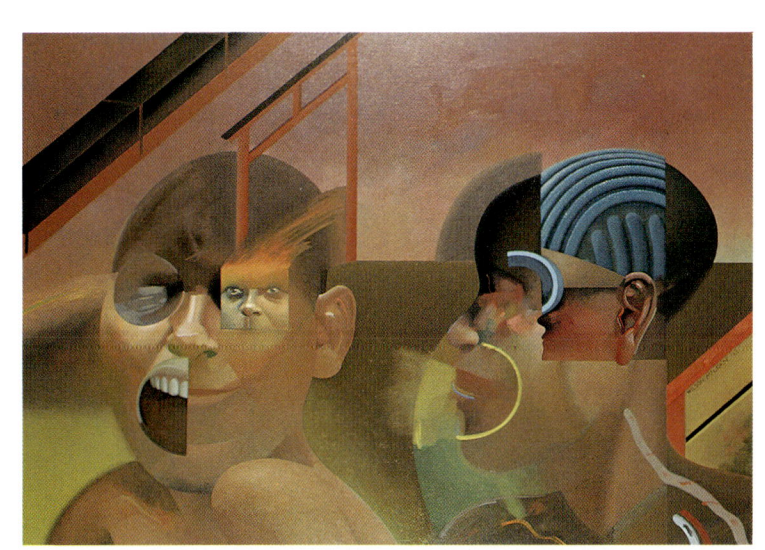

Represented by Artist

James McMullan　　　ジェームス・マクマラン

1-4. a. watercolor
1-4. b. poster

1-4.a. 水彩絵具
1-4.b. ポスター

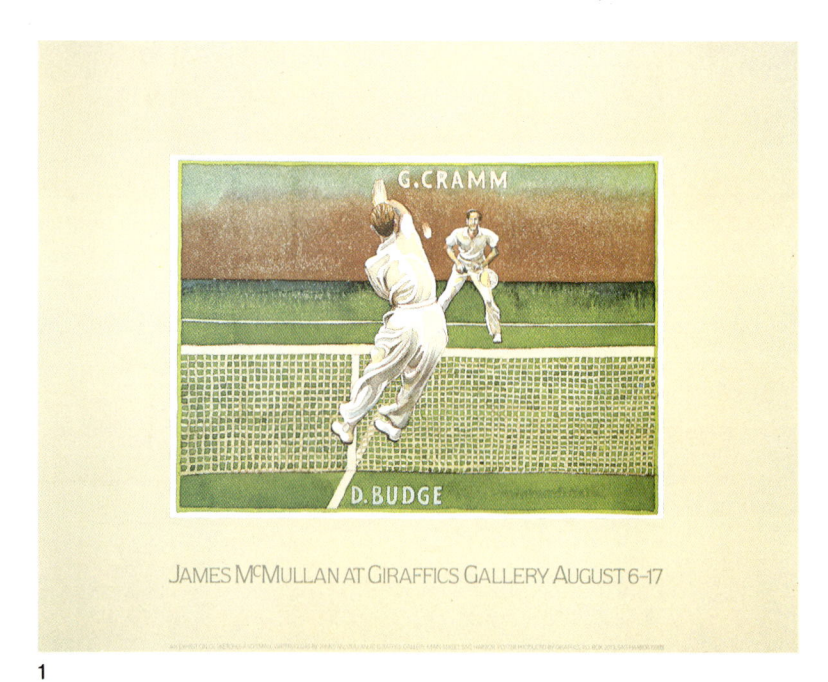

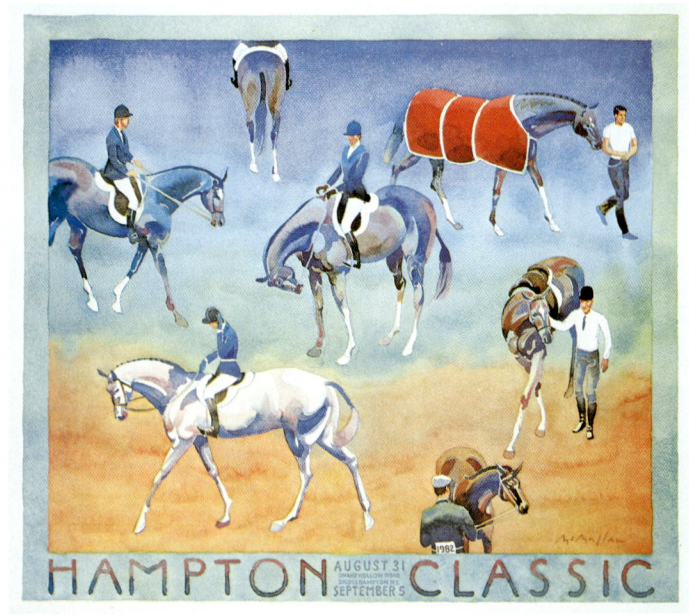

Represented by Artist

Frank Mediate

1. a. gouache b. story book
2. a. ink & color film b. poster
3. a. ink & dyes b. travel brochure

フランク・メディエイト

1. a. ガッシュ b. 書籍イラスト
2. a. インク、カラーフィルム b. ポスター
3. a. インク、染料 b. 旅行パンフレット

Represented by Artist

Paul Meisel

1. a. pen and ink and watercolor b. Boston Globe, magazine section, article on French culture c. 1983
2. a. marker and watercolor b. poster for exhibition at Central Park Zoo, New York City c. 1983
3. a. pen and ink and watercolor b. unpublished, for artist's portfolio c. 1983
4. a. pen and ink and watercolor b. unpublished, for artist's portfolio c. 1983

ポール・ミーゼル

1. a. ペン,インク,水彩絵具 b. 雑誌イラスト c.1983年
2. a. マーカー,水彩絵具 b. ポスター c.1983年
3. a. ペン,インク,水彩絵具 b. ポートフォリオ c.1983年
4. a. ペン,インク,水彩絵具 b. ポートフォリオ 1983年

Represented by Artist

Gary Mele

1. WHITE CANE DAY a. pastel, enamel, & graphite on paper b. personal work of artist c. 1983
2. a. graphite, pastel, and enamel b. personal work of artist c. 1983
3. MISSING KIN a. pastel, enamel on paper b. fiction story for Northeast magazine c. 1983

ゲーリー・メール

1. a. パステル，エナメル，グラファイト鉛筆、紙 b. 未発表作品 c.1983年
2. a. グラファイト鉛筆，パステル，エナメル b. 未発表作品 c.1983年
3. a. パステル，エナメル，紙 b. 雑誌イラスト c.1983年

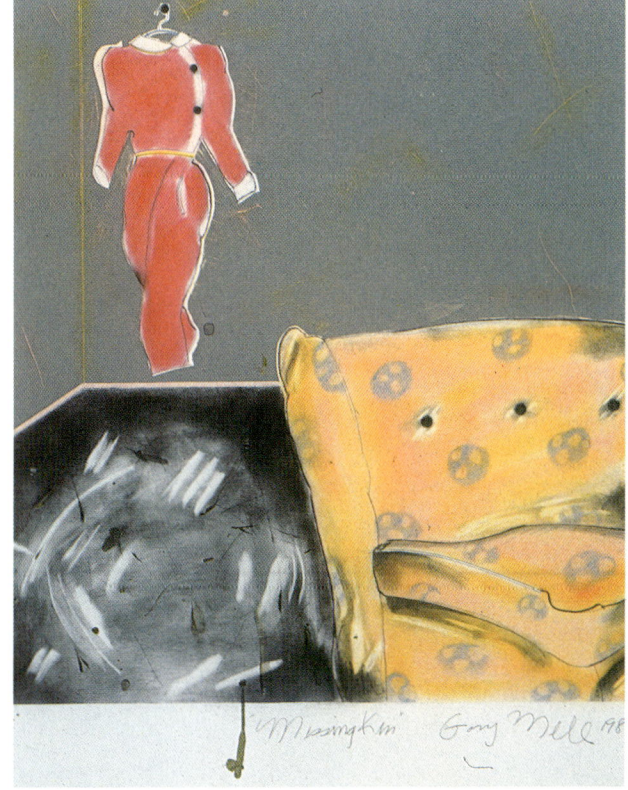

Represented by Artist

Paul Melia

1. a. watercolor on gesso b. personal painting c. 1983
2. a. gouache and acrylic b. one of 8 days for Baldwin Piano & Organ Co. c. 1982
3. PELICANS a. acrylic and inks on illustration board b. personal painting c. 1980
4. a. watercolor on gesso b. for Marathon in horse magazine c. 1983

ポール・メリア

1. a.水彩絵具, ジェッソ b.未発表作品 c.1983年
2. a.ガッシュ, アクリル絵具 b.広告イラスト c.1982年
3. a.アクリル絵具, インク, イラストレーションボード b.未発表作品 c.1980年
4. a.水彩絵具, ジェッソ b.雑誌イラスト c.1983年

188

Represented by Artist

Rick Meyerowitz

1. THE "PARANOIASAUR" a. watercolor and colored pencil on paper b. from the book "Dodosaurs" the Dinosaurs that didn't make it. c. 1983
2. BASEBALL "FLAKE" a. watercolor and colored pencils on paper b. Esquire magazine c. 1981
3. SAMURAI HAIRCUT! a. watercolor and colored pencils on paper b. Bananas Magazine c. 1979
4. GUSTO a. watercolor and colored pencil on paper b. gusto poster c. 1982

リック・マイヤーウィッツ

1. a. 水彩絵具, 色鉛筆, 水彩画紙 b. 書籍イラスト c. 1983年
2. a. 水彩絵具, 色鉛筆, 水彩画紙 b. 雑誌イラスト c. 1981年
3. a. 水彩絵具, 色鉛筆, 水彩画紙 b. 雑誌イラスト c. 1979年
4. a. 水彩絵具, 色鉛筆, 水彩画紙 b. ポスター c. 1982年

Represented by Artist

Gary Meyer

1. VISCICORP POSTER a. gouache on illustration board with brush and airbrush b. poster c. 1982
2. OLDE ENGLISH 800 a. gouache on illustration board with brush and airbrush b. poster and billboard c. 1981
3. CHICAGO ALBUM COVER "CHICAGO" a. gouache on illustration board with brush and some airbrush b. album cover and poster c. 1979

ゲーリー・メイヤー

1. a. ガッシュ, イラストレーションボード, 画筆, エアブラシ b. ポスター c.1982年
2. a. ガッシュ, イラストレーションボード, 画筆, エアブラシ b. ポスター, ビルボード c.1981年
3. a. ガッシュ, イラストレーションボード, 画筆, エアブラシ b. レコードジャケット, ポスター c.1979年

Represented by Artist

4. "MUTANT" MOVIE POSTER a. gouache on illustration board with brush and airbrush b. movie poster and ad art c. 1983

Wendell Minor

ウェンデル・マイナー

1. SHOELESS JOE a. acrylic on masonite b. book jacket c. 1982
2. MASTER OF THE MOOR a. acrylic on masonite b. book jacket c. 1983
3. SEASON OF YELLOW LEAF a. acrylic on masonite b. book jacket c. 1983

1. a. アクリル絵具, メゾナイト b. 書籍表紙 c. 1982年
2. a. アクリル絵具, メゾナイト b. 書籍表紙 c. 1983年
3. a. アクリル絵具, メゾナイト b. 書籍表紙 c. 1983年

Represented by Artist

Paul Moch

1. a. watercolor on illustration board with airbrush b. spot illustration of Punk Santa for Playboy magazine c. 1983
2. a. watercolor on illustration board with airbrush b. spot illustration of Grace Jones for Playboy magazine c. 1982
3. a. watercolor on illustration board with airbrush b. spot illustration of Ronald Reagan for Playboy magazine c. 1983

ポール・モック

1. a. 水彩絵具, イラストレーションボード, エアブラシ b. 雑誌イラスト c.1983年
2. a. 水彩絵具, イラストレーションボード, エアブラシ b. 雑誌イラスト c.1982年
3. a. 水彩絵具, イラストレーションボード, エアブラシ b. 雑誌イラスト c.1983年

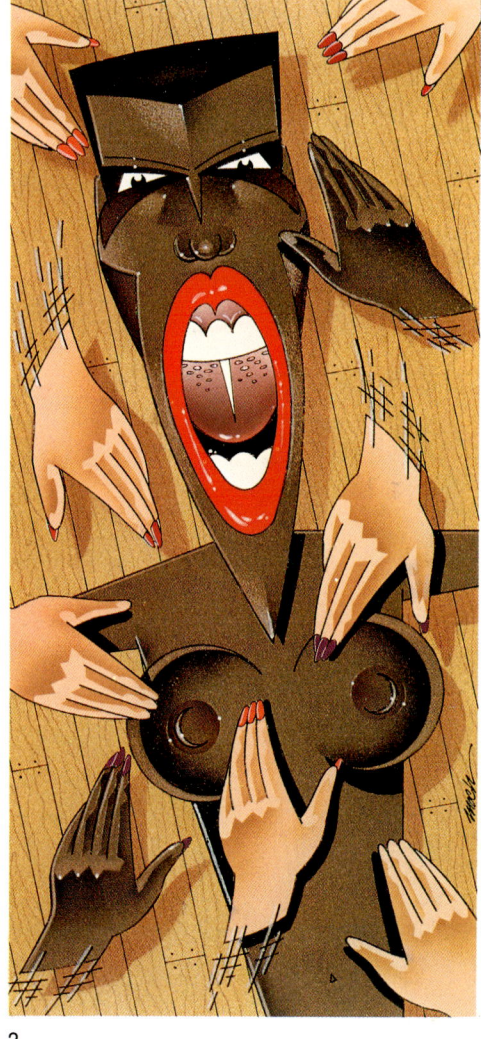

Represented by Artist

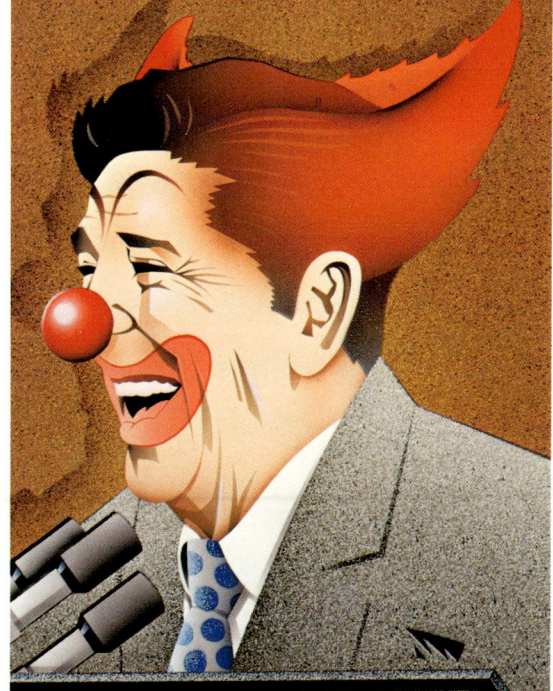

Marilyn Montgomery

1. a. vynil acrylic with airbrush b. video package cover c. 1984
2. BLACK ICE a. vynil acrylic with airbrush b. record album cover c. 1982
3. FEATHER RIVER a. Liquitex acrylic painting c. 1980

マリリン・モンゴメリー

1.a. ビニールアクリル絵具, エアブラシ b. ビデオパッケージ c.1984年
2.a. ビニールアクリル絵具, エアブラシ b. レコードジャケット c.1982年
3.a. アクリル絵具 c.1980年

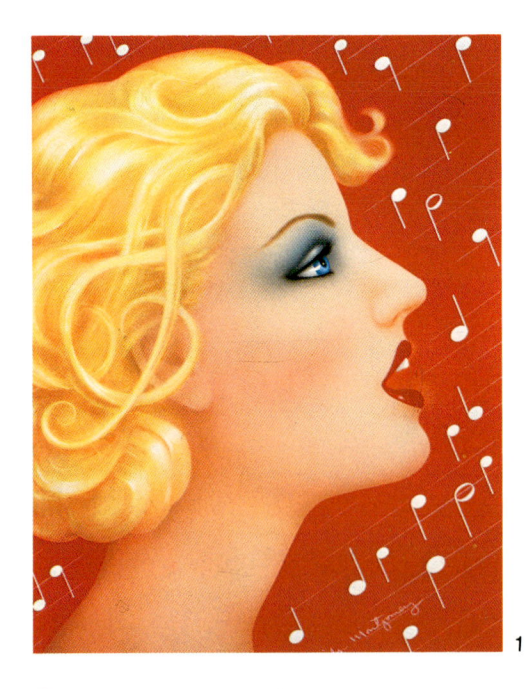

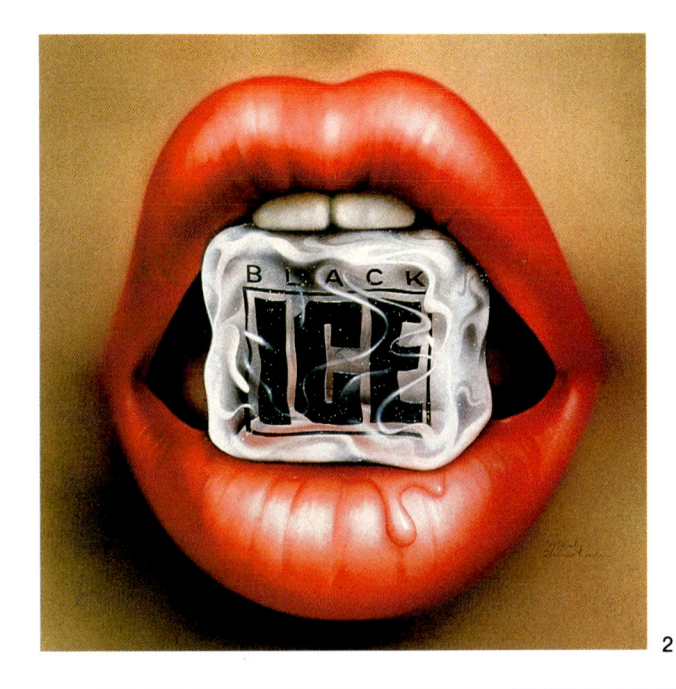

Represented by Artist

David Montiel

1. a. acrylic on canvas with brush b. two-page spread for Family Computing Magazine Scholastic Publications c. 1983
2. a. acrylic on canvas with brush b. cover of book entitled "Lying Now" by Diane Johnson for Random House Publishers c. 1982
3. a. acrylic on canvas with airbrush b. advertising poster for Kennex Tennis Shoes c.1983
4. a. acrylic on canvas with brush b. cover of Fortune magazine for Time Inc. c. 1982

デイヴィッド・モンティエール

1. a. アクリル絵具，キャンバス，画筆 b. 雑誌イラスト c. 1983年
2. a. アクリル絵具，キャンバス，画筆 b. 書籍表紙 c. 1982年
3. a. アクリル絵具，キャンバス，エアブラシ b. ポスター c. 1983年
4. a. アクリル絵具，キャンバス，画筆 b. 雑誌表紙 c. 1982年

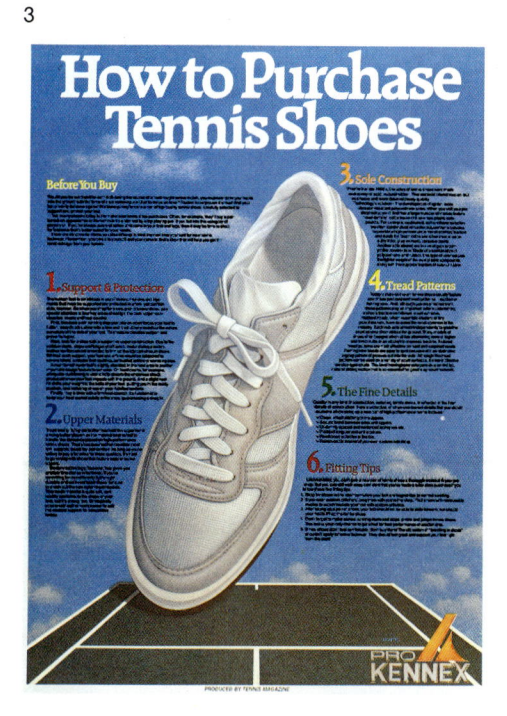

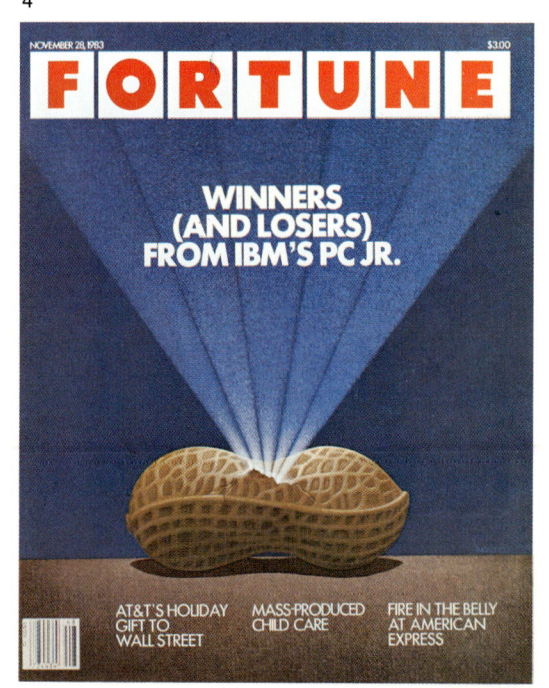

Represented by Artist

Jacqui Morgan

1. a. dyes on Arches paper b. theater poster or "The Tap Dance Kid" c. 1983
2. a. cast paper with mixed media b. cover illustration for Today's Art and Graphics c. 1980
3. a. cast paper with mixed media b. poster for exhibition of "Miss America" Icons. one of seven in the series c. 1980
4. a. watercolor on Whatman paper b. reflective surfaces for "Watercolor for Illustration" book c. 1983

ジャッキー・モーガン

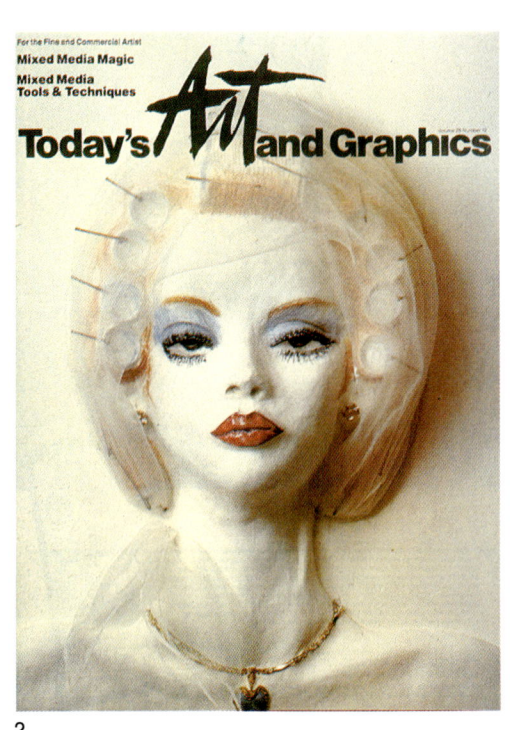

1. a. 染料, 水彩画紙　b. ポスター　c. 1983年
2. a. キャスト紙, その他　b. 雑誌表紙　c. 1980年
3. a. キャスト紙, その他　b. ポスター　c. 1980年
4. a. 水彩絵具, 水彩画紙　b. 書籍イラスト　c. 1983年

Represented by Artist

Frank K. Morris

1. a. acrylic, pencil & markers b. editorial article on home birthday, for Memphis magazine c. 1983
2. a. acrylics, inks and pencil b. cover for New York magazine. cover story was entitled "Second Ave, Romance" article about singles bars and the people who frequent them in N.Y. City c. 1980
3. a. acrylics b. hardcover for book of short stories entitled "A Visit From the Foot Binder" published by Simon Schuster c. 1983

フランク・K・モリス

1. a. アクリル絵具, 鉛筆, マーカー b. 雑誌イラスト c. 1983年
2. a. アクリル絵具, インク, 鉛筆 b. 雑誌表紙 c. 1980年
3. a. アクリル絵具 b. 書籍表紙 c. 1983年

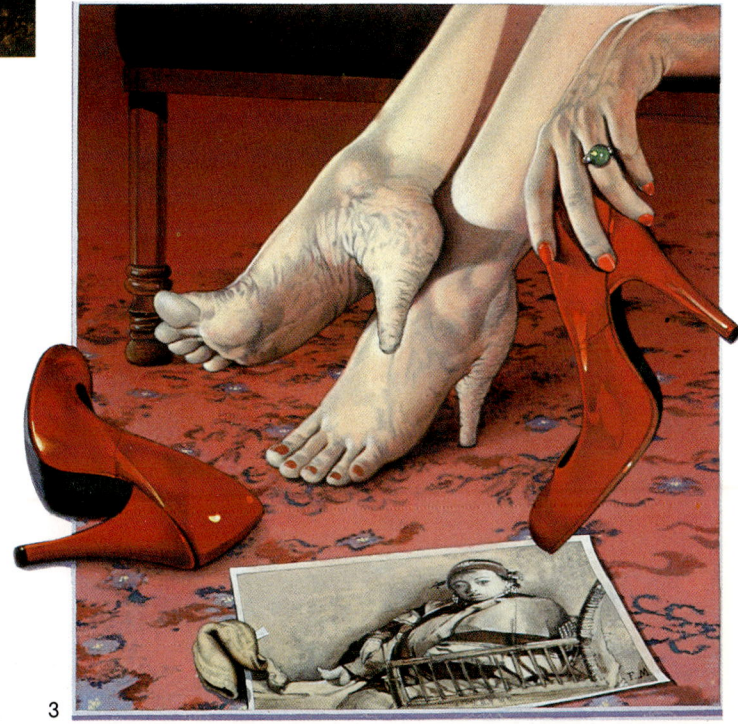

Represented by Artist

Dennis Mukai

1. SLIPPERY WHEN WET a. ink on crescent board with airbrush b. promotional for the Dot Printer c. 1981
2. THANK YOU a. ink on crescent board with airbrush b. thank you card for Paper Moon Graphics c. 1982
3. GOING FOR BAROQUE a. ink on crescent board with airbrush b. article in Oui magazine c. 1980

デニス・ムカイ

1. a. インク，クレセントボード，エアブラシ b. 広告イラスト c. 1981年
2. a. インク，クレセントボード，エアブラシ b. グリーティングカード c. 1982年
3. a. インク，クレセントボード，エアブラシ b. 雑誌イラスト c. 1980年

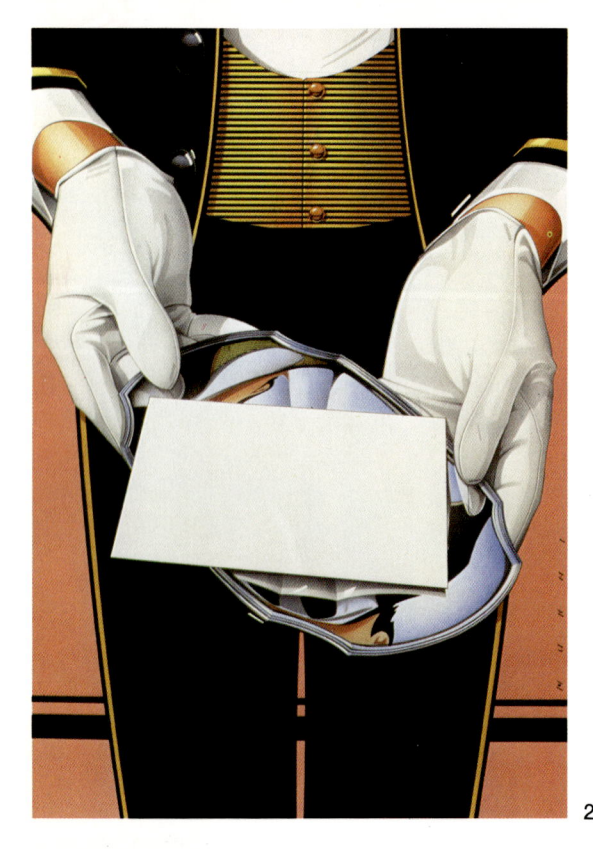

Represented by Artist

Tak Murakami

1. LION a. clay, cut paper, wire, acrylic paint b. cover for textbook SKATES AND ROLLER SKATES, published by Laidlaw Brothers c. 1983
2. SCARECROW a. cut paper, clay, wood, wire, acrylic paint, string b. cover for textbook POCKETS AND PATCHES, published by Laidlaw Brothers c. 1983
3. DRAGON a. clay, cut paper, wire, straw basket, acrylic paint b. cover for textbook BASKETS AND BALLOONS, published by Laidlaw Brothers c. 1983
4. WIZARD/GENIE a. cut paper, clay, wire acrylic paint, cotton b. cover for textbook WIZARDS AND WISHES, published by Laidlaw Brothers c. 1983

タク・ムラカミ

1. a. 粘土，切り紙，針金，アクリル絵具 b. テキストブックの表紙 c. 1983年
2. a. 切り紙，粘土，木，針金，アクリル絵具，ひも b. テキストブックの表紙 c. 1983年
3. a. 粘土，切り紙，針金，わらのバスケット，アクリル絵具 b. テキストブックの表紙 c. 1983年
4. a. 切り紙，粘土，針金，アクリル絵具，コットン b. テキストブックの表紙 c. 1983年

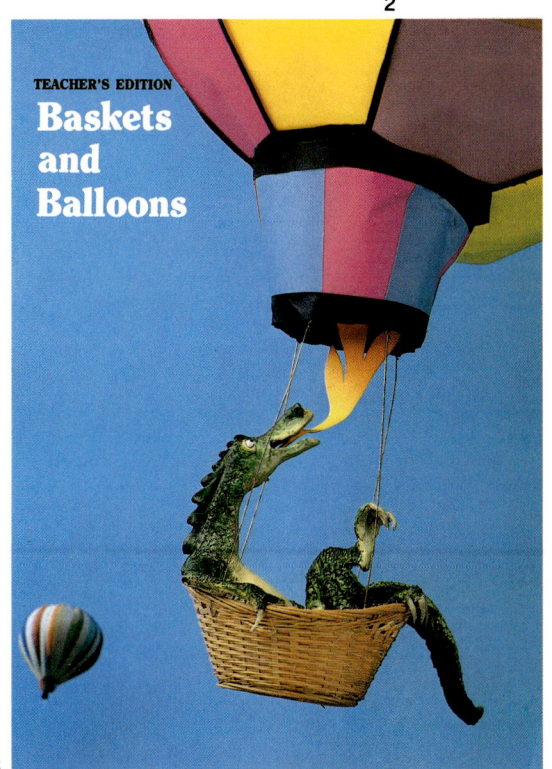

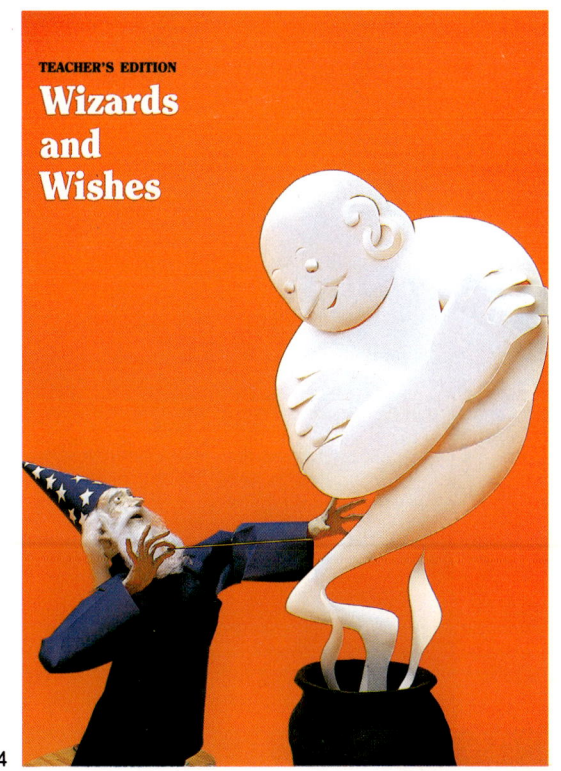

Represented by Artist

Bill Nelson

1. JOY AND PATHOS a. colored pencil on charcoal paper b. illustration for poster announcing a celebration of the arts c. 1982
2. ONE MAN SHOW a. colored pencil on matte board b. illustration for poster for a one man show of artist's illustration work c. 1981
3. ROCKING ROY a. colored pencil on charcoal paper b. cover of THROTTLE, HALLOWEEN ISSUE (a local tabroid newspaper) c. 1983
4. PINHEADS a. colored pencil on matte board b. poster for self-promotion for a printer c. 1982

ビル・ネルソン

1. a. 色鉛筆, 木炭紙 b. ポスター c.1982年
2. a. 色鉛筆, マットボード b. ポスター c.1981年
3. a. 色鉛筆, 木炭紙 b. 地方紙の表紙 c.1983年
4. a. 色鉛筆, マットボード b. セルフプロモーション c.1982年

Represented by Artist

Will Nelson

1. APPLES a. gouache on illustration board b. Pacific Northwest magazine, "Apples of Washington" c. 1983
2. TRACK SHOES a. gouache on illustration board b. Playboy magazine, "The Ultimate Athlete" c. 1983
3. DIVING HELMET a. transparent watercolor on D'Arches rag paper b. private collection, "Locker 23" c. 1982

ウイル・ネルソン

1. a. ガッシュ，イラストレーションボード b. 雑誌イラスト c.1983年
2. a. ガッシュ，イラストレーションボード b. 雑誌イラスト c.1983年
3. a. 透明水彩絵具，ダーチェスラグペーパー b. 個人所蔵作品 c.1982年

Represented by Artist

Meredith Nemirov

1. MEXICAN DANCERS a. watercolor b. portfolio c. 1981
2. BARBRA IN MOROCCO a. watercolor b. portfolio piece c. 1982
3. LA FAMILIA DE MI ESPOSO a. watercolor. 3-D diorama b. personal piece c. 1983

メレディス・ネミロフ

1. a. 水彩絵具　b. ポートフォリオ　c. 1981年
2. a. 水彩絵具　b. ポートフォリオ　c. 1982年
3. a. 水彩絵具，三次元透視画　b. 個人作品　c. 1983年

Represented by Artist

Barbara Nessim

1. AMERICAN WOMEN: THE CLIMB TO EQUALITY a. watercolor, pen, ink b. Time magazine cover: the image expresses all women's struggle, black and white, through sweat, tears and thoughtful evaluation and reevaluation c. 1982
2. FANCY DANCER-BOBBI HUMPHREY a. pen and ink, watercolor b. record album cover. Bobbi Humphrey-United Artists blue note c. 1975
3. GIDON KREMER/ROMANTIC MINIATURES VIOLIN a. pastel b. CBS Record album cover c. 1980
4. "COLORS-COMING UP" NEW MAKEUP COLORS FOR FALL 1982 a. gouache and collage b. Madmoiselle magazine, Condé Nast Publications to show new makeup colors for fall 1982 c. 1982

バーバラ・ネッシム

1. a. 水彩絵具, ペン, インク b. 雑誌表紙 c.1982年
2. a. ペン, インク, 水彩絵具 b. レコードジャケット c.1975年
3. a. パステル b. レコードジャケット c.1980年
4. a. ガッシュ, コラージュ b. 雑誌イラスト c.1982年

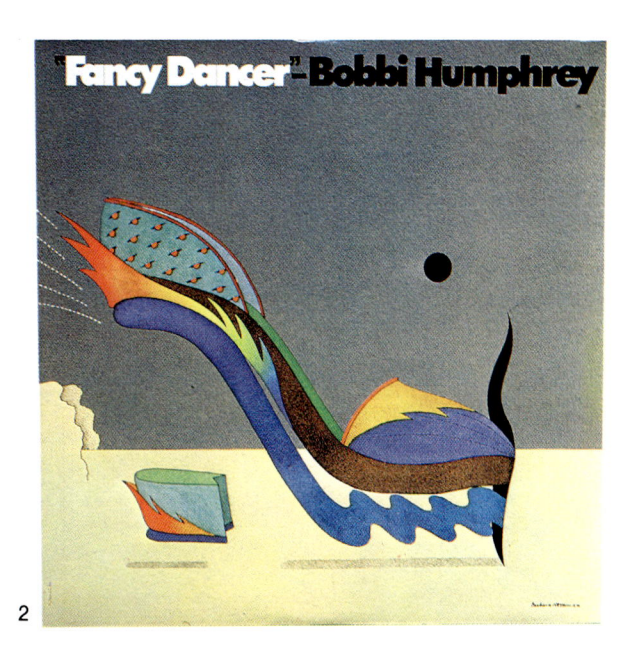

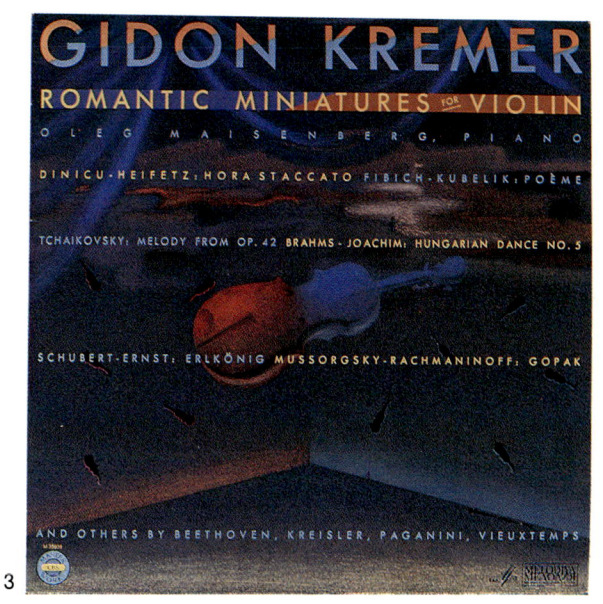

Represented by Artist

Susan Nethery　スーザン・ナザレー

1. a. Luma dyes and ink, pen, brush b. portfolio piece c. 1984
2. a. Luma dyes and ink, pen, brush b. Department of Water and Power poster c. 1981
3. a. Luma dyes and ink, pen, brush b. Dollar Sense magazine, editorial c. 1983

1. a.カラーインク，インク，ペン，画筆 b.ポートフォリオ c.1984年
2. a.カラーインク，インク，ペン，画筆 b.ポスター c.1981年
3. a.カラーインク，インク，ペン，画筆 b.雑誌イラスト c.1983年

Represented by Artist

Mel Odom

1. THE YAKUZA a. pencil, dyes, and gouache b. illustration for Playboy magazine c. 1984
2. a. pencil, dyes, and gouache b. nonfiction piece in Blueboy magazine c. 1978
3. A FRINGE OF LEAVES a. pencil, dyes, and gouache b. Penguin Books. unpublished c. 1983

メル・オドム

1. a. 鉛筆, 染料, ガッシュ b. 雑誌イラスト c.1984年
2. a. 鉛筆, 染料, ガッシュ b. 雑誌イラスト c.1980年
3. a. 鉛筆, 染料, ガッシュ b. 書籍イラスト c.1983年

Represented by Artist

J. Rafal Olbinski

1. a. acrylic on canvas with brush b. New York times magazine cover c. 1983
2. a. acrylic on canvas with brush b. poster announcing TV program "The New Tech. Times" c. 1983
3. a. acrylic on canvas with brush b. record cover for two operas by Richard Wagner; "Mastersinger" and "Götten Dammerung" for RCA records c. 1983
4. a. acrylic and colored pencil on canvas with brush b. book cover for the mystery by Richard Hoyt "30 for Marry" by Viking Press Pub. c. 1983

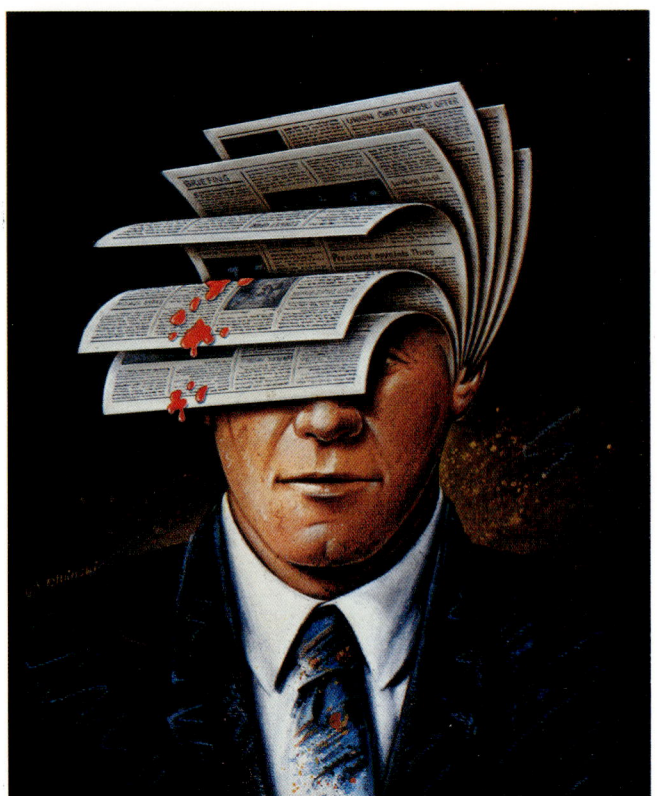

Represented by Artist

Jim Owens

1. a. airbrush b. book cover c. 1983
2. a. airbrush and watercolor b. magazine cover c. 1982
3. a. pencil b. self-promotion c. 1984
4. a. airbrush and watercolor b. Video Game magazine cover c. 1983

ジム・オーエンス

1. a. エアブラシ b. 書籍表紙 c. 1983年
2. a. エアブラシ，水彩絵具 b. 雑誌表紙 c. 1982年
3. a. 鉛筆 b. セルフプロモーション c. 1984年
4. a. エアブラシ，水彩絵具 b. 雑誌表紙 c. 1983年

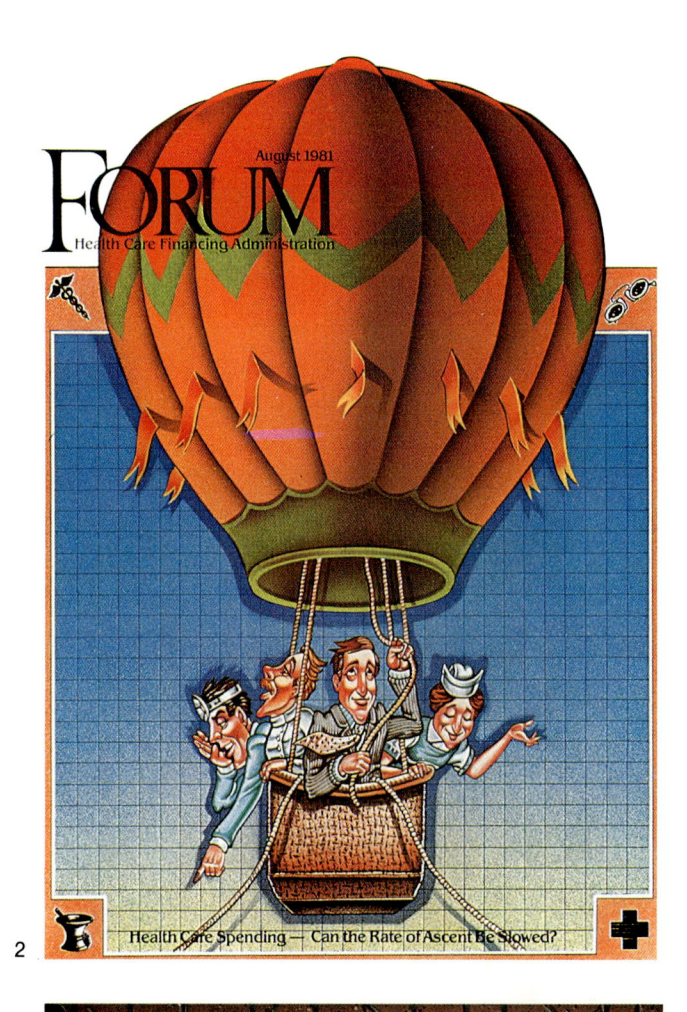

Represented by Artist

Jack Pardue

ジャック・パルデュー

208

1. a. casein b. bookcover, Bradbury Press c. 1983
2. a. casein b. Professional Pilots magazine cover c. 1983
3. a. casein b. Time-Life books c. 1981
4. a. pastel on lines b. Gallery painting c. 1983

1. a.カゼイン b.書籍表紙 c.1983年
2. a.カゼイン b.雑誌表紙 c.1983年
3. a.カゼイン b.書籍イラスト c.1981年
4. a.パステル b.ギャラリー展示作品 c.1983年

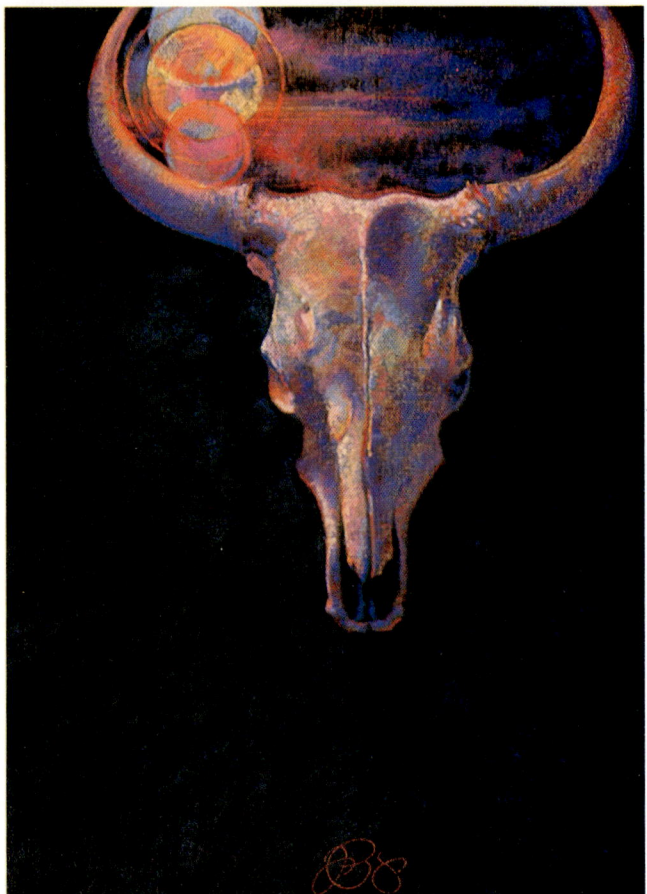

Represented by Artist

Al Parker アル・パーカー

1. a. collage of cut paper and colored pencil on flesh areas over watercolor b. Boys' Life magazine

1. a. 切り紙のコラージュ，色鉛筆，水彩絵具 b. 雑誌イラスト

Represented by Artist

2. a. carbon pencil on watercolor paper b. catalogue of Kit Parker Films c. 1984
3. a. xeroxed girls in pen and ink b. catalogue of Kit Parker Films c. 1984
4. a. watercolor with pencil b. portrait of Helen Keller. commemorative envelope for United States mail c. 1982

2.a.鉛筆，水彩画紙 b.映画カタログの扉ページ・イラスト c.1984年
3.a.ペン，インク，b.映画カタログの扉ページ・イラスト c.1984年
4.a.水彩絵具，鉛筆 b.記念封筒 c.1982年

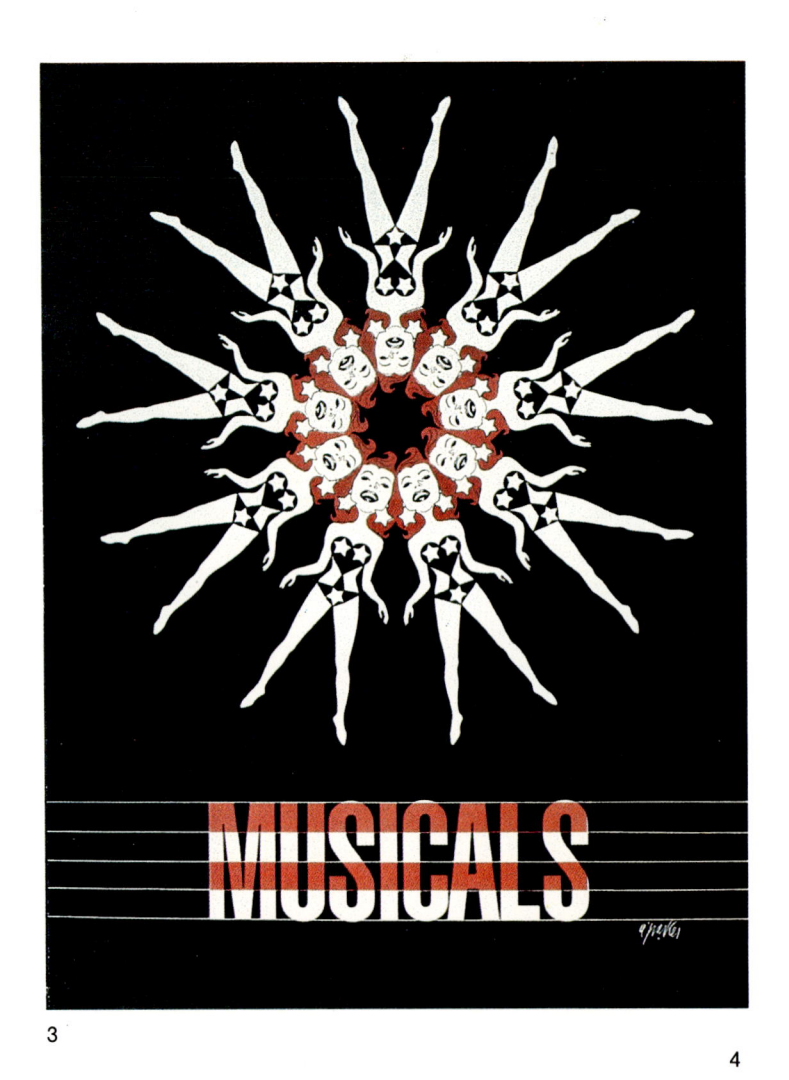

Represented by Artist

5. a. pen and ink b. catalogue of Kit Parker Films c. 1984
6. a. felt tip pen b. catalogue of Kit Parker Films c. 1984
7. a. brush and ink with xeroxed copies b. catalogue of Kit Parker Films c. 1984

5.a. ペン，インク b.映画カタログの扉ページ・イラスト c.1984年
6.a. フェルトチップペン b.映画カタログの扉ページ・イラスト c.1984年
7.a. インク，画筆，ロゴのコピー b.映画カタログの扉ページ・イラスト c.1984年

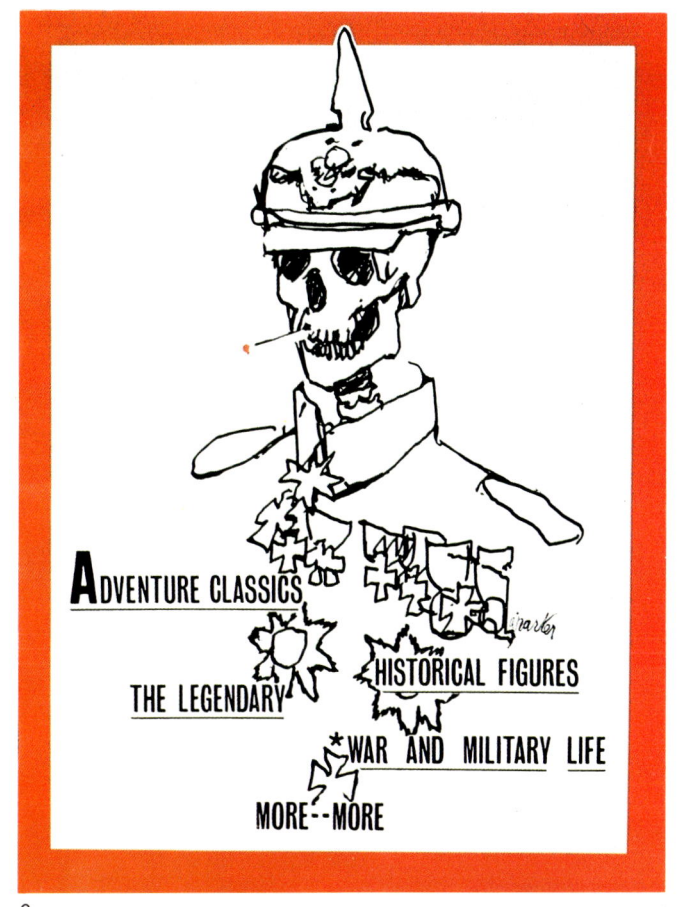

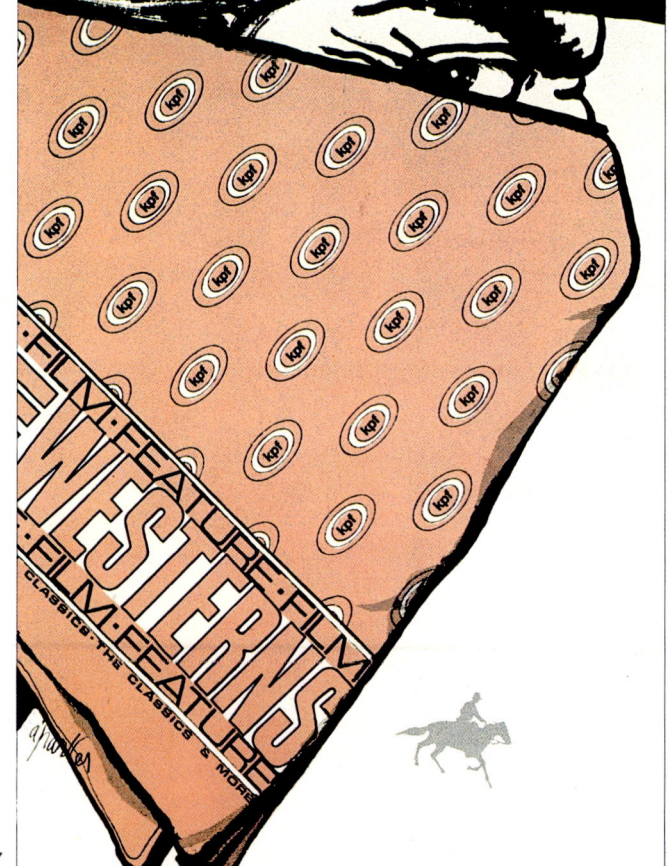

Represented by Artist

Gary Patterson

1. HALF-DAY BOAT a. pen and ink, watercolor b. puzzle, print and calendar c. 1979

2. TOUCHDOWN a. pen and ink, acrylic on cold press illustration board b. print for commercial sale c. 1984
3. MAN VS. MOUNTAIN a. pen & ink, acrylic and color inks on illustration board b. calendar and print for commercial use c. 1984
4. THRILL OF VICTORY a. pen & ink and color inks b. print for commercial sales c. 1977
5. DEDICATION a. pen and ink, color inks b. magazine illustration and print c. 1981

2.a. ペン，インク，アクリル絵具，コールドプレス・イラストレーションボード　b. プリント　c. 1984年
3.a. ペン，インク，アクリル絵具，カラーインク，イラストレーションボード　b. カレンダー，プリント　c. 1984年
4.a. ペン，インク，カラーインク　b. 雑誌イラスト，版画　c. 1977年
5.a. ペン，インク，カラーインク　b. 雑誌イラスト，プリント　c. 1981年

Represented by Artist

Bob Peak

1. MERLIN a. watercolor and pastel b. movie poster for "Excalaber". client: Orion Pictures c. 1982

ボブ・ピーク

1.a. 水彩絵具, パステル　b. 映画ポスター　c. 1982年

Represented by Artist

2. a. watercolor and pastel b. painting for "The Academy of Motion Picture Arts and Sciences" c. 1983

2. a. 水彩絵具, パステル b. プロモーション c. 1983年

Represented by Artist

216

3. JOHN SINGER SARGENT a. oil on paper b. private collection of the artist c. 1979
4. ASPEN TREES IN WINTER a. watercolor b. private collection c. 1980

3. a. 油彩絵具, 紙 b. プライベートコレクション c. 1979年
4. a. 水彩絵具 b. プライベートコレクション c. 1980年

3

4

Represented by Artist

217

5. a. mixed media. gouache b. movie poster for "Pennies From Heaven". client: MGM c. 1981

5.a.ガッシュほか b.映画ポスター c.1981年

Represented by Artist

Jim Pearson

1. a. Sculpey modeling compound, wood, wire, and acrylic b. Sunshine Magazine illustration c. 1984
2. a. Sculpey modeling compound, wood, wire, and acrylic b. Cal Today Magazine cover c. 1982
3. a. Sculpey modeling compound, wood, wire, and acrylic b. self-promotional sample c. 1981
4. a. Sculpey modeling compound, wood, wire, and acrylic b. Cal Today magazine cover c. 1983

ジム・ピアソン

1. a. スカルペイ，混合物，木，針金，アクリル絵具 b. 雑誌イラスト c.1984年
2. a. スカルペイ，混合物，木，針金，アクリル絵具 b. 雑誌表紙 c.1982年
3. a. スカルペイ，混合物，木，針金，アクリル絵具 b. セルフプロモーション c.1981年
4. a. スカルペイ，混合物，木，針金，アクリル絵具 b. 雑誌イラスト c.1983年

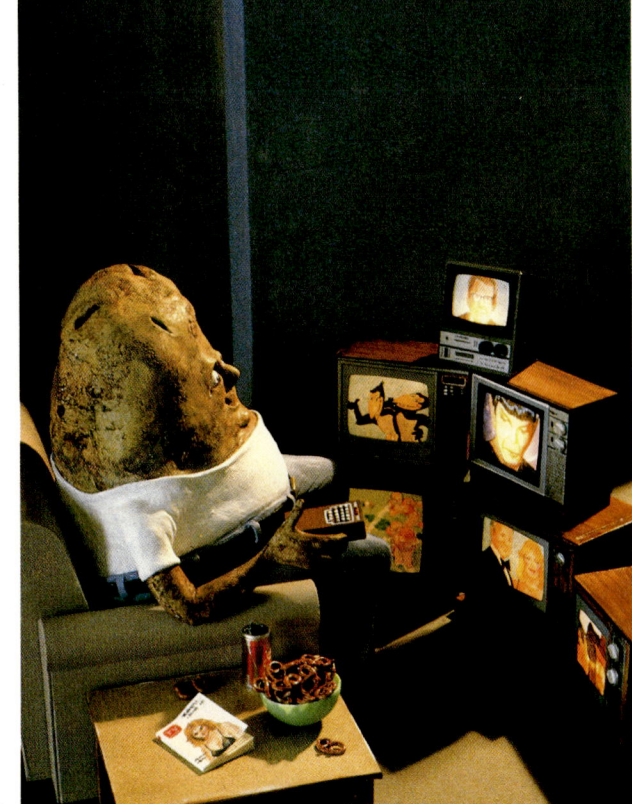

Represented by Artist

Everett Peck

1. a. pen and ink with gouache b. Dino Trilogy #1 c. 1984
2. a. pen and ink with vynil color b. moving announcement c. 1983
3. a. pen and ink with vinyl color b. Heaven Retail Stores (Greeting card) c. 1983

Represented by Artist

Judy Pederson

1. LADY ON A STRIPED CHAIR a. pastel b. greeting card c. 1982
2. LADY IN THE GARDEN a. pastel b. editorial — Avenue magazine c. 1983
3. TEA & COOKIES a. pastel b. greeting card c. 1983
4. GIRL WITH PEARS a. pastel b. personal work c. 1982

ジュディ・ペダーソン

1. a. パステル b. グリーティングカード c. 1982年
2. a. パステル b. 雑誌イラスト c. 1983年
3. a. パステル b. グリーティングカード c. 1983年
4. a. パステル b. 未発表作品 c. 1982年

Represented by Artist

Robert Peluce

1. MAN IN CAN a. acrylic on canvas board c. 1979
2. LIFE BOX a. acrylic on canvas c. 1978
3. UNTITLED a. acrylic on canvas c. 1982

ロバート・ペルース

1. a. アクリル絵具, キャンバスボード c.1979年
2. a. アクリル絵具, キャンバス c.1978年
3. a. アクリル絵具, キャンバス c.1982年

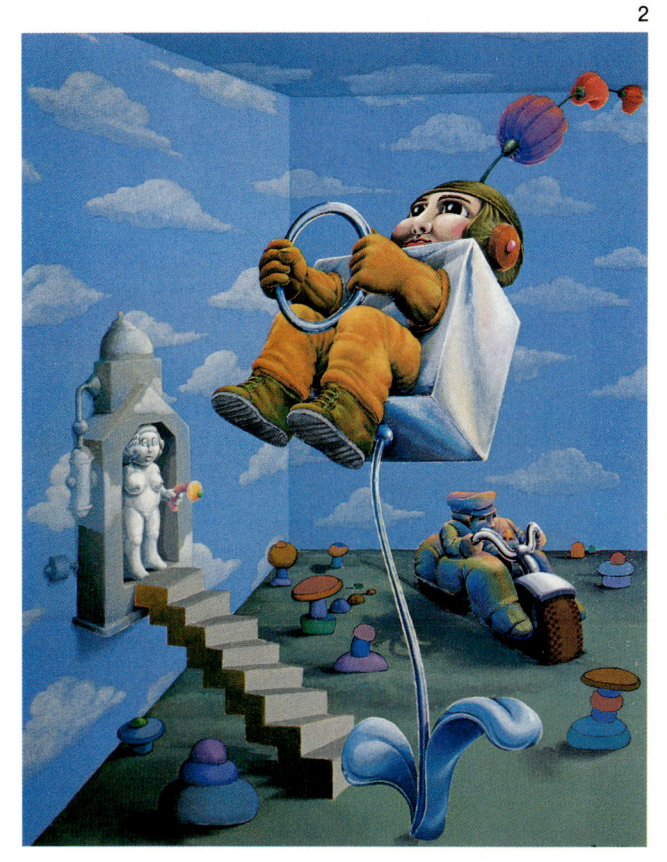

Represented by Artist

Julie Peterson

1. HERBAL TEA LABEL a. Dr. Martins dyes, bleach and acrylic airbrush b. tea package label c. 1980
2. SEASON GREETINGS SAN FRANCISCO FORTY NINERS a. acrylic airbrush and dyes b. Christmas card for San Francisco Forty Niners football team c. 1981
3. PARSLEY PATCH a. Dr. Martins dyes & acrylic airbrush b. point of purchase poster promoting Parsley Patch Herb & Spice Blends c. 1983
4. CRUISE SHIP a. dyes and airbrush b. magazine advertisement for cruise company c. 1980

ジュリー・ピーターソン

1. a.カラーインク，漂白剤，アクリル絵具，エアブラシ b.紅茶のパッケージラベル c.1980年
2. a.アクリル絵具，エアブラシ，染料 b.クリスマスカード c.1981年
3. a.カラーインク，アクリル絵具，エアブラシ b.ポスター c.1983年
4. a.染料，エアブラシ b.雑誌広告 c.1980年

Represented by Artist

Clive Piercy

1. COMPUTER WOMAN a. mixed media b. illustration for Shape magazine c. 1982
2. a. collage b. for Vanity Fair magazine
3. HITS FROM HEAVEN a. airbrush and line b. album cover c. 1983
4. HOT SEAT ILLUSTRATION a. gouache b. advertisement for furniture store London c. 1980

クライブ・ピアーシー

1. a. 各種画材　b. 雑誌イラスト　c. 1982年
2. a. コラージュ　b. 雑誌イラスト
3. a. エアブラシ　b. レコードジャケット　c. 1983年
4. a. ガッシュ　b. 広告イラスト　c. 1980年

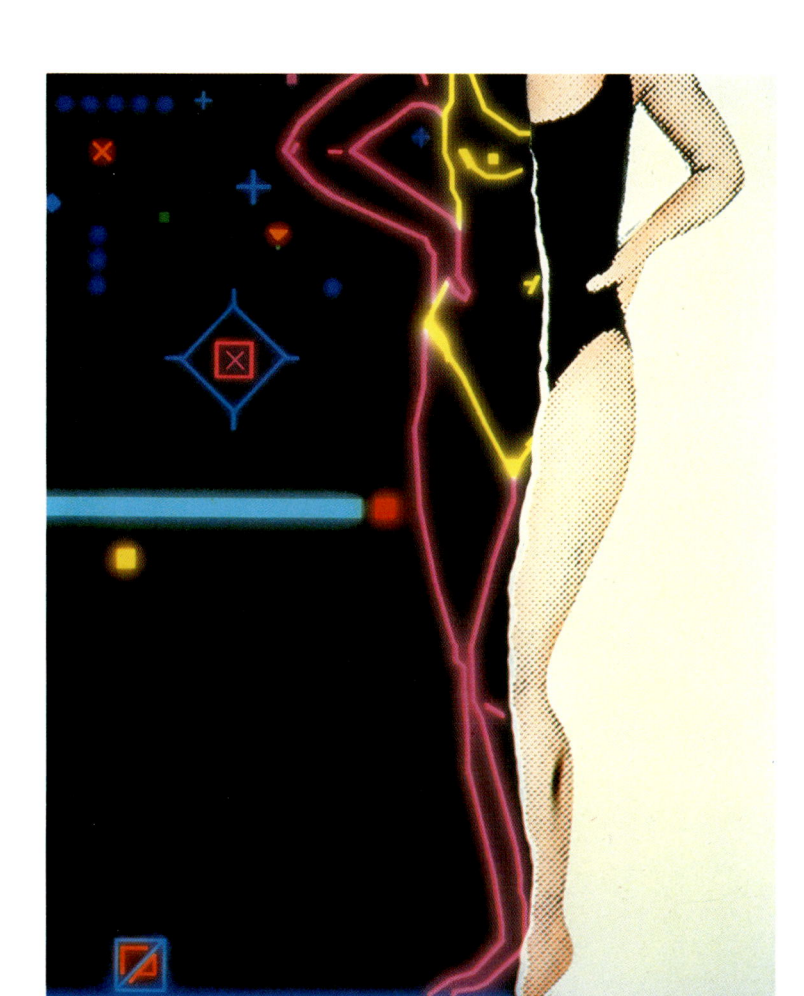

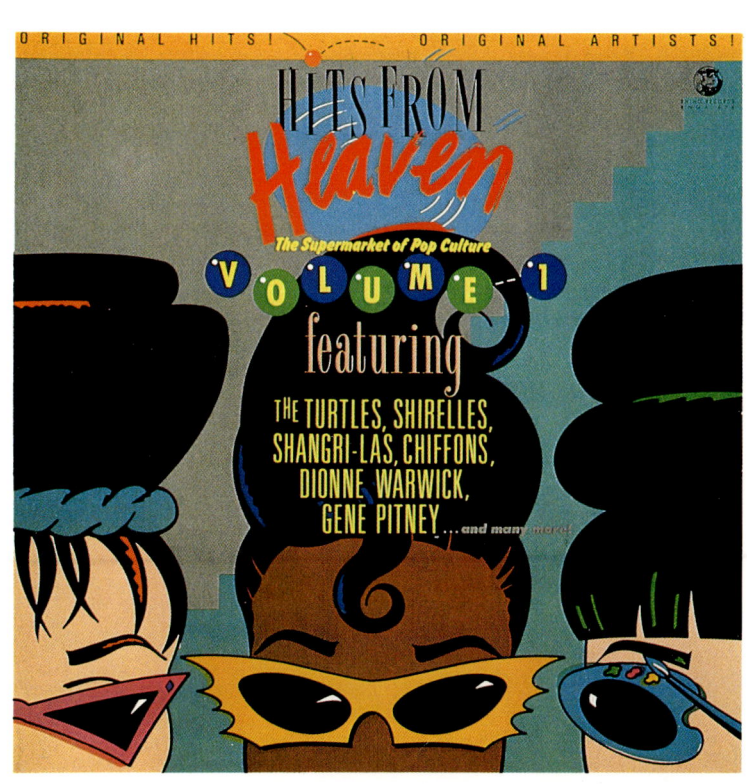

Represented by Artist

Jerry Pinkney

1. JELLY POLL MORTON a. watercolor b. calendar for Smirnoff c. 1982
2. G. WASHINGTON a. watercolor b. R.O.T.C. c. 1978

ジェリー・ピンクニー

1. a. 水彩絵具 b. カレンダー c. 1982年
2. a. 水彩絵具 b. R.O.T.C. c. 1978年

1

2

Represented by Artist

3. COLEMAN HAWKINS a. watercolor b. calendar for Smirnoff c. 1983
4. KID ORY a. watercolor b. calendar for Smirnoff c. 1982
5. BIG BROTHERS, BIG SISTERS a. watercolor b. Marathon World. c. 1982

3.a. 水彩絵具　b. カレンダー　c. 1983年
4.a. 水彩絵具　b. カレンダー　c. 1982年
5.a. 水彩絵具　b. エディトリアル　c. 1982年

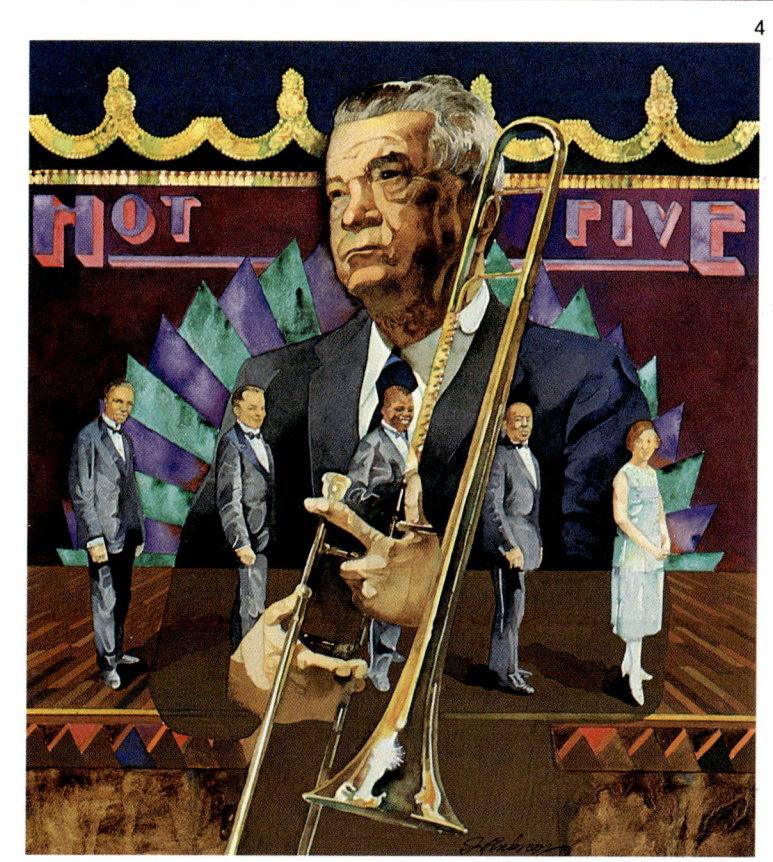

Represented by Artist

Paola Piglia

1. a. watercolor and crayon b. editorial illustration for Ms. magazine. article about rape called "Pig Latin" c. 1984
2. a. watercolor and crayon b. Ms. magazine. editorial illustration for article called "The Bastard Child" c. 1983
3. a. watercolor and crayons b. self-promotional card c. 1983

1. a. 水彩絵具, クレヨン b. 雑誌イラスト c. 1984年
2. a. 水彩絵具, クレヨン b. 雑誌イラスト c. 1983年
3. a. 水彩絵具, クレヨン b. カード (セルフプロモーション) c. 1983年

Represented by Artist

Scott Pollack

1. a. airbrushed dyes and color pencils b. advertisement for Larson Bateman & McAlister Advertising. These are five scientists that were going crazy before they discovered a digital sound speech lab computer c. 1983

2. a. airbrushed dyes and color pencils b. advertisement for Backer & Spielvogel Advertising c. 1983

スコット・ポラック

1. a. エアブラシ染料, 色鉛筆　b. 広告イラスト　c. 1983年
2. a. エアブラシ染料, 色鉛筆　b. 広告イラスト　c. 1983年

Represented by Artist

Ivan Powell

アイバン・パウエル

228

1. JUGGLER a. charcoal, pastel, colored pencil b. self-promotion c. 1983

1.a. チャコール, パステル, 色鉛筆 b. セルフプロモーション c. 1983年

Represented by Artist

2. SAXOPHONE a. charcoal, pastel, colored pencil b. self-promotion c. 1981
3. PIANO a. charcoal, pastel, colored pencils b. piano concert poster c. 1983
4. BILL EVANS a. charcoal, pastel, colored pencils b. book of the Month Club. record album c. 1983
5. FASHION a. pastel, colored pencils b. self-promotion c. 1983

2. a. チャコール，パステル，色鉛筆 b. セルフプロモーション c.1981年
3. a. チャコール，パステル，色鉛筆 b. ポスター c. 1983年
4. a. チャコール，パステル，色鉛筆 b. 書籍イラスト，レコードジャケット c.1983年
5. a. パステル，色鉛筆 b. セルフプロモーション c. 1983年

Represented by Artist

Don Ivan Punchatz

ドン・アイバン・パンチャッツ

230

1. RUNNING ON EMPTY a. acrylic on Mylar drafting film b. self-promotion c. 1984
2. ANCIENT EVENINGS a. acrylic on mylar film b. Playboy magazine. Illustration for the novel "Ancient Evenings" c. 1983

1. a. アクリル絵具, マイラードラフティングフィルム b. セルフプロモーション c.1984年
2. a. アクリル絵具, マイラーフィルム b. 雑誌イラスト c.1983年

1

2

Represented by Artist

231

3. UNICORN a. acrylic on mylar film b. record album cover for readings by Harlan Ellison c. 1984
4. RIVER WORLD a. acrylic on myler drafting film b. book jacket c. 1981

3.a.アクリル絵具, マイラーフィルム b.レコードジャケット c.1984年
4.a.マイラードラフティングフィルム b.書籍表紙 c.1981年

3

4

Represented by Artist

Bill Prochnow

ビル・プロクノー

232

1. VALENTINE a. pen & ink, watercolor b. magazine article about finding true love c. 1984
2. TOOLS OF THE TRADE a. pen & ink, watercolor b. one of a series for Communication Arts magazine c. 1980
3. ATLAS a. pen & ink, watercolor b. magazine article about maps c. 1981

1. a. ペン，インク，水彩絵具　b. 雑誌イラスト　c. 1984年
2. a. ペン，インク，水彩絵具　b. 雑誌イラスト　c. 1980年
3. a. ペン，インク，水彩絵具　b. 雑誌イラスト　c. 1981年

Represented by Artist

Dan Quarnstrom

1. a. acrylic on illustration board with zip-a-tone b. poster for Levis
2. a. ink on paper with pen and brush b. editorial illustration for a restaurant
3. PEOPLE ON ROLLER SKATES a. ink on paper with brush and pen b. advertisement for a roller skate maker, showing their product being used in the local neighborhood, in this case Venice, California
4. RADIO a. ink on paper with brush and pen b. trade advertisement for Lionel Richie record

ダン・クウォンストローム

1. a.アクリル絵具 イラストレーションボード。ジップ・ア・トーン技法 b.ポスター
2. a.インク, ペン, 紙 b.エディトリアル
3. a.インク, ペン, 紙 b.広告イラスト
4. a.インク, ペン, 紙 b.広告イラスト

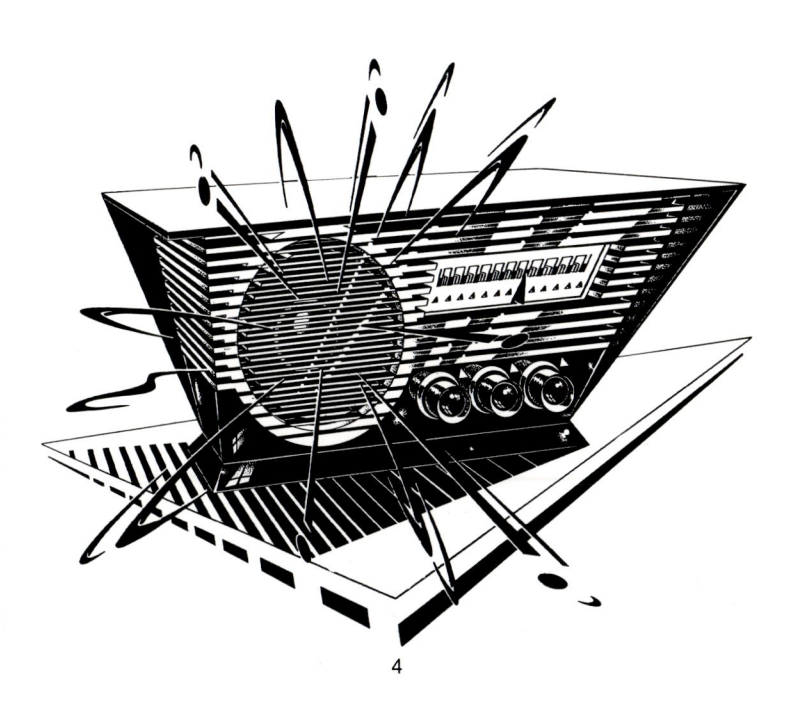

Represented by Artist

Mike Quon

1-12. CHINESE ZODIAC a. ink on rice paper with pen and brush b. Upper and Lower Case magazine, article c. 1981-1982
1. RAT 2. OX 3. TIGER 4. RABBIT 5. DRAGON 6. SNAKE 7. HORSE 8. RAM 9. MONKEY 10. ROOSTER 11. DOG 12. BOAR

マイク・クウォン

1-12.a.インク, わら紙, ペン, 画筆 b.雑誌イラスト c.1981-1982年
十二支 1.子 2.丑 3.寅 4.卯 5.辰 6.巳 7.午 8.未 9.申 10.酉 11.戌 12.亥

Represented by Artist

William Reynolds　　ウィリアム・レイノルズ　　　237

1. a. airbrush and pastel b. self promotion c. 1980
2. a. acrylic, oil on pastel. oil wash b. personal promotion c. 1982
3. a. oil and acrylic. oil wash b. personal c. 1983

1. a. パステル，エアブラシ　b. セルフプロモーション c.1980年
2. a. アクリル絵具，パステル，油彩絵具。ウォッシュ技法　b. セルフプロモーション　c.1982年
3. a. 油彩絵具，アクリル絵具。ウォッシュ技法　b. 未発表作品　c.1983年

Represented by Artist

William Rieser

1. a. pastel on newsprint b. selfpromotion c. 1984
2. a. pastel on charcoal paper b. ad for Levis c. 1983
3. a. pastel, pencil, pantone film on illustration board b. album cover for RCA Records c. 1983
4. a. pastel, pencil, pantone film on charcoal paper b. artwork illustrating the Josie Cotton Song entitled "Johnny Are You Queer?" c. 1983

ウィリアム・リーサー

1. a.パステル，新聞用紙 b.セルフプロモーション c. 1984年
2. a.パステル，チャコールペーパー b.広告イラスト c. 1983年
3. a.パステル，鉛筆，カラートーン，イラストレーションボード b.レコードジャケット c.1983年
4. a.パステル，鉛筆，カラートーン，チャコールペーパー b.イメージイラスト c.1983年

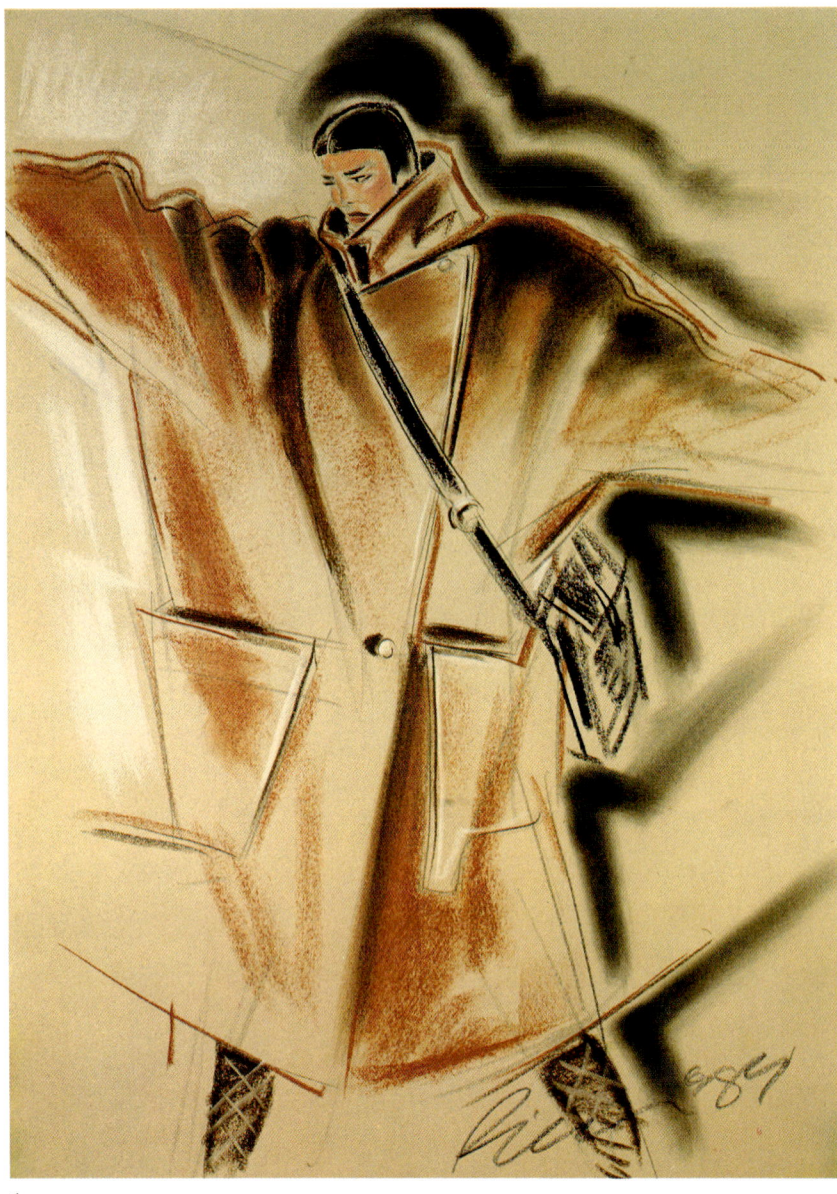

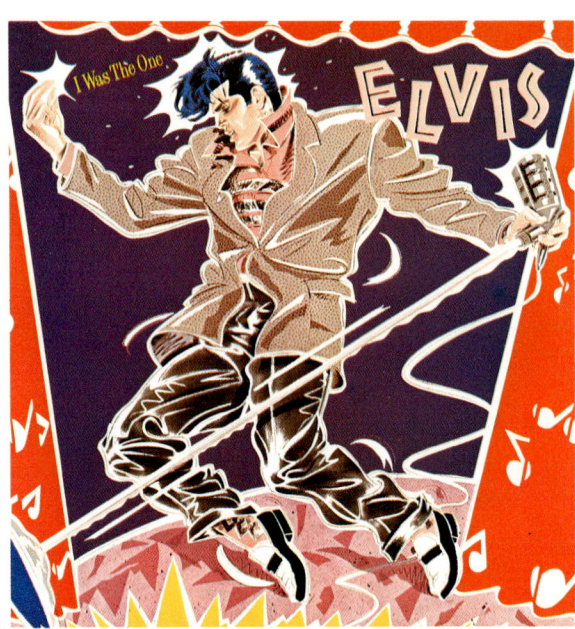

238

Represented by Artist

Frank Riley

1. a. watercolor with airbrush b. poster Electronic Fun magazine c. 1983
2. a. watercolor with airbrush b. cover for Electronic Fun magazine c. 1983
3. a. watercolor with airbrush b. advertisement for E-Z Wider Rolling Paper c. 1983

フランク・ライリー

1. a. 水彩絵具, エアブラシ b. ポスター c. 1983年
2. a. 水彩絵具, エアブラシ b. 雑誌表紙 c. 1983年
3. a. 水彩絵具, エアブラシ b. 広告イラスト c. 1983年

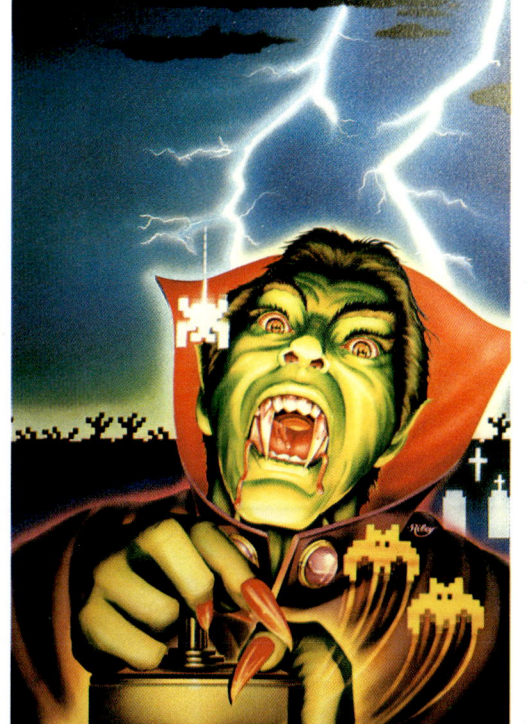

Represented by Artist

Robert Risko

1. ELIZABETH TAYLOR & RICHARD BURTON a. designers gouache on illustration with airbrush b. VANITY FAIR c. 1983
2. MARILYN MONROE a. designers gouache on illustration board with airbrush b. no client c. 1982
3. WOODY ALLEN a. designers gouache on illustration board with airbrush b. TIME unpublished c. 1983
4. DIANA ROSS a. designers gouache on illustration board with airbrush b. VANITY FAIR c. 1982

ロバート・リスコー

1. a. ガッシュ，イラストレーションボード，エアブラシ b. 雑誌イラスト c.1983年
2. a. ガッシュ，イラストレーションボード，エアブラシ b. 未発表作品 c.1982年
3. a. ガッシュ，イラストレーションボード，エアブラシ b. 雑誌イラスト(未発表) c.1983年
4. a. ガッシュ，イラストレーションボード，エアブラシ b. 雑誌イラスト c.1982年

Represented by Artist

Stanley Roberts

1. a. lithograph. colored pencil, watercolor b. portfolio c. 1977
2. a. watercolor, Luma dyes, and colored pencil on matboard b. self-promotion c. 1983
3. a. pencil and colored pencil on mat board b. portfolio c. 1982

Represented by Artist

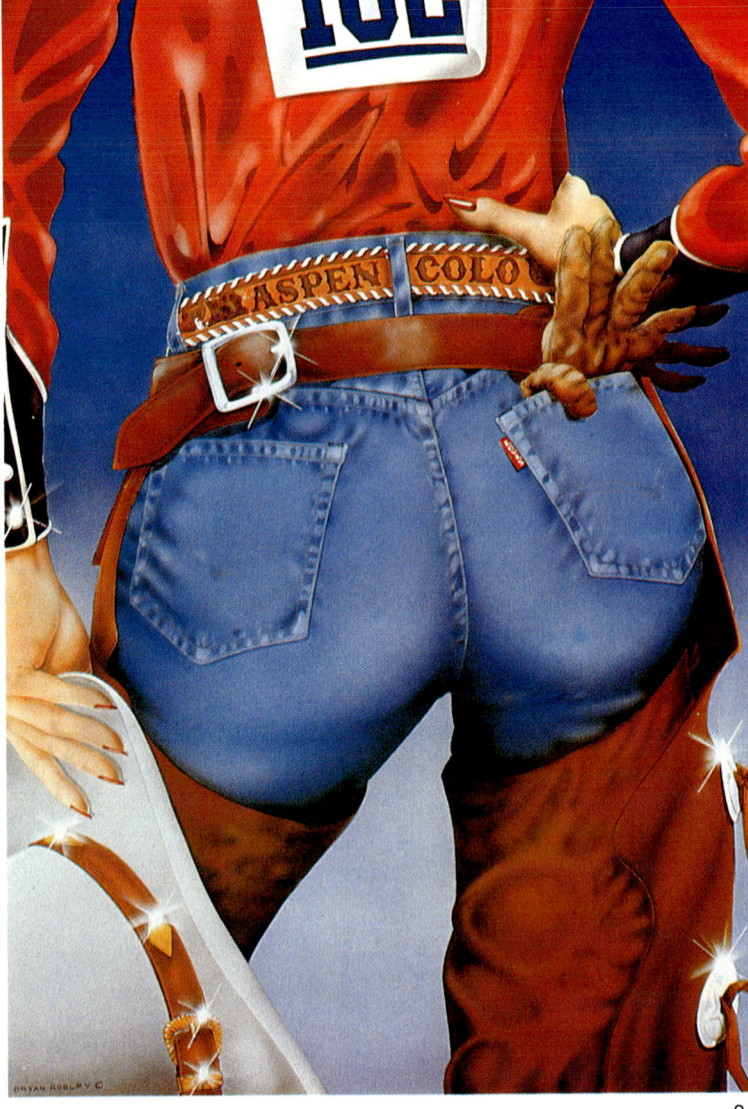

Bryan Robley

1. a. acrylics on frosted mylar with airbrush b. winter Olympic poster for Salomon Ski Equipment, France c. 1983
2. a. acrylics on frosted mylar with airbrush b. design and illustration for poster, Aspen Rodeo c. 1982
3. a. acrylics on frosted mylar with airbrush b. design and illustration for poster for Sun Valley Center for the arts & Humanities c. 1981
4. a. acrylics on frosted mylar with airbrush b. promotional and advertising poster for retail store c. 1983

Represented by Artist

Robert Rodoriguez

1. a. acrylics on paper with brush, some airbrush b. poster for the Los Angeles Brewery of Budweiser Beer c. 1983
2. a. acrylics on illustration board with brush and airbrush b. poster for a west coast airline whose planes were painted yellow c. 1981
3. a. acrylics on paper with brush and airbrush b. '84 Olympics visitor's guide to Los Angeles, title page c. 1984

ロバート・ロドリゲス

1. a. アクリル絵具，紙・画筆，部分的にエアブラシ b. ポスター c.1983年
2. a. アクリル絵具，イラストレーションボード，エアブラシ，画筆 b. ポスター c.1981年
3. a. アクリル絵具，紙，画筆，エアブラシ b. ガイドブックの扉イラスト c.1984年

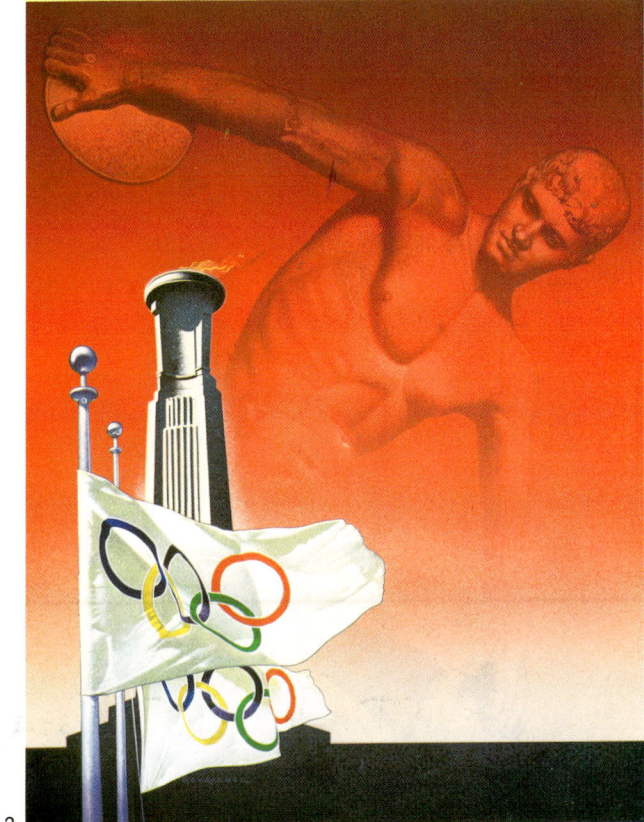

Represented by Artist

Mario Rossetti

1. a. pen and ink on board. crosshatching
   b. album cover c. 1981
2. a. pencil on gesso board. tone drawing
   b. magazine interview- John Glenn- 1984 U.S. Presidential Candidate c. 1983
3. a. pencil on gesso board. tone drawing
   b. magazine interview –Gary Hart– 1984 U.S. Presidential Candidate c. 1983

マリオ・ロゼッティ

1. a.ペン, インク, ボード b.レコードジャケット c.1981年
2. a.鉛筆, ジェッソボード b.雑誌イラスト c.1983年
3. a.鉛筆, ジェッソボード b.雑誌イラスト c.1983年

Represented by Artist

John Rush

1. a. gouache on linen board with airbrush b. poster for Anheuser-Bush Co. c. 1983
2. a. gouache on gessoed panel with wash and airbrush b. Advertising Age magazine cover c. 1983
3. a. gouache on linen board. mainly drybrush b. Psychology Today magazine c. 1980
4. a. gouache on linen board. mainly drybrush b. Pharmaceutical advertising c. 1981

ジョン・ラッシュ

1. a. ガッシュ, リネンボード, エアブラシ b. ポスター c. 1983年
2. a. ガッシュ, ジェッソパネル, エアブラシ。ウォッシュ技法 b. 雑誌表紙 c. 1983年
3. a. ガッシュ, リネンボード。主にドライブラッシュ技法 b. 雑誌イラスト c. 1980年
4. a. ガッシュ, リネンボード。主にドライブラッシュ技法 b. 広告イラスト c. 1981年

Represented by Artist

Tracy Sabin

1. TRACY SABIN a. silkscreen. hand-cut rubylith b. self-promotion poster for artist c. 1983
2. CATS a. offset lithography. hand-cut rubylith b. poster for Mirage Editions c. 1983
3. GORDON SCREEN PRINTING a. silk screen hand-cut rubylith b. self-promotion poster for Gordon Screen Printing c. 1983
4. TANABATA a. silk screen. hand-cut rubylith b. illustration used in promotional materials for the Tanabata festival at Japanese Village Plaza, Los Angeles c. 1981

トレーシー・サビン

1. a. シルクスクリーン　b. セルフプロモーション用ポスター　c. 1983年
2. a. オフセットリトグラフ　b. ポスター　c. 1983年
3. a. シルクスクリーン　b. セルフプロモーション用ポスター　c. 1983年
4. a. シルクスクリーン　b. ロサンゼルス日本人街・七夕祭りのプロモーション・イラスト　c. 1981年

Represented by Artist

Jim Salvati

1. WOODEN SHIPS a. mixed media b. Crosby Stills, Nash book c. 1984
2. MASTER BREW a. mixed media b. Tim Bogert cover. Takoma Records c. 1984
3. AUTOMATIX a. acrylic b. MCA Records cover c. 1983

ジム・サルバティ

1. a.各種画材 b.書籍イラスト c.1984年
2. a.各種画材 b.レコードジャケット c.1984年
3. a.アクリル絵具 b.レコードジャケット c.1983年

Represented by Artist

Emanuel Schongut

エマニュエル・ショングット

248

1. REBECCA a. watercolor and pencil on watercolor paper b. for Mobil Masterpiece Theater advertising & posters. also used at book cover for Avon Books
2. LEDA + THE SWAN a. pencil and watercolor on watercolor paper b. for Pushpin Graphic
3. a. watercolor wash and pencil on watercolor on watercolor paper b. for Pushpin Graphic

1. a. 水彩絵具, 鉛筆, 水彩画紙 b. ポスター, 書籍表紙
2. 鉛筆, 水彩絵具, 水彩画紙 b. プッシュピン・グラフィック
3. a. 水彩絵具のウォッシュ, 鉛筆, 水彩画紙 b. プッシュピン・グラフィック

Represented by Artist

Daniel B. Schwartz

1. a. watercolor b. poster for Mobil Masterpiece Theater c. 1981
2. a. watercolor b. poster for Mobil Masterpiece Theater c. 1983
3. a. watercolor b. editorial illustration of circus performance c. 1979
4. a. watercolor b. painting for Heinz Annual Report c. 1983

ダニエル・B・シュワルツ

1. a. 水彩絵具 b. ポスター c.1981年
2. a. 水彩絵具 b. ポスター c.1983年
3. a. 水彩絵具 b. エディトリアル c.1979年
4. a. 水彩絵具 b. 企業年次報告書 c.1983年

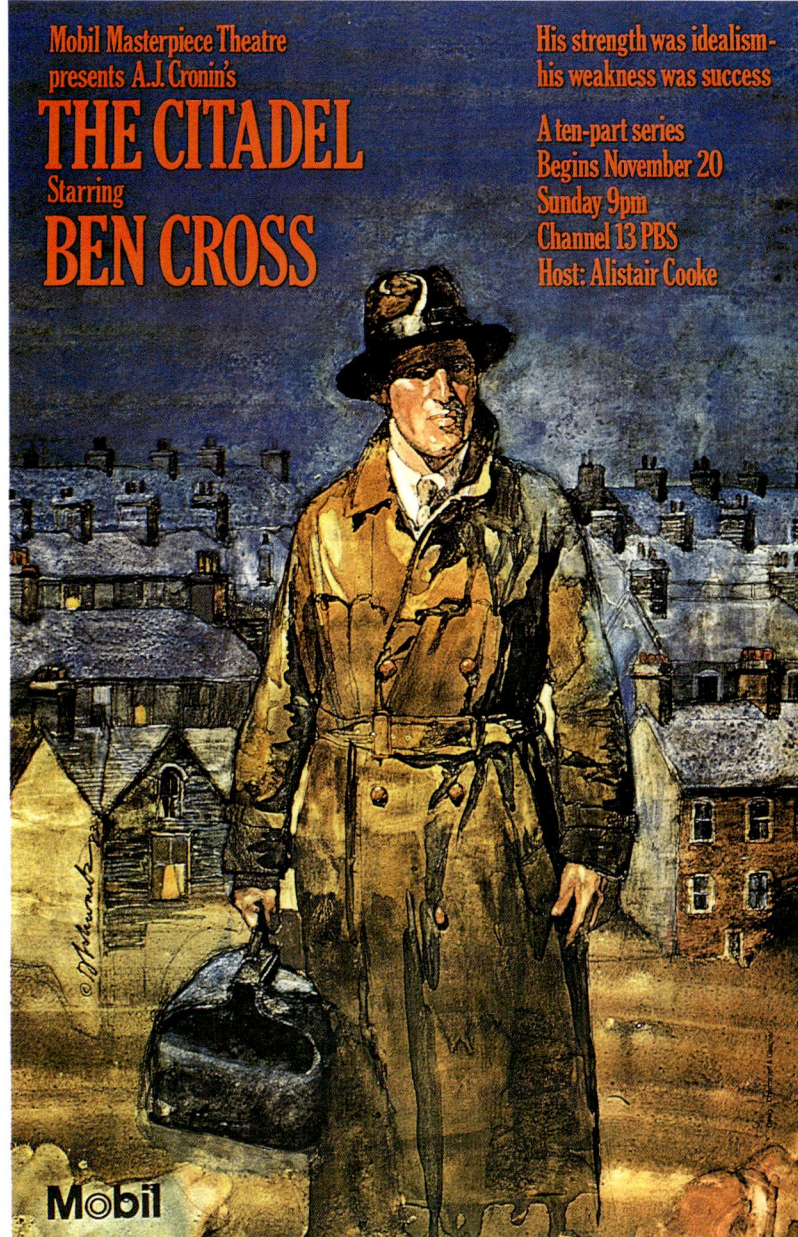

Represented by Artist

Jeffery Seaver

1. a. pen and ink, colored pencils b. Oui magazine, for article on automobile recalls due to defects c. 1980
2. a. pen and ink, colored pencils b. unpublished rendering of solar-powered hamburger stand, later published by Quest magazine in a review of the artist's works c. 1980
3. a. pen and ink, dyes and wash, colored pencils b. Video Review magazine, on the difficulty of repairing broken videotapes c. 1982

ジェフェリー・シーバー

1. a.ペン,インク,色鉛筆 b.雑誌イラスト c.1980年
2. a.ペン,インク,色鉛筆 b.雑誌イラスト c.1980年
3. a.ペン,インク,染料,ウォッシュ技法,色鉛筆 b.雑誌イラスト c.1982年

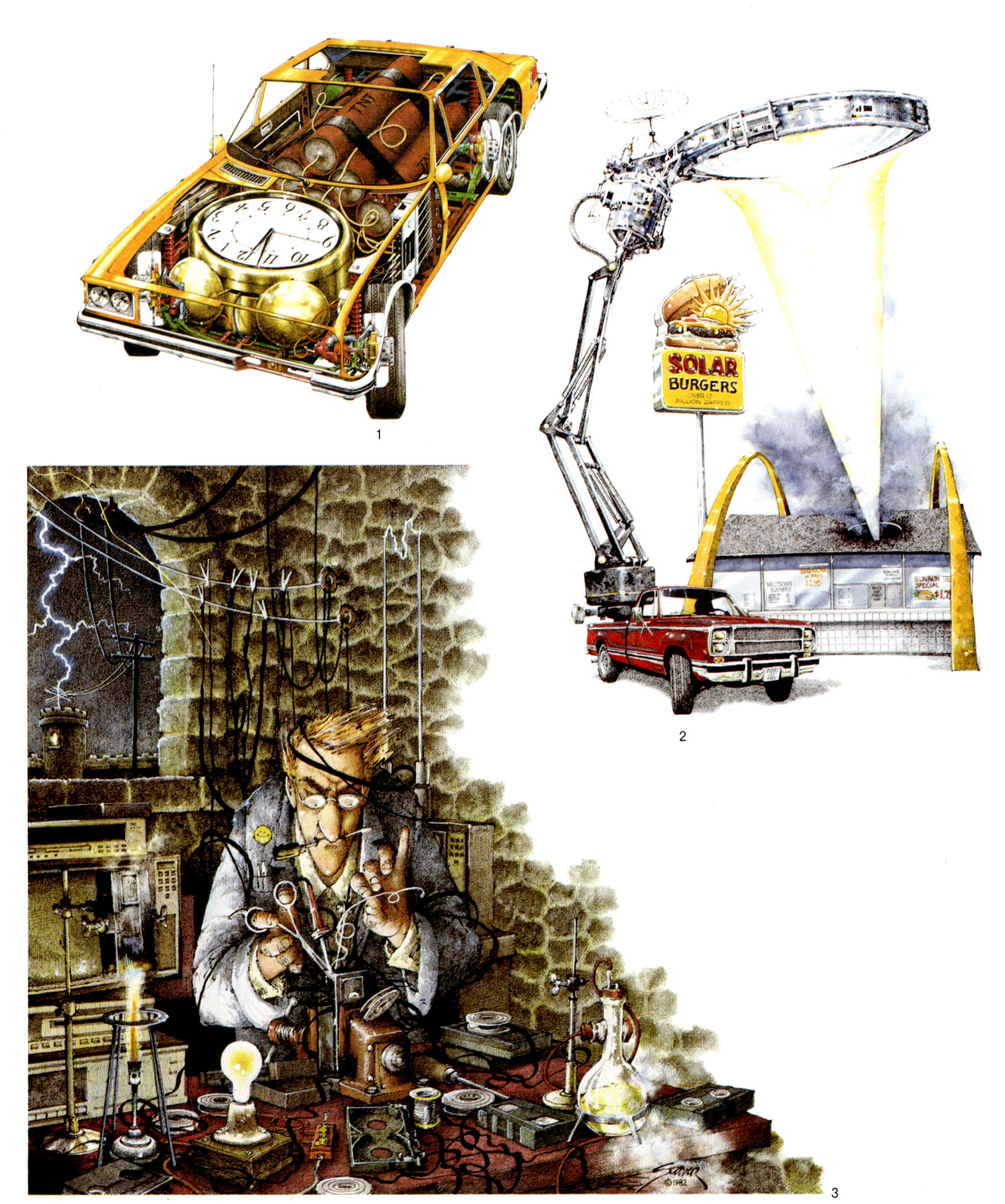

Represented by Artist

Isadore Seltzer

1. a. acrylic paint b. Newsweek magazine cover c. 1983
2. a. acrylic and watercolor b. movie poster c. 1984
3. a. acrylic paint b. movie poster c. 1984

イサドア・セルツァー

1. a. アクリル絵具　b. 雑誌表紙　c. 1983年
2. a. アクリル絵具，水彩絵具　b. 映画ポスター c. 1984年
3. a. アクリル絵具　b. 映画ポスター　c. 1984年

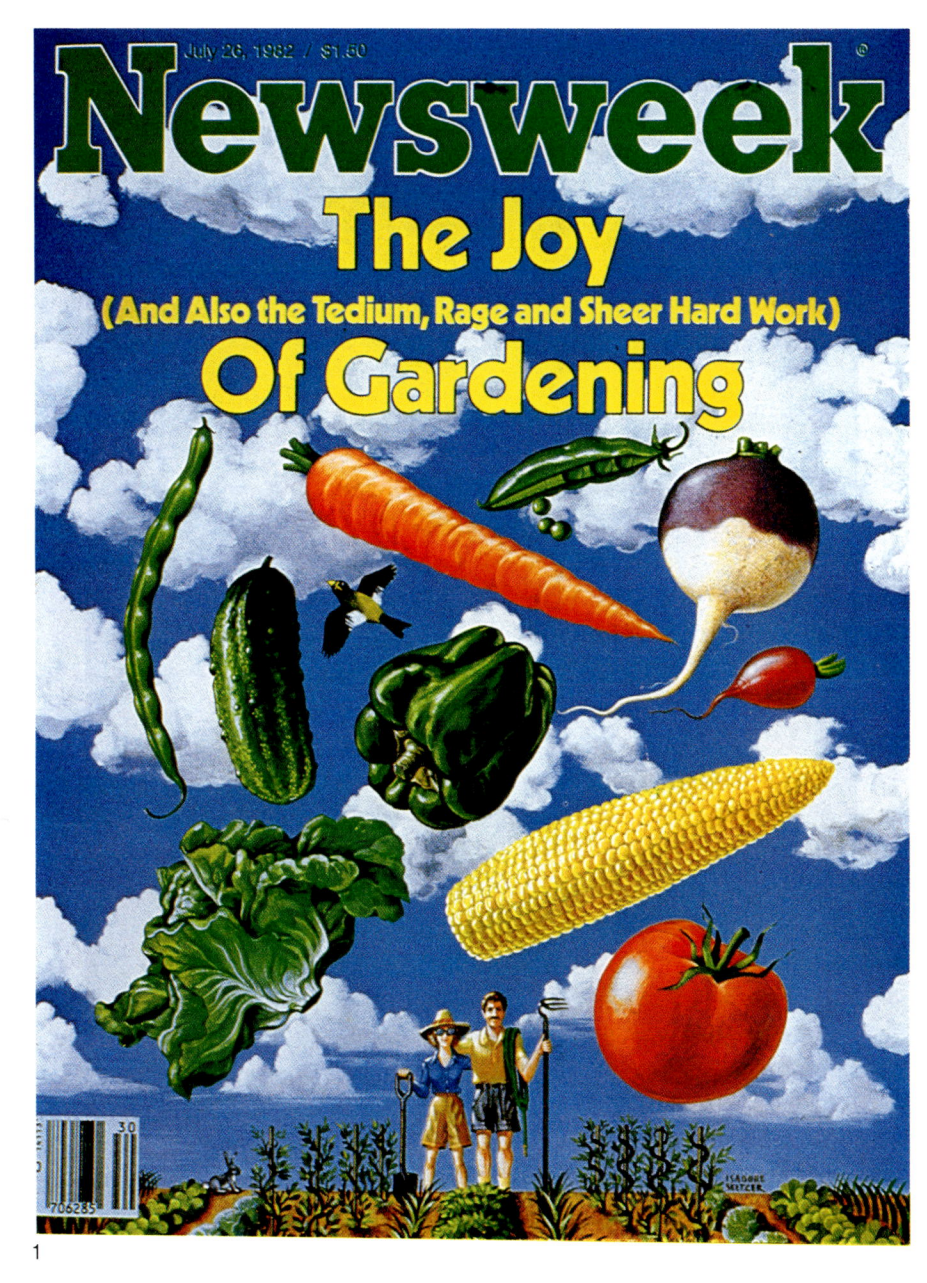

Represented by Artist

R.J. Shay　　　　　　　R.J.シェイ　　　　　　　　　　　　　　　252

1. a. pen, ink, color ink b. editorial
2. a. pen, ink, color ink b. magazine cover
3. a. pen, ink, color ink b. editorial

1.a.ペン, インク, カラーインク　b.エディトリアル
2.a.ペン, インク, カラーインク　b.雑誌表紙
3.a.ペン, インク, カラーインク　b.エディトリアル

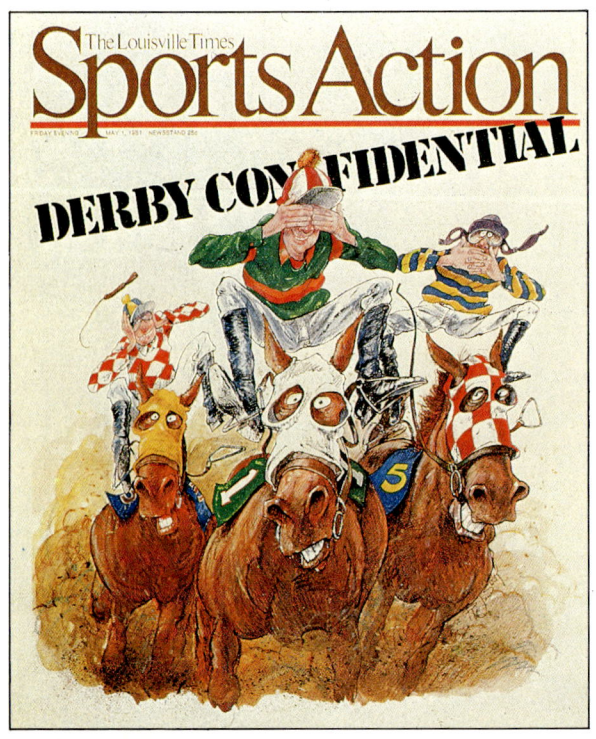

Represented by Artist

Mamoru Shimokochi

1. a. acrylic and ink with airbrush b. album cover. United Artists Records, Inc. (unpublished) c. 1982
2. a. ink with airbrush b. Beckman poster agency: Pat Soo Hoo Designers, Inc. c. 1983
3. a. acrylic with airbrush b. West Week Client: Pacific Design Center c. 1983
4. a. ink with airbrush b. Client: Orange County Advertising Federation c. 1982

マモル・シモコウチ

1. a. アクリル絵具, インク, エアブラシ b. レコードジャケット(未発表) c. 1982年
2. a. インク, エアブラシ b. ポスター c. 1983年
3. a. アクリル絵具, エアブラシ b. エディトリアル c. 1983年
4. a. インク, エアブラシ b. 広告イラスト c. 1982年

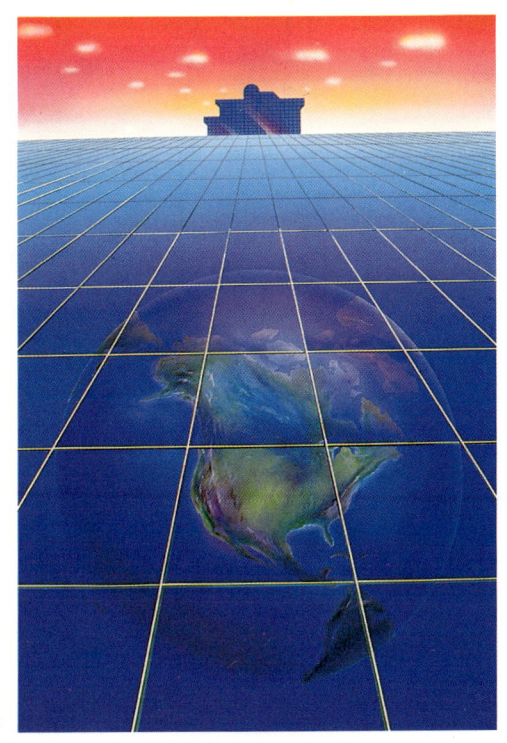

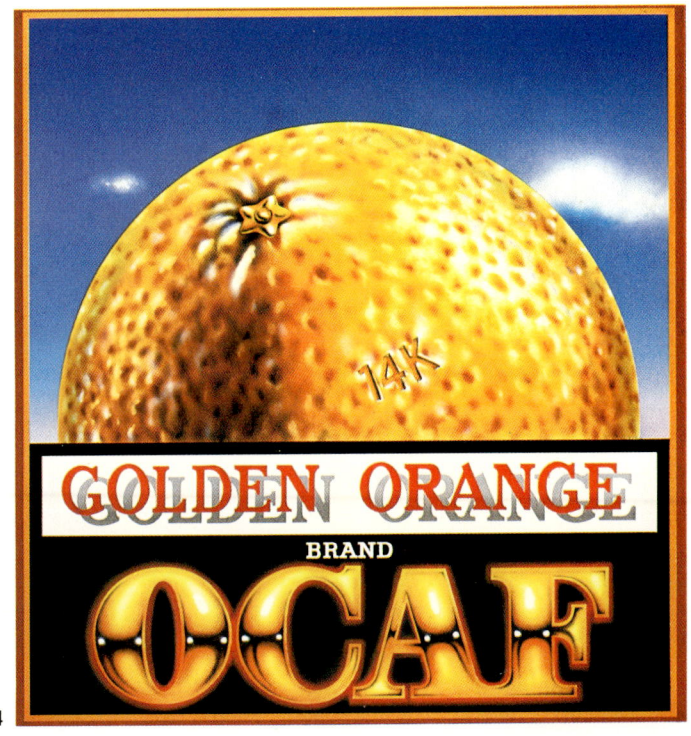

Represented by Artist

William A. Sloan

1. ELIZABETH TAYLOR a. acrylic on canvas b. self-promotion c. 1983
2. THE NATURAL MAN a. ink and cellotak b. book cover for Viking Penguin Publishing c. 1983
3. VENICE SIMPLON ORIENT EXPRESS a ink and cellotak b. travel promotion poster c. 1982

ウィリアム・A・スローン

1. a. アクリル絵具, キャンバス b. セルフプロモーション c.1983年
2. a. インク, セロタック b. 書籍表紙 c.1983年
3. a. インク, セロタック b. ポスター c.1982年

Represented by Artist

Doug Smith

1. a. scratchboard b. full page newspaper ad for food chain c. 1983
2. a. scratchboard b. promotional poster for Altman & Manley advertising agency c. 1982
3. a. scratchboard b. feature illustration for article in New England Life Insurance Co.'s in House magazine c. 1982
4. a. scratchboard b. spread for Boston Glove's Sunday magazine c. 1981

ダグ・スミス

1. a. スクラッチボード b. 新聞広告イラスト c.1983年
2. a. スクラッチボード b. ポスター c.1982年
3. a. スクラッチボード b. 企業社内誌イラスト c.1982年
4. a. スクラッチボード b. 雑誌イラスト c.1981年

255

Represented by Artist

Jes Smithback

1. ROSE AND NORMAN a. Prisma color pencil and transparent dyes with airbrush b. gift c. 1981
2. INDIAN a. pen and ink on gesso board b. limited edition prints c. 1980
3. GANDHI a. gouache on gesso board. wash b. portfolio piece c. 1983
4. MATCH POINT a. gouache and transparent dyes on gesso board. wash b. portfolio piece c. 1982

ジェス・スミスバック

1. a. 色鉛筆, 染料, エアブラシ b. ギフト c. 1981年
2. a. ペン, インク, ジェッソボード b. 限定版画 c. 1980年
3. a. ガッシュ, ジェッソボード。ウォッシュ技法 b. ポートフォリオ c. 1983年
4. a. ガッシュ, 染料, ジェッソボード。ウォッシュ技法 b. ポートフォリオ c. 1982年

Represented by Artist

Greg Spalenka

1. ANIMAL PURSUIT a. oils & acrylics strictly with brush work. many glazes. solvents and sprays b. Honda Motorcycle. unpublished c. 1983
2. JACK LAMBERT a. oils & acrylics strictly with brush work. many glazes. solvents and sprays b. Pro magazine c. 1983
3. a. oils & acrylics strictly with brush work. many glazes. solvents and sprays. b. P.C. World magazine-article on alternative forms of communication c. 1983

グレッグ・スパレンカ

1. a. 油彩絵具、アクリル絵具、画筆。グラッシ技法を多用。ソルベント、スプレイ b. ホンダオートバイ（未発表作品） c. 1983年
2. a. 油彩絵具、アクリル絵具、画筆。グラッシ技法を多用。ソルベント、スプレイ b. 雑誌イラスト c. 1983年
3. a. 油彩絵具、アクリル絵具、画筆。グラッシ技法を多用。ソルベント、スプレイ b. 雑誌イラスト c. 1983年

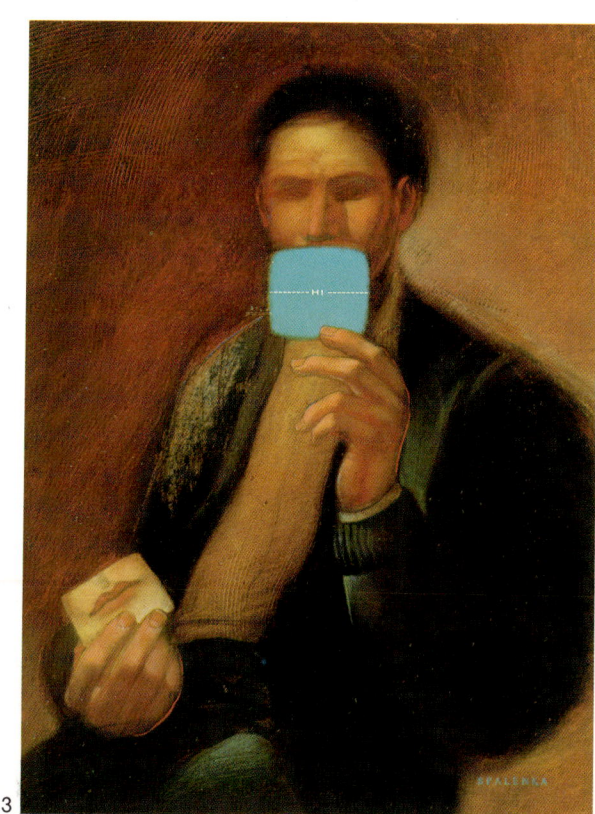

Represented by Artist

Randy Spear

1. HOW MUCH PROTEIN? CONSIDER THE GORILLA a. acrylics on illustration board with airbrush and handpaint b. editorial double page for Joe Wieder's Muscle and Fitness magazine c. 1983
2. AMERICA YOUR OVER WEIGHT! a. acrylic on illustration board with airbrush and handpaint b. self-promotion c. 1981
3. STOCKING A BODYBUILDER'S FURNACE a. acrylic on illustration board with airbrush and handpaint b. editorial double page spread for Joe Wieder's Muscle and Fitness magazine c. 1983

ランディ・スピア

1. a. アクリル絵具, イラストレーションボード, エアブラシ, 画筆 b. 雑誌イラスト c. 1983年
2. a. アクリル絵具, イラストレーションボード, エアブラシ, 画筆 b. セルフプロモーション c. 1981年
3. a. アクリル絵具, イラストレーションボード, エアブラシ, 画筆 b. 雑誌イラスト c. 1983年

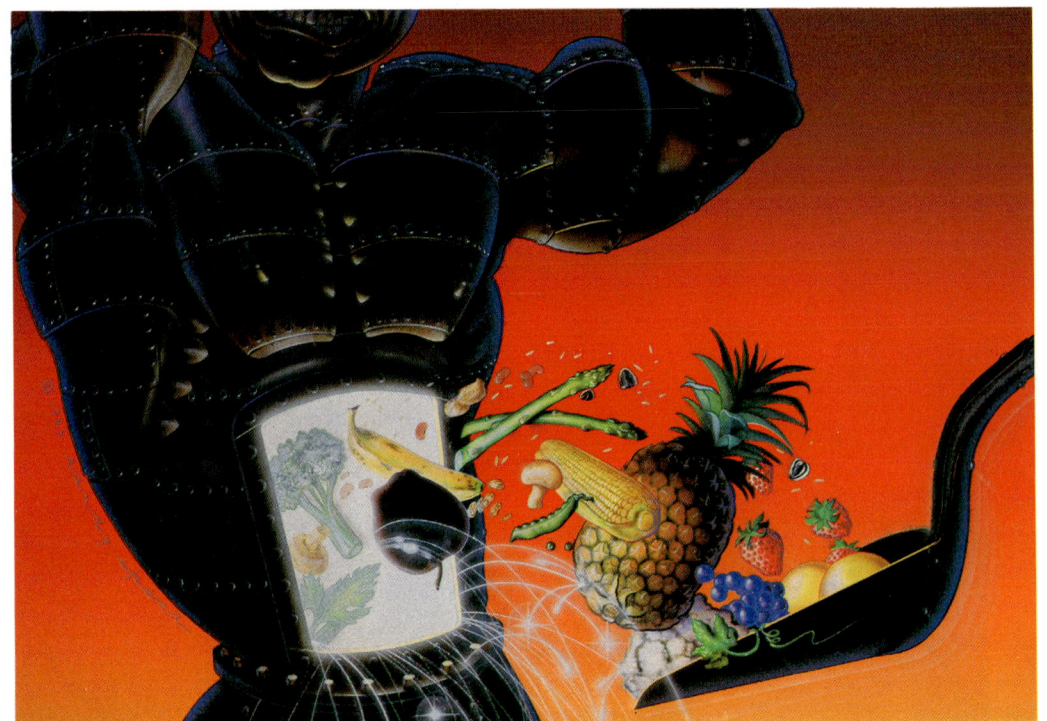

Represented by Artist

Barron Storey

1. a. mixed media b. editorial, National Geography magazine c. 1982
2. a. mixed media b. record album cover
3. a. mixed media b. poster for Mohawk Paper Company c. 1976
4. a. mixed media b. editorial, Flying magazine c. 1979

バロン・ストアリー

1. a. 各種画材 b. エディトリアル c. 1982年
2. a. 各種画材 b. レコードジャケット
3. a. 各種画材 b. ポスター c. 1976年
4. a. 各種画材 b. エディトリアル c. 1979年

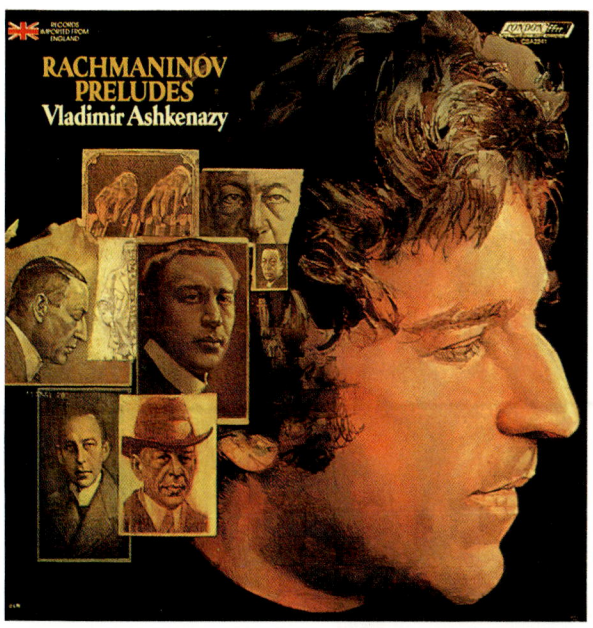

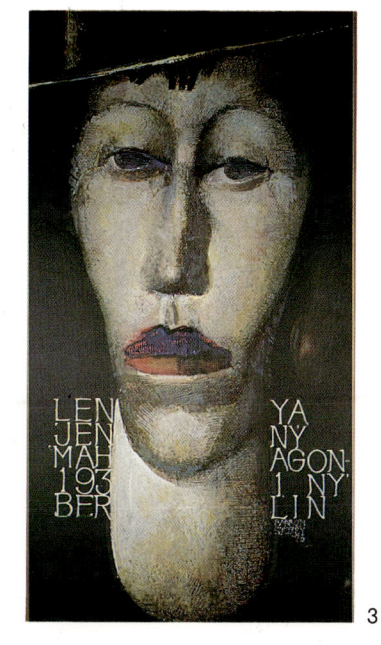

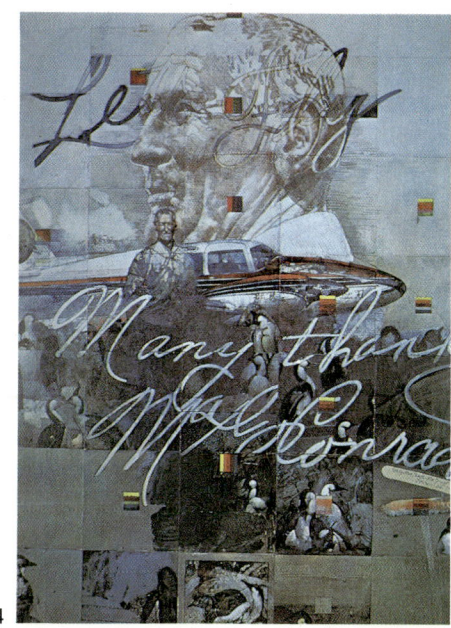

Represented by Artist

George Stavrinos

1. a. graphite on paper b. New York magazine illustration for article on designer, Mary McFadden c. 1980
2. a. graphite on paper b. fashion ad for designer, Devereaux c. 1980
3. a. graphite on paper b. fashion ad for Bergdorf Goodman for Sunday N.Y. Times and French Vogue. Designer; Tarlazzi c. 1983
4. a. graphite on paper b. fashion ad for Barney's Dept. Store for N.Y. Times c. 1978
5. a. Graphite on paper b. Fashion promotion for Oscar de La Renta shirts c. 1982
6. a. graphite on paper b. fashion ad for Bergdorf Goodman for "M" magazine c. 1983

ジョージ・スタヴリノス

1. a.グラファイト鉛筆, 紙 b.雑誌イラスト c.1980年
2. a.グラファイト鉛筆, 紙 b.広告イラストc.1980年
3. a.グラファイト鉛筆, 紙 b.広告イラストc.1983年
4. a.グラファイト鉛筆, 紙 b.広告イラストc.1978年
5. a.グラファイト鉛筆, 紙 b.プロモーション c.1982年
6. a.グラファイト鉛筆, 紙 b.広告イラストc.1983年

Represented by Artist

Represented by Artist

Dugald Stermer デュガルド・スターマー 262

1. "CALIFORNIA LIVING" VANISHING NURSE a. watercolor and graphite on Arches watercolor paper b. cover for a newspaper Sunday magazine in San Francisco, illustrating an article on the nursing profession c. 1983

1.a. 水彩絵具, グラファイト鉛筆, 水彩画紙 b. 雑誌表紙 c. 1983年

2. "CALIFORNIA LIVING" STORK a. watercolor and graphite on Arches paper b. cover for a newspaper Sunday magazine in San Francisco, illustrating an article on artificial insemination c. 1982
3. BIRDS OF ALASKA a. watercolor and graphite on Arches paper b. Consumer magazine advertisement promoting tourism in Alaska c. 1983
4. SIERRA a. watercolor and graphite on Arches paper b. cover of the Sierra Club's magazine illustrating an article on endangered plants and animals in the United States c. 1982
5. LEVI'S 501 BLUEJEANS a. watercolor and graphite on Arches paper b. Consumer magazine advertisement for the original Levi's 501 jeans c. 1983

2. a. 水彩絵具, グラファイト鉛筆, 水彩画紙 b. 雑誌表紙 c. 1982年
3. a. 水彩絵具, グラファイト鉛筆, 水彩画紙 b. 雑誌広告 c. 1983年
4. a. 水彩絵具, グラファイト鉛筆, 水彩画紙 b. 雑誌表紙 c. 1982年
5. a. 水彩絵具, グラファイト鉛筆, 水彩画紙 b. 雑誌広告 c. 1983年

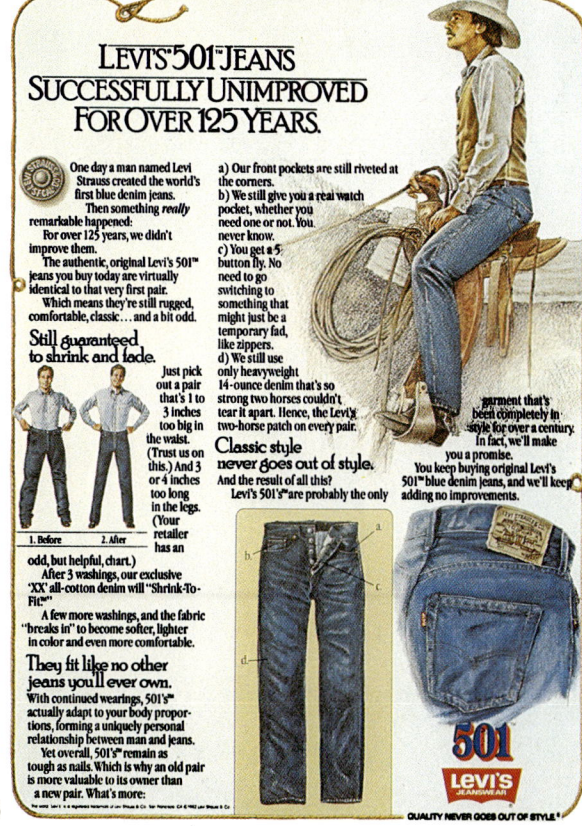

Represented by Artist

Susan Sumichrast

1. ONE HORSE OPEN SLEIGH a. fabric over cardboard. trees are hand sewn, snow is machine sewn b. Christmas card for Portal Publications, also appeared as magazine cover c. 1982
2. SHOES IN MEDICINE CHEST a. box constructed out of cardboard then covered with satin. All objects in box were created out of fabric. pieces were hand and machine sewn and stuffed. b. New Realities magazine. article titled "Consciousness in Running" c. 1980
3. FISH AND VEGETABLES a. completely hand sewn and stuffed b. unpublished piece to show food represented in fabric c. 1981
4. HOLIDAY SHOPPING a. three dimensional piece completely covered in fabric. dollhouse objects b. Vantage Point magazine c. 1983

スーザン・スミックラスト

1. a. 厚紙, ファブリック。木は手縫い, 雪はミシンがけ b. クリスマスカード, 雑誌表紙 c. 1982年
2. a. ファブリック, サテンで覆った厚紙の箱。手縫い, ミシンがけをし, キルト仕上げ b. 雑誌に発表 c. 1980年
3. a. すべて手縫い, キルト仕上げ b. 未発表作品 c. 1981年
4. a. ファブリック, ドールハウスの小物 b. 雑誌に発表 c. 1983年

Represented by Artist

George Suyeoka

1. ST. GEORGE AND THE DRAGON a. various fruits, wires, smoke b. Abbott Laboratories "K-Lor" calendar art c. 1984
2. ALLADIN a. various fruits, wires, cotton b. Abbott Laboratories "K-Lor" Calendar art c. 1984
3. W.C. FIELDS AND BOTTLES a. bottles, wood, ads b. self-promotion, Chicago Sourcebook c. 1982–83
4. OCTPUS a. wire, clay, paper, plastic, paint b. Scott Foresman Reader Book cover c. 1980

1. a. 果物, 針金, 煙 b. カレンダー c. 1984年
2. a. 果物, 針金, 綿 b. カレンダー c. 1984年
3. a. びん, 木, 広告ラベル b. セルフプロモーション c. 1982〜1983年
4. a. 針金, 粘土, 紙, プラスティック, ペンキ b. 書籍表紙 c. 1980年

Represented by Artist

Brock Swanson

1. a. watercolor on paper. three color glaze b. self portrait c. 1982
2. a. watercolor on paper. three color glaze b. exhibition c. 1983
3. a. watercolor on paper. three color glaze b. released poster form c. 1978

ブロック・スワンソン

1. a. 水彩絵具, 紙。三色グラッシ b. 自画像 c. 1982年
2. a. 水彩絵具, 紙。三色グラッシ b. 展覧会出品作品 c. 1983年
3. a. 水彩絵具, 紙。三色グラッシ b. ポスター c. 1978年

266

Represented by Artist

Nick Taggart

1. SUNSET LOOKING TOWARDS GRIFFITH PARK OBSERVATORY a. acrylic on paper b. view from the studio c. 1983
2. OLIMPIC JAVERIN THROWER a. acrylic on paper c. 1983
3. HEROINE a. serigraph in 3 colors on paper b. "Eye" magazine #8 c. 1983

Represented by Artist

Yuriko Takata

1. a. watercolor & ink on paper b. prospective poster design c. 1983
2. a. watercolor & ink on paper b. poster for retail sale c. 1983
3. a. watercolor & ink on paper b. piece for Gallery exhibition c. 1983
4. a. watercolor & ink on paper b. prospective poster c. 1984

ユリコ・タカタ

1. a. 水彩絵具，インク，紙 b. ポスターデザイン c. 1983年
2. a. 水彩絵具，インク，紙 b. ポスター c. 1983年
3. a. 水彩絵具，インク，紙 b. ギャラリー展示品 c. 1983年
4. a. 水彩絵具，インク，紙 b. ポスターデザイン c. 1984年

Represented by Artist

Robert Tanenbaum

1. a. casein b. annual report c. 1983
2. a. casein b. national movie poster c. 1983
3. a. casein b. national ad — Levi's c. 1983

1.a. カゼイン絵具　b. 企業年次報告書　c.1983年
2.a. カゼイン絵具　b. 映画ポスター　c.1983年
3.a. カゼイン絵具　b. 広告イラスト　c.1983年

Represented by Artist

C. Winston Taylor

1. FORCE FIVE a. acrylic, airbrush background b. movie poster c. 1982
2. LONEWOLF McQUARE a. acrylic with airbrush b. movie poster for Orion Pictures c. 1984
3. INSIDE MOVES a. acrylic with airbrush background b. movie poster c. 1982
4. THE PIRATE MOVIE a. acrylic, airbrush background b. 20th Century-Fox movie poster c. 1983
5. USA OLYMPIC PRACTICE BALL a. acrylic b. American Basketball Association client: UOIT. International Poster Publication c. 1982

C・ウィンストン・テイラー

1. a.アクリル絵具，背景でエアブラシ b.映画ポスター c.1982年
2. a.アクリル絵具，エアブラシ b.映画プロモーション c.1984年
3. a.アクリル絵具，背景でエアブラシ b.映画ポスター c.1982年
4. a.アクリル絵具，背景でエアブラシ b.映画プロモーション c.1983年
5. a.アクリル絵具 b.ポスター c.1982年

Represented by Artist

2

3

4

5

Represented by Artist

Aki Tomita

アキ・トミタ

1. a. oil b. paperback cover c. 1980
2. a. oil b. paperback cover c. 1981
3. a. oil b. paperback cover c. 1982

1.a. 油彩絵具 b. ペーパーバック表紙 c. 1980年
2.a. 油彩絵具 b. ペーパーバック表紙 c. 1981年
3.a. 油彩絵具 b. ペーパーバック表紙 c. 1982年

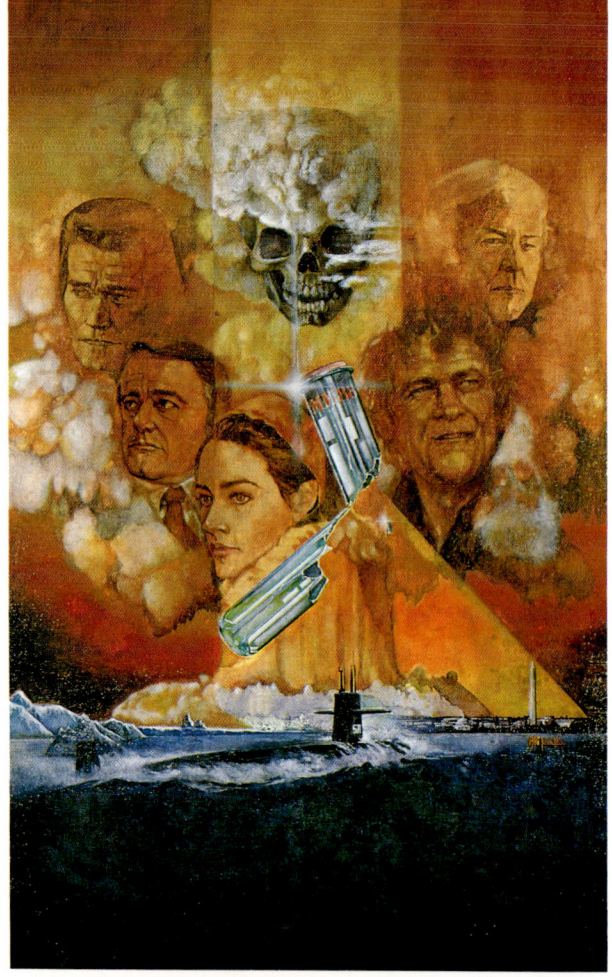

Represented by Artist

Tom T. Tomita

トム・T・トミタ

1. a. acrylic with airbrush b. illustration for book "Fame" c. 1982–1984
2. a. acrylic with airbrush b. illustration for book "Fame" c. 1982–1984
3. a. acrylic with airbrush b. magazine advertisement. Computer Game — Data-soft Inc. c. 1982–1984

1. a.アクリル絵具，エアブラシ b.書籍イラスト c. 1982年〜1984年
2. a.アクリル絵具，エアブラシ b.書籍イラスト c. 1982年〜1984年
3. a.アクリル絵具，エアブラシ b.雑誌広告 c.1982年〜1984年

Represented by Artist

Dale C. Verzaal

1. a. acrylic and Prisma pencils b. poster illustration for INTEL c. 1982
2. a. acrylic and Prisma pencils b. self promotion c. 1983
3. a. acrylic and prisma pencils b. self promotion c. 1977

デール・C・ヴァゼール

1. a. アクリル絵具, 色鉛筆 b. ポスター c. 1982年
2. a. アクリル絵具, 色鉛筆 b. セルフプロモーション c. 1983年
3. a. アクリル絵具, 色鉛筆 b. セルフプロモーション c. 1977年

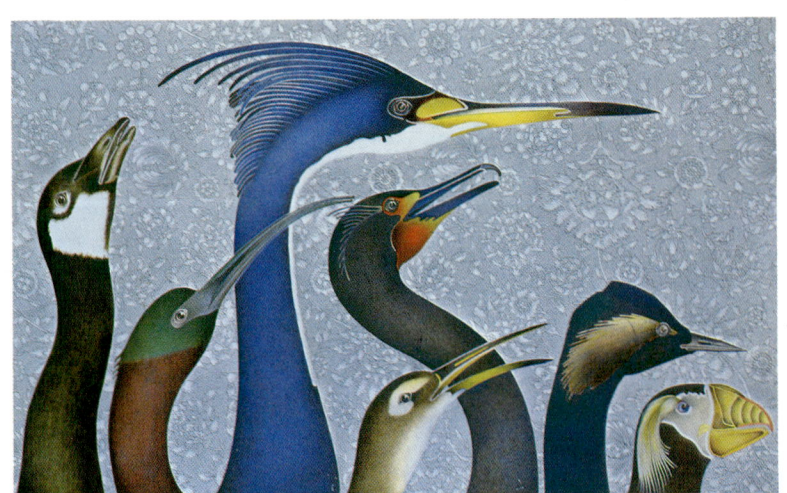

274

Represented by Artist

Fran Vuksanovich

1. a. dyes and color pencils b. self promotion c. 1984
2. a. dyes and color pencils b. self-promotion c. 1982
3. a. dyes and color pencils b. self-promotion c. 1982

Represented by Artist

William Vuksanovich

1. a. watercolor on illustration board b. self-promotion c. 1979
2. a. oil on canvas b. self-promotion c. 1983
3. a. oil on canvas b. self-promotion c. 1980
4. a. oil on canvas b. self-promotion c. 1979
5. a. oil on canvas b. self-promotion c. 1984

ウィリアム・ヴクサノヴィッチ

1. a. 水彩絵具, イラストレーションボード b. セルフプロモーション c. 1979年
2. a. 油彩絵具, キャンバス b. セルフプロモーション c. 1983年
3. a. 油彩絵具, キャンバス b. セルフプロモーション c. 1980年
4. a. 油彩絵具, キャンバス b. セルフプロモーション c. 1979年
5. a. 油彩絵具, キャンバス b. セルフプロモーション c. 1984年

Represented by Artist

3

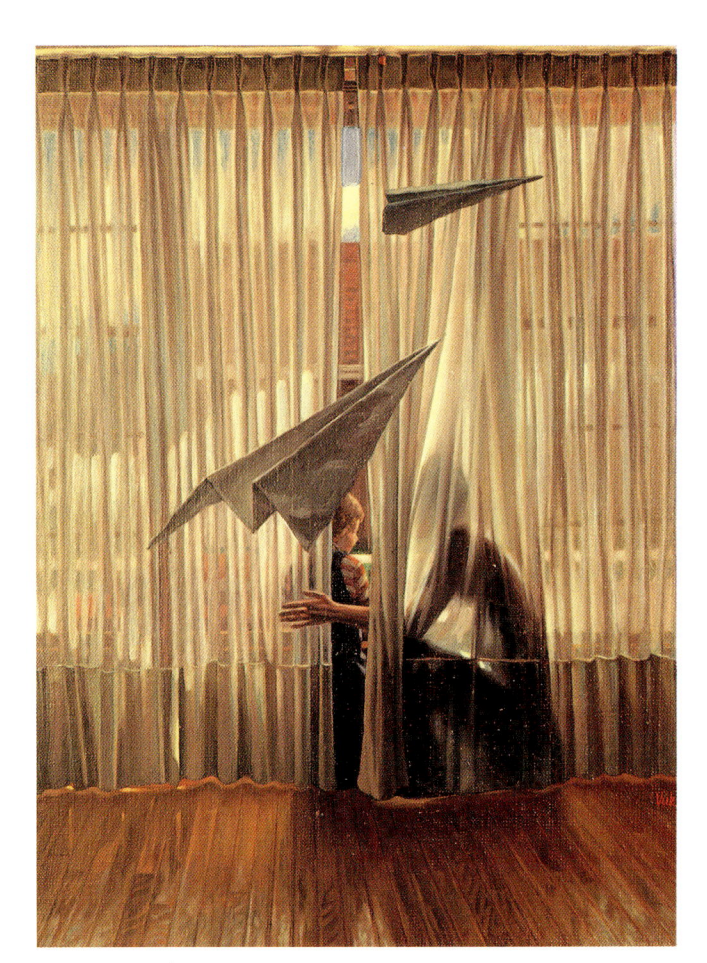

4

5

Represented by Artist

Jeff Wack　ジェフ・ワック　278

1. a. acrylics b. Playboy magazine c. 1981
2. a. acrylics b. magazine article on stress c. 1983
3. a. acrylics b. movie poster. 20th Cent. Fox c. 1982

1. a.アクリル絵具　b.雑誌イラスト　c.1981年
2. a.アクリル絵具　b.雑誌イラスト　c.1983年
3. a.アクリル絵具　b.映画ポスター　c.1982年

Represented by Artist

Robert L. Wade

1. DOMINOES, PUSH-UPS AND HAND-ROLLED CIGARETTES: 90 DAYS IN THE WARDEN'S PARTYHOUSE WRITTEN BY FREDDIE BOSCO a. pen, ink and wash on illustration board b. to illustrate story about life in the country prison c. 1982
2. WATERHOLE a. alkyd and mixed media on illustration board b. self promotion c. 1984
3. THE AGONY OF AIDS: ONE MAN'S STORY WRITTEN BY MAUREEN HARRINGTON a. acrylic and pencil on wet media acetate. four color hand separation b. to illustrate article on the disappear and frustration in the life of an AID's victim c. 1983

1.a.ペン，インク，イラストレーションボード b.エディトリアル c.1982年
2.a.アルキド絵具，その他，イラストレーションボード b.セルフプロモーション c.1984年
3.a.アクリル絵具，鉛筆，ウェットメディア・アセテート。4色ハンドセパレーション b.エディトリアル c.1983年

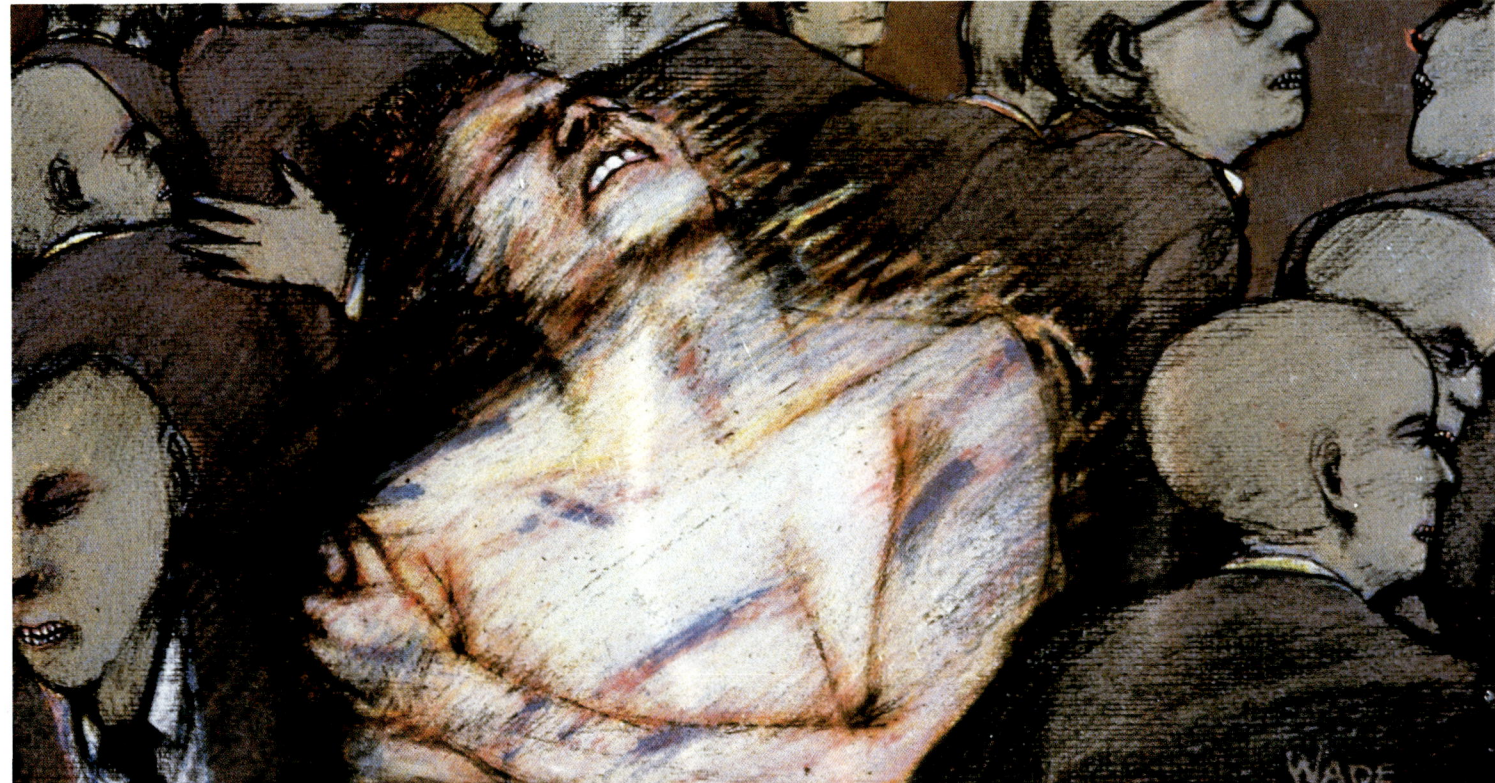

Represented by Artist

Richard Waldrep リチャード・ウォルドレップ

1. a. colored pencil on mat board b. Time-life album cover c. 1983
2. a. colored pencil on mat board b. Time-life Album cover c. 1983
3. a. airbrush dyes b. brochure for Haryland Institute College of Art c. 1983
4. a. Prisma color pencil b. best products c. 1981

1. a. 色鉛筆，マットボード b. レコードジャケット c. 1983年
2. a. 色鉛筆，マットボード b. レコードジャケット c. 1983年
3. a. エアブラシ用カラーインク b. カタログ c. 1983年
4. a. 色鉛筆 b. 広告イラスト c. 1981年

Represented by Artist

Stan Watts　スタン・ワッツ

1. INAMORATA a. Prisma color pencil and acrylic airbrush on prepared masonite b. album art. artist; Poco. rock rylics illustrated in "Radio Eyes" c. 1983

1.a. 色鉛筆, アクリル絵具, メゾナイト　b. レコードジャケット　c. 1983年

Represented by Artist

2. COUNT BASIE a. Prisma color pencil & acrylic airbrush on prepared masonite board b. biographical portrait. Playboy Jazz Festival c. 1983
3. PETE THE PIT PUNK a. Prisma color pencil and acrylic airbrush on prepared masonite board b. for Papermoon c. 1984
4. QUIET RIOT a. Prisma color pencil and acrylic airbrush on prepared masonite b. album art. CBS Records c. 1983

2. a. 色鉛筆, アクリル絵具, エアブラシ, メゾナイト b. 肖像画 c. 1983年
3. a. 色鉛筆, アクリル絵具, エアブラシ, メゾナイト b. グリーティングカード c. 1984年
4. a. 色鉛筆, アクリル絵具, エアブラシ, メゾナイト b. レコードジャケット c. 1983年

Represented by Artist

5. ONE NIGHT WITH A STRANGER a. Prisma color pencil and acrylic airbrush on prepared masonite b. '84 Grammy nominated for Best Album Art — album cover for Martin Briley c. 1984

5.a. 色鉛筆, アクリル絵具, エアブラシ, メゾナイト
b. レコードジャケット c. 1984年

Represented by Artist

Robert Weaver

ロバート・ウィーバー

284

1. a. acrylic on bristol b. a book-in-progress called New York New York — a collection of some 150 paintings consisting of 8 or 10 page, 2 level sequences showing contrasting aspects of New York c. 1982

1. a. アクリル絵具，ブリストル紙 b. 書籍イラスト
c. 1982年

Represented by Artist

2. a. acrylic on bristol b. From "New York New York" c. 1982
3. a. acrylic on bristol b. from "New York New York" c. 1982
4. a. acrylic on bristol b. from "New York New York" c. 1982

2. a. アクリル絵具, ブリストル紙 b. 書籍イラスト c. 1982年
3. a. アクリル絵具, ブリストル紙 b. 書籍イラスト c. 1982年
4. a. アクリル絵具, ブリストル紙 b. 書籍イラスト c. 1982年

Represented by Artist

5. a. acrylic on bristol b. from "New York New York" c. 1982

5. a. アクリル絵具, ブリストル紙 b. 書籍イラスト c. 1982年

Don Weller

ドン・ウェラー

1. a. dyes and watercolor on rag paper b. call for entries poster for Illustration West Exhibition c. 1980

1.a. 染料, 水彩絵具, ラグペーパー(上質紙) b. ポスター c.1980年

287

Represented by Artist

2. a. dyes and watercolor on rag paper b. poster for sale. San Graphics c. 1981

2.a. 染料, 水彩絵具, ラグペーパー b. ポスター c. 1981年

288

2

Represented by Artist

3. a. color was indicated on an overlay and supplied by the printer in the form of benday screens of process colors b. poster to an announce an exhibition of work by Don Weller in Spokane c. 1980
4. a. Dr. Martin's dyes on rag paper. trees; carved from a pink pearl erasor, stamped, the imprint enlarged photomechanically and applied to the illustration repeatedly. white spray paint blasted over the "trees". b. travel poster for Western Airlines c. 1982
5. a. dyes and watercolor on rag paper b. poster for sale. Sun Graphics c. 1980

3. a. オーバーレイ b. ポスター c.1980年
4. a. カラーインク, ラグペーパー b. ポスター c.1982年
5. a. 染料, 水彩絵具, ラグペーパー b. ポスター c. 1980年

Represented by Artist

Jim White

ジム・ホワイト

290

1. CHICAGO a. mixed media on board with brush and airbrush b. used by Paper and Printing Co. c. 1983

1.a. 各種絵具, ボード, 筆, エアブラシ b. 広告イラスト c. 1983年

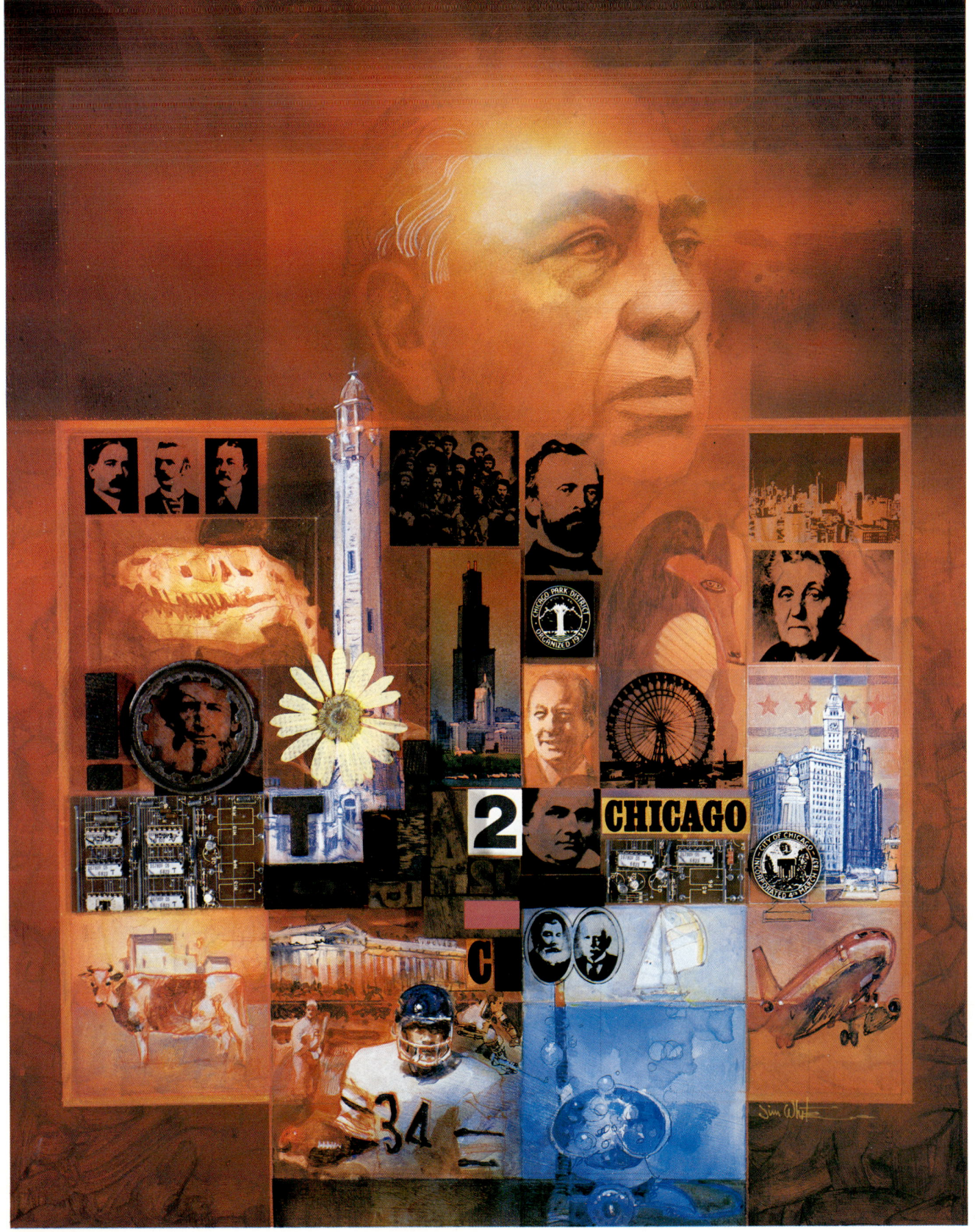

Represented by Artist

2. CUMMINS DIESEL a. mixed media on board with brush and airbrush b. art for Cummins calendar c. 1983

3. INDIAN a. watercolor and colored ink on paper with airbrush b. poster for promotion c. 1983

4. HEART a. watercolor and ink on paper. washes & colored line b. promotional piece for Studio c. 1983

2.a. 各種絵具, ボード, 筆, エアブラシ b. カレンダー c. 1983年
3.a. 水彩絵具, カラーインク, 紙, エアブラシ b. ポスター c. 1983年
4.a. 水彩絵具, インク, 紙, ウォッシュ技法 b. スタジオのプロモーション c. 1983年

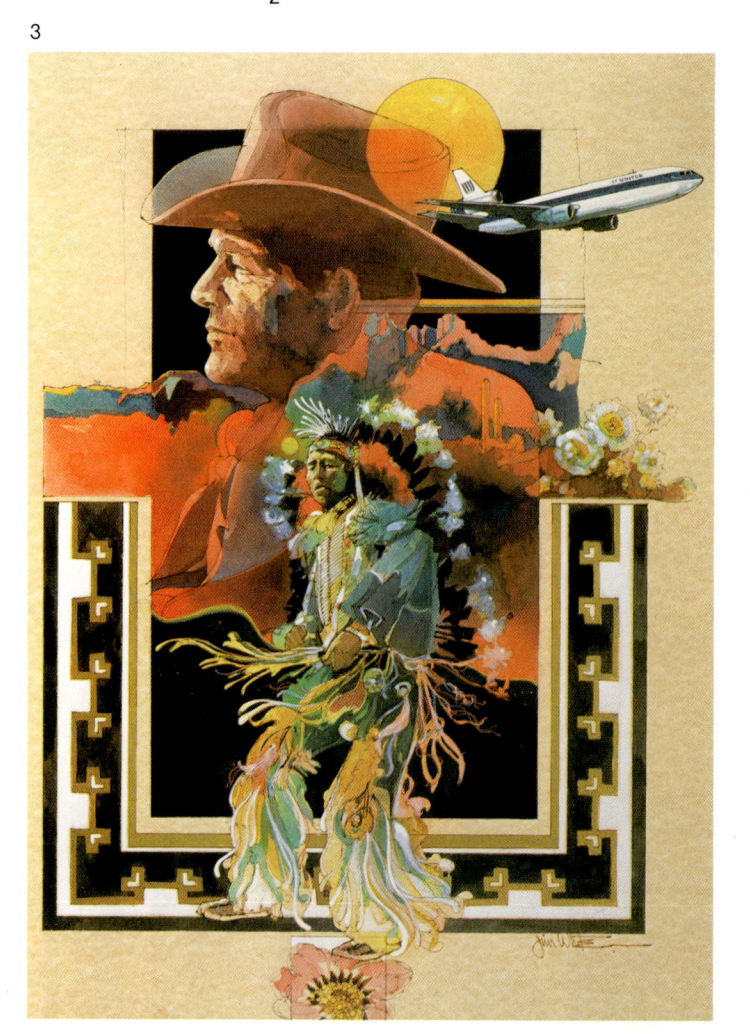

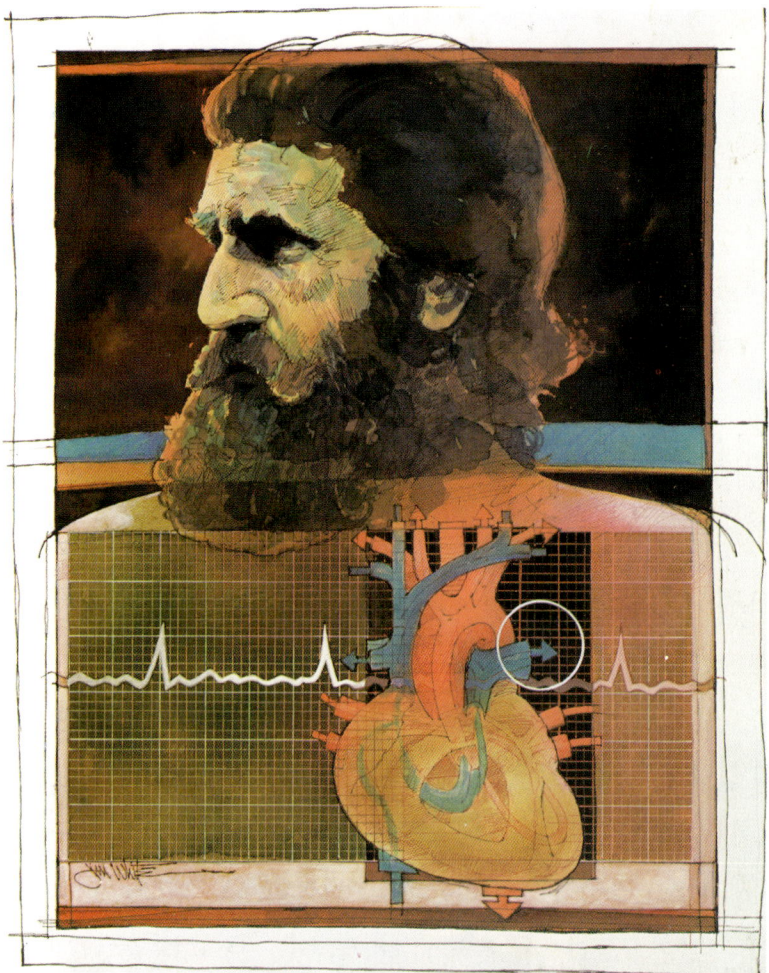

Represented by Artist

Kim Whitesides

1. a. acrylic on strathmore board with airbrush b. Paper Moon post card – San Francisco c. 1983
2. a. watercolor on strathmore board with airbrush b. editorial spread. Texas Monthly magazine c. 1983
3. a. acrylic on strathmore board with airbrush b. music catalog cover. Miller Beer c. 1983

キム・ホワイトサイズ

1. a. アクリル絵具, ストラスモアボード, エアブラシ b. ポストカード c. 1983年
2. a. 水彩絵具, ストラスモアボード, エアブラシ b. 雑誌イラスト c. 1983年
3. a. アクリル絵具, ストラスモアボード, エアブラシ b. カタログ表紙 c. 1983年

Represented by Artist

Terry Widener

1. a. oil on canvas b. illustration for self-promotion poster c. 1983
2. a. oil on canvas b. illustration for self-promotion mailer c. 1984
3. a. oil on canvas b. illustration for an article in Boston magazine about a murder that took place in a small neighborhood store c. 1983

テリー・ワイドナー

1. a. 油彩絵具，キャンバス b. セルフプロモーション・ポスター c.1983年
2. a. 油彩絵具，キャンバス b. セルフプロモーション・DMイラスト c.1984年
3. a. 油彩絵具，キャンバス b. 雑誌イラスト c.1983年

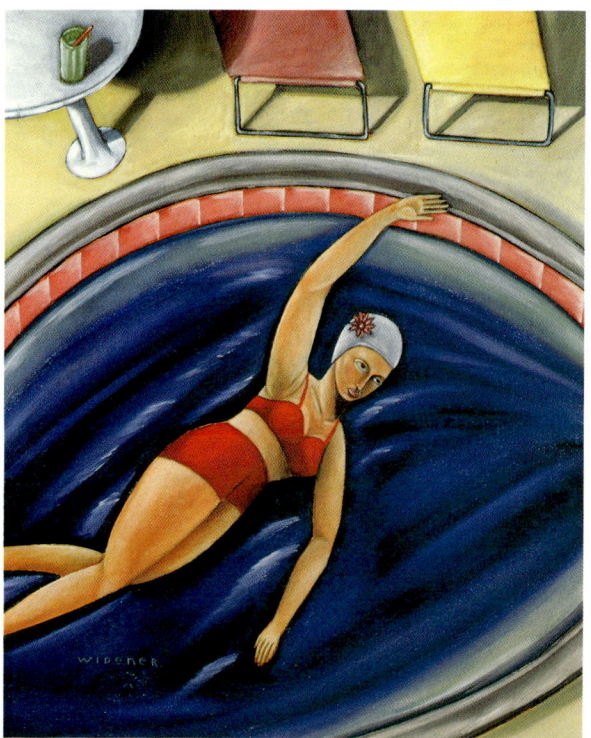

Represented by Artist

Larry C. Winborg

1. a. mixed media b. computer game cover for Texas Instruments Inc. c. 1983
2. a. mixed media b. illustrative story for Audubon Society magazine c. 1982
3. a. mixed media b. illustrative story for Sports Illustrated magazine c. 1983

1. a. 各種画材 b. コンピューターゲームのカバー c. 1983年
2. a. 各種画材 b. 雑誌イラスト c. 1982年
3. a. 各種画材 b. 雑誌イラスト c. 1983年

Represented by Artist

Ron Wolin

1. a. wood block printed with oil based ink. after printing, watercolors and airbrush were used b. calendar poster for a company called Graphic Processing c. 1979
2. 1943 MY WIFE a. wood block print with oil based ink. watercolors and airbrush were used after printing b. one of a series of 20 woodcuts from a series on the Holocaust, which was done to commemorate the Holocaust Museum in Los Ageles c. 1983
3. 1930 ALL STARS a. wood block printed with oil based inks. after printing, watercolor and airbrush were used b. an editorial story on all star baseball players of the past for Hughes Air West magazine c. 1980

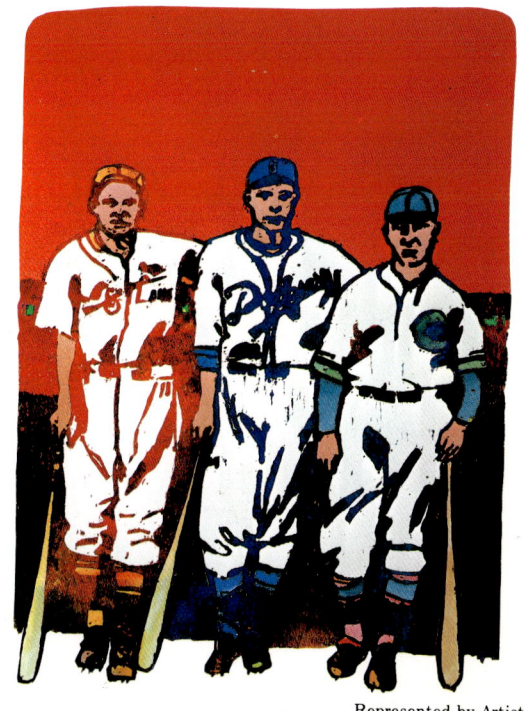

Represented by Artist

Bruce Wolfe

1. a. oils b. for Mastercraft Press as a promotional piece for their new press and later used as a poster for the S.F. Chamber orchastra concert in Lake Tahoe c. 1983
2. a. oil paint b. tea box of Celestial Seasonings Tea. c. 1983
3. a. oils b. Olympic ad by Southern Pacific c. 1983
4. a. oils b. A San Miguel series of classic's. for magazine prints and later made into a television ad. c. 1982
5. a. oils b. cover of S.F. Communication Arts magazine to promote an article they did about Bruce... c. 1982

ブルース・ウルフ

1. a.油彩絵具 b.プロモーション, ポスター c.1983年
2. a.油彩絵具 b.紅茶のパッケージ c.1983年
3. a.油彩絵具 b.広告イラスト c.1983年
4. a.油彩絵具 b.雑誌イラスト, TV広告 c.1982年
5. a.油彩絵具 b.雑誌表紙 c.1982年

Represented by Artist

Represented by Artist

Teresa Woodward

1. ZAPATA'S HORSE —"EL CABALLO DE ZAPATA" a. gouache-Opaque watercolor b. one of a series of drawings an paintings based on "The Mexican Revolution" for a future exhibit c. 1983
2. GREEK DANCERS a. watercolor b. promotional campaign to promote a real estate development that featured Mediterranean style architecture c. 1983–1984
3. BEACH GIRLS AND SURFERS a. gouache opaque watercolor b. self-promotion c. 1983

テレサ・ウッドワード

1. ガッシュ, 水彩絵具 b. 展示会出品予定作品 c. 1983年
2. a. 水彩絵具 b. プロモーション・キャンペーン用イラスト b. 1983～1984年
3. a. ガッシュ, 水彩絵具 b. セルフプロモーション c. 1983年

Represented by Artist

Gary Yealdhall ゲーリー・ヤードホール

1. a. airbrush b. postcard for AT&T c. 1983
2. a. airbrush b. postcard for AT&T c. 1983

1. a. エアブラシ b. ポストカード c. 1983年
2. a. エアブラシ b. ポストカード c. 1983年

Represented by Artist

James Courtney Zar

1. BILLY BALL a. acrylic on illustration board with airbrush background b. poster for Oakland A's c. 1981
2. LOU FERRIGNO AS "THOR" a. acrylic on illustration board with airbrush background c. 1981
3. CRAIG MORTON a. acrylic on illustration board with airbrush background b. poster for Denver Broncos c. 1981

ジェームス・コートニー・ザール

1.a. アクリル絵具，イラストレーションボード。背景にエアブラシ b. ポスター c.1981年
2.a. アクリル絵具，イラストレーションボード。背景にエアブラシ c.1981年
3.a. アクリル絵具，イラストレーションボード。背景にエアブラシ b. ポスター c.1981年

Represented by Artist

Brian Zick

1. artist's portrait
2-7 a. all work done mostly with dyes, but also with acrylic, ink, gouache, Prisma pencil on illustration board using airbrush, paintbrush, X-acto knife, I.N.T., and silkscreen
2. GIRL IN STOCKINGS b. originally personal work, picked up by Paper Moon Graphics for use as greeting card, key ring
3. NEW YORK FOLDOUT b. conned Paper Moon into using this as greeting card
4. RED LEATHER JACKET b. self-promotion
5. BLUE JEANS b. advertisement, poster, hang tag for Sasson Jeans, couldn't unload it on to Paper Moon
6. EARTHQUAKE b. originally magazine cover for New West magazine, subsequent use by Paper Moon Graphics as greeting card
7. BEERBELLY b. slipped this one into Paper Moon line

ブライアン・ジック

1. アーティスト近影
2〜7.a. 染料，アクリル絵具，インク，ガッシュ，色鉛筆，イラストレーションボード，エアブラシ，画筆，ナイフ，I.N.T.，シルクスクリーン
2. b. グリーティングカード
3. b. グリーティングカード
4. b. セルフプロモーション
5. b. 広告イラスト，ポスターなど
6. b. 雑誌表紙。後にグリーティングカード，かぎ環
7. b. グリーティングカード

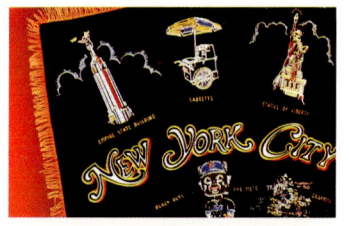

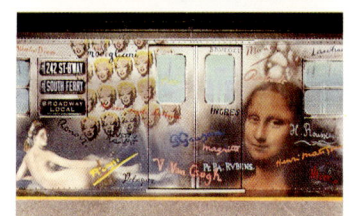

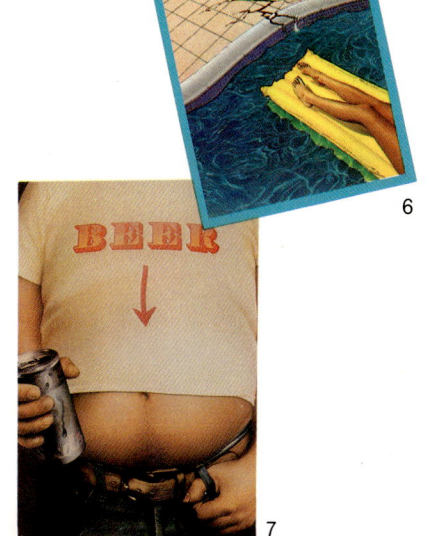

Represented by Artist

John Zielisnki

1. a. colored pencil, acrylic b. editorial illustration for South Western Barrel magazine c. 1984
2. a. colored pencil, acrylic b. editorial illustration for an article on Acid Rain c. 1982
3. a. colored pencil, acrylic b. cover illustration for Chicago magazine c. 1982
4. a. colored pencil, acrylic b. editorial illustration for ABA Journal c. 1983

ジョン・ジーリンスキー

1. a. 色鉛筆, アクリル絵具 b. 雑誌イラスト c. 1984年
2. a. 色鉛筆, アクリル絵具 b. 雑誌イラスト c. 1982年
3. a. 色鉛筆, アクリル絵具 b. 雑誌表紙 c. 1982年
4. a. 色鉛筆, アクリル絵具 b. 雑誌イラスト c. 1983年

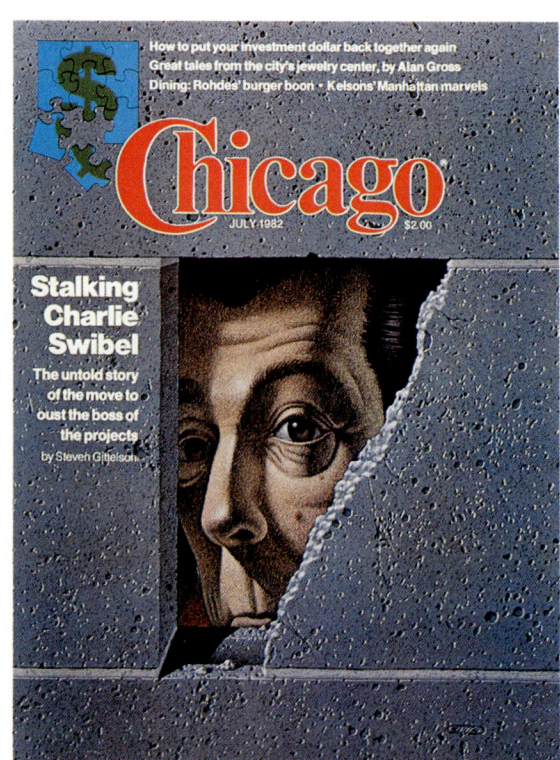

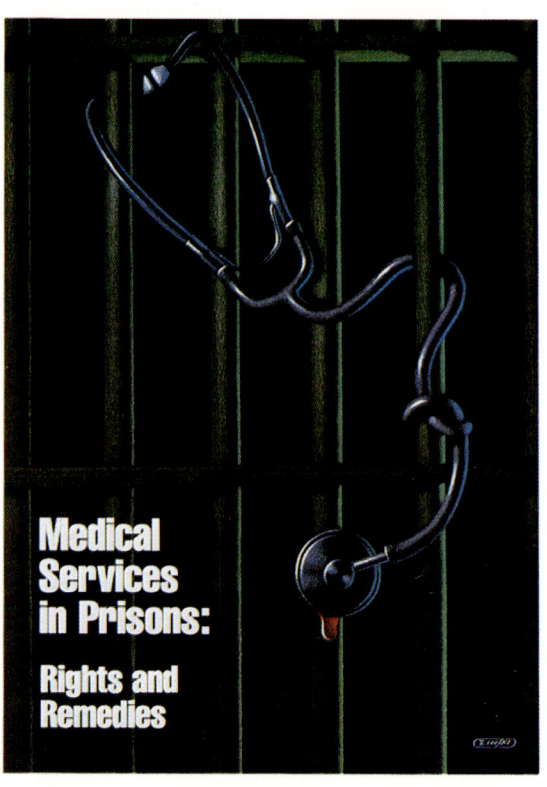

Represented by Artist

Andy Zito

1. SUPERBOWL XVI a. acrylic with airbrush b. 16th NFL Superbowl image, for posters, programs, and tickets c. 1981
2. LEARNING TO LOVE a. acrylic on canvas with brush b. album cover for Rodney Franklin c. 1982
3. SIMPLE IS SOMETIMES BEST a. acrylic with airbrush b. National Semiconductor magazine to show simpler connectors, etc. are also available c. 1981
4. STRONGER THAN EVER a. acrylic with airbrush b. Rose Royce album cover c. 1982

アンディ・ジート

1. a. アクリル絵具, エアブラシ b. ポスター, プログラム, 入場券 c.1981年
2. a. アクリル絵具, キャンバス, 画筆 b. レコードジャケット c.1982年
3. a. アクリル絵具, エアブラシ b. 雑誌イラスト c.1981年
4. a. アクリル絵具, エアブラシ b. レコードジャケット c.1982年

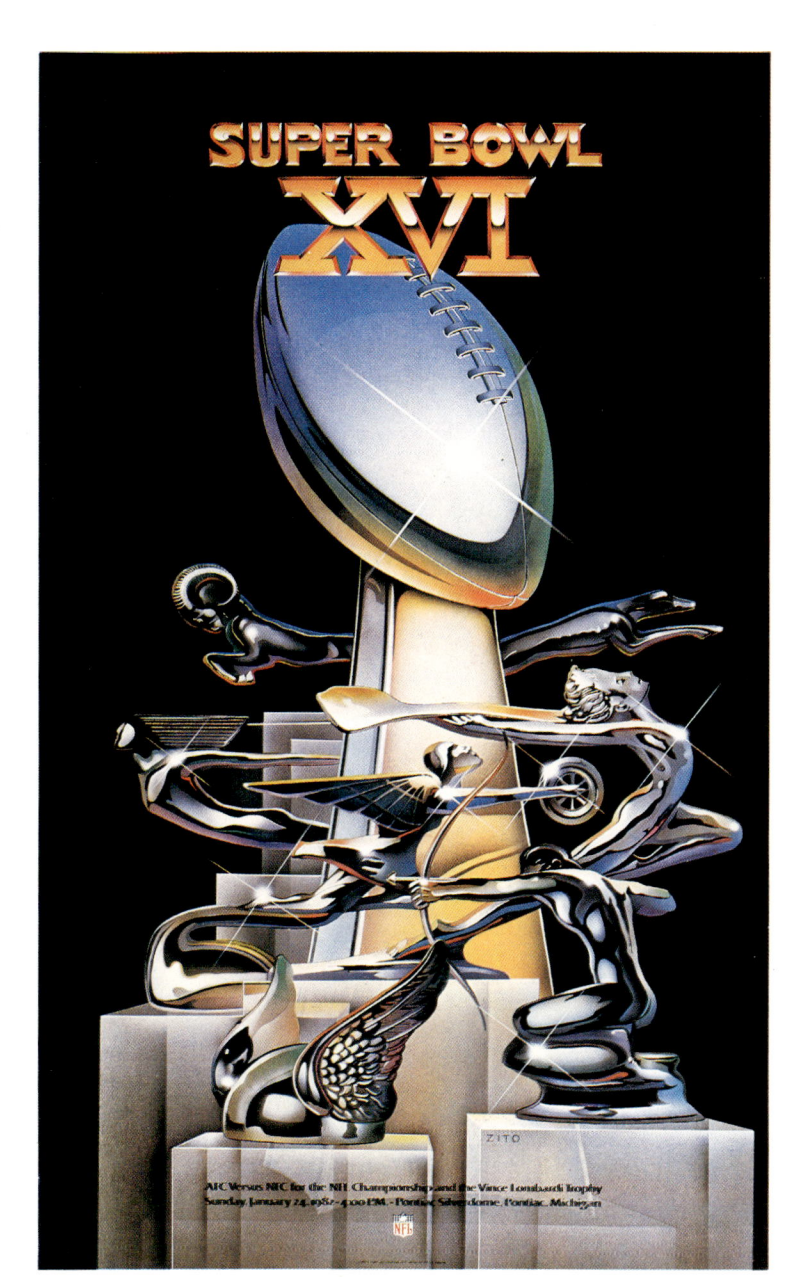

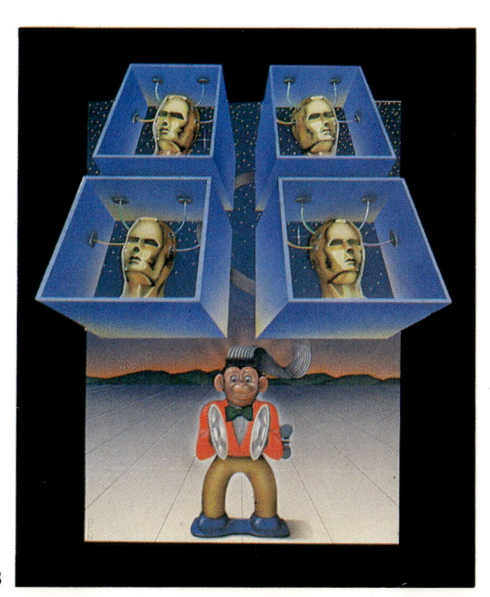

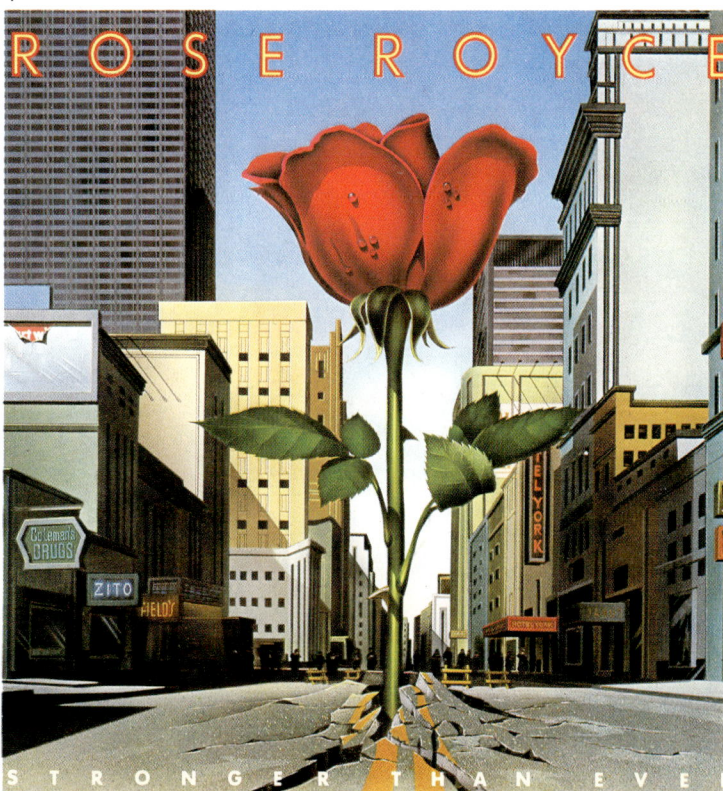

Represented by Artist

Index
索引

作家紹介

ジュリアン・アレン 10

イギリスのケンブリッジに生まれる。ケンブリッジ大学美術学部を卒業後、ロンドンにあるセントラル・アート・スクールに学んだ。ジャーナリスト兼アーティストとしてロンドン・サンデー・タイムズ誌の編集にあたる。1973年には、ニューヨーク・マガジンの編集長クレイ・フェルカー氏らの招きにより、ニューヨークに渡り、1977年まで同社に勤めた。現在はフリーランスのイラストレーターとしてニューヨークで活躍している。

マーシャル・アリスマン 11-13

1938年、ニューヨーク州ジェームスタウンに生まれる。ブルックリンのプラッツ・インスティテュート卒。一時ゼネラルモーターズにグラフィックデザイナーとして勤めたが、ヨーロッパ遊学後、ニューヨークのスクール・オブ・ビジュアル・アートで教え、イラストレーション学部、メディア学部の部長を歴任した。現在はフリーランスのイラストレーター。ニューヨーク・タイムズやタイム誌、『プレイボーイ』等の雑誌や本のイラストに従事。ニューヨーク・アート・ディレクターズ・クラブなどから数々の賞を受けている。

トム・バレンジャー 14

オクラホマに生まれ、カンサスおよびサンフランシスコで美術を学ぶ。その後テキサス大学で教鞭を執るかたわら、フリーランスのイラストレーターとして南西部を中心に活躍をしている。ニューヨークのイラストレーターズ・クラブ展で受賞したのをはじめ、数々の賞を受ける。エクソン石油等の広告を手がけ、ごく最近はTVコマーシャルのためのイラストレーションを完成させたばかりである。

ミッシェル・バーンズ 15

1956年、ミズーリ州スプリングフィールドの生まれ。フランスのレコード会社のジャケット・イラストを手がけていたが、現在はトラベル・レジャー、デンバー・ポスト、ウェストワード、ブロムスベリー・リビュー、メディソン＆エンフェンスなどの企業から仕事を請けている。作品を展覧会などにも発表している。コロラド州デンバーに在住。

ジェームス・バークレイ 16

1941年、ニューヨーク生まれ。ソサエティ・オブ・イラストレーターズの数々の年度賞のほか、ニューヨーク、シカゴ、ニュージャージーの各AD展で受賞している。マッキンリー山脈をデザインした15セントの航空郵便切手や、1984年度のアメリカ大使館展のポスターなどの作品で知られ、現在は限定刷り版画やワーナーブラザーズ映画のポスター、ライフ・タイム、ダブルデイなどの仕事を手がけている。作品はブリッジ・ギャラリーやハドソン・リバー美術館などで展示、アメリカ内務省、郵政省などに所蔵されている。

バスコーヴ 17

ニューヨーク・タイムズ、『ライフ』『ミズ』『フォーチュン』などの雑誌やマグロウヒル社などの本のイラストを手がける。各地のイラストレーターズ・クラブから数々の賞を受賞。またニューヨーク・アート・ディレクターズ・クラブからも賞を受けている。イエール大学の人類学研究所に寄稿したり、プレイボーイ美術館のスタッフ・アーティストとして活躍した経歴もある。

レオナード・バスキン 18

1922年にニュージャージー州ニューブランズウィックで生まれる。イエール大学で美術を学ぶ。彫刻や絵画で重要な賞を次々と受ける。1957年には東京国際版画ビエンナーレで大原美術館賞も受けた。主にニューヨークで活動し、個展を何度か行なっており、1977年にカナダのトロント、オンタリオで個展を開催したのを皮切りに、アメリカ以外の土地にも進出をはかっている。

ドン・バウム 19

1922年、ミシガン州エスカナーバで生まれる。ミシガン州立大学、シカゴ大学等で学んだのち、ルーズベルト大学、ハイドパーク・アートセンターで教鞭をとる。1973年にはブラジルでサンパウロビエンナーレの理事もつとめた。シカゴを中心に多数の個展、グループ展を行なっている。

ルード・J 20-21

1947年にドイツのブラウンシュバインで生まれる。両親はポーランド系。1951年にアメリカに渡り、1965年までニューヨーク州のロチェスターに、その後はカリフォルニア、ボストンと移り、現在はカリフォルニアのロサンゼルスに在住。美術に関しては特別の教育は受けなかった。セールスマンやトラックの運転手、店員、教会の堂守など苦労の時代を経たあと、よきパトロンを得て現在の道に至っている。

デイヴィッド・M・ベック 22-23

1950年、イリノイ州スプリングフィールドに生まれる。『プレイボーイ』誌、ラッキー・ストライク・シガレット、シカゴ・WLS放送、ユナイテッド航空、クラフト、マクドナルドなど数多くの企業のイラストの仕事に従事してきた。ニューヨーク・ソサエティ・オブ・イラストレーターズやシカゴ美術展などで賞を受けている。現在は、イリノイ州シカゴに在住して活躍している。

ロジャー・ビアワース 24

1946年、カリフォルニア州の生まれ。子ども向けの本や雑誌、グリーティング・カード、各企業の広告の仕事と幅広く活躍。ソサエティ・オブ・ロサンゼルス・イラストレーターズやアメリカン・インスティチュート・オブ・グラフィック・アートなどで数々の賞を受けている。作品はソサエティ・オブ・ロサンゼルス・イラストレーターズやロサンゼルス・アート・ディレクターズ・クラブ等の展覧会に出品。現在はアメリカン・イクスプレス、スズキ、カーネーション食品、マクドナルドなどの仕事をしている。

デイヴ・バング 25

1939年ミズーリ州セントルイスに生まれ、シェイナード美術大学を卒業。ロスアンゼルス・タイムズやさまざまな雑誌のデザイン・ディレクターを勤め、またカリフォルニア美術大学などで講師の経験もある。ソサエティ・オブ・ニューヨーク・イラストレーターズや、ソサエティ・オブ・ロスアンゼルス・イラストレーターズ、その他数多くの雑誌にその作品を発表。現在はイラストの仕事の傍ら、本を出版したり、デザイン・コンサルタント、およびデザイン教育と幅広い活動を行なっている。

ブロート・ブローズ 26-28

1951年オランダ、ホックカークに生まれ、ロッテルダムにあるグラフィック・スクールを卒業。ワシントン・ポストや『タイム』誌、CBSレコード、バドワイザー、IBMなど、論説文のイラストから広告に至るまで、多くの作品を手がける。1982年にはミネソタ・アート・ディレクターズ・クラブで金・銀賞を受賞、1983年にはコネチカット・アート・ディレクターズ・クラブで金賞を受賞。また、各地のイラストレーター協会で3つの銀賞をはじめ、数えきれないほどの賞を受けている。

マイケル・D・ブラウン 29

1940年カリフォルニア州フレートン生まれ。ワシントンポスト、『フォーチュン』『ニューズウィーク』『スポーツ・イラストレイテッド』など新聞・雑誌のイラストやパラマウント映画のポスター、記念切手の図柄など数多くの作品がある。ニューヨークおよびメトロポリタン・ワシントンのアート・ディレクターズ・クラブから多くの賞を受け、1983年にはニューヨーク・ソサエティ・オブ・イラストレーターズから銀賞を送られた。現在も雑誌や多くの企業からの仕事に追われている。

トレーシー・W・ブリット 30

1955年インディアナ州インディアナポリス生まれ。レコードジャケットや企業の年次報告書、広告などのイラストを手がけてきた。最近、ニューヨーク・ソサエティ・オブ・イラストレーターズより受賞。また、日本旅行展示会に作品を発表し、賞を受けている。現在も、マッキャン エリクソン、デルモンテ・フード、バンク・オブ・アメリカなど、数多くの企業の広告イラストに従事している。

ルー・ブルックス 31

1944年ペンシルバニア州フィラデルフィアに生まれる。ニューヨーク・タイムズや『タイム』『フォーチュン』『スポーツ・イラストレイテッド』などさまざまな新聞・雑誌や、CBSレコード、エクソンなど、多くの企業のイラストに従事する傍ら、ニューヨークのスクール・オブ・ビジュアル・アートなどでイラスト部門の講師を勤める。ソサエティ・オブ・イラストレーターズ第26回展の審査員、1983年には同会主催の新イラスト展で審査員長を勤める。自身もソサエティ・オブ・ニューヨーク・イラストレーターズなどさまざまな協会で受賞。

フィリップ・バーク 32

1956年ニューヨーク州バッファロー生まれ。ニューヨーク・タイムズや『タイム』『ヴォーグ』『ネーション』誌をはじめとする多くの新聞・雑誌のイラストに従事。1980年および1981年にはニューヨーク・ソサエティ・オブ・イラストレーターズより、また、1982〜'83年にはアメリカン・イラスト年鑑の賞を受けている。出身地のバッファローのカーネギー文化センターで個展。現在も雑誌イラストの仕事に従事している。

スティーヴン・バッツ 33

1952年カリフォルニア州ロサンゼルスの生まれ。サンリオ、グレイサー・フォックスの映画ポスターや出版社の本のイラストなどを手がけてきたが、現在は、バーリントン出版社、マッテル、フィルム・ベンチャー・インターナショナルなどの仕事に従事している。

キャサリン・コールダーウッド 34

1945年ニューヨーク州オッデンバーグに生まれる。『プレイボーイ』『エスクワイア』や『アート・マガジン』『アート・ニュース』などの美術雑誌のイラストを描いている。シカゴ、ロサンゼルス、インディアナポリス、出身地のニューヨーク州の各都市の展覧会に出品。ソサエティ・オブ・アート・ディレクターズ・クラブ第26回展をはじめとするさまざまな美術展で受賞している。ニューヨーク州ロチェスターのナザレス・カレジ、シラキュース大学の助教授である。

カーク・コールドウェル 35

1951年カリフォルニア州パサデナに生まれる。テレビコマーシャルや『オーシャン・マガジン』など雑誌のイラストに従事。サンフランシスコのソサエティ・オブ・コミュニケーティング・アート、アメリカ・インスティチュート・オブ・グフィック・アートなどで賞を受けている。

ジャスティン・キャロル 36

1953年テキサス州ヒューストンに生まれる。14歳の頃からフリーランスのイラストレーターとして仕事をしてきた。テキサス大学やロサンゼルスのアート・センター・カレッジでデザインを学ぶ。現在もロサンゼルスでエアブラシ・イラストとグラフィック・デザインのスペシャリストとして、フリーランスで活躍している。

ロン・チャン 37

1958年カリフォルニア州サンフランシスコに生まれる。雑誌『フォーカス』や『オーシャン・マガジン』『カリフォルニア・リビング・マガジン』、ランブラーレコード、バンク・オブ・アメリカなど、幅広く仕事をしている。1980年から1982年にはAIGAなどから受賞、1981年にはサンフランシスコのソサエティ・オブ・コミュニケーティング・アートより表彰されている。

エリック・チャン 38-39

1935年ホンコンに生まれる。オーストラリアのメルボルンにあるロイヤル・メルボルン・テクニカル・カレッジで広告デザインを学び、また、ロサンゼルスのシェイナード・アート・インスティチュートにも在籍して美術を専攻した。ロサンゼルスで23年間働き、その後ポスターの仕事に専念。現在は航空機をテーマとしたポスターの仕事を手がけている。

ジム・チェリー 40

1948年ワシントン州クラクラに生まれる。アトランティック・レコードやアリスタ・レコードなどのジャケットの表紙、ヘビー・メタル、『セブンティーン』『サイエンス・ダイジェスト』などの雑誌や、NBC、CBSおよびABC放送などのイラストの仕事に従事。1982年度のアメリカン・ソサエティ・オブ・イラストレーターズ主催の展覧会をはじめ、ロサンゼルス・アート・ディレクターズ・クラブなどから数々の賞を受けている。

スティーヴン・チョーニー 41

1951年ワシントンD.C.に生まれる。特別に美術教育は受けなかったが、1922年のロサンゼルスでのコマーシャルの仕事を皮切りに、アニメーション・デザイナーとしての頭角を現わしてきた。ユニバーサル映画、MGM、20世紀フォックス、ワーナー・ブラザーズなどの映画キャンペーンのための作品や、CBSやABC放送のコマーシャルなど幅広く活動している。

ジェームス・C・クリステンセン 42-43

1942年カリフォルニア州カルバーシティの生まれ。各レコード会社のレコードジャケットや本の表紙、『オムニ』など雑誌のイラストなどに従事。NASA25周年記念展をはじめ、多くの展覧会に作品を発表、絵画展覧会などで数々の賞を受けている。また、作品は国内の博物館だけでなく、メキシコ、イギリス、スペインなどの博物館にも収められている。

シーモア・クワスト 44-47

1931年ニューヨークに生まれる。クーパー・ユニオンでイラストレーションとグラフィック・デザインを学ぶ。現代の視覚芸術に世界的影響を与えたプッシュ・ピン・スタジオの創立者の一人。広告、レコードジャケット、アニメーション、本、雑誌、パッケージング等々と、その活動は多岐にわたる。『プッシュ・ピン・グラフィック』誌の発行者であり、アートディレクターでもあった。また、アメリカ本土だけでなく、ヨーロッパ、日本、ブラジルと世界各国の展覧会に出品し、パリのルーブル美術館で表彰された経歴もある。

ケイ・クレイ 48-49

1936年インディアナ州ロチェスターの生まれ。ヘロン美術学校、インディアナ大学などで学ぶ。母校のヘロン美術学校、インディアナ大学をはじめ多くの学校で美術の講師を勤める。インディアナ州展覧会やインディアナ州アーティスト展などで数多くの賞を受けている。インディアナポリス美術館やインディアナ・セントラル大学などで個展。

フランソワ・クロトー　50

1952年パリで生まれる。ベルギーで美術と建築を学んだのち1970年に渡英し、カー・デザイナーとしてスタートを切る。1975年突然写真家に転向したかと思うと、77年以降はグラフィックデザインを始めるなど、多才なところを見せる。1980年の大規模な個展を皮切りに、本格派のイラストレーターとしてニューヨーク、ハンブルグ、パリを拠点にインターナショナルな活躍を続けている。

ボビー・コクラン　51

インディアナ州ニュー・アルバニーに生まれる。1973年、ミズーリ州セントルイスのワシントン大学卒業。イラストレーターであり、デザイナーである。イリノイ州のシカゴを基点として、全米にわたって活躍している。グラフィック部門では、これまでに数多くの賞を受けている。

アラン・E・コバー　52-53

ニューヨークに生まれる。バーモント大学、スクール・オブ・ビジュアル・アートで学ぶ。イラストレーターズ・ワークショップの代表者である。ソサエティ・オブ・イラストレーターズやアーティスト・ギルドより多くの賞を受けている。『ライフ』『ルック』『タイム』『ハーパーズ』誌などのエディトリアル、IBM、CBS、エクリン、ゼロックス、パンナム、GE社等の広告を手がけ、高い評価を受けてきた。

シャーリーン・コリコット　54

1937年ロサンゼルスに生まれる。フリーランスになって15年たつが、ロサンゼルスのアート・ディレクターズ・クラブ記念賞、ニューヨーク・ソサエティ・オブ・イラストレーターズの優秀賞など、その作品に対しては高い評価が寄せられてきた。レコードジャケット、書籍・雑誌のカバーイラストなど、多種多様な仕事を手がけている。

クリフォード・アラ・コンダック　55

1930年マサチューセッツ州に生まれる。コロンビア・レコード、『プレイボーイ』誌などのイラストを手がけ、現在はCBSレコード、チバ・ガイギーなどの仕事に従事。ソサエティ・オブ・ニューヨーク・イラストレーターズおよびアメリカン・インスティチュート・オブ・グラフィック・アートより賞を受けている。ニューヨーク、サンフランシスコ、ワシントンD.C.などの各都市で作品展を毎年のように行なっている。

クリス・コンサーニ　56

1935年ワシントンD.C.に生まれる。アート・センター・カレッジでデザインを学ぶ。MCAレコードのジャケット・イラストや、キャピタルレコードのポスター、ウォルト・デズニーのビデオ広告などを手がけたが、現在はロサンゼルスに在住、MCAレコード、キャピタル・レコード、コロンビア映画、エーブル・コンピューター、サン・ジャイアンツなど、各企業の仕事をしている。母校の第12回展で受賞、また1983年にはマギー賞を受けている。

ホセ・クルーズ　57

1955年にメキシコのタンピコで生まれる。現在はテキサスのダラス在住。テキサス・インスツルメント、ゼロックスなどの企業の仕事のほか、『ペントハウス』『タイム』『マネー』など種々の雑誌のイラストを手がけている。また、ソサエティ・オブ・ニューヨーク・イラストレーターズの年度賞をはじめ、デザイン、アートディレクションなどで数々の賞を受けている。

レイ・クルーズ　58

1933年ニューヨークに生まれる。プラット・インスティチュートやクーパー・ユニオンなどで学ぶ。広告イラストの分野で活躍しているが、生態学や動物保護などにも関心を持つユニークな作家である。アーティスト・レップのビッキー・モルガンと共同制作をした最初の作家として有名である。グラフィック・アーティスト・ギルドの会員。

トム・カリー　60

1945年にテキサス州コレマンで生まれる。アメリカン航空、アップル・コンピューターなどの企業の広告や、各種雑誌のイラストに従事してきたが、現在も『テキサス・マンスリー』『アメリカン・ウェイ・マガジン』などで活躍している。作品はニューヨーク・ソサエティ・オブ・イラストレーターズ展やオースチン・グラフィックアート協会展などに出品し、これまでにもいくつかの賞を受けている。

ジェリー・ダッズ　60

大西洋岸中部地方のイラストとデザインのスタジオとして有名なユーカリプタス・ツリー・スタジオの社長。1965年、メリーランド州バルチモアにこのスタジオを設立し、以来、デザイナーおよびイラストレーターとしても活躍している。フィラデルフィア美術大学を卒業し、ニューヨーク・アート・ディレクターズ展でその才能を認められた。主なるクライアントは、アメリカ海軍、NASA、バルチモア市、『T.V.ガイド』『ジョン・ホプキン』誌、『MTTテクニカル・リビュー』などである。

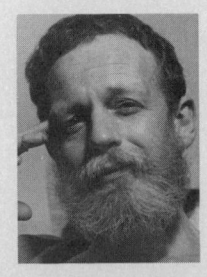

トム・デイリー　61

1938年にニューヨークで生まれる。ゼネラル食品、シネマックス、コロンビア映画、サンシャイン・バーカーズなどの大手企業をはじめ、CBSレコード、『プレイボーイ』や『マッコール』誌などのイラストも手がける。ソサエティ・オブ・ニューヨーク・イラストレーターズやソサエティ・オブ・ニューヨーク・アート・ディレクター・クラブから賞を受けている。作品はニューヨーク歴史協会やワシントンのスミソニアン博物館などにも展示され、シカゴのプレイボーイ・コレクション、スミソニアン・コレクションなどに所蔵されている。

アラン・ダニエルズ　62-63

1947年カリフォルニア州ロサンゼルスに生まれる。作品は非常に多く、現在もプレイボーイ、バージン・レコード、20世紀フォックス、英国航空、コアーズ・ビールなどのイラストを描いている。ロンドンやハンブルグなどの各都市で展覧会を行なってきたが、ブリティッシュ・イラストレーターズから賞を受けている。

ボー・ダニエルズ　64

1951年カリフォルニア州ロサンゼルスに生まれる。イラストレーターとしてこれまで数多くの件事をしてきたが、現在はホンダ、オリオン映画、プレイボーイ、ロックウェルなど各種企業のイラストを描いている。スミソニアン展で受賞。ロンドンのハミルトン・ギャラリーなどでも作品を発表した。スミソニアン博物館には作品が収められている。

ビル・デイヴィス　65

1940年、カリフォルニア州ロサンゼルスに生まれる。イラストレーターでデザイナー。『クリケット・マガジン』の表紙やマクミラン社の子供絵本のイラスト、NBC等のテレビのアニメーション・コマーシャルなど、幅広く活躍している。エミー賞をはじめ、ニューヨーク・ソサエティ・オブ・イラストレーターズやロサンゼルス・ソサエティ・オブ・イラストレーターズから賞を受けている。

ポール・デイヴィス　　　　　　　　　　　　66-68

1938年、オクラホマ州セントラホマに生まれる。アメリカ国内の大手出版社および海外の多くの雑誌のカバーや挿絵、レコード・ジャケットやパッケージ、ポスターなどを手がけている。ポスターでは、ニューヨーク・シェクスピア・フェスティヴァルの劇場ポスターが特に有名で、作品としてはほかにもリトグラフ、彫刻、アニメフィルム、書籍等があり、多彩である。また、イラストレーションとデザイン部門では各地の協会やクラブ展で数多くの賞を得ている。その名声はアメリカ全土に限らずヨーロッパ、日本、ソ連などにも知られている。

マイケル・J・ディーズ　　　　　　　　　　69

1956年、バージニア州ノーホークに生まれる。1974～'78年、プラッツ・インスティテュートで美術を専攻、1978年にはロンドンのバイアン・ショウ美術大学にも学んだ。在学中からフリーランスのイラストレーターとして、ドイル・ダン、リーダース・ダイジェスト、デイリー・プレス、レディース・ホーム・ジャーナル、フランクリン・ワット等、出版社やエージェンシーなどの仕事を手がけている。1981年よりニューヨーク・ファーム・オブ・アーティスト・アソシエーションの代表、かたわらスクール・オブ・ビジュアル・アートの講師をつとめている。

チャールズ・D・ドゥマール　　　　　　　　70

1959年、ニューヨークに生まれる。美術に関しては特別な教育を受けなかったが、1980年に、東海岸の大手のデザインスタジオのスタッフとして映画の宣伝のイラストを手がけて以来、その才能を認められるようになり、現在は、ワーナーブラザーズやユニバーサル映画、CBSテレビ局などの仕事を担当している。映画やテレビに共通するようなリアリズムとみずみずしい感受性とがブレンドされたような作風に定評がある。

ハーベイ・ディナースタイン　　　　　　　　71

1928年にニューヨーク州ブルックリンで生まれる。アカデミー・オブ・ファインアートより金賞、国際労働者協会より年間最優秀雑誌表紙賞など多数の賞を受賞。クライアントには『アトランティック・マガジン』『エスクァイア』『フォーチュン』『プレイボーイ』、ニューヨーク・タイムスなどの雑誌社、新聞社、RCAレコードなどの有名会社が名を連ねる。1983年にはシンデン・ギャラリーで展示会を行なっている。

ジョン・テイラー・ディズミュークス　　　　72

1953年生まれ。A&Mレコードのアルバム・カバーや、ワーナーブラザーズ、ユニバーサル、オリオン、RCAなどの映画、サンヨー、リーバイス・ジーンズウェア、コーア・ビールなどの企業、アメリカ・ナショナル・フットボール・リーグのポスターを手がけている。アート・ディレクターズ・クラブやイラストレーターズ・クラブから多くの賞を受ける。サンフランシスコとニューヨークの画廊で作品を展示、ヨーロッパ、日本にもコレクターがいる。

デニス・ディートリッヒ　　　　　　　　　　73

1954年生まれ。ピッツバーグ・インスティテュートを卒業後、スクール・オブ・ビジュアル・アート、ソサエティ・オブ・グラフィックアートのビジネス・スクールなどで学ぶ。フリーランスのイラストレーターとして、『アウトドア・ライフ』『ゴルフ』『タイム・ライフ』の雑誌やAT&Tなどの広告を手がけている。ソサエティ・オブ・グラフィック・アーティストのニューヨーク委員会の委員をつとめる。また、漫画家協会会員。

パティ・ドライデン　　　　　　　　　　　　74

1950年、ペンシルバニア州ピッツバーグに生まれる。これまでにEMIやRCAレコードのアルバム・カバーをはじめ、『ハーパーズ』『エスクァイア』『ニューズウィーク』など雑誌のイラストを描いてきたが、現在も『ヴォーグ』『ヴァニティ・フェア』等の仕事を手がけている。

アンドレイ・デュディンスキー　　　　　　　75

1945年ポーランドのソポットに生まれる。『タイム』『ボストン・グローブ』『サタデー・ナイト』『サンデー・タイムス』などの雑誌の表紙や挿絵、ポスターなどの仕事をしてきたが、現在もニューヨーク・タイムズや『タイム』誌、『テキサス・マンスリー』『マネー』などのイラストを手がけている。

アレックス・エベル　　　　　　　　　　　　76

1932年、メキシコに生まれる。両親はドイツ系。1956年、アメリカの市民権を取得。レコード・ジャケットや書籍の表紙、多くの雑誌、広告イラスト等を仕事としてきたが、現在も『サイエンス・ダイジェスト』『ボーイズ・ライフ』『プレイボーイ』『ウイ』『ペントハウス』などの雑誌イラストのほか、パラマウント映画の広告等を手がけている。ニューヨークのコロンブス画廊で展覧会。ケリー賞、アンディ賞、ロサンゼルス・ソサエティ・オブ・イラストレーターズ賞、アート・ディレクターズ・クラブ賞など、多くの受賞歴がある。

ジャック・エンデウォルト　　　　　　　　　77

1935年、ニューヨークに生まれる。2年の軍隊生活のあと、スクール・オブ・ビジュアル・アートに学ぶ。1961年からフリーランスのイラストレーターとなり、デル、エーボン、バンタム等のペーパーバックのカバーや『タイム・ライフ』『レディス・ホーム・ジャーナル』等、雑誌のイラスト、その他イベリア航空やデュポン等、多くの企業の広告イラストを手がけている。1976年にはイラストレーターズ協会主催のアメリカ建国200年記念展示に出品。現在は母校の講師をつとめる。

ジョン・イーストマン　　　　　　　　　　78-79

UCLAを卒業。ファッション・イラストレーター、アートディレクターとして世に出たが、のちにイラストレーターに転向した。特に女性をデフォルメした作品は、その美しさで全米を魅了し、一連のリトグラフは多くのファンに愛蔵されている。

ジェームス・R・エンディコット　　　　　　80

1946年、カリフォルニア州バーナーディノに生まれる。キャピタル・レコードのジャケット、『アップル・コンピューター』誌などのイラストや広告を手がけてきたが、現在も『アトランティック・マンスリー』『タイム』『ペントハウス』誌などの仕事が多い。1983年にはニューヨーク・アートディレクターズ・クラブ展で受賞。また同年と翌1984年のニューヨーク・イラストレーターズ・クラブ展でも賞を受けている。

アンカ・エンテ　　　　　　　　　　　　　　81

1949年、インドネシアのソロンに生まれる。シェブロンやIBMなどの広告、および『月刊バークレイ』誌などの雑誌のイラストに従事。サンフランシスコ芸術協会などから多くの賞を受けている。また彼女はサンフランシスコのソマ・ギャラリーの創立者の一人でもある。彼女の名声を得た作品の多くは、現在、サンフランシスコの周辺の人びとに愛蔵されている。

ビル・アーズランド　　　　　　　　　　　　82

アイオワ州デモワネに生まれた。アイオワ州立大学を卒業。アイオワ・アート・ディレクターズ・クラブ、タルサ・アート・ディレクターズ・クラブや、第21回から第24回までのニューヨーク・ソサエティ・オブ・イラストレーターズやシカゴ・ソサエティ・オブ・イラストレーターズの主催する展覧会に出品している。現在はミネソタ州のスティルウォーターでスタジオを構えて活躍中。

ルイ・エスコベード 83
1952年テキサス州のスィートウォーターに生まれる。ペーパームーン・グラフィックやタイム・ライフ・レコードなどの仕事を手がける。ニューヨーク・ソサエティ・オブ・イラストレーターズで金メダル、ダラスのソサエティ・オブ・ビジュアル・コミュニケーションズより銀メダルを受賞している。現在は『ボーイズライフ』『アトランティックマガジン』、ジュリアード・プレスなどの仕事に従事。

ジム・エヴァンス 84
1947年イリノイ州シカゴに生まれた。アート・センター・カレッジ・オブ・デザイン卒。ランブラー、コンチネンタル航空、ペーパーム―ン・グラフィックス、ウォルトディズニー・プロダクション、美津濃などの仕事を手がける。ニューヨーク・アート・ディレクターズ・クラブ展をはじめとして、ロサンゼルス、また東京などでも意欲的に作品を発表している。

テレサ・ファソリーノ 85
1946年、ニューヨーク州ポート・チェスターに生まれる。これまでにも大手の雑誌や単行本、および広告のイラストを手がけてきた。ニューヨーク・ソサエティ・オブ・イラストレーターズやニューヨーク・アート・ディレクターズ・クラブ主催の展覧会などに出品。受賞歴多数。現在も『エスクァイア』『タイム・ライフ』『プレイボーイ』『テレビガイド』などの雑誌を中心とした仕事をしている。

アン・フィールド 86
1956年、イギリスのサセックス、ブリントンで生まれる。ロンドンの主要ファッション雑誌のイラストに従事してきたが、現在も『カリフォルニア』誌やセミ・レコードなどの仕事を請けている。作品はパステルやクレヨンを使ったファッション画が多い。

ヴィヴィアン・フレッシャー 87
1956年、ニューヨーク生まれ。パーソンズ・デザイン学校を卒業。主としてパステルや木炭、油絵具などを用いたイラストを描く。『タイム』『ヴォーグ』『フォーチュン』などの雑誌をはじめ、エレクトラ・レコード、CBSレコード、ランダムハウスの単行本、ニューヨーク・タイムズなどの仕事も手がけている。1984年には、イラストレーターズ協会より金メダルを受賞。また、1985年初頭に封切られる映画の『Almost you』では、彼女の作品が起用されている。

ディック・フラッド 88
ゼネラル・モータース、ユナイテッド航空など、大手企業の広告イラストや漫画のほか、単行本・新聞・テレビのイラストや漫画も手がける。かつて、編集者やレポーターと一緒に、新聞のイラストや漫画についての研究をしたこともあって、数多くの政治漫画なども描いている。

ロバート・フロアザーク 89
1950年、ワシントンD.C.に生まれる。CBSレコードやランダムハウス、バンタム・ブックス、バランタイン・ブックス、ニュー・アメリカン・ライブラリー、エース・ブックスなど種々の企業のイラストに従事。各地の展示会で作品を発表し、賞や賞金を受けている。現在もワーナー・ブラザーズ映画などの大手企業の仕事を請けて活躍中。

パトリック・フロシェ 90
1943年、ミシガン州デトロイトの生まれ。カリフォルニア州パサデナのアート・センター・デザイン・カレッジを卒業。主に本のイラストやデザインの仕事を手がけている。ニューヨーク・ソサエティ・オブ・イラストレーターズやアメリカ・イラスト展、グラフィック・アーティスト・ガイド展などで受賞。ミシガン州の各都市で展覧会を開催している。作品は、ミシガン州やイリノイ州在住の愛好家たちの手に収められている。

フィル・フランケ 91
1955年、ブルックリンに生まれる。ハイスクールを卒業後、プラッツ・インスティテュートの美術学校に学び、1977年に学位を受ける。ソサエティ・オブ・イラストレーターズ賞をはじめ、受賞歴多数の実力派。フリーランスのイラストレーター兼映画会社のアートディレクターとして活躍する生粋のニューヨーカーである。

ダグマール・フリンタ 92
1956年、ニューヨークに生まれる。CBSレコードや『タイム』『フォーチュン』、ハーパー・アンド・ロウ、サイモン・アンド・シュスターなどの出版社のイラストを手がけた。ニューヨーク・ソサエティ・オブ・イラストレーターズをはじめ、ニューヨーク・アート・ディレクターズ・クラブ、アメリカ・イラストレーション展などで数々の賞を受けている。現在も雑誌のイラストに追われる傍ら、ロード・アイランドのデザイン学校で講師を勤めている。

ニコラス・ガエターノ 93
1944年にコロラド州コロラドスプリングで生まれる。家族とともにニューヨーク州ロングアイランドに移り、そこで少年時代を過ごす。ロサンゼルスのアートセンターに学んだ。今日までにソサエティ・オブ・イラストレーターズやアメリカン・インスティテュート・オブ・グラフィック・アート、アンディ賞など数々の賞を受けてきた。現在は『タイム』『フォーブス』『ニューヨーク・マガジン』などのエディトリアル、TVアニメーション、ソニー、イースタン航空の企業プロモーションなど、多方面からその才能を認められて活躍している。ニューヨーク在住。

バーナード・フックス 94-95
イラストレーションの世界では、すでに伝説的な人である。ミズーリ州セントルイスのワシントン大学に学んだ。『スポーツ・イラストレイテッド』『ニュー・ヨーカー』『レディス・ホーム・ジャーナル』『TVガイド』等、大手出版社の仕事を手がけ、ニューヨーク・ソサエティ・オブ・イラストレーターズの賞をはじめとするありとあらゆる賞を手にして、1975年、イラストレーターとしては最年少で名誉の殿堂入りをした。ケネディ・ライブラリーには、彼が描いたありし日のJ・F・ケネディの2点の肖像画が掛けられている。

スタンリー・W・ガリ 96-97
1912年、サンフランシスコで生まれる。美術学校卒業後、イラストレーターの道に入ったが、彼を一躍有名にしたのは、野生動物・森林保護をテーマにしたウェアハウザー社のコレクションである。これらの作品は現在に至るまで数多くの書籍・雑誌、百科辞典に載せられている。彼はまた26種類の合衆国郵便切手のデザインも手がけており、1982年にはそれまでの業績が評価され、ニューヨーク・ソサエティ・オブ・イラストレーターズの名誉の殿堂入りをした。現在彼はスペイン植民地時代のカリフォルニア史をテーマに、新たな作品を描いている。

ニクソン・ギャロウェイ 98-99
カリフォルニアに生まれる。第二次大戦中、海軍の航空隊に務め、1949年にアート・センター・スクールを卒業した。アメリカ各地で催された展覧会で数々の賞を受けている。スミソニアン博物館、ホワイトハウス、空軍博物館、ロサンゼルス・カントリー博物館などにも作品が展示された。ロサンゼルス・ソサエティ・オブ・イラストレーターズの会長を勤めたこともある。休日にはスキーを楽しんだり、カリフォルニアの海でボートをこいだりするのが趣味。

ジョン・ガマッシュ　100

1945年、マサチューセッツ州ガードナーに生まれる。『アトランティック・マンスリー』『ギャラリー・マガジン』などのイラストやホートン・ミフリン社などの単行本の表紙および各種企業の広告の仕事に従事。ニューヨーク・ソサエティ・オブ・イラストレーターズの第20回および第24回展において受賞、そのほかハッチ賞、ニューヨーク・アドヴァタイジング・クラブのアンディ賞やマサチューセッツ州西部のアドヴァタイジング・クラブなどからも各種の賞を受けている。

ジョン・ガンパート　101

1944年、ニューヨークに生まれる。ランダムハウス、ダブルデイ、デル等、大手出版社の仕事のほか、ニューヨーク・タイムズ、CBSなどのイラストも手がけている。最近のものとしては、プレイボーイなどの雑誌イラストのほか、1984年度のジャズ・カレンダーがある。

ジョー・ガーネット　102

シカゴ・アート・インスティチュート、テキサス工科大学、ロサンゼルス・シェイナード・アート・インスティチュートなどで学ぶ。フリーランスでテレビ、雑誌、新聞誌のイラストやデザインの仕事を行なったり、カリフォルニア州立大学でイラストの講師を勤めたこともある。デトロイト、ロサンゼルス、サンディエゴなどで開催されたアート・ディレクターズ・ショーに数々の作品を発表。1975年、デトロイトのショーでは金メダルを獲得している。

ジェリー・ガーステン　103

1927年、ニューヨーク市に生まれる。クーパー・ユニオン・アート・スクールで学ぶ。『タイム』『ニューズウィーク』『マネー』『プレイボーイ』などの雑誌やシティ・バンクのテレビコマーシャルなど、多くの企業のイラストを手がける。ニューヨークのソサエティ・オブ・イラストレーターズや、ニューヨークのアート・ディレクターズ・クラブ、アメリカン・インスティテュート・オブ・グラフィック・アートなどから賞を受けている。ニューヨークのスペクトラム・ギャラリーなどで作品を発表。

ジョージ・ギュースティ　104-106

イタリアのミラノに生まれる。同市のブレラ美術学校を卒業。スイスの市民権を取り、自分のスタジオをチューリッヒに持っている。1938年アメリカに来て、現在はアメリカの市民権も取得。フリーランスでのアーチスト、デザイナーとして『タイム』や『フォーチュン』などの雑誌をはじめ、各種企業の広告などのイラストを手がける。さまざまな展覧会において、10数個の金メダルと80以上の賞を獲得している。企業や政府のイラストのコンサルタントなども勤める。ニューヨークのアート・ディレクターズ・クラブその他多くの協会の会員として、現在も活躍。

ロバート・ギュースティ　107

1930年、スイスのチューリッヒに生まれる。アトランティック・レコード、CBSレコードなどのジャケット、『タイム』『テレビガイド』『サイエンス・ダイジェスト』など雑誌のイラスト、ゼロックス社やIBM社の広告などの仕事に従事。ニューヨーク・ソサエティ・オブ・イラストレーターズやアート・ディレクターズ・クラブなどで多くの賞を受けている。現在も『タイム』、バークレイ銀行、出版社のランダムハウスなどの仕事を請けている。

ミルトン・グレイサー　108-111

1929年、ニューヨークに生まれる。フルブライト奨学金を受けてイタリアのボローニアの美術アカデミーに学び、故ジョルジュ・モランディ氏からエッチングの指導を受ける。1954年、シーモア・クワスト、エド・ソレル、レイノルド・ラフィンとプッシュピン・ブラフィックを設立。1968年にはクレイ・フェルカーと雑誌『ニューヨーク』を創刊し、編集代表とデザインディレクターを1977年までつとめた。1979年、ニューヨーク・アート・ディレクターズ・クラブの名誉の殿堂入りを果たす。現在も多くの企業のCI計画やプロモーションなどの仕事を請けている。

アレクサンダー・ニジコー　112

1966年から、『タイム』『ニューヨーク・マガジン』『スポーツ・イラストレイテッド』『マッコール』などの大手出版社の雑誌やNBC、モーゼル・オイル等、多くの企業のイラストの仕事に従事。ソサエティ・オブ・イラストレーターズより、1975年および1979年の2回、金賞を受賞している。その他、『カリフォルニア・マガジン』より優秀賞を、広告の部ではアンディ賞を受けた。また、モリス博物館の第39回展覧会でも受賞をするなど、各地でその実力が認められている。

ラファエル・ゴゥテルス　113

1958年、ベルギーのブリュッセルに生まれる。キャピタル・レコード、『カリフォルニア・マガジン』『シェイプ・マガジン』『ロサンゼルス・マガジン』などのイラストを手がけている。ロサンゼルスのイラストレーターズ協会展で受賞。ブリュッセルのギャラリー75などで作品を展示。現在はロサンゼルスに在住して活躍している。

ペネローペ・ゴットリーブ　114

アート・センター・カレッジ・オブ・デザインに学ぶ。フリーランスのデザイナー、イラストレーターとして、ABC、NBC、CBSや、『ロサンゼルス』誌や『プレイガール』誌などの雑誌およびパスポート・ウイスキー、マニュファクチャー銀行、シズラー・ステーキ・ハウスなど、各種企業のイラストの仕事を手がける。1976年より1981年にかけて、各地のイラストレーター協会主催の展覧会で、数々の賞を獲得している。

ジェームス・グラカ　115

1948年、オハイオ州アクロンに生まれる。アートセンター・カレッジ・オブ・デザインに学ぶ。母校の国際アルミニ展で最優秀賞を受け、イラストレーターとしてのデビューのきっかけとなった。現在はイラストレーター、デザイナーとして活躍。主なるクライアントに20世紀フォックス映画、NBCテレビ、トヨタ、ユナイテッド航空、ウェスタン航空などがあり、各種企業の広告イラストとデザインを手がけている。

アレッサ・グレース　116

『タイム』『ライフ』、およびニューヨーク・タイムズなどの新聞や雑誌でおなじみのイラストレーターである。1981年には、フランスの子ども向けの本のイラストも手がけている。ニューヨークのマジソン・アベニューにあるグラハム・ギャラリーで、彼女の作品はよく展示されている。

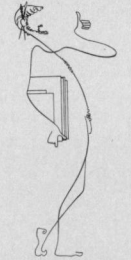

デーリック・グロス　117

1947年、オハイオ州デイトンに生まれる。各種雑誌や企業広告用ポスターのイラストやアートディレクション等を手がけている。1980年にはフランスで開かれた国際ポスター・コンテストで賞を受け、ほかにもいくつかの受賞歴がある。現在も『フレックス』誌などの雑誌を中心として活躍している。ニューヨークのレスリー・ローマン・ギャラリーで作品を展示。

ボブ・グラハム　118-119

1947年、テキサス州に生まれる。ノース・テキサス州立大学で美術を専攻。その後、マサチューセッツ州のプロビンスタウンにわたり、印象派のヘンリー・ヘンシューに教えを請う。数年後、独立してジョージア州アトランタにスタジオを構えた。そこでの4年間に数多くの肖像画を描いてきたが、最近、ニューオーリアンズに転居した。彼はパステル、油絵具とさまざまな材料と手法を用いている。一つの作品に3週間もかけることがある。美術クラブや各種学校で講師の経験もある。

デイヴィッド・グローヴ　　120-121

　1940年、ワシントンD.C.に生まれる。バンク・オブ・アメリカ、スタンダード・オイル、アメリカ海軍、ウォルトディズニー・プロダクション、ウェスタン航空など各種企業のイラストの仕事に従事。ニューヨークのソサエティ・オブ・イラストレーターズやロサンゼルスのソサエティ・オブ・イラストレーターズで金賞、優秀賞を受賞。その他ニューヨーク、パリなど各地で開かれる展覧会等にも意欲的に作品を出品している。1983年にはサンフランシスコのアカデミー・アート・ギャラリーで個展を開いた。

スティーヴン・ガルナーシア　　122

　1953年、コネチカット州フェアフィールドに生まれる。レコード・ジャケット、単行本、雑誌のイラストや映画ポスターなど数多くの仕事を手がけてきた。ニューヨークのソサエティ・オブ・イラストレーターズや、ニューヨーク・アート・ディレクターズ・クラブ、アメリカン・インスティテュート・オブ・グラフィック・アートなどから毎年のように賞を受けている。現在も主としてニューヨーク・タイムズや『ボストン・グローブ・マガジン』『スポーツ・イラストレイテッド』など、雑誌の仕事に従事している。

ヘレン・ゲータリー　　123

　1957年にパリで生まれる。パリの美術学校を卒業後渡米し、ニューヨークのスクール・オブ・ビジュアル・アートでエッチングとリトグラフを学ぶ。ニューヨーク、シアトル、フランスで毎年個展を開いている。クライアントも順調についており、フランスでは『エル』『ギャップ』、アメリカでは『ペントハウス』『インタビュー』『カメラアート』など主要雑誌が彼女の作品をとりあげている。1981年にはCEBA優秀賞を受賞した。

クニオ・ハギオ　　124-125

　1947年、イリノイ州シカゴに生まれる。『プレイボーイ』『ペントハウス』20世紀フォックス、パラマウント映画、CBS、バドワイザーなどの仕事を請けている。ニューヨークのソサエティ・オブ・イラストレーターズで金賞・銀賞を受賞。また、ニューヨークのアート・ディレクターズ・クラブなどからも銀賞を受けている。

H・トム・ホール　　126-127

　1932年、ペンシルバニア州リドレイパークに生まれる。子供絵本や雑誌のイラストを皮切りに、クノッフ社より出版した『金のトンボ』という本の絵を描く1年半を日本で快適に過ごした。そのあと大人の本を手がけ、バンタム・ブックス、エーボン・ブックス、ワーナー・ブックス、その他サタデー・イヴニング・ポストや『リーダーズ・ダイジェスト』などの仕事をしている。フィラデルフィアの美術学校で個展、ニューヨークのソサエティ・オブ・イラストレーターズでグループ展。同協会の年度展で受賞している。

エイブ・ガーヴィン　　128

　1959年にUCLAを卒業後、いくつかのデザイン学校で学び、イラストレーターの道に入る。マスコミ界だけでなく、旅行、食品、金融、住宅、エレクトロニクスなど幅広い分野のクライアントから支持を受けている。また、1977年にマギー賞、1980年にオレンジカウンティ広告財団よりオレンジ賞を獲得しており、イラストレーション界の主だった賞にはすべて顔を出している。

ジョン・ハマガミ　　129

　1955年、日本の奈良に生まれる。2歳のときに渡米。インクにアクリル絵具、エアブラシを併用する技法で、『プレイボーイ』などの雑誌、ユニバーサル映画、グリーティングカードのペーパームーン等々、いろいろな企業のいろいろなイラストを手がけている。

キャシー・ヘック　　130

　1956年、テキサス州サン・アントニオで生まれる。テキサス大学で広告デザインを学ぶ。卒業後、1978年にジム・ヘック氏と結婚し、79年にアートディレクターとしてヤング・アンド・ルビカム社に入社する。1981年同社を退社し、フリーランスのイラストレーターとして再出発し、「アートディレクターズ・アニュアル」優秀賞などを受賞。テニス、料理、アンティック収集が趣味だという。テキサスとニューヨークで仕事をしている。

ジョー・ハイナー，キャシー・ハイナー　　131

　ジョー・ハイナーは1951年、メリーランド州アバーディーンに生まれ、キャシー・ハイナーは1952年ユタ州のソルト・レイク・シティに生まれる。小学校6年以来のコンビで、現在もユタ山スタジオで一緒に働いている。ABCレコード、20世紀フォックス映画、また『タイム』『ヴォーグ』『マッコール』等各種雑誌のイラストやビルボード、ポスター、パッケージデザイン、グリーティングカードなどいろいろな仕事に従事してきた。彼らはさまざまな展覧会において賞を受けている。ニューヨーク現代美術博物館にも作品が展示されている。

アルバート・ハーシュフェルド　　132-133

　1903年、セントルイスの生まれ。彫刻家として出発したが、のちにイラストレーターに転じた。ニューヨーク・タイムズ日曜版のイラストで多くの人たちに親しまれている。『ホリデー』『ヴォーグ』『ライフ』『ルック』などの雑誌やサタデー・イヴニング・ポストなどの仕事に従事。彼の作品はメトロポリタン美術館、現代美術館、フォッグ美術館、ブルックリン美術館など、アメリカの主要な美術館に数多く収められている。また、ニューヨークのマーゴ・フェイデン・ギャラリーには、彼の半世紀にわたる作品が展示してある。

マーティン・ホフマン　　134

　1935年にフロリダ州セント・オーガスティンで生まれる。1969年から1971年までマイアミ大学で美術とドローイングを教える。NASAスペースシャトル計画、ハーレーダビットソン・モーターサイクル、全米鉄鋼協会、味の素のプロモーションなどに参加、そのほか『プレイボーイ』『フォーチュン』などの仕事を手がけている。ほとんど毎年のように個展、グループ展を開き、精力的な創作活動を行なっている。

ジャミー・ホーガン　　135

　1958年、ニュー・ハンプシャー州リンカーンの生まれ。ニューヨーク・ソサエティ・オブ・イラストレーターズの第25回展や、ボストン・アート・ディレクターズ・クラブなどで受賞。現在はデジタル・エクイープメント社をはじめ、『ボストン・グローブ』『ニュー・エイジ・ジャーナル』『テキサス・マンスリー』などの雑誌イラストを手がけている。

ブラッド・ホランド　　136-137

　オハイオ州フレモントの出身。美術に関しては特別な教育は受けなかったが、『タイム』『ライフ』、ニューヨーク・タイムズなどの新聞、雑誌から、フランクリン図書館のジャック・ロンドンの本のイラストなども手がけている。また、1982年には、13セント切手のクレージー・ホースのデザインも彼の手になる。ニューヨークのソサエティ・オブ・イラストレーターズやアート・ディレクターズ・クラブより受賞。

ホリー・ホリントン　　138

　1950年に生まれる。1968-69年、ウェスト・サセックスの美術学校でファッション・デザインを学び、1968-72年、バーミンガム美術大学に進んで学位を取る。服の店をはじめるが、2年ほどして西ドイツのミュンヘンに移り住み、広告デザインの仕事に従事。その後アメリカに渡り、本格的にイラストレーターとして活躍するようになる。英国の『ヴォーグ』誌、『プレイガール』、ロッド・ダイアー、MCAレコード、A&Mレコード、パラマウント、マッキャン・エリクソンなどの仕事を手がけている。

312

キャサリン・ホルト 139

1969−71年、南カリフォルニア大学、その後ロサンゼルスのアート・センター・カレッジ・オブ・デザインに学ぶ。フリーランスのイラストレーターとしてニューヨーク・タイムズ、『ヴォーグ』『フォーチュン』などの出版物や、RCAレコード、CBSレコードなどの企業の仕事を行なう。その他、ニューヨークのスクール・オブ・ビジュアル・アートの講師を勤めたり、アート・ディレクターやファッション・コーディネーターとしても幅広く活躍している。

ロバート・ハント 140

1952年、カリフォルニア州バークレーに生まれる。バンク・オブ・アメリカ、テキサス・インスツルメント、バンタム・ブックス、デル出版などの企業のイラストを手がける。ロサンゼルス・ソサエティ・オブ・イラストレーターズおよびウェスタン・アート・ディレクターズ・クラブから賞を受けている。

ビル・イムホフ 141

1944年、カリフォルニア州ロサンゼルスに生まれる。レコード・ジャケットや雑誌や単行本の表紙、ポスター、スタジオ・アートなどの仕事をしている。

グレン・イワサキ 142

ロサンゼルスに生まれる。1972年にフリーランスとなり、デザイン・スタジオ、広告会社、レコード会社、そして雑誌などの仕事に従事。1979−81年、アートディレクターとしてボウマー・ノーブル出版社の仕事をし、1981年からはナショナル・フットボール・リーグの衣裳や28のクラブのキャラクター商品等のアートディレクターをつとめた。最近は建築要覧や数学入門書などの本のイラストを手がける。ロボットや機械などの絵が多く、ペン、インク、水彩絵具、カラーペンシルなどさまざまな方法を用いて制作している。

バリー・ジャクソン 143

空軍の軍人家庭に育ったため、子供時代は各地を転々としたが、主にカリフォルニアに住んだ。早くから自分に絵の才能があることに気づき、大学で絵を学ぼうと思い立つ。アートセンター・カレッジ・オブ・デザインを卒業した後、映画「アメリカンポップ」と「指輪物語」の背景イラストレーションにたずさわる。1980年にフリーランスとして独立し、映画のキャンペーンを中心に仕事を続けている。

キャシー・ヤコブ 144

1947年、ニューヨーク市に生まれる。カリフォルニア州立大学で修士号を取得。卒業後イラストレーションの道に入る。国立水彩画協会、グラフィック・アーティスト・ギルドのメンバーでもある彼女は、特に水彩画で多くの賞を受賞している。個展、グループ展は全米各地で行なわれ、いずれも好評を博している。

ジェイ 145

1949年生まれ、北イリノイ大学芸術学部を卒業。その後、母校の北イリノイ大学で修士号を取得している。現在はフリーランスのイラストレーターとして仕事をしている。

ユージン・カーリン 146-147

1918年、ウィスコンシン州で生まれ、シカゴ、ニューヨーク、コロラドなど各地の美術学校で学ぶ。卒業後、サンフランシスコ美術館、アロンソ・ギャラリーなどで個展を行なう一方、『フォーチュン』『エスクワイア』『リーダーズ・ダイジェスト』等の主要雑誌に次々と作品を発表し、AIGAで優秀賞、アート・インスティテュート（シカゴ）でクライド・M・カー賞などを受賞した。1954年以降、現在もスクール・オブ・ビジュアルアートで教えている。

ロニー・スー・ジョンソン 148

1950年、ニュージャージー州プリンストンに生まれる。父方はエレクトロニクス・エンジニア、母方が代々芸術家という家系で、幼少のころから音楽や芸術に目ざめ、ピアノ、ヴァイオリン、ビオラ等を習い、高校のオーケストラに入り、プリンストン大学では多くの室内楽で演奏した。オハイオ州のウースター・カレッジに通い、のち、ミシガン大学で建築とデザインを学び、スチュアートカントリー・デイ・スクールで教鞭をとったあと、プロのイラストレーターとなる。その後、ニューヨークのスクール・オブ・ビジュアル・アートで学んだりもした。

ジョイ・M・キルロイ 149

1957年、マサチューセッツ州ボストンの生まれ。パーカー・ブラザーズ、ポラロイド、マクドナルド、ハワード・ジョンソンなどの企業や、『ヤンキー・マガジン』等の雑誌イラストを手がけている。ニューヨーク・ソサエティ・オブ・イラストレーターズ展で受賞。

チョル・サ・キム 150

1958年、日本の福岡県に生まれる。滋賀県へ移り、大阪中の島美術学院に2年間通学。のちアメリカへ渡って、サンフランシスコのアカデミー・オブ・アートに4年間学ぶ。1983年、同校の奨学金、翌1984年にはニューヨークのイラストレーターズ・ソサエティから奨学金を受ける。現在は出版社のハーコート・ブレース、バーナード・ホーズ広告などの仕事を請けている。

テア・クリロス 151

ニューヨークに生まれる。エイボン化粧品、レディー・マンハッタン・シャツ、ハドソンデパート、キャンディーズ・シューズ、『グッド・ハウスキーピング・マガジン』などのイラストを手がけてきた。ニューヨーク・ソサエティ・オブ・イラストレーターズ展などから賞を受けている。現在も『レディーズ・ホーム・ジャーナル』などで活躍。

リチャード・M・クレグラー 152

1946年、ミネソタ州セント・ポールに生まれる。ヒューストン大学に学び、のちミシガン州のクランブロック・アカデミー・オブ・アートで学位を取得。1973年にカリフォルニア州ロサンゼルスに移り、ロンドン・レコードのジャケット・イラストを手がけたりして、1979年にスタジオを構えた。ロサンゼルス・アート・ディレクターズ賞やニューヨーク・アート・ディレクターズ賞等、いくつかの受賞歴がある。現在はITT、ABCテレビ、20世紀フォックス映画、コンチネンタル航空などのクライアントを抱えて仕事をしている。

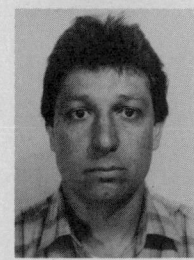

ジョン・A・カーツ 153

1942年にイリノイ州シカゴで生まれる。アート・インスティテュート・オブ・シカゴを卒業し、1969年初めての個展を開く。雑誌『プレイボーイ』とは縁が深く、80年10月号の"Loon Lake"のイラストで、翌年アート・ディレクターズ・クラブとソサエティ・オブ・パブリケーション・デザイナーズの優秀賞を連続受賞した。1984年はアート・インスティテュート・オブ・シカゴの第80回グループ展に出品。

ボブ・カーツ　154-155

カリフォルニア州ロサンゼルスに生まれる。シェイナード・アート・インスティテュート卒業。カーツ&フレンドを主宰。エンターテインメント映画やテレビ・コマーシャル映画のプロデューサー、ライター、デザイナー、ディレクターとして幅広く活躍している。ニューヨーク近代美術館、サンフランシスコ美術館、ロサンゼルス郡立美術館等には作品が永久保存されている。ロサンゼルスのソサエティ・オブ・イラストレーターズ展、ポーランド・クラコウの国際短編映画祭やニューヨーク国際映画祭などで数々の賞を受けている。

デイブ・ラフローア　156

コロラド・インスティテュート・オブ・アートを卒業。在学中よりシカゴの広告会社レオ・バーネットの仕事を手がける。卒業後、『デンバー』『ロサンゼルス』『キャンパス・ライフ』などの雑誌をはじめ、多くの仕事に取り組んでいる。デンバーのアート・ディレクターズ・クラブなどから賞を受けている。1983年には、彼の所属するマスグレイブ・アンド・フレンズによるカリフォルニア・ワイン・フェスティバルのポスターが好評を博した。

ジム・ラム　157

1946年にモンタナ州ハミルトンで生まれる。『コミュニケーション・アート』誌で優秀賞、ソサエティ・オブ・イラストレーターズ賞など数々の賞を受賞。映画ポスター、書籍・雑誌のカバーイラスト、カレンダー、企業プロモーションなど、さまざまな仕事を手がけてきた。現在は上記の仕事のほかにマクドナルドのキャンペーンなどを担当している。彼の作品は、ホワイトハウス、ペンタゴン、スミソニアンなどの各美術館がコレクションしている。

ソール・ランバート　158

1928年にニューヨークのブロンクスで生まれる。ブルックリン大学を卒業後、イタリアのフィレンツェへ渡り、美術学校で学ぶ。イスラエルへ行き、2年間滞在してアメリカに戻った。1960年からフリーランスとなり、AIGA、ニューヨークのソサエティ・オブ・イラストレーターズ、アートディレクターズ・クラブなどから多数の賞を受けている。

ジョアン・ランディス　159

1928年、オハイオ州クリーブランドに生まれる。エクソン、IBM、アメリカ歴史協会などの仕事をこなし、最近では合衆国の郵便切手や『レディース・ホーム・ジャーナル』誌のイラスト、カレンダーなどのイラストなども描いている。作品はアメリカ国内だけでなく、ヨーロッパにも渡っている。

バーニー・レティック　160-162

1919年、コネチカット州ニューヘブンに生まれる。1942年イエール大学を卒業し、イラストレーションと絵画の世界に入る。1940年代後期から1960年にかけて、『コリアーズ』『タイム』『リーダーズ・ダイジェスト』等のカバーイラスト、ゼネラル・エレクトリック、コカコーラ、ゼネラル・モーターズ社のキャンペーンに作品を提供し、名声を確立した。肖像画や静物における彼のリアリズムは、1970年、一群の映画ポスターに発揮された。「天国からのチャンピオン」「ファールプレイ」「アルカトラズからの脱出」などは、映画ポスター史上に残る作品ばかりである。

ベット・リバイン　163

1951年、カリフォルニア州ハリウッドに生まれる。アート・センター・カレッジ・オブ・デザインを卒業。1983年にはカリフォルニア州立大学で開かれた現代イラストレーター・グループ展に出品している。作品の一部は、ブライアン・ジックやデニス・ムカイなどの個人の愛好家に収められている。

ティム・ルイス　164

1937年、ミシガン州に生まれる。アメリカの大手企業の広告や、書籍・雑誌・新聞などのイラストを手がけている。また、作品はアメリカン・インスティテュート・オブ・グラフィック・アート、ニューヨーク・ディレクターズ・クラブ、シカゴ・ディレクターズ・クラブなどの展覧会に出品、出版物に収録されている。

エド・リンドロフ　165

1943年、カリフォルニア州ロングビーチに生まれる。アメリカ国内および海外の大手企業の広告のイラストを中心に、その他、本や雑誌のイラストも手がけてきた。ニューヨーク・ソサエティ・オブ・イラストレーターズや、ニューヨーク・アート・ディレクターズ・クラブ、アメリカン・インスティテュート、オブ・グラフィック・アート（AIGA）、コミュニケーション・アート等の展覧会に出品、受賞している。現在はAIGA、ニューヨーク・ソサエティ・オブ・イラストレーターズ、グラフィック・アーティスト・ギルド会員。

スー・ルウェリン　166

1946年、オハイオ州デイトンに生まれる。テキサス州にある北テキサス州立大学を卒業。『ヴォーグ』『サンデー』や『ダラス・ライフ』『アメリカン・ウェイ』などの雑誌のイラストの仕事に従事。ダラスやニューヨークばかりでなく、パリやカナダのトロントなどの展示会にも作品を出品している。また、ロサンゼルスのメトロ・ギャラリーなどで個展も開いた。

ジョン・ライクス　167

1952年にカリフォルニア州ロングビーチで生まれる。1979年にヨーロッパへ渡り、83年まで各地を描いて旅をする。現在はイラストレーターだけでなく、ファインアートの分野でも活躍している。映画やTVにも出演しており、異色派俳優としても有名である。

ダニエル・マフィア　168

1937年フランスに生まれる。1957年アメリカに渡り、アメリカ国民となる。『タイム』『プレイボーイ』『エスクワイア』などの雑誌のイラストを手がけてきた。ニューヨーク・ソサエティ・オブ・イラストレーターズ主催の展覧会で銀メダルを獲得している。現在も、『タイム』『レッドブック』『フォーチュン』などの雑誌を中心に活躍。トランプ・タワーやウェスト・ブロードウェイ・ギャラリーなどで個展を開いている。

グレッグ・マンチェス　169

1955年にケンタッキーで生まれる。西ミネアポリス美術デザイン大学に通ったが、今日の地位をつくりあげた要素は、独学で習得したものがむしろ多いようである。短期間だが、カリフォルニア美術工芸大学でも学んだ。ミネアポリス大学卒業後、ヘルマン・デザイン・アソシエーツという会社でイラストレーターとして2年ほど働く。その後フリーランスとして独立したが、シカゴでダン・セルと出会い、現在に至る。

リチャード・マンテル　170

1941年、オハイオ州に生まれる。モービル、U.S.インフォメーション・サービスなどのポスターや、『タイム』誌、ランダムハウス、サイモン&シュスター社などの書籍の表紙、およびエレクトラ・レコードのジャケット・イラストを手がける。ニューヨーク・ソサエティ・オブ・イラストレーターズ、アメリカン・インスティテュート・オブ・グラフィック・アート、ニューヨーク・アート・ディレクターズ・クラブなどから賞を受けている。現在も本や雑誌のイラストを中心に活躍している。

マーク・メレック　171

1956年、テキサス州ダラスに生まれる。ニューヨーク・タイムズをはじめとする雑誌やハーパー＆ロー社の本のイラスト等に従事。1982年と1983年には、イラストレーター協会より賞を受けている。作品にはユーモアあふれるものが多い。

シンシア・マーシュ　172

1948年にマサチューセッツ州ボストンで生まれる。現在までに約50の個展、グループ展をこなし、1982年にヴェスタ賞、1984年にニューグラント賞を受ける。A＆M、CBS、MCAなどの各レコード会社や、『プレイガール』『アート・アンド・アーキテクチュア』誌、マイケル・サルスベリ・デザイン、ロッド・ダイアなどのための仕事をしている。彼女の作品は歌手のジョニー・ミッチェルや、カリフォルニア州立大学等がコレクションしている。

ジョン・J・マルチネス　173

1950年、フロリダ州マイアミに生まれる。ニューヨーク・タイムズや『GQ』誌、RCAレコードなどのイラストに従事。ソサエティ・オブ・アメリカン・イラストレーターズやニューヨーク・アート・ディレクターズ・クラブなどにも作品を出品している。作品のいくつかは、スミソニアン美術館、国会図書館などに収められている。

マーヴィン・マテルソン　174

1947年、ペンシルバニア州フィラデルフィアに生まれる。『タイム』『ニューズウィーク』『ペントハウス』『プレイボーイ』などの雑誌や、デル、バンタム、ワーナー、バークレイなどの各出版社の単行本イラストをはじめ、メリル・リンチ、リンカーン、マーキュリーなどの企業の広告に至るまで幅広く活躍している。イラストレーターズ協会やニューヨーク・アート・ディレクターズ・クラブなどから受賞。

ビル・メイヤー　175

1951年、アラバマ州バーミンガムで生まれる。テネシー州メンフィス、ニューヨーク、ジョージアと転居したが、1972年にリングリング美術学校を卒業。アトランタのグラフィック・グループに属して4年間仕事をし、その後ホール・ホン・スタジオと共同して多くの経験を積んだ。1980年以降、フリーランサーとしてアトランタで活躍している。

デイヴッド・M・マッティングレー　176-177

1956年、コロラド州フォート・コリンズに生まれる。幼少時より絵に興味を抱き、コロラド・インスティテュート・オブ・アート、アート・センター・カレッジ・オブ・デザインなどに学ぶ。ウォルト・ディズニー・スタジオで働き、その時の作品「ブラック・ホール」がアカデミー賞を受賞。その後、フリーランスとして、本や雑誌、20世紀フォックスやユニバーサル映画、あるいはまたトッコ・オイル会社などの企業からイラストの仕事を請けている。

ジェリー・マクドナルド　178

1940年にオレゴン州コルバリスで生まれる。オレゴン大学で絵画、ドローイング、印刷を学び、大学院進む。この間、講師としてドローイングやカリグラフィを教える。卒業後フリーランスとなり、『ローリング・ストーン』『プレイボーイ』『ウォール・ストーリート・ジャーナル』のカバーおよびエディトリアル、CBSレコード、シェブロン、バンク・オブ・アメリカ、ヤマハのプロモーション等を手がけてきた。ウェスタン・アート・ディレクターズ年度賞、ソサエティ・オブ・コミュニケーション・アート賞などを数回にわたり受賞している。

カレン・M・マクドナルド　179

1956年にノースカロライナ州ローリーで生まれる。アトランタ・カレッジ・オブ・アートで絵を学ぶ。1980年に同校を卒業。イラストレーターとなる。2年後、フロリダ・ガルフ・コースト・アートセンター展で3位に入賞し、幸運なスタートを切り、『サンフランシスコ・マガジン』『PC・ワールド』『ウェストマガジン』などの仕事を手がけるようになる。IBMをはじめとするアメリカの大手企業が彼女の作品をコレクションしている。

ミック・マクギンティ　180

1952年、アイオワ州シオックスに生まれる。ロサンゼルスに移り、アート・センター・デザイン・カレッジに学ぶ。卒業後デザイン・スタジオで働き、やがて独立して、ドクター・ペッパーやリーバイスなどの企業、レコード・アルバムの表紙、ワーナー・ブラザーズ、20世紀フォックスなどの映画キャンペーンイラストなどの仕事を手がける。繊細な筆のタッチと、色彩の豊かさが作品からうかがわれる。コミュニケーション・アート・ソサエティなどで受賞。

マーク・マクマホン　181

シカゴを中心に雑誌、書籍、企業年次報告書、カタログなど、いろいろな形で作品を発表している。クライアントには『スポーツ・イラストレイテッド』、シカゴ・トリビューン、コカコーラなど、アメリカの主要な企業や出版社が名を連ねる。シカゴとコロラドをテーマにした一連のポスターと版画は、彼の名を一躍有名にした。スタンダードオイル、NASA、米国空軍等が彼の作品を永久保存のコレクションに決めている。

ウィルソン・マクリーン　182

1937年、スコットランドに生まれる。15歳でイラストレーターとしてイギリスのシルクスクリーン・ショップに勤め、1966年にニューヨークに移ったが、ロンドン、コペンハーゲンで働いたこともある。『タイム』『スポーツ・イラストレイテッド』『ペントハウス』『エスクワイア』などの仕事を手がけてきた。ソサエティ・オブ・イラストレーターズから金賞を3回、銀賞を7回受け、その他多くの受賞歴がある。マンハッタンのスクール・オブ・ビジュアル・アートやケント州立大学で教鞭をとったこともある。夫人は写真家のローズマリー・フォワード。

ジェームス・マクマラン　184

1934年、中国の青島で生まれる。ニューヨークのプラッツ・インスティチュートに学ぶ。雑誌、レコード・ジャケット、書籍カバー、ポスター、広告イラスト、アニメフィルムなど、幅広い創作活動を行なっている。アーティストかつ職人としての質の高さを保ちながら、文字や言葉をどう絵に組み込ませたらよいかを知っている数少ないイラストレーター、デザイナーとして著名である。アメリカン・インスティチュート・オブ・グラフィック・アート、アート・ディレクターズ・クラブなどから受賞。スクール・オブ・ビジュアル・アートで教えている。

フランク・メディエイト　185

コロラド州プエブロで生まれた。ウォルト・ディズニー・プロダクション、トミー玩具、ユニオン石油など大手企業のイラストの仕事に従事している。アメリカ西部イラスト展の最優秀賞などを受賞。

ポール・ミーゼル　186

1955年、ニューヨーク州フリーポートに生まれる。『ニューヨーク』誌、ボストン・グローブ、ニューヨーク・タイムズなどの新聞・雑誌をはじめ、カレンダーなどのイラストを手がけている。アート・ディレクターズ・クラブのバレンタイン・デー展覧会などにも作品を出品している。ニューヨークのリゾヴリィ・ギャラリーでエッチング展。

ゲーリー・メール 187

1960年、ニューヨーク市で生まれる。1981年にニューヨーク・ソサエティ・オブ・イラストレーターズ年度賞を受賞。AGIレコードの仕事を経て、『TWAアンバサダー・マガジン』『ノースイースト・マガジン』『セルフ・マガジン』『ニュース・マガジン』『エスクワイヤ』などのクライアントを得た。ニューヨークのマスターイーグル・ギャラリーで展覧会を行なっている。

ポール・メリア 188

1929年にオハイオ州デイトンで生まれる。H&Hアートスタジオでイラストレーターとして働き、1976年にフリーランスとなる。西部オハイオ水彩協会秋期展で1位を5回受賞するなどの実績をかわれて、ボールドウィンピアノ、ジェネラルタイヤ、ジェネラルエレクトリックなど多数のクライアントを得た。オハイオを中心に、個展・グループ展も盛んに行なっている。

リック・マイヤーウイッツ 189

1943年、ニューヨーク市に生まれる。16歳のときから仕事としてイラストを描いていた。アメリカ国内にとどまらず、広くヨーロッパ、オーストラリアなど世界各国の企業のイラストの仕事に従事してきた。諷刺画でおなじみである。日本で展覧会を開いたこともある。現在は『世界の鳥』という本を書いている。近く出版の予定。

ゲーリー・メイヤー 190-191

1934年にミズーリ州のブーンビルで生まれる。映画「ザ・ディープ」「ジョーズ3D」のプロモーション、シカゴやジャクソンズ、ビーチボーイズのレコードジャケットを担当し、現在の地位を築いた。ソサエティ・オブ・イラストレーターズ、アートディレクターズ・クラブ、TIMAなどから数えきれないほどの賞を受けている。現在もユニバーサル・ピクチャーズ、MGM、ディズニー、リーバイスなど、世界に名だたるクライアンドを得て、創作を続けている。

ウェンデル・マイナー 192

1944年、イリノイ州オーロラの出身。『アトランチッチ・マガジン』『マッコール・マガジン』のサイモン&シュスターの出版する本のイラストに従事。ニューヨーク・アート・ディレクターズ・クラブやソサエティ・オブ・イラストレーターズなど各種協会より賞を受けている。国会図書館やアリゾナ歴史財団などに作品が収められている。

ポール・モック 193

1959年、イリノイ州シカゴに生まれる。『プレイボーイ』『シカゴ・マガジン』『マネー・メーカー』『インサイド・スポーツ・マガジン』『サクセス・マガジン』など、雑誌を中心とした仕事を手がけている。アメリカン・ソサエティ・オブ・グラフィック・アートのカバー・ショーで受賞。

マリリン・モンゴメリー 194

ペッパーディン大学およびアート・センター・カレッジ・オブ・デザインを卒業。ウォルト・ディズニー・プロダクションやハナ・バーベラなどで陰のアーティストとして働いてきた。フリーランスのイラストレーターになってからは、MCAレコードなど大手企業の広告の仕事を手がけたり、ロサンゼルス・シティ・カレッジで講師を勤めたりしている。1981年にはソサエティ・オブ・イラストレーターズより賞を受けている。エアブラシを使った作品がお得意である。

デイヴィッド・モンティエール 195

1949年、メキシコのモレロスに生まれる。『ビジネスウィーク・マガジン』や『ディスカバー・マガジン』などの雑誌の表紙や、チバ・ガイギー社の薬剤パンフレット・カバーのイラストなどを多く手がけている。ニューヨークのソサエティ・オブ・イラストレーターズをはじめとして各種展覧会において賞を獲得している。

ジャッキー・モーガン 196

ニューヨークのプラット・インスティテュートで学び、ハンター・カレッジで学位を取る。現在はプラット・インスティテュートで教壇に立つ。ソサエティ・オブ・イラストレーターズやフェデラル・デザイン・カウンシルなどで50を超す賞を受けている。ワルシャワ国際ポスタービエンナーレで入賞するなど、国際的にも活躍し、また、ヨーロッパ各地の大学や美術学校に招かれて講演する機会も多い。彼女の作品はスミソニアン・インスティテュート、ワルシャワ美術館等がコレクションしている。

フランク・K・モリス 197

1950年、テネシー州メンフィスに生まれる。ポール・ペンツナーに師事し、メンフィス・アート・アカデミーやメンフィス州立大学で学ぶ。もとは広告のデザイナー兼ディレクターであったが、デザイン・スタジオを設立してアート・センター・デザイン・カレッジに入学してからはイラストの方に転じた。現在はフリーランスで、『ニューズウィーク』『ニューヨーク・マガジン』や、ABC放送などの仕事に従事している。ソサエティ・オブ・イラストレーターズ展やコミュニケーション・アート展には、毎年のように作品を出品している。

デニス・ムカイ 198

1956年、日本の広島に生まれる。パサディナ・カレッジ、アート・センター・デザイン・カレッジに学ぶ。プレイボーイ・ジャズフェスティバルのプログラム・カバーや、「メリークリスマス・ミスター・ローレンス」などの映画ポスターを手がけてきた。現在は『プレイボーイ』誌やグリーティングカードのペーパー・ムーン・グラフィックの仕事をしている。ソサエティ・オブ・イラストレーターズより受賞。

タク・ムラカミ 199

1933年、カリフォルニア州アナヘイムに生まれる。『シカゴ』『シカゴ・トリビューン』『ロータリアン』などの雑誌や『エンサイクロペディア・ブリタニカ』など百科事典のイラストに従事。ニューヨーク・ソサエティ・オブ・イラストレーターズや、シカゴ・アート・ディレクターズ・クラブなどから賞を受ける。現在も各種企業の広告イラストを手がけている。

ビル・ネルソン 200

1946年、バージニア州リッチモンドに生まれる。『ニューズウィーク』や『ワシントン・ポスト』などの表紙をはじめ、『テレビ・ガイド』『プレイボーイ』『エスクワイア』などの雑誌イラストのほか、CBS放送、マクドナルド、モービル石油、パーカー・ブラザーズなど大手企業の広告なども幅広く手がける。ニューヨークのソサエティ・オブ・イラストレーターズから銀メダル、アートディレクターズ・クラブより金メダルを受けている。

ウイル・ネルソン 201

1932年、アイダホ州ツイン・ホールズの生まれ。RCAレコードやダウ・ケミカルなどの各種企業のイラスト、広告の仕事等に従事してきた。シカゴ・アート・ディレクターズ・クラブ、アカデミック・アーティスツ・アソシエーションなどから賞を受けている。ニッカーボッカー・クラブやノースウエスト水彩画協会などの展覧会に作品を発表。現在のクライアントには、MGM、バンク・オブ・アメリカなどがある。

メレディス・ネミロフ　202

1955年、ニューヨーク市に生まれる。ＲＣＡレコードアルバムの表紙や、レブロン、エイボンなど化粧品のパッケージ・デザイン、『マネー』誌やバーガー・キングなどの広告キャンペーン、『レッド・ブック』やニューヨーク・タイムズのイラストと幅広い活動をしている。1977年以降、毎年の展覧会に作品を発表、1983年は、ニューヨークのソサエティ・オブ・イラストレーターズ年度展などに出品した。

バーバラ・ネッシム　203

1939年にニューヨーク州ニューヨーク市で生まれる。1960年にプラット・インスティテュートを卒業、翌年ソサエティ・オブ・イラストレーターズから初めての賞を受賞して以来、同協会の特別賞を含めて100以上の賞を獲得している。スクール・オブ・ビジュアル・アートやプラッツ・インスティテュートで教壇に立つ一方で、アメリカ、東欧諸国、ドイツ、日本、韓国の雑誌などにも意欲的に作品を発表し続けている。

スーザン・ナザレー　204

1939年、カリフォルニア州コビナの生まれ。カーネーション食品やトミー玩具、ゼロックス社のためのイラストから、ユニオン石油やマックスファクターの広告、ハーコート・ブレース、マクミランなどの出版社の児童書イラストと幅広く活躍。アメリカン・インスティテュート・オブ・グラフィック・アートなどから賞を受けている。また、ロサンゼルス・アート・ディレクターズ・クラブなどの展覧会にも作品を出品している。

メル・オドム　205

1950年、バージニア州リッチモンドに生まれる。幼少時よりウォルト・ディズニーやテレビなどの影響を受け、その後バージニア州立大学でファッション・イラストレーションを専攻。また、イギリスに渡り、リード・ポリテクニック・インスティテュートでも学んでいる。雑誌や本および企業の広告のイラストに従事。ソサエティ・オブ・イラストレーターズから二度受賞。その他クーパー・ヒューイット美術館のグループ展などで作品を展示発表している。日本でも画集が出版されている。

J・ラファル・オルビンスキー　206

1945年、ポーランドに生まれる。ジャズ・フェスティバルのポスターや、ユネスコ、ポーランド映画、ＣＢＳレコードの表紙などを手がけてきた。フランスで開かれた世界ポスター・コンテストでは第一位に、またオーストリアでの世界ジャズ連盟主催のコンテストでも一位を獲得している。現在はニューヨークに在住し、ニューヨーク・タイムズ、『タイム』、ＲＣＡレコードなどのイラストに従事している。作品の一部はポーランドのワルシャワやパリ、ニューヨークのカーネギー財団などに納められている。

ジム・オーエンス　207

シラキュース大学やアート・スチューデント・リーグなどで学ぶ。1978年から1981年の3年間、バージニア・ビーチの"スタッフ・スタジオ"でデザインやイラストの仕事に従事。ＡＴ＆Ｔ、デュポン、マクドナルド、『ビデオゲーム・マガジン』などのイラストを手がける。シラキュース・ソサエティ・オブ・コミュニケーティング・アートなどから金賞・銀賞を受けている。

ジャック・パルデュー　208

ノースカロライナ州ローリイに生まれる。少年時代、家族の肖像やアンティックカーを描いて早くもその才能を現わし、フロリダ州サラソタのリングリング美術学校を出てからはフリーランスの画家、イラストレーターとして活躍している。現在はワシントンに在住。40歳。ホワイトハウスに展示されているカウボーイハットのジョージ・ワシントンの肖像画は特に有名である。また、タイム・ライフ・ジャズアルバム・シリーズのジャズミュージシャンの肖像などで知られる。今も1800年代のカウボーイとアメリカンインディアンをテーマにした作品を精力的に描く。

アル・パーカー　209-211

1927年にバージニア州ノーフォークで生まれる。1948年から1952年までシカゴのアート・インスティテュートに通う。卒業後、ニューヨークのアトリエ・セブンティーンに入り、イラストレーターとしてスタートした。その作品は内外から高い評価を受けている。アメリカ建国200年記念ポスター・ビエンナーレに参加している他、児童向き絵本のさし絵なども多く描いている。現代アメリカのもっとも偉大なイラストレーターの一人であり、カレン・E・コバー、バーナード・フォックス、マーク・イングリッシュなどを育てたことでも知られる。

ゲーリー・パターソン　212-213

1941年にカリフォルニア州ロサンゼルスで生まれる。スポーツものを得意としており、合衆国スポーツアーティスト年度賞などを受賞している。これまでに『ゴルフ・マガジン』『スキー・マガジン』、ソニー、ラングラー、ＣＢＳＴＶなどの仕事を手がけてきた。最近は1984年度夏期・冬期オリンピックポスターをはじめ、アメリカ国内だけでなく広くヨーロッパにまでクライアントを得て活躍している。

ボブ・ピーク　214-217

コロラド州デンバーで生まれた。カンサスのウィチタ州立大学とロサンゼルスのアートセンター・カレッジ・オブ・デザインを卒業後、フリーランスのイラストレーターとして出発し、以来はなばなしく活躍して、今世紀最高最大とまでいわれている超大物である。彼の作品は『スポーツ・イラストレイテッド』『ＴＶガイド』『コスモポリタン』など主要雑誌に載せられ、グッドリッチゴム、ウィンストン・シガレットなどの大企業がクライアントである。「マイ・フェア・レディ」「キャメロット」「ザッツ・エンターテイメント」など大作映画の広告美術を担当した。

ジム・ピアソン　218

1956年、カリフォルニア州サン・メテオに生まれる。パシフィック・プレス社出版の雑誌『サン・ホセ・マーキュリー・ニュース』のほか、『サンシャイン・マガジン』『トゥデイ』『リッスン・マガジン』などのイラストを手がけている。

エヴァレット・ペック　219

1950年、カリフォルニア州サンディエゴの生まれ。ＣＢＳレコードのアルバム表紙、20世紀フォックス映画のポスター、モービル石油社などのアニメーションデザイン、ニューヨーク・タイムズ、『プレイボーイ』など新聞・雑誌のイラスト等、幅広く活躍している。ロサンゼルス・ソサエティ・オブ・イラストレーターズ、フィラデルフィア・アート・ディレクターズ・クラブ、ロサンゼルス・アートディレクターズ・クラブなどから数々の賞を受ける。作品の一部は、ワシントンのスミソニアン・インスティテュートにも収められている。

ジュディ・ペダーソン　220

1957年、ニューヨークのブルックリンに生まれる。いろいろな本の表紙や、グリーティング・カード、その他エディトリアル関係のイラストを手がける。現在はランダム・ハウス、サイモン＆シュスター、サンライズ出版社、タイムライフ、ニューヨーク・タイムズなど、本や雑誌や新聞のイラストを中心に活躍している。

ロバート・ペルース　221

1937年、ニューヨーク市に生まれる。クルツ＆フレンドのアニメ・フィルムのデザインや、レイチュル・ベリー化粧品の宣伝およびパッケージ・デザイン、ホールマーク・カードのイラストなどを手がける。ロサンゼルスのソサエティ・オブ・イラストレーターズや、アート・ディレクターズ・クラブなどから賞を受けている。

ジュリー・ピーターソン　222

1954年、カリフォルニア州パロ・アルトに生まれる。ペーパー・ムーン社のグリーティング・カードのイラストや、アポ財団法人のポスターなどの仕事を手がける。団体展に出品のほか、個展も行ない、第18回ロサンゼルス・ソサエティ・オブ・イラストレーターズ展などでは賞を受けている。

クライヴ・ピアシー　223

1955年、イギリスのチェルトナムに生まれる。ブライトン・カレッジ・オブ・アート・アンド・デザインを卒業。ビジュアル・コミュニケーションで学位を取る。1977年から81年までイギリスBBCテレビのデザイナーをつとめたが、現在はロサンゼルスに住み、ダイヤー・カーン社のアートディレクターとして活動している。ブリティッシュ・アソシエーション・オブ・イラストレーターズと、ザ・ニュー・アメリカン・イラストレーション・ショーで受賞している。

ジェリー・ピンクニー　224-225

1939年、ペンシルバニア州のフィラデルフィアで生まれる。切手のデザインを多く手がけており、ハリエット・タブマンやマーティン・ルーサー・キングJrらが彼の手によって切手の上によみがえった。『コミニュケーション・アート』『アメリカン・アーティスト』等の雑誌が彼の作品を取りあげており、ジェネラルエレクトリック、カナダドライ、メイシーデパート、NASAや、デル、ハーパー＆ロウなどの出版社がクライアントとしてついている。また、個展・グループ展をボストン美術館、ロードアイランド黒人選民教会等で行ない、いろいろな賞を受けている。

パオラ・ピグリア　226

1955年、イタリアのチューリンで生まれる。『エスクァイア』『ローリング・ストーン』『ミズ』『セブンティーン』デイリー・ニューズ等のエディトリアル・イラストのほか、企業のプロモーション・ポスターなどを手がけている。アメリカン・イラストレーション、グラフィス・ショーで受賞。

スコット・ポラック　227

1958年、ニューヨークで生まれる。雑誌『ランナー』『ビジネス・ウィーク』『ウォールストリート・ジャーナル』『アウトドア・ライフ』『スキー』等のエディトリアルイラスト、あるいはプロモーションを目的とした広告イラストを中心に活動を続けている。

アイバン・パウエル　228

1936年にフロリダ州のマイアミで生まれる。ニューヨークのソサエティ・オブ・イラストレーターズ、アート・ディレクターズ・クラブから賞を受けている。シラキュース大学とパーソンズ・スクール・オブ・デザインで教える一方、『フォーチュン』『スポーツ・イラストレイテッド』『ニューヨーク・タイムズ』などに作品を発表してきた。現在はアトランティック・レコード、アメリカン・エクスプレス、IBM、『ワーキングウーマン』誌などをクライアントに得て創作を続けている。

ドン・アイバン・パンチャッツ　230-231

1936年に生まれ、スクール・オブ・ビジュアル・アート、クーパー・ユニオン・スクール・オブ・ファインアートで教育を受ける。いくつかの会社で働いた後、1966年フリーランスになり、1970年には自分のスタジオを持つ。全米各地のアート・ディレクターズ・クラブ、ソサエティ・オブ・イラストレーターズより受賞。IBM、エクソン、レミントン、『エスクァイア』『プレイボーイ』『サイエンス・ダイジェスト』など、トップクラスのクライアントに作品を提供、特に『タイム』誌のカバーイラストはスミソニアン・インスティチュートのコレクションとなっている。

ビル・プロクノー　232

1947年にアリゾナ州ホルブロックで生まれる。本や雑誌のイラストを中心に仕事をしており、現在も『スポーツ・イラストレイテッド』『ウェスト・マガジン』『カリフォルニア・アカデミー・サイエンス』『オーシャン・マガジン』などに作品を提供している。アメリカン・インスティチュート・オブ・グラフィックアート、AIGA、ニューヨーク・ソサエティ・オブ・イラストレーターズなどから多くの賞を受けている。

ダン・クウォンストローム　233

1951年、カリフォルニア州ウィリッツで生まれる。雑誌『ウイ』『プレイボーイ』のエディトリアルイラストや、グリーティング・カードの最大手ペーパームーン社の仕事を手がける。現在はウォルト・ディズニー・プロダクションや主要映画会社をクライアントに持ち、活動を続けている。

マイク・クウォン　234-235

1947年、ロサンゼルス生まれのグラフィックデザイナー、イラストレーター。雑誌やレコードジャケットのカバーイラスト、パッケージなど広範囲の仕事をし、現在もメリルリンチ、『タイム』『ニューズウィーク』などをクライアントに持っている。ロサンゼルスのアート・ディレクターズ・クラブ、AIGA、ソサエティ・オブ・イラストレーターズなどから各賞を受賞している。

スコット・レイノルズ　236

1956年、ミシガン州ランシングに生まれる。アメリカン・エクスプレスの年次報告書や、ライフ・タイム・レコードのジャケットなどを手がけ、現在も『テキサス・マンスリー』、ニューヨーク・タイムズ、ザ・ダラス・タイムス・ヘラルド等の雑誌や新聞にイラストを描いている。ニューヨーク・アート・ディレクターズ・クラブ、ダラス・アート・ディレクターズ・クラブなどから受賞。

ウィリアム・レイノルズ　237

1952年にノースカロライナ州グリーンズボロで生まれる。リパブリック航空のポスターやコントロール・データの絵などを手がけ、現在はIBMなどの大手コンピュータ会社をクライアントに持って、主にニューヨークで活動している。ニューヨーク・ソサエティ・オブ・イラストレーターズ展や、1980年度デイトン広告ベストポスター賞などを受けている。

ウィリアム・リーサー　238

1954年、ウィスコンシン州マディソンで生まれる。リーバイス・ジーンズなどの広告キャンペーン、RCAレコードなどのジャケットの制作、『プレイボーイ』誌のエディトルアルイラスト等を手がける。現在も大手雑誌社、レコード会社をクライアントに持ち、旺盛な活動振りを見せている。

フランク・ライリー　239

1949年、ニュージャージー州のペーターソンで生まれる。インダストリアルデザインを学んだ後、美術に転向し、ニューヨークのスクール・オブ・ビジュアル・アートに通学、フリーランスのイラストレーターとなる。ニューヨークのアート・ディレクターズ・クラブからアンディ賞を受けているほか、ソサエティ・オブ・イラストレーターズなどでも受賞。現在は妻や息子と共にニュージャージー州のホーソーンに住んでいる。

ロバート・リスコー 240

1956年、ペンシルバニア州エルウッド・シティに生まれる。彼の作品はブラッド・ベネディクトの一連の著書『フェイム』『ラブ』『クール・キャット』のほか、『アメリカン・イラストレーション 2』、雑誌では『バニティフェア』『タイム』『ヴォーグ』『プレイボーイ』、ニューヨーク・タイムズなどで見ることができる。ニューヨーク・ソサエティ・オブ・イラストレーターズの年度展などにも出品。

スタンレー・ロバーツ 241

1956年、マサチューセッツ州ケンブリッジ生まれ。ニューヨーク・ソサエティ・オブ・イラストレーターズ年度展とグラフィック・デザインUSAで受賞している。クライアントにはプレンティス・アソシエーション、LTXなどが名を連ねる。ロードアイランド州のウッズ・ゲリー・ギャラリーで個展。

ブライアン・ロブレー 242

1949年、カリフォルニア州ロサンゼルス生まれ。ロバート・ケネディ事件の裁判の模様を伝えたイラストが評価され、フリーランスのイラストレーター、デザイナーとしてスタートする。スキーチームのメンバーとして活躍した経験を生かし、動き、構造の微妙なバランスを絵に取り入れている数少ないイラストレーターである。ニューヨーク・ソサエティ・オブ・イラストレーターズの会員でもある彼は、1981年以来20を越える重要な賞を受賞している。現在もロス・オリンピックのポスターや、フランスのスキー会社のための限定版画などを制作している。

ロバート・ロドリゲス 243

1947年ルイジアナ州ニューオーリアンズに生まれる。ニューヨーク・ソサエティ・オブ・イラストレーターズの年間優秀賞、カラー新聞広告賞で第一位、アカデミー賞レコードジャケット部門にノミネートされるなど、数々の賞を受ける。その創作活動もポスター、カレンダー、広告イラスト、グリーティング・カード、エディトリアルなどと幅広い。現在のクライアントはバドワイザー・ビール、ウォルト・ディズニーなど、そうそうたる顔ぶれである。

マリオ・ロセッティ 244

1951年にペンシルバニア州アレンタウンで生まれる。ニューヨーク・ソサエティ・オブ・イラストレーターズの年間賞を受賞している。レコードジャケットの制作のほかに、『ニューヨーク・タイムズ・マガジン』など主要雑誌に作品を発表している。

ジョン・ラッシュ 245

1948年、インディアナ州インディアナポリスで生まれる。『エスクワイア』『プレイボーイ』『ペントハウス』『サイエンス・ダイジェスト』誌や、ランダムハウス、バンタム・ブックス、バレンタイン・ブックスなどに作品を提供し、ほかにIBM、スタンダードオイル、デュポン等の広告プロモーションのイラストも描いている。ソサエティ・オブ・イラストレーターズで金賞ほか各賞を受賞。

トレーシー・ザビン 246

1948年にオレゴン州ユージンで生まれる。オレゴン大学でラ・ベルタ・クラウス氏について学び、次いでイタリアのミラノ、フィレンツェへ渡る。帰国後ブリガム・ヤング大学で学位を取り、卒業後グラフィックデザイナー、およびイラストレーターとしてスタートをする。アニメーション・フィルムやショッピングセンターの仕事を手がけ、1973年には初の個展を開く。1981年にニューヨーク・ソサエティ・オブ・イラストレーターズ年度展に作品「たなばた」を出品、その実力を認められた。

ジム・サルバティ 247

1957年、カリフォルニア州ロサンゼルスに生まれる。ベル・テレフォン、ビュイック等への広告イラストや、主要レコード会社のレコード・ジャケットの仕事をする。現在は仕事の幅をさらに広げて20世紀フォックスのポスターや、アメリカ最大のグリーティング・カードの会社ペーパームーン・グラフィックスのポストカード制作にも意欲的に取り組んでいる。

エマニュエル・ションクット 248

1938年、ニューヨーク州モンティセロで生まれる。プラット・インスティチュートを卒業後、ニューヨーク・ソサエティ・オブ・イラストレーターズ、AIGA等から受賞。劇場用ポスター、絵本、あるいは『エスクワイア』『コスモポリタン』『レッドブック』『ニューヨーク・タイムス・マガジン』のエディトリアル、CBSレコードのプロモーションなどの仕事を手がけている。

ダニエル・シュワルツ 249

1929年生まれの生粋のニューヨーカーである。『ライフ』『スポーツ・イラストレイテッド』『マッコールズ』『レッドブック』『タイム』『ニューズウィーク』など主要誌に作品を発表し、モービル石油、H.J.ハインツといった大会社のプロモーションにも協力している。過去に8回の個展を開いている。イラストレーターズ協会賞を初めとする各賞で8つの金賞を獲得している実力派である。

ジェフェリー・シーバー 250

1952年、ネブラスカ州オマハに生まれる。大手出版社ならびにニューヨーク・タイムズ、『フォーチュン』、アメリカン・エクスプレス、『ビジネスウィーク』などを含む大手企業500社の広告イラストを手がけてきた。ニューヨーク・ソサエティ・オブ・イラストレーターズ展や、各地のアートディレクターズ・クラブなどから多くの賞を受けている。東京でアメリカン・ユーモア・イラスト展が開かれたときにも出品している。

イサドーア・セルツァー 251

1930年、ミズーリ州セントルイスで生まれる。ロサンゼルス・シティ・カレッジ、シェイナード・インスティチュート、アートセンターで学び、兵役を終えた後、イラストレーターとして出発する。スクール・オブ・ビジュアル・アート、シラキュース大学、パーソンズ等で教えながら、コブコ、デュポン、N.W.、アイヤーなどの仕事を手がけてきた。彼の仕事の50パーセントは広告イラストであり、かつて教え子であったADたちとの仕事を非常に楽しんでいるという。ソサエティ・オブ・イラストレーターズ展やアート・ディレクターズ展、AIGAなどから受賞。

R・J・シェイ 252

1950年生まれ。南イリノイ大学で美術を学び、1972年からイラストレーターとして活躍している。ミズーリ州セントルイス在住。

マモル・シモコウチ 253

1942年、日本で生まれる。1963年に留学のため渡米。バークレイ・ユニファイド・スクール、その後アートセンター・カレッジ・オブ・デザインで学ぶ。卒業後、ソール・バス・アソシエイツにグラフィックデザイナーとして入社、この間、味の素、ユナイテッド航空の仕事を手がける。1974年に独立して事務所を持ち、フリーランスのイラストレーター、グラフィックデザイナーとして活躍している。ロサンゼルス在住。

ウィリアム・スローン　254

1954年、ペンシルバニア州フィラデルフィアで生まれる。旅行ポスターや、アート・エクスポ・ニューヨークのポスター、『レッドブック』などの雑誌イラストを手がけてきたが、現在もエイボン化粧品、レブロン、ニューヨーク・タイムズ等のクライアントを持って仕事をしている。ニューヨーク・ソサエティ・オブ・イラストレーターズ展、ニューヨーク・アート・ディレクターズ展などで賞を受けている。

ダグ・スミス　255

1952年、ニューヨーク州ニューヨークで生まれる。ボストン・グローブ紙、『ボストン・マガジン』『ローリング・ストーン』『クロスカントリー・スキーヤー』など、新聞・雑誌のイラストを中心に仕事をしている。ニューヨーク・ソサエティ・オブ・イラストレーターズ展、アート・ディレクターズ・クラブ展などで受賞。

ジェス・スミスバック　256

1948年にカンサス州ウェリントンで生まれる。ファースト・ナショナル・バンク、ユナイテッド・ナショナル・バンクなどの企業プロモーションに多くたずさわってきた。現在もこの路線で、中南部中心に創作活動を続けている。ウィチタ・アート・ディレクターズ賞を受賞している。

グレッグ・スパレンカ　257

1958年、カリフォルニア州アルカディアで生まれる。『ローリング・ストーン』『カリフォルニア・マガジン』などの依頼を受けて仕事をしてきた。現在も雑誌のカバーおよびエディトリアルイラストを中心に、独自の世界を展開している。1983年には初めての個展を開いた。ニューヨーク・ソサエティ・オブ・イラストレーターズ展で年度賞を受けている。

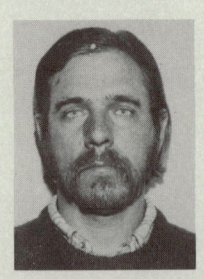

ランディ・スピア　258

1958年にカリフォルニア州ロサンゼルスで生まれる。主に雑誌のカバーイラストを多く手がけており、現在はさらに枠を広げて、レコードジャケットや広告イラスト、企業プロモーションなどの仕事も行なっている。

バロン・ストアリー　259

1940年、テキサス州ダラスに生まれる。ロサンゼルスのアート・センター・スクールとニューヨークのスクール・オブ・ビジュアル・アートに学ぶ。フリーランスのイラストレーターとして活躍。1976年にはソサエティ・オブ・イラストレーターズ展で金賞、1977年にはアート・ディレクターズ・クラブで最優秀賞、その他多くの賞を受けている。彼の作品では、国立肖像画ギャラリーに収められている一連の肖像画が有名である。母校のアートセンター・カレッジ・オブ・デザインとシラキュース大学、ニューヨークのプラット・インスティテュートで教壇に立った。

ジョージ・スタブリノス　260-261

1948年、マサチューセッツ州ボストンに生まれる。ニューヨークを中心に、デパートのイメージイラストや、エディトリアルで次々に作品を発表している。1981年には個展を開催。彼の作品はフィリップ・モリス・コーポレーション、メトロポリタン美術館に集められている。1984年、ニューヨーク・ソサエティ・オブ・イラストレーターズ展で年度賞を受賞。

デュガルド・スターマー　262-263

1936年、カリフォルニア州ロサンゼルスに生まれる。リーバイス、バンク・オブ・アメリカ、メジャー雑誌の仕事を手がけるかたわら、『芸術革命』『絶滅した生物』『絶滅した植物』の3冊の著書をものしている。フリーランスのイラストレーター、雑誌の編集者として忙しい毎日を送りながら、4冊目の著書に取り組んでいる。AIGA、ソサエティ・オブ・イラストレーターズ、アメリカン・イラストレーションなどで各賞を受賞。

スーザン・スミックラスト　264

1946年にミネソタ州ミネアポリスに生まれる。ユニークな布絵を次々に発表し、ニューヨーク・ソサエティ・オブ・イラストレーターズ展で5回連続受賞の実績を持つ。クライアントにはアメリカの主要雑誌が名を連ね、アート・ディレクターズ・クラブではソフト・スカルプチャーのクラスを受け持ち、講議も行なっている。

ジョージ・スエオカ　265

1926年、ハワイのホノルル生まれ。ニューヨーク・ソサエティ・オブ・イラストレーターズ展年間賞、シカゴ・アーティスト・ギルド、AIGAなど各賞を受賞。『プレイボーイ』『ワールドブック』など、さまざまな出版社や広告会社をクライアントに持ち、仕事をしている。シカゴ・パブリック・ライブラリー、プレイボーイ国際旅行ショーなどで作品の展示会も行なっている。

ブロック・スワンソン　266

1948年、ワシントン州スポーケン生まれ。現在はニューオーリアンズで生活しているが、それまではナイロビ、カブール、ラパス、パリ、ハワイと各地を転々とし、6000点以上の肖像画、絵画を描いてきた。現在はフィルム・ビデオ会社などをクライアントに持ち、創作活動を続けている。

ニック・タガート　267

1954年にイギリスのチェシャイアに生まれる。ケンブリッジ・アート・カレッジを1975年に卒業後、ロンドンで2年間働き、1977年にロサンゼルスに渡る。ポスター、雑誌のエディトリアルイラスト、書籍のカバーイラスト、レコードジャケット、ファブリックデザインと、その活動は幅広い。個展やグループ展も何回か行なっている。日本ではナイアガラレコードの真属アーティストとしても知られている。

ユリコ・タカタ　268

1957年、カリフォルニア州ロサンゼルス生まれ。透明感あふれる植物の絵は、雑誌のカバーイラストやグリーティング・カード、ポスター、陶器デザインなどに好んでとりあげられている。彼女の作品はバンク・オブ・アメリカ、IBM、VISA、ウェスタン・エレクトリック等がコレクションしている。

ロバート・ターネンバウム　269

1936年、ミズーリ州チリコッシで生まれる。ワシントン大学卒。ロサンゼルスおよびニューヨークのソサエティ・オブ・イラストレーターズ展賞受賞。彼を有名にしたのは、ハワード・ヒューズの等身大肖像画と、TV番組「ルーツ」「センテニアル」のための一連の作品である。現在も日立、MGM、リーバイス、デニーズ、ワーナーブラザーズ・レコードなどの仕事をひきうけている。

C・ウィンストン・テイラー　270-271

1943年にオクラホマ州オクラホマで生まれる。ワーナーブラザーズ、20世紀フォックス、ウォルトディズニー、CBSテレビなど、アメリカのトップランクの企業の仕事を手がけてある。ロサンゼルスのソサエティ・オブ・イラストレーターズの最優秀賞、ウェスタン・パブリケーション・アソシエーションのマギー賞を受賞。

アキ・トミタ　272

1944年、東京で生まれる。渡米後、"サイラ"年度賞を受賞。映画のポスターやペーパーバックのカバーイラストなどを多く手がけている。

トム・T・トミタ　273

1952年、神奈川県藤沢市で生まれる。武蔵野美術短期大学を出て渡米、サンフランシスコのアカデミー・オブ・アート・カレッジに学ぶ。映画のポスターやグリーティング・カード、雑誌のカバーイラスト、ビルボードに才能を発揮してきた。現在はフリーランスでNBCテレビ、CBSテレビ、20世紀フォックス映画、『コンピューター・マガジン』などをクライアントに持ち、創作活動を続けている。ロサンゼルス・ソサエティ・オブ・イラストレーターズの優秀賞を受賞。

デール・C・ヴァゼール　274

1952年に生まれる。イースト・カロライナ大学で学位を取得後、1977年にインディアナ州立大学、1979年にアリゾナ州立大学で芸術学科助教授として教鞭をとり、現在に至る。この間、フリーランスのイラストレーター、グラフィックデザイナーとして、数多くの作品を産み出してきた。クライアントには、ファースト・インターナショナル・バンク、『アリゾナ・ハイウェイ・マガジン』などがある。

フラン・ヴクサノヴィッチ　275

1941年、シカゴで生まれ、以来、同市に居住している。アメリカン・アカデミー・オブ・アートで人物画と油彩画を3年間学んだ。彼女の作品の多くは、鉛筆とカラーインクで描かれている。

ウイリアム・ヴクサノヴィッチ　276-277

1938年にユーゴスラビアのベルグラードで生まれる。13歳の時アメリカに渡ってきてシカゴに落ち着く。アメリカン・アカデミー・オブ・アートに3年、スクール・オブ・プロフェッショナル・アートの夜間部に2年通い、イラストレーションの道に入る。クライアントにはマクドナルド、『プレイボーイ』『ペントハウス』、クラフト、ケロッグなどがついている。

ジェフ・ワック　278

1956年、カリフォルニア州オレンジで生まれる。映画、雑誌、レコード、テレビ・アニメーションなど、企業プロモーションの仕事に従事。アート・センター・アルミニからいくつかの賞を受けている。

ロバート・L・ウェード　279

1955年、テネシー州チャタヌガに生まれる。1976年にアート・オン・ペーパー展で入賞の実績を持つ。1983年には『アメリカン・イラストレーション 2』に登場。エディトリアルを主な活動範囲とし、現在も『ニューヨーク・タイムス・マガジン』や『テキサス・マンスリー』、デンバー・ポストなど主要出版社や新聞社に作品を提供している。

リチャード・ウォルドレップ　280

ジョージア大学でデザインとイラストレーションを学び、学位を取得。ジェリー・ダッズら4人のイラストレーターがつくっている"ユーカリの木"スタジオに1976年に参加、現在は副社長を兼任する。イラストレーターズ・アニュアル、グラフィス・アニュアル等のイラストレーション部門で認められ、現在はワシントンポスト、マクドナルド、パーカー・ブラザーズ、ペントハウス、タイム・ライフなどのクライアントの仕事を続けている。

スタン・ワッツ　281-283

1952年にオクラホマ州ポンカ・シティで生まれる。最初、学校新聞や鑑などの漫画家として出発したが、水彩画の教師ジーン・ダガティに出会ってから絵画に転向する。その後2年間、イラストレーターのドン・アイバン・パンチャッツのもとで修業し、フリーランスのイラストレーターとなる。映画「ハウリング」のポスターで1982年度キーアート第1位、1983年・84年にグラミー賞ベストアルバム・アート部門で最終ノミネートされた。リーバイス、RCAレコード、ペーパームーン、20世紀フォックス、『プレイボーイ』などのクライアントを持つ。

ロバート・ウィーバー　284-286

1924年にペンシルバニア州ピッツバーグに生まれる。ピッツバーグのカーネギー・インスティテュート・テクノロジー、ニューヨークのアートスチューデント・リーグ、イタリアのベニスにも学ぶ。1957年に『エスクワイア』誌が最初に彼の作品をとりあげて記事を載せて以来、数々の個展やグループ展、ソサエティ・オブ・イラストレーターズでの金賞で不動の名声を築いた。現在も『ライフ』『ルック』『フォーチュン』『グラフィス』『スポーツ・イラストレイテッド』等の雑誌の仕事や単行本なども手がけて、精力的に活躍している。

ドン・ウェラー　287-289

アメリカのイラストレーション、デザイン界の重鎮である。ワシントン州の東部に生まれ育ち、ワシントン大学で美術を専攻した。ロサンゼルスのデザイン・スタジオで働いたあと、1965年に独立、フリーランスとなり、1973年にはデザイン工房"ウェラー・インスティチュート"を設立した。UCLAやアートセンター・カレッジ・オブ・デザインでも教鞭をとっている。この30年間、大手出版社の主要雑誌はもとより、大手企業の広告や年次報告書その他の仕事を精力的に手がけ、多くの賞を獲得している。

ジム・ホワイト　290

1947年にミズーリ州ワイアットで生まれる。ニューヨーク・ソサエティ・オブ・イラストレーターズ、中西部ショー、シカゴ・デザイン&イラストレーション・ショーなどで受賞。『プレイボーイ』や『ペントハウス』誌などの仕事のほか、カレンダーやポスター、広告なども手がけている。現在のクライアントには、前記のほか、インターナショナル・ハーベスター、スイフト・フーズなどがついている。

キム・ホワイトサイズ　292

1941年ユタ州のローガンで生まれる。1969年から1981年にかけてニューヨーク・アート・ディレクターズ・クラブの優秀賞を数回、1969年から1975年にかけて、ソサエティ・オブ・イラストレーターズ賞を数度、受賞している。『ローリング・ストーン』『タイム』『プレイボーイ』などのカバーイラスト、ポスターやレコードジャケット、リーバイスの広告イラスト等の仕事を手がけている。

テリー・ワイドナー　293

1950年、オクラホマ州のタルサで生まれる。ペプシコーラのいろいろな広告、ダラス・ジャズオーケストラのプロモーションポスターなどを手がける。現在もアメリカン・エアラインや『ボストン・マンスリー』『テキサス・マンスリー』等の雑誌に作品を提供し続けている。アメリカン・イラストレーション、ソサエティ・オブ・イラストレーターズ、グラフィス・アニュアル、プリント・マガジン、アートディレクターズ・クラブなどの各賞を受賞。

ラリー・C・ウィンボーグ　294

1942年にアイダホ州のアイダホ・フォールで生まれ、ユタ州立大学に学ぶ。ニューヨーク・ソサエティ・オブ・イラストレーターズ年度展、グラフィス・アニュアルなどに発品を発表。オデュボーン・ソサエティ、コカコーラ、ヘレン・カーティス、IBM、ITT、『スポーツ・イラストレイテッド』などの仕事をしている。

ロン・ウォーリン　295

1942年にニューヨーク市ブルックリンで生まれる。映画「グレイストーン」のポスター、UCLAの壁画を手がけ、現在もMGA、ホンダ、UCLA、トヨタ、『ライフ』誌、ダブルディ・ブックスなどをクライアントに得て創作活動を続けている。グラフィス・アニュアル、AIGA、ニューヨークとロサンゼルスのソサエティ・オブ・イラストレーターズから各賞を受賞。

ブルース・ウルフ　296-297

1941年にカリフォルニア州ロサンゼルスで生まれる。ロサンゼルス・アート・ディレクターズ・クラブ展でいくつかの賞、またアウトドア広告賞、西海岸展の最優秀賞、ソサエティ・オブ・イラストレーターズなどからも数々の賞を受けている。現在のクライアントにはリーバイス、ペーパームーン、プレイボーイ、バンク・オブ・アメリカなどアメリカのビッグカンパニーが名を連ねる。

テレサ・ウッドワード　298

カリフォルニア州サンディエゴに生まれる。サメラメントで美術を学び、その後シェイナード・アート・インスティチュート、UCLAのアートセンター・カレッジ・オブ・デザイン、南カリフォルニア大学にも通った。卒業後、フリーランスのイラストレーター、デザイナーの道を歩き、テレビジョン、パッケージング、ポスター、書籍・雑誌イラスト等の仕事をしている。ロサンゼルス・ソサエティ・オブ・イラストレーターズの会長をつとめた。カリフォルニア州立大学、南カリフォルニア大学、アートセンター・カレッジ・オブ・デザインでも教壇に立つ。

ゲーリー・ヤードホール　299

1980年に"ユーカリの木"スタジオに参加した26歳の新進イラストレーターである。メリーランド・インスティチュート・オブ・アートを卒業後、講師としてそこに残るかたわら、フリーランスとしてスタートする。グラフィス・アニュアルなどで認められ、ワシントン・アート・ディレクターズ・クラブ・ショーなどで最優秀賞を受ける。クライアントにはマクドナルド、サンシャイン・クッキーズなどのほか、『ビデオゲーム』『ナショナル・ジオグラフィック』『U.S.ニュース&ワールド・レポート』などの雑誌をもっている。

ジェームス・コートニー・ザール　300

1941年にカリフォルニア州のサン・ペドロで生まれる。サンペドロ・ハイスクール、バレー・カレッジに学び、フットボール選手として活躍した。1976年にロサンゼルス市主催の建国200年記念展で1位に入賞し、1983年にはアメリカン・カウボーイ・アソシエーションから金賞を受けるなど、彼の作品には高い評価が寄せられている。彼の代表作はアメリカのプロフットボールのチームポスターであるが、同時にファインアートの画家として、フランク・シナトラやスティーブ・ガーベイなど、著名人の肖像画を多く描いている。

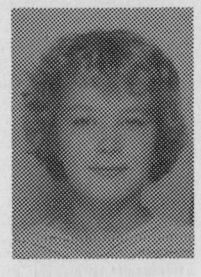

ブライアン・ジック　301

1949年、カリフォルニア州ロサンゼルス生まれ。大手航空会社やデパート、映画スタジオ、ソフトドリンク、銀行、パンティストッキング、ブルージーンズ等々、多岐にわたるクライアントの仕事を手がけている。彼女の作品はアーティスト仲間や出版社、好事家が所蔵している。

ジョン・ジーリンスキー　302

1954年にシカゴで生まれる。シカゴ・アカデミー・オブ・ファインアート卒業後、イラストレーターズ・ワークショップ、ミルトン・グレイサー・ワークショップで働く。『ワールド・ブック・エンサイクロペディア』『エンサイクロペディア・ブリタニカ』などの辞典、書籍、『プレイボーイ』『トリビューン』などの雑誌に作品を提供している。

アンディ・ジート　303

1964年から3年間、アート・センター・カレッジ・オブ・デザインに学び、のちロサンゼルスにスタジオを持ち、フリーランスのイラストレーターとして活躍している。ニューヨーク・アート・ディレクターズ・クラブ、AIGA、ロサンゼルスおよびニューヨークのソサエティ・オブ・イラストレーターズから賞を受ける。現在はCBSレコード、ペーパームーン・グラフィックス、テキサス・インスツルメント、マッキャンエリクソンなどをクライアントを抱えて制作を続けている。

★作家紹介欄に掲載した肖像写真のうち、次の方々の写真撮影者は以下のとおりです。

Leonard Baskin:　Photo © Kennedy Galleries, Inc.
Kathleen Calderwood:　Photo © 84 Phill Matt
Jim Cherry:　Photo; Bob Haft
Tom Daly:　Photo; Pam Morrison
Patty Dryden:　Photo © Joyce Ravid
Jim Evans:　Photo; Steve Sakai
Teresa Fasolino:　Photograph Courtesy of PLAYBOY Magazine: © 1984 PLAYBOY
Nicholas Gaetano:　Photo © Timothy Greenfield-Sanders
John Gamache:　Photo; Yuval Shousterman. Slang Photo Center
David Grove:　Photo; Jeanne Milligan
Richard Mantel:　© George Ancona 1981
James McMullan:　Photo; Duane Michals
Wendell Minor:　Photo; Florence Minor
Barbara Nessim:　© Seiji Kakazaki
Mel Odom:　Photo; Robert Mapplethorpe
J. Rafal Olbisnki:　Photo; Czeslaw Czaplinski © All Rights Reserved
Robert Peluce:　© Shelli Kurtz 1979
Don Ivan Punchatz:　Photo © 1984 Don Ivan Punchatz
Tracy Sabin:　Photo; William Hawks
Kim Whitesides:　Photo; Andrew Vracin

Artists profile

A

Julien Allen 10
Born Cambridge, England. Studied at Cambridge College of Arts, then the Central School of Art, London. Worked for the London Sunday Times magazine as a journalist-artist. In 1973 came to New York at the invitation of Clay Felker (the publisher of New York magazine) and Milton Glaser. Resigned from New York magazine in 1977, have since been freelancing.

Marshall Arisman 11–13
Exhibitions.
1983 One Man Show, Parco View Gallery, Tokyo Japan
1983 One Man Show, Harcourts Contemporary, San Francisco CA
One Man Show, Sindin Gallery, N.Y.C., N.Y.
1982 One Man Show, Galerie Phillippe Guimiot, Bruxelles, Belgium
One Man Show, Harcourts Contemporary, San Francisco, CA
1981 Hansen Gallery, N.Y.C., N.Y.
Images of Labor, N.Y.C., N.Y.
One Man Show, Sindin Galleries, N.Y.C., N.Y.
1980 One Man Show, Kutztown Museum, Kutztown, PA
1979 One Man show, Sindin Galleries, N.Y.C., N.Y.
1978 7th International Poster Biennale, Warszawa, Poland
1977 One Man Show, Corridor Gallery, N.Y.C., N.Y.
1975 Musee des Arts Decoratifs, Louvre, Paris
Musee des Beaux Arts, Bordeaux, France
1969 Brooklyn Museum Annual Print Show, N.Y.C., N.Y.
1968 Listening to Pictures Exhibition, Brooklyn Museum, N.Y.C., N.Y.
1966 New Talent Show, Rochester University, Guest
1965 Group Painting Show, Allan Stone Gallery, N.Y.C., N.Y.
1964 One Man Show, York Gallery, N.Y.C., N.Y.
Editorial
1970 to present Contributor of political drawings Op-Ed page, New York times
1978 to present Contributor of political drawings for The Nation
1977–1978 Contributor of political drawings "Urban Journal" Arisman, Politicks Magazine
1973 to present Editorial drawings for Esquire magazine, Playboy, Psychology Today, Omni, New York Times magazine, Sports Illustrated, Time magazine covers, Rolling Stone, Penthouse, California magazine
Books
"Frozen Images:" drawings by Marshall Arisman, published 1973, Visual Arts Press, N.Y.C.
"Art of the Times" edited by J.C. Suares Universe Books, N.Y.
"Artist of Christmas Cards" compiled by Steven Heller, A&W publishers, N.Y.C.
"Images of Labor" preface by Joan Mondale, The Pilgrim Press, N.Y.C.
Awards
Ida Haskill award for study and travel in Europe
1979 Illustrator of the Year award Playboy Magazine
1979 Gold Medal Society of Publication Designers
American Institute of Graphic Artists, Graphis Annual and Graphis Poster Awards, Communication Arts Annual, New York Art Director's Club Awards, Print Casebook Award
Articles
1982 "Marshall Arisman", Communication Arts
"Marshall Arisman," Illustration Magazine, Tokyo, Japan
"Les 'Frozen Images' d' Arisman" Art International, Lugano, Suisse
"Marshall Arisman" Where Flesh and Steel Mesh, Omni Magazine
1979 "The Art of Marshall Arisman," Graphis Magazine
"Extra Issue" Idea Magazine
Collections
Natonal Museum of American Art (Smithionian Institute, Washington, D.C.)
Brooklyn Museum Permanent Painting Collection
Brooklyn Museum Permanent Collection Drawings and Prints
Time Corporation (Smithsonian Institute, Washington, D.C.)
Mr. John Gilroy, Mr. Thomas B. Morgan, Mrs. Mary Rockfeller Morgan, Mr. Jacques Carpentier (Paris), Mr. & Mrs. Malcolm Kirk, Mr. Bob Guccione, Ms. Kathy Keeton, Mr. Bob Garland, Mr. & Mrs. Ronald Travisano, Mr. John Berg, Mr. & Mrs. Lance Wyman, Mr. & Mrs. Earl Hoyt, Mr. & Mrs. Michael Oliver, Mr. & Mrs. Avery Corman, Mr. Stuart Cutshall
Appointments
1970 to present Co-chairman, Media Department, School of Visual Arts
1969–70 Chairman Design/Illustration Department, School of Visual Arts
1964 to present Faculty of the School of Visual Arts, N.Y.C.

B

Tom Ballenger 14
Tom Ballenger, a native of Oklahoma, attended the Art Students League, The Kansas City Art Institute, and the San Francisco School of Fine Arts. He is a freelance illustrator and has worked in San Fransisco, Houston, Chicago and New York, and currently works out of Austin, where he also teaches at the University of Texas.
He has had illustrations in the Los Angeles, Denver, Dallas-Ft. Worth, and Houston Art Director's Club Exhibitions, and The Society of Illustrators Exhibition in New York, winning numerous awards including eight Best of Show Addy Awards. His work has been represented in Art Direction Magazine's "Creativity on Paper" Exhibit and CA Magazine's Annual Competition. He has done work for Exxon, Texas Monthly Magazine, and various advertising agencies in the Southwest. Recently he has completed several animated TV commericals.
He is exclusively represented by Jane Lander Associates.

Michelle Barnes 15
Place of Birth: Springfield, Missouri
Date of Birth: Sep. 23, 1956
Awards: None as yet
Past Works: Album cover for "Deliene Disques", Paris
Present Clients: Travel & Leisure, The Denver Post, Westword Bloomsbury Review, Medicine & Enfance
Exhibitions: Panache Gallery, Colorado Women & the Arts
Collections: Private Collectors

James Barkley 16
Place of Birth: New York
Date of Birth: 4/19/1941
Awards: Society of Illustrators Annual Show: #10, 11, 12, 13, 14, 15, 16, 18, 21, 22
New York A.D. Show, Chicago A.D. Show
New Jersey A.D. Show
The One Show
Gold Medal S.I. Show-11 Award of Excellence
S.I. Show-10
Past Works: Commissioned to design 15¢ Mt. Mckinley Air Mail Stamp for U.S. Postal Dept.
Commissioned to do Poster for U.S. Embassy Exhibition 1984 Illustrated 10 Childrens Books: Sounder: Winds: Why the Wind God Wept: Etc.
Present Clients: Time Life, ITC, HBO, Doubleday, Warner Bros., Most Advertising Agencies, Book Pub. and Limited Edition Prints, Movie Posters
Exhibitions: The Bridge Gallery, The Katonah Gallery, The Hudson River Museum, The Somers Town Gallery
Collections: U.S. Dept. of the Interior, U.S. Postal Service, U.S. Air Force Collection

Bascove 17
Exhibitions:
1982–83 Art & Design Gallery, N.Y., N.Y.
1982 Political Art Exhibition, Marymount College, N.Y., N.Y.
1980 One Man Show, New York Art Directors' Club, N.Y., N.Y.
Editorial:
1968–72 Contributor to Atlantic Monthly, Harper's, Redbook, Macmillan, Doubeday
1977–79 Contributor to L'Expansion, MIM's, Marie France, Marie Claire
1972-Present Contributor to the New York Times, Esquire, Ms., Life, The Progressive, Fortune, Chief Executive, Crown Publishers, Random House, Harcourt, Brace, Jovanovitch, Viking Press, Arbeiderspers, Penguin Books
Books:
"Crime and Punishment", Eastern Press, Westport, Conn.
"The Green Hero", Four Winds Press, New York, N.Y.
"Free to be You and Me", McGraw Hill, New York, N.Y.
Articles:
"Bascove — Back to Basics", Print Magazine, 1973
"Bascove", Graphis Magazine, 1981
"New York Design", Print Magazine, 1982
Awards:
1975–84 Silver Medal, New York Art directors' Club
Numerous Society of Illustrators Awards for Excellence
Graphis Annual Awards
Communication Arts Annual Awards
New York Art Directors' Club Awards
Print Casebook Awards
Appointments:
1970–72 Yale University, Department of Anthropology, Contributing Artist
Peabody Museum, Staff Artist
1974–75 Department of Education, Washington, D.C., Project Manager and Contributing Artist

Leonard Baskin 18
1922 Born, August 15, New Brunswick, New Jersey
1939–40 Attended New York University School of Architecture and Allied Arts.
1941 Received scholarship to Yale University School of Fine Arts.
1947 Received Louis Comfort Tiffany Foundation Fellowship for sculpture.
1957 Received O'Hara Museum Prize, Japanese National Museum of Tokyo.
1961 Received Grant, National Institute of Arts and Letters, New York
Received Alonzo C. Mather Prize, Art Institute of Chicago.
1962 Exhibition: The Royal Watercolor Society with St. George's Gallery.
1965 Received Pennsylvania Academy of the Fine Arts Widener Medal.
1966 Exhibition: Peale House, Pennsylvania Academy of the Fine Arts, Philadelphia.
1969 Received Medal, National Institute of Arts and Letters, New York.
1971 Exhibition: Kennedy Galleries, New York.
1976–77 One-man shows: "Leonard Baskin/An Exhibition of Sculpture, Watercolors, Drawings and Gaphics" Prince Arthur Galleries, Toronto, Ontario, Canada.

Don Baum 19
Date of Birth: June 2, 1922
Place of Birth: Escanaba, Michigan
Education: Michigan State College, Art Institute of Chicago, School of Design (Chicago), University of Chicago
Teaching: Chairman of Art Department, Roosevelt University, Chicago; Hyde Park Art Center, Chicago as a Painting Instructor
Professional experience: Board Member and Director of Exhibitions at the Hyde Park Art Center Gallery, Chicago; American Commissioner of United States Entry in Sao Paulo Biennale, Sao Paulo, Brazil (1973); awarded commission for work of art at new State of Illinois Building, Chicago (1983); award for outstanding contribution in the arts, Cliff Dweller's Club, Chicago (1977); others
Numerous one-man and group exhibitons
One-man exhibitions at Ziegfield Theater, Chicago; Kalamazoo Art Institute, Kalamazoo, Michigan; The Players' Guild, Chicago; Max Segal Bookstore, Chicago; John L. Hunt Gallery, Chicago; Betsy Rosenfield Gallery, Chicago; others
Group exhibitions including "Portraits of LBJ", Richard Gray Gallery, Chicago; "Fantasy and Figure: Chicago Art Since World War II" The American Federation of Arts, New York; "The House that Art Built", California State University, Fullerton; "Habitats", Paul Klein Gallery, Chicago; many others mostly in Chicago and northern Midwest.

Lou Beach 20–21
Born — March 8, 1947 in Göttingen, Germany of Polish parents. Came to U.S. in 1951 — lived in Rochester, N.Y. until 1965. Moved to Calif. in late 60's, then to Boston in Early 70's. Returned to Calif., 1975. No formal art training. Held many jobs — salesman, truck driver, store manager, machine shop foreman, church sexton. For 2 years was supported by art patrons. A swell guy, he is married and has one child 3 1/2 years old who draws better than he does.

David M. Beck 22–23
Place of Birth: Springfield, Illinois
Date of Birth: Dec. 25, 1950
Awards: New York Society of Illustrators Annual Show, The Annual Chicago Show
Past Works: Illustrations for Playboy magazine, Allnet combined Networks, Lucky Strike Cigarettes, Owens-Illinois, Masonite Corp., WLS-TV/Chicago, United Airlines, Kraft Inc., Abbott Laboratories, Kellog's, MacDonalds, Miller Brewing Co.

Roger Beerworth 24
Place of Birth: Oxnard, California
Date of Birth: Sep. 16, 1946
Awards: Awards of Merit — Los Angeles Society of Illustrators
Certificate of Excellence (Children's Illustration) — American Institute of Graphic Arts
Award of Excellence — Communication Arts magazine
Belding Cup — Art Directors Club of Los Angeles
Past Works: Children's Books, Pop-Up books, Greeting Cards, Magazines, Advertisements, etc.
Present Clients: Tomu Tous, National Football League, Carnation Foods, McDonalds, American Express, Paper Moon Graphics, Suzuki
Exhibitions: Society of Illustrators of Los Angeles, Los Angeles Art Directors Club

Dave Bhang 25
Born: St. Louis Missouri, Sep. 8, 1939
School: Chouinard Art Institute
Experience: Playboy Magazine, Asst. Art Director
Mattel Toys, Designer, R & D Department
Los Angeles Times, Design Director, Home Magazine
Warner Bros. Records, Art Director
California Institute of The Arts, Design Instructor
Gifted Childrens Program, L.A.C.C., Gymnastics Instructor
Otis/Parsons School of Design, Design Instructor, Illustration Instructor
Los Angeles Herald Examiner, Designer on Special Project of Re-designing the format for The Sunday Herald.
Dave Bhang Design and Illustration since 1970.
Work Published: Graphis Annual, PhotoGraphis, Graphis Record Album Covers, C.A. Magazine, A.I.G.A., Society of Illustrators, New York, The One Show, New York, A.D.L.A., Los Angeles, Society of Illustrators, Los Angeles
Personal Articles: Idea Magazine (Japan) Issue 119, "Nine Los Angeles Designers",
Idea Magazine Special Issue, "Graphic Designers on The West Coast"
Vision (Japan), "American Artists Today"

Idea Magazine (Japan) Special Issue, "California Graphics"
Current Projects: Writing and Illustrating a personal book, Editorial Design consultation, Illustrations, Teaching

Bralt Bralds 26—28

Born: 1951 Hoogkerk, Holland.
Education: Grafische School, Rotterdam, Holland.
Published Work in Editorial: Penthouse, Redbook, The Atlantic Monthly, Oui, Washington Post, Time Magazine, Esquire, Science Digest, Mother Jones, Inside Sports
Advertising: Levi's, Hitachi, Celestial Seasoning, CBS Records, Atlantic Records, Peoplexpress Airlines, Maxell, Memorex, Gilbey's Gin, Siogwork Farben, Nike, Budweiser, IBM.
Publishing: Alfred E. Knopf, Simon & Schuster, Ballantine, Avon.
Articles: Graphis #215; "Braldt Bralds".
Awards: A Gold and Silver Award from the Minnesota Art Directors Club for Best Illustration 1982. A Gold award from the Connecticut Art Directors Club for Best Illustration 1983.
Three Silver Medals from the Society of Illustrators, numerous Awards of Merit from the Society of Illustrators, numerous awards for excellence from Communication Arts, the American Institute for Graphic Arts.
Numerous publications in Graphis Annuals, European Illustration, American Illustration, Idea Magazine, the New York ADC Annual, Desi Annual, and the ADCN Annual, Holland.
Group Shows: 1982-1983 "NEW YORK ILLUSTRATION EXPRESS" — Japan Travel Show.
1983-1984 "SOCIETY OF ILLUSTRATORS SILVER ANNIVERSARY/BEST COLLECTION" — Japan Travel Show.
1983-1984 Society of Illustrators Travel Show; American Art Colleges.

Michael D. Brown 29

Date and Place of Birth: February 20, 1940; Fullerton, California
Awards: The Art Directors Club (New York) 1978-1983, Silver Medal (1981)
Society of Illustrators (New York) 1978-1983, Silver Medal (1983)
Communication Arts (California) The Art Annual, 1977-1982, The CA Annual, 1978-1980
Graphis (Switzerland) Annual, 1976-1983, Poster Annual, 1981, 1982, Photographis 1982
Print Regional Design Annual 1981-1983
The Art Directors Club of Metropolitan Washington 1973-1982 2 Silver Medals 1973, Gold Medal 1974, Gold Medal 1976, Gold Medal 1981, Gold Medal 1982, 2 Silver Medals 1982
Past Works: 4 commemorative postage stamps for the U.S. Postal Service commemorating the 50th anniversaries of the Federal Deposit Insurance Company, Federal Credit Unions, Soil and Water Conservation and the National Archives. Advertising campaigns for IC Industries, the Washington Post; editorial illustrations for the Atlantic Monthly, Fortune, Newsweek, Sports Illustrated, Money; posters for Paramount Pictures.
Present Clients: Present clients include Booz-Allen Hamilton, Exxon, I.C. Industries, AT&T, American Institute of Architects, Western Electric Corp., TV Guide, American Express, ABC News, Money
Exhibitions: N/A
Collections: N/A

Tracy W. Britt 30

Place of Birth: Indianapolis, Indiana
Date of Birth: December 29, 1955
Awards: most recently New York Society of Illustrators Annual Show and the Japanese Travel Show, ORIGINAL AMERICAN ILLUSTRATION 1982-83
Past Works: general commercial illustration including album covers, advertising, and annual reports for various agencies and corporations
Present Clients: various agencies including McCann Erickson Inc; J. Walter Thompson USA; Foote, Cone & Belding/Honig, Inc. for their clients including Chevron, Del Monte Foods, and Bank of America
Exhibitions: most recently the Japanese Travel Show ORIGINAL AMERICAN ILLUSTRATION
Collections: Private collections of clients and corporations

Lou Brooks 31

Place and Date of Birth: Philadelphia, Pennsylvania 9-5-44
Education: Self taught
Awards: Society of Illustrators, New York City
American Illustration, New York City
Graphics Design: USA
American Institute of Graphic Arts, New York City
Clients: Most major publications including Playboy (illustrations plus comic strips written and illustrated for "Playboy Funnies"), Time, New York Times, People, Rolling Stone, Forum, Vanity Fair, McCall's, Fortune, Sports Illustrated, Adweek
Other clients include Exxon Corp., Atari, Inc., Nintendo, Inc., MTV Music Television, CBS Records, Parker Brothers, Heaven, and an extensive line of greeting cards for Ruby Street
Miscellaneous: Jury Chairman for the New Illustration Show 1983, Society of Illustrator
Jury member for the Society of Illustrators 26th Annual Show
Co-founder of "The Zipatones", a comedy rock band which includes fellow illustrator Elwood Smith and cartoonists Bill Plympton and Mark Allan Stamaty
Organized and produced the Artists and Models Ball '81 for the Graphic Artists Guild, New York Chapter
Produced and performed comedy art on Manhattan Cable TV
Writes a video column for Stop
Taught illustration at the School of Visual Arts, New York City
Lectured at various art schools in New York City

Philip Burke 32

Born: Buffalo, New York, 11. 27. 1956
Awards: New York Society of Illustrators Annual Show 1980, 1981
American Illustration Annual 1982, 1983
Past Works: Illustrations for Village Voice, The Progressive, New York Magazine, New Times, Time Magazine, The Nation, New York Times, SOHO News, Harper's, Vanity Fair, Vogue, Pantheon Books, New York Daily News, and many others
Present Client: VANITY FAIR Magazine — Conde' Nast Publications Inc.
Exhibitions: Carnegie Cultural Center, Buffalo New York

Steven Butz 33

Born: Los Angeles, CA. Feb. 27, 1952
Past Works: 'The Glacier Fox' movie poster, Sanrio
Book of 20,000 Leagues Under the Sea — Raintree Publishers
Present Clients: Film Ventures Intn'l Mattel, Barrington Publishers

C

Kathleen Calderwood 34

Born: 1945 — Ogdensburg, New York
Awards: American Illustration 1982-83; 1983-84
Playboy Magazine's Best Fiction Illustrator
Art Directors Club 62nd Annual Exhibition
"Chicago 80", Communications Collaborative, Inc.
National UDCA Design Competition
University of Rochester — Lillian Fairchild Award
Society of Publication Designers Awards Exhibition
Art Directors Club of New York (the 'One Show')
Italian Designers Annual
Rochester Finger Lakes Exhibition — B. Forman Award; Rumrill Hoyt Award
Past Works & Features: Playboy Magazine, Esquire Magazine, Lampoon, New West, Graphics Annual, Art Direction Magazine, Arts Magazine, American Artist, Art News, Communication Arts
Present Clients: Playboy Magazine, Hutchins, Young & Rubicam, Associate Professor at Nazareth College, Rochester, NY, Syracuse Universtity, Syracuse, NY
Exhibitions: Alan Stone Gallery, New York, NY
"The Reality of Illusion", Two year traveling exhibition originated by the University of Southern California which appeared at major galleries throughout the U.S. (Chicago Museum of Contemporary Art. Hirschorn Museum, Herbert Johnson Museum, Cornell University, Oakland Museum, Newberger Museum, etc.)
"The Small Scale in Contemporary Art", Art Institute of Chicago, Chicago, Illinois
Everson Museum of Art, Syracuse, NY
Schuman Gallery, Rochester, NY
"Illustration Faculty Exhibition" Syracuse University, Lubin House, New York, NY
"Uncommon Visions", Memorial Art Gallery (National Exhibition), Rochester, NY
"Untitled, Invitational Exhibition of Works by six nationally known Rochester women, Tower Fine Arts Gallery, SUCB at Brockport, NY
"Alumni", Bevier Gallery, Rochester Institute of Technology, Rochester, NY
"Viscom Faculty Show", Lowe Gallery, Syracuse University, Syracuse, NY
"Artists Look at Art", University of Kansas
"Women's Art Symposium", Turman Art Gallery, Indiana State University
"Painting and Sculpture Today", Indianapolis Museum of Art Indianapolis, Indiana
"The Presence and Absence in Realism", Brainard Art Gallery, Potsdam, NY
"Unordinary Realities", Xerox Square Exhibition Center, Rochester, NY
"Aspects of Realism", State University College, Oswego, NY
"Beyond Illustration", PEI exhibition originated at the New York Cultural Center and appeared in 52 major cities in the U.S. and Europe
Comara Gallery, Los Angeles, California

Kirk Caldwell 35

Place of Birth: Pasadena, California 7/5/51
Awards: San Francisco Society of Communicating Arts
American Institute of Graphic Arts (work seen in American Illustration)
Print Annuals 1982 & 1983
Past Works: Portrait of Mr. S & Mr. W for S&W foods TV commercial
Present Clients: Oceans Magazine/Chevron
Exhibitions: Executive offices of Foote, Cone & Belding

Justin Carroll 36

Born 1953 in Houston, Texas. Started doing freelance illustration at 14 years old. Attended the University of Texas and Art Center College of Design in Los Angeles. Currently Freelancing in Los Angeles.

Ron Chan 37

Place of Birth: San Francisco, California
Date of Birth: October 8, 1958
Awards: AIGA/California Design 1980-1982, 1981 Society of Communicating Arts
Partial Client: Bank of America; Landor Associates; Rambler Records; Goodby, Berlin & Silverstein; Teleflora; San Francisco Symphony; Focus Magazine; Sierra Magazine; California Living Magazine; San Jose Mercury; Mother Jones; Oceans Magazine; Atari Connection
Exhibitions: J Walter Thompson

Eric Chan 38—39

California graphic designer and illustrator, studied advertising design at the Royal Melborne Technical College in Melbourne, Australia and Chouinard Art Institute in Los Angeles.
He has worked in the Los Angeles area for 23 years. Since 1979 he has worked in the area of Dimensional Assemblages and Poster Graphics. He is currently producing a series of limited edition posters on aviation theme.

Jim Cherry 40

Place of Birth: Walla Walla, Washington
Date of Birth: Jan. 31, 1948
Awards: Four Pieces in "New Illustration" show American Society of Illustrators 1982
Illustration Award Winner, Los Angeles Art Directors Club in 1982, work has been featured in "Art Direction", "Print", and "Graphis" magazines.
Past Works: He has done a wide range of design & illustration projects — designed store fronts & signage, T-shirts, including one for Andy Warhol's visit to the Seattle Art Museum, LP covers for Atlantic Records & Arista Records, a poster for rock group "TOTO".
magazines he has worked for: Heavy Metal, Gentlemen's Quarterly, Seventeen, Science Digest, K- Power, Family Computing, Home Video, Contact!, and games.
Other clients: Harper & Row, Nike Tennis Shoes, NBC, CBS & ABC, and Estee-Lauder Cosmetics, also Lois Jeans.
Present Clients: ABC, Amiga Video Games, Seventeen magazine

Steven Chorney 41

Steven Chorney was born in Washington, D.C., November 24, 1951. After moving to Los Angeles, his first experience in commercial art came in 1972 as an animation designer. Although without formal education in art, Chorney's strong sense of design and sophistication is reflected in his diverse accomplishments in animation, lettering and illustration. Specializing in the entertainment industry, Steven has produced the key art for motion picture campaigns for Universal, MGM, 20th Century Fox and Warner Brothers, as well as the screen title art and animation for "The Sting II" and television advertising for CBS and ABC. Other clients include Levi's, Carnation, McDonalds and Raid.

James C. Christensen 42—43

Place of Birth: Culver City, California
Date of Birth: 9.26.1942
Awards: National Small Painting Exhibition (1st place purchase), Utah Bienniel (painting award), Springville Art Museum April Salon (Silver medal), Mormon Festival of the Arts (6 purchase awards), World Fantasy Convention (best in show)
Past Works: Album Covers, Radio Shack and Covenant Recordings; Book Covers, Berkely Books, Ace Books, Pocket Books, Underwood-Miller, Arkham House, Simon & Schuster; Omni Magazine; Southwest Art Magazine, Mountain West Magazine, Expression Magazine.
Present Clients: Berkely Books, Omni Magazine, Time-Life Books
Exhibitions: 25th Anniversary of NASA Show: Space Art, Fact and Fantasy, Cleveland Museum of Natural History;

"Fantasies of the Sea", National Aquarium, Baltimore Maryland; Society of Illustrators; American Illustration; Museum of the Southwest, Midland Texas; Springville Art Museum, Utah; "This World and Others" Exhibition, Canton Art Institute, Canton Ohio; Lido Gallery, Park City, Utah; Allen Husberg Gallery, Sedona, Arizona; Pendragon Gallery, Annapolis, Maryland.
Collections: Brigham Young University Collection; Museum of the Southwest; Springville Museum of Art; National Small Painging Collection; represented in over 50 major private collections in U.S., Mexico, Fngland, and Spain.

Seymour Chwast 44–47

Seymour Chwast was born in New York City in 1931 and is a graduate of Cooper Union, where he studied illustration and graphic design. He was a founding partner of he celebrated Push Pin Studios whose distinctive style has had a worldwide influence on contemporary visual communications. In 1982 he and Alan Peckolick formed a new company, Pushpin Lubalin Peckolick, of which Mr. Chwast is a partner.
Mr. Chwast's clients include leading corporations, advertising agencies and publishing companies both here and abroad. His designs and illustrations have been used in advertising, animated films, corporate and environmental graphics, record covers, books, magazines, posters and packaging. He has created a variety of type faces and has designed and illustrated more than a dozen children's books. He was publisher and art director of the Push Pin Graphic, a bi-monthly magazine with subscribers all over the world, and formed the Push Pin Press, which originated and produced a wide range of books. He also created background images for productions of Candide and The Magic Flute.
He works in a variety of styles and media. His work has been exhibited in major galleries and museums in the U.S., Europe, Japan and Brazil. Mr. Chwast and Push Pin were honored at the Louvre in Paris in a two-month retrospective exhibition entitled "The Push Pin Style." His most recent shows were in the Galerie Delpire in Paris, Kunstegewerbe Museum in Zurich and the Gutenberg Museum in Mainz, West Germany.
Mr. Chwast's work has been the subject of numerous magazine and newspaper articles. IDEA, Japan's leading graphic arts magazine, published a complete issue on his work, and he was the subject of a special feature in the Frankfurter Allgemeine Zeitung magazine. He has received many design awards, is the recipient of the coveted St. Gauden's Medal from Cooper Union, and was elected to the Art Director's Hall of Fame. His posters are in the permanent collection of New York's Museum of Modern Art, The Cooper-Hewitt Museum of the Smithsonian Institution, the Library of Congress and the Gutenberg Museum.
Mr. Chwast teaches at the Cooper Union Art School, and has served as vice-president of the American Institute of Graphic Arts. He is a member of the Alliance Graphique Internationale and a frequent lecturer to student and professional groups.
He lives and works in the Gramercy Park area of New York and his favorite skyscraper is the Chrysler Building.

Kay Clay 48–49

Born: June 8th, 1936– Rochester, Indiana
Education: B.A.E., M.A.E., Herron School of Art; Post-Graduate Work, Indiana University
Teaching Experience: Art Department Head, Crispus Attucks High School; Painting Instructor, Herron School of Art; Drawing Instructor, Indiana University Purdue University Indianapolis; Figure Drawing, Indianapolis Art League; Guest Lecturer on Academic Drawing in conjunction with the show, Prix De Rome, Indianapolis Museum of Art (Summer, 1984)
Awards: Tri-Kappa State Art Award; Herron Undergraduate Award in Painting; Wolcott Graduate Award for Travel and Study in Europe; Lilly Grant for Post Graduate Study, Indiana University; Outstanding Art Educator Award given by the National Art Education Association (1981)
Painting Awards: Indiana Artist Show, Michiana Biennial, Wabash Valley Show, 500 Festival of the Arts, Indiana State Fair, Ball-State National Drawing Show
Exhibited: Indiana University, Indianapolis Art League, Indianapolis Museum of Art, Indiana State Museum
One Woman Shows: Ransburg Gallery, Indiana Central University, Jewish Community Center, Lockerbie Gallery, Indianapolis Museum of Art (Spring, 1984)

Francois Cloteaux 50

1952 Born in the heart of Paris
1969 St. Luc de Tournai Art School in Belgium Academical Arts and Architecture
1979 London
Designer at Jon Bannenberg, does the small jobs. Mainly drawing cars, car interiors, etc...
1973 Builds cars
Still designing at Bannenberg's but also working as a freelance stylist for rich car lovers. (Peter Stengel's Rolls-Royce Show.)
also takes a job as freelance art director for Guest Int. Designing booklet for Computer Sales.
1974 First interesting Exhibition of Technical Arts.
Mainly plastics. Electronic sculptures designed to look interesting, transparent Hi-Fi units, etc. Zarach of Sloane St. May 1974
1975 Freelance photographer
Starts getting impressed by lighting.
Gives up industry products, quits everything, opens a small studio in Bryanston Mews East in London W.I.
1976 Photography. Small exhibitions everywhere
Advertising agencies, well-known shops, restaurant, etc... Did many freelance jobs in this year. Some clients were Rolls-Royce, Keelers Instruments and friends at Guest Int.
1977 Hamburg
Freelance graphic artist
1978–79 Freelance jobs 100% Graphic Arts. No cars, no Hi-Fi, no camera, but Airbrush...
1980 Exhibition
250 large illustrations or paintings, books full of sketches, posters, postcards, etc. Absolute success. Great promotion for a really good show.
Since then Francois Cloteaux delivers highest quality paintings for highest quality clients at highest quality agencies. And the life goes on. The exhibition drawings are constantly renewed and are sent every three months to different galleries.
1982 Freelance illustrator and designer in New York, Hamburg and Paris. In America he is represented by Jane Lander Associates.

Bobbye Cochran 51

Bobbye Cochran is an illustrator and graphic designer. She has won numerous awards and received international acclaim in the area of graphic communication. Based in Chicago, Illionois, she is represented throughout the United States.

Alan E. Cober 52–53

Place of Birth: New York City
Education: University of Vermont, School of Visual Arts, Pratt Graphics Center
Military: U.S. Army including Special Warfare School, Fort Bragg, North Carolina
Teaching: Silvermine College of Art, Parson's School of Design, President of Illustrators Workshop
Awards: Artist of the Year 1965 (Artists Guild of New York), New York Times Ten Best Illustrated Books (Winters Eve 1969, Mr. Corbetts Ghost, 1968), Society of Publication Designers gold and silver awards; New York Society of Illustrators and other medals
Shows: Brooklyn Museum 100 years of American Illustration New York Historical Society 200 Years of American Illustration Whitney Museum: Color Many one-man shows, collections
Magazine clients: Life, Look, Time, Newsweek, Sports Illustrated, Inside Sports, Atlantic, Harpers, Science Digest, McCalls, Rolling Stone, Esquire, others
Advertising: IBM, CBS, NBC, ITT, Exxon, Gulf, Mobil, Texaco, Conoco, Xerox, Eastern, TWA, Pan American, American, GE, others
Many articles have appeared abut Alan Cober including articles in American Artist, Gebrauchsgraphik, Delta Sky, TWA Ambassador and other graphics trade magazine.

Sharleen Collicott 54

Born in LosAngeles in 1937, Sharleen has been a freelance illustrator for 15 years. During the summer of 1983, she taught at Otis/Parson. Her works have appeared on the record covers of Liberty-United Artists, Universal and Casablanca Records and Film Works. Also, her works have appeared in such books and magazines as: THE ENORMOUS LEAP OF ALPHONSE FROG (Nash Publishers), ELEMENTARY MATH SERIES (Addison-Wesley Publishers), AN ELEPHANT in MY BED (Follett Publishers), PSYCHOLOGY TODAY, PLAYBOY, NATIONAL WILDLIFE FEDERATION and many others. Among the many awards that she has received are: Memorial Award (1971) Art Directors Club of Los Angeles, Awards of Excellence, Illustrators XV (New York Society of Illustrators), Graphis Annual (1971–73), Distincitive Merit (14th Annual, Communicating Art of San Diego) and many others.

Clifford Ara Condak 55

Place of Birth: Haverhill, Mass.
Date of Birth: April 8th, 1930
Awards: Included in most annual shows held by New York Society of Illustrators: (received Award of Special Merit a few years back.) and American Institute of Graphic Arts, "A.I.G.A." (N.Y.C.)
Past Works: Pharmecuticals, and Columbia Records, Playboy magazine
Present Clients: CBS Records, Ciba-Giegy
Exhibitions: Kunstlerhaus Salzburg, Aug. '53, Spring Show: Painting, City Center Gallery '55, Group Show, Painting. Roko Gallery ('60?) Group Show, Steindler Gallery (1961) Group Show, 1962 One-Man Show) San Francisco Mus. of Contemp. Art – ('65? group) Gallery of Modern Art, Wash. D.C. ('65 Group), Visual Arts Gallery, NY. (One-Man Show '64–'65) Katonha Gallery, N.Y. (One-man Show '69 –'70?), Allentown Art Museum, Allentown, Penn. (One-Man Show '77) Large Permanent Oil on Canvas on the wall of theater 'J.I. Rodale' Theater: ("Show-Biz") 22'H 55'L, ('77) Allentown, Penn. O.K. Harris Gallery, N.T.C. Group Show, '65–'66? Mus. of Modern, N.Y.C., Painting in (Group Show) '64 – '67 'Lettering & The Artist's Hand'
Collections: Allentown Museum of Art: A'town, Penn.
Mrs. Alfred List Collection: N.Y.C. & L.I., Mrs. J.I. Rodale of Penn. & N.Y.C., Museum fo Erotic Art: San Francisco Ca.

Chris Consani 56

Place of Birth: District of Columbia Washington D.C.
Date of Birth: Feb. 3, 1955
Awards: Art Center College of Design 12th Annual Alumni Exhibition of Design and Art. 1983 Maggie Awards
Past Works: Album cover MCA Records, Poster Capitol Records, Spread ad Disney Video, Campaign Able Computers
Present Clients: MCA Records, Capitol Records, Columbia Pictures, Disney Video, Able Computers, Sun Giant
Education: Art Center College of Design

Jose Cruz 57

Born in Nuevo Laredo, Tamp., Mexico on April 12, 1955.
Awards: Print's Regional Deisgn Annual
New York Society of Illustrators Annual Show, Graphis, American Illustration Annual, Art Direction, Art Directors 61st Annual
Past Works: Ohio Plain Dealer, T.W.A. Ambassador Magazine, D Magazine, Texas Instruments, Xerox, Creative Software, Penthouse Magazine, Radio Shack, Children's Computer Workshop
Present Clients: Meetings and conventions Mag., Time Magazine, Mony Magazine, Atlantic Monthly, Texas Monthly, 13–30 Corporation
Currently represented by: Carol J. Hohmann Southwest U.S.A. Phylis Flood/Pushpin, Lubalin, and Peckolick

Ray Cruz 58

Ray Cruz is a native New Yorker who attended Big Apple schools including Pratt Institute and Cooper Union. He graduated the latter in 1957. Ray's work experience in various fields of design propelled him to his present involvement in advertising illustration. He is a member of the Graphic Artist's Guild. Special interests include ecology and, more specifically, animal conservation. Ray hs the distinct honor of being the first artist to work with Vicki Morgan, Artist Rep.

Tom Curry 59

Place of Birth: Coleman, Texas
Date of Birth: July, 12, 1945
Awards: New York Society of Illustrators Show, Communication Arts Annual, Graphis Annual, Print Magazine Regional Annual, New York Art Directors Show
Past Works: Advertinzing illustrations for American Airlines, Apple Computer, Selsun Blue Shampoo, Steak and Ale of America. Magazine covers for Texas Monthly, Financial World, D Magazine.
Presetn Clients: Texas Monthly, Boy's Life, American Way Magazine, The Cleveland Plain Dealer,The Dallas Times Herald.
Exhibitions: New York Society of Illustrators Show, Austin Graphic Arts Society, Bozell and Jacobs Advertizing Gallery.
Collections: Private collectors from the Los Angeles Times, Texas Monthly, and American Airlines.

D

Jerry Dadds 60

44; President and co-founder of Edcalyptus Tree Studio; Designer/illustrator; received BFA in advertising design from the Philadelphia College of Art. Recognision in the New York Art Director's Show, Creativity, Upper and Lower Case Magazine, Best in Baltimore, Graphis, Print Regional Issue, Chicago Art Director's Annual, Washington Art Director's Show.
Clients: Maryland Dept. of Economic & Community Development, Equitable Trust, Health Care Financing Administration, W.R. Grace – Davison Chemical Co., Food & Drug Administration, The Pride of Baltimore, The Maryland Port Authority, National Aquarium in Baltimore, U.S. Navy, NASA, Baltimore City, T.V. Guide, Changing Times, Johns Hopkins Magazine, MIT Technology Review
Eucalyptus Tree Studio is a Baltimore based illustration and design studio recognized as one of the foremost in the Mid-Atlantic region. Founded in 1965, the organization has expanded to meet a growing list of clients in government, in dustry, advertising, and the public sector. Helping with this promotion are representatives in New York and Chicago.

Tom Daly 61

Born in New York City on Oct. 11, 1938, has won the Gold Medal from the NY Art Directors Club, an Award of Excellence from the N.Y. Society of Illustrators, and is represented quite of ten in their annual show. He has done both print and TV commercials. Working for most of the top advertising agencies in the United States. His clients have included General Foods, Cinemax, Columbia Pictures, Sunshine Bakers, I.T.T. as well as editorial paintings and designs for Good House Keeping, CBS Records, Playboy and McCall's magazine.
His work has been exhibited at the N.Y. Historical Society and by

the Smithonian Institute in Washington D.C.
Works are owned by the Playboy Collection in Chicago and the Smithonian Collection of American Poster Art.

Aran Daniels 62—63
Place of Birth: Loa Angeles, California
Date of Birth: Nov. 25, 1947
Awards: British Illustrators
Past Works: too numerous
Present Clients: Playboy Virgin Records, 20th Century Fox, most major movie houses. Britsh Airways, Coors Beer.
Exhibitions: Hamiltons,London. Gogartochon, Hamburgh. Collectors Choice, California. Midland Group Nottingham England. off the wall, London.

Beau Daniels 64
Place of Birth: Los Angeles, CA
Date of Birth: Apr. 24, 1951
Awards: Smithonian Exhibit.
Past Works: working illustrator works too numerous to mention
Present Clients: Honda, Vivitar, Orion Pictures, Revell, Playboy, Rockwell Int.
Exhibitions: Hamilton Gallery, London
Collections: Smithonian Institute

Bill Davis 65
Place of Birth: Los Angeles, California
Date of Birth: May 18, 1949
Awards: Emmy Award, New York Society of Illustrators Annual Show, Society of Illustrators of Los Angeles Annual Show
Past Works: Cover for Cricket Magazine
Children's Illustrations for "MacMillan and Co. Publishing Inc."
Sports Illustration for "Gillette"
"More to Come" artwork for NBC's "The Tonight Show"
Film shorts for "NBC, The First Fifty Years" and "NBC, The First Fifty Years, A Closer Look" Magazine illustrations for "The Children's Television Workshop"
Design of many animated television commercials through the "Kurtz & Friends Animation" organization. Record album & book package for the McDonald's Corp."
Present Clients: "Kurtz & Friends Animation", "Children's Television Workshop"
Exhibitions: New York Society of Illustrators Annual Show
Society of Illustrators of Los Angeles Annual Show

Paul Davis 66—68
Born 10 February 1938 Centrahoma, Oklahoma.
Awards for illustration and design number in the hundreds from the American Institute of Graphic Arts. The Society of Illustrators, Art Directors Clubs throughout the United States, and professional reviews and exhibitions in America and abroad. Some major awards:
1972 Silver Medal from the Primera Bienal de Artes Graficas, Museo de Tertulia, Colombia, S. A.; 1973 Gold Medal, Art Directors Club of New York; 1974 Gold Medal, Art Directors Club of New York and Silver Medal, Art Directors Club of Dallas; 1974 Asahi Newspaper Advertising Award, Mainichi Newspaper Advertising Award and Dentsu Advertising Award; 1980 Bronze medal, 8th International Poster Biennale, Warsaw; 1981. 3rd Prize Taidmuseum Poster Exhibition, Lahti, Finland.
Past works include illustrations for the pages and covers of almost every major American publication and many abroad, and in books, on record albums, packaging, and posters. His theater posters for Joseph Papp's New York Shakespeare Festival are especially well known. He also has produced lithographs, sculpture, animated films, and books.
Present clients include Merzario, Inc., the Italian shipping company for whom he is producing 25 paintings for an illustrated edition of "Moby Dick"; the New York Shakespeare Festival for whom he has just completed a poster for "The Human Comedy"; the Mobil Corporation; the New York Arts and Business Council; the Big Apple Circus: etc.
His work has appeared in numerous one-man and group exhibitions in North and South America, Europe and Japan, and is shown regularly at the Nishimura Gallery in Tokyo. A retrospective of 150 paintings was held at the Museum of Modern Art in Kamakura in 1975, and later traveled to the Museum of Modern Art in Kyoto, the Museum of Modern art in Gumma, and the opening of Centre Pompidou in Paris in 1977. His work is in the collections of the National Portrait Gallery in Washington, D.C.; the Museum of Modern Art Poster Collection; the Museum of Racing, Saratoga, New York; Guild Hall Museum, East Hampton, New York; the Tochigi Prefectural Museum of Fine Art, Japan; Museo Bogarin, El Tigre, Venezuela; the American Embassy in Moscow; General Electric Company;Exxon; Bollafi Arte; The Paris Review; Aid Association for Lutherans; and many private collectors.

Michael J. Deas 69
Michael J. Deas was born in Norfolk, Virginia in 1956, and raised in both New Orleans, Louisiana and Long Island, New York. Between 1974 and 1978 he studied fine arts at Pratt Institute and, during 1978, at the Byam Shaw College of Art in London. While in college he began freelance illustrating for various publishers and agencies, which have included Doyle Dane & Bernbach, Readers Digest, the Dial Press, Ladies Home Journal, and Franklin Watts. His work has been featured in the Graphis Annual as well as in exhibitions at the Society of Illustrators and the Art directors Club. Since 1981 he has been represented by the New York Firm of Artists Associates. Currently, he is an instructor at the School of Visual Arts and resides in Brooklyn Heights, New York.

Charles D. deMar 70
Charles deMar was born in New York City, October 1, 1959, the son of a successful textile designer. As a "self-taught" illustrator, Charles began his professional career in November, 1980, when he was introduced to the highly specialized field of motion picture advertising as a staff illustrator for a major east-coast design studio. In 1982 charles left his Connecticut home for Los Angeles, where he currently resides. deMar brings to his work an intriguing blend of realism and sensitivity as he captures the likenesses of motion picture and television celebrities alike. Clients include Warner Brothers, Universal Pictures, Polygram Pictures, CBS Television and many others.

Harvey Dinnerstein 71
Place of Birth: Brooklyn, New York, U.S.A.
4.3.1928
Awards: Temple Gold Medal, Penna. Academy of Fine Arts, 1950. Tiffany Foundation Grant, 1948, 1961
Hassam Purchase Award, American Academy and Institute of Arts and Letters, 1974, 1978
Ranger Purchase Award, National Academy of Design, 1976
Art and the Law Purchase Award, West Publishing Co. 1982, 1983
Best Labor magazine cover of the year, AFL/CIO International Labor Press Assoc., 1982
Arthur Ross Award, Classical America, 1983
Clients: Atlantic Magazine, Esquire Magazine, Fortune Magazine, New York Magazine, New York Times, Playboy Magazine, RCA Records
Exhibitions: Sindin Galleries, New York City, 1983

John Taylor Dismukes 72
Date of Birth: October 24, 1953
Awards: John Taylor Dismukes has recieved numerous awards from the art directors and illustration clubs. He is in private colllections in The United States, Europe and Japan.
Past Works: Album covers for A&M records, robot designs for several major motion pictures as well as logo and program design for the National Football League of Amercia
Present Clients: Warner Brothers Pictures, Universal Pictures, Orion Pictures, Sanyo, RCA, Levi's Jeanswear, Coors Beer, National Football League
Exhibitions: Gallery of Erotic Art, San Francisco, California; Image West Gallery, Los Angeles, California; Crocker Art Gallery, Sacramento, California; San Diego State University Gallery, San Diego, California; Gallery 101, New York City, N.Y.
Collections: John is private collections in the United States, Europe and Japan

Dennis Dittrich 73
Work History: Freelance illustrator 11/81 to Present.
Clients include: Outdoor Life, Golf, Physics Today, Communications of the A.C.M., Institutional Investor and Scholastic Magazines; Leber-Katz Advertising, McAffrey and McCall Advertising; Equitable, Time/Life, and AT&T
Education: 1979 Graduate Art Institute of Pittsburgh
1979-82 School of Visual Arts
1979-82 Graphic Artists Guild Business School
1983 New School for Social Research
Professional Affiliations: Graphic Artists Guild—Currently serving on New York Board, Grievance Committee and Illustrators Steering Committee
Cartoonists Guild
Personal: Date of Birth 11/10/54

Patty Dryden 74
Plac of birth: Pittsburgh, Pennsylvania.
Date of Birth: 11/22/1950.
Awards: None.
Past Works: Album covers for E.M.I., R.C.A., Arista, A. and M. Magazines include Harpers, Esquire, New York Magazine, Atlantic Monthly, Rolling Stone, Atlantic Monthly, Rolling Stone, Newsweek.
Present Clients: Vogue Magazine, Vanity Fair Magazine, T.W.A., Redbook.
Exhibitions: None
Collections: None

Andrzej Dudzinski 75
Place of Birth: Sopot, Poland
Date of Birth: 14.12.1945
Awards: None
Past Works: Covers for Satruday Night, Boston Globe Magazine, Time, Vanity Fair (unpublished), Racquet Quarterly, poster for Parsons School of Design, illustrations for Sunday Times Magazine, Tatler, Vogue, Rolling Stone, The New York Times, New York Magazine, Harpers, Geo
Present Clients: The Atlantic, Avenue, The Boston Globe, GQ, Money, Ms, Racquet Quarterly, Science '84, the New York Times, Time, The Times, Texas Monthly

E

Alex Ebel 76
Place of Birth: born in Mexico from German Parentage, an American Citizen since 1956
Date of Birth: 11.14.1932
Awards: Kelly Award, Andy Award, Society of Illustrators of Los Angeles, The 1978 San Francisco Show, The San Francisco Society of Communicating Arts, The Art Director Club, The American Institute of Graphic Arts, Chicago Soc. of Communicating Arts, The Society of Illustrators of New York, etc.
Past Works: Record Album Covers, Book Covers, Science, Magazine and Advertising Illustration
Clients: Science Digest, Boys' Life, Playboy, Oui, Penthouse, Hustler, Paramount Pictures, Country wide Advertising Agecies.
Exhibitions: Columbus Gallery, New York
Collections: Several Private Collectors

Jack Endewelt 77
Born in New York City in 1935, he studied at the School of Viual Arts after serving for two years in the army.
He has worked as a free-lance illustrator since 1961, and his accounts have included: Dell; Avon; Bantam Books, where his work appaeared on numerous paperback covers; Time/Life Books, for whom he worked on "The Emergence of Man" series; the Franklin Library; Holt, Rinehart and Winston; and other childrens' book publishers. He has also worked for may magazines such as the Ladies' Home Journal, the Atlantic Monthly, and foreign publications including Town Magazine in Britain and Idea Magazine in Japan. His advertising accounts have included Iberian Airlines, Dupont, Audi and several pharmaceutical companies.
In 1976, his work was celebrated by its inclusion into the Society of Illustrators' "200 Years of American Illustration" exhibit and he has participated in most of the Society of Illustrators annual exhibitions since 1961.
He has been a instructor at the School of Visual Arts since 1968.

John Eastman 78—79
After graduating UCLA, John Eastman started as a fashion illustrator and art director, then became a freelance illlustrator. His illustrations of ladies are placed a high value from all over America. Especially, a sereal of his lithographs have numerous collectors. He has a studio at the foot of mountain which one can overlook Hollywood Boulevard.

James R. Endicott 80
Place of Birth: San Bernardino, Califolnia
Date of Birth: Dec. 6, 1946
Awards: New York Art Directors Show 1983. New York Society of Illustrators Show 1983 & 1984.
Past Works: Album covers for Capitol Records, Ads for Benton and Bowles Advertising, Oligevy and Mather Advertising, J. Walter Thompson Advertising, and Apple Computer Magazine.
Present Clients: Atlantic Monthly Magazine, National Football League Properties, Time Magazine Inc., Price/Waterhouse Inc., Capitol Records Inc., and Penthouse Magazine
Exhibitions: McVey Gallery, Los Angeles & Los Gatos, California
Collections: Capitol Records and Westways Magazine

Anka Ente 81
Place of Birth: Sorong,Indonesia
Date of Birth: 11/3/49
Awards: Communication Arts (CA) magazine, San Francisco Society of Communicating Arts (SFSCA), Design Award for Architechural Tensile, San Mateo Art Council Award for painting.
Past Works: Clients include: Chevron, Intel, Berkeley Monthly Magazine, MCA Corporation, Sunflower Tea, Shaklee Corporation, IBM Counseling, Activision Inc, Alaskan Travel & Kit Hinrichs (Jonson-Pederson-Hinrichs & Shakery Design).
Present Clients: Castle & Cook (Dole Division)
Exhibitions: Lucien Labaudt Gallery, (SOMA) South of Market Artists.
Note: Anka was favorably critiqued by Thomas Albright at the Lucien Labaudt Gallery and has been a founding member of the SOMA Gallery in San Francisco.
Collections: Several of Anka's paintings have been purchased by local area residents of San Francisco, which has earned her much prestige where personal art is concerned.

Bill Ersland 82

Illustrator Bill Ersland is a native of Des Moines, Iowa. He received his B.S. degree from Iowa State University. He has participated in many juried exhibits including Iowa Art Directors, New York Advertising Club, Tulsa Art Directors, 21st, 22nd, 23rd, and 24th Society of Illustrators, Annual National Exhibitions in New York City, and Chicago '79, '80, and '82 Annual Graphic Shows. He lived and worked in the Waterloo-Cedar Falls ara for over ten years. He now has a studio in Stillwater, Minnesota.

Louis Escobedo 83

Place of Birth: Sweetwater, Texas
Date of Birth: Aug. 20, 1952
Awards: Gold Medal – New York Society of Illustrators
Silver Medal – Dallas Society of Visual Communications
Past Works: Paper Moon Graphics, Time/Life Records
Present Clients: Boy's Life, Atlantic magazine, Gilliard Press, Miner Brewing Co.
Exhibitions: None
Collections: None

Jim Evans 84

I was born in Chicago, Illinois on Dec. 31, 1947. My schooling included Art Center College of Design and Cal Arts. In recent years I have done numerous Album covers, Movie Posters and Advertising Illustrations for all the major companies in Los Angeles. My clients have included Wrangler of Tokyo, Carnation Products, Continental Airlines, Paper Moon Graphics, Levi's, Walt Disney Productions, New World Pictures, Mizuno, and Life Link Intl. I have appeared in the New York Art Directors Annual, Idea Magazine, Jpanese Illustrator, Communication Arts, and Art Direction Magazine. My work has also appeared in the books, Air Powered, Phonographics, The Album cover Album, and The Blu-Book. Art exhibitions that I have appeared in recently include The Phonographics Exibition (L.A.), The American Airbrush Art Exhibition (TOKYO), a show titled 100 Unpublished Works by 50 Published Illustrators (L.A.) and a show at The Museum of Modern Art featuring T-Shirt Art (N.Y.). My original paintings have been bought primarily by private collectors.

F

Teresa Fasolino 85

Born: 1946, Port Chester, New York
Awards: Numerous Society of Illustrators Awards for Excellence; Graphis Annual; Society of Publication Design Awards of Merit
Past Works: Illustratons for most major national magazines, ad agencies and book publications
Present Clients: Esquire; Grand Union; Life; Playboy; Time/Life Books Inc.; TV Guide
Exhibitions: 1976: 200 Years of American Illustration, New York Historical Society, New York
1981: Religion Into Art, Pratt Manhatten Center, New York and Arkansas Art Center
1982–83: European Illustration, National Theatre, London
1983: Contemporary American Illustration and Design, Butler Art Institute, Youngstown, Ohio
Scoeity of Illustrators, New York
Art Directors Club of New York
Collections: Grand Union

Ann Field 86

Place of Birth: Brighton, Sussex, England.
Date of Birth: 29th February 1956
Past Works: All major fashion magazines in London, England.
Present Clients: Emi Records, Parachute (Fashion store), California magazine

Vivienne Flesher 87

Born: 1956 in N.Y.C.
School: Parsons School of Design
Primarily working in pastels, oils, and charcoal
Clients: Time, Rollingstone, New York Magazine, Texas Monthly, Vogue, Fortune, The Boston Globe, Bloomingdales, Macys, Bendels, Electra Records, CBS Records, The New York Times, Random House, recently finished a book for William Morrow & son, one of the books illustrations won a gold metal at the Society of Illustrators 1984. Several paintings are to be used in an upcoming movie "Almost You" to be released in early 1985, has been featured in Graphis 229 and teaches a portfolio class at School of Visual Arts.

Dick Flood 88

Profession: Advertising Illustrations and Cartoons for Digital
1980 Equipment Corporation, General Motors, Sears, United Airlines, Groen, Country Companies, United States Forest Service, Federal Emergency Management Agency, etc.
Book Illustration and Cartoons
The Legal Guide for the Family, By Donald Very, J.G. Ferguson Publishing Co., 111 East Wacker, Chicago, Il. (Literary Guild selection)
Teaching Involved Parenting, by Bill Wagonseller and Richard McDowell Research Press, Champaign, Il.
Getting Better Results from the Meetings You Run, by Michael Renton, Research Press, Champaign, Il.
Stress and How to Live With It, by Dr. Jerry Robinson, Meredith Corporation, Des Moines, Iowa
Courtroom Artist, On-the-spot drawings of U.S. Senate for CBS Evening News. Also assigned by CBS Network News to courtroom cases in Chicago, Detroit, Cleveland, St. Louis, Topeka, and Omaha.
Drawings of court cases for ABC Network News have appeared on World News Tonight, Good Morning America, and Nightline.
Positions: Assistant Editorial Art Director. San Jose Mercury-News, 750 Ridder Park Drive, San Jose, California.
1977–79 Working with editors and reporters to develop illustrations and cartoons to complement and attract attention to newspaper's editorial content.
1965–77 Political Cartoonist/Editorial Artist. San Jose Mercury-News
Political cartooning: Drawings on national issues covered the period from Vietnam to Watergate. Local and State issues included a special emphasis on environmental concerns such as saving of San Francisco Bay and protection of the California coastline.
Courtroom artist: On-the-Spot drawings at the trials of Angela Davis, Patty Hearst, John Lindley Fraser and others.
Special assignments: Monterey Jazz Festival, Hospital Emergency Room, Working on murder investigations to produce likeness of suspect from verbal descriptions provided by withness during hypnosis.

Robert Florczak 89

Born: 1950 in Washington D.C.
Awards: 1st prize National Scholastic Art Awards
1st prize West Village Outdoor Art Festival
Full Scholarship to Cooper Union N.Y.
Past Clients: CBS Records, Nonesuch Records, Random House, Bantam Books, Ballantine Books, New American Library, Ace Books, Del Rey, Franklin Mint.
Present Clinets: Young & Rubicam, Embassy Pictures, Warner Bros. Pictures.
Shows: Newman Galleries, N.Y.; Galleries Three N.Y.
Collections: Ruggiero Ricci, Eugene Fodor.

Patric Fourshé 90

Born: April 10, 1943 in Detroit, Michigan, graduated from Art Center College of Design in Pasadena, California.
Awards: Graphic Artist Guild Annual Shows
New York Society of Illustrators Annual Shows
American Illustration Annual Shows
Exhibitions: Scarab Club Annual Exhibitions, Detroit, Michigan
Return to Realism... Detroit Realists, Rochester, Michigan
Michigan Invitational Flint, Michigan
Collections: P. Candor – Robillard Birmingham, Michigan
Ms. Margaret Otremba Chicago, Illinois
Joseph & Helen Ostremba Harper Woods, Michigan
W. Lyle Davis Foundation Southfield, Michigan
Polk Laffoon IV Detroit, Michigan
Associate Professor of Advertising Design at Center for Creative Studies, Detroit, Michigan.
He is currently writing, designing and illusrating a book on surprising delusions in Contemporary American Life, called "Clap-Trap, Poppycock, Blather Cackle".

Phil Franké 91

Phil Franké was born in Brooklyn in 1955. After completing high school at St. Francis Prep School he attended art school at Pratt Institute, receiving his BFA in 1977.
Mr. Franké holds the position of art director, for motion picture advertising, at Diener Houser Bates. He is also a free-lance illustrator.
As an illustrator, Phil has had work exhibited in Creativity; the Society of Illustrators, Illustrators 21 and many other awards. Some of the many clients he works for are: I.C. Industries (annual report), ABC newspaper ads, BBD & O, N.W. Ayer, Doyle, Dane, Bernbach (GTE), AC & R Advertising (AURGEN), pharmaceutical advertisements, INA Insurance and many other national clients & agencies. He also does work for magazines (Field & Stream, Science Digest etc.) & books (Bradbury Press).
Mr. Franké is married and lives in Babylon, N.Y.
He is represented by Jane Lander Associates.

Dagmar Frinta 92

Born: October 16, 1956 in New York City, N.Y.
Awards: New York Art Director's Club
New York Society of Illustrators Annual Shows
Communication Arts Annuals
American Illustration Annuals
Creativity Annuals
Graphis Annuals
Past Works: CBS Records – Mobil Oil Corporation
Sony Television – Time Magazine
Fortune Magazine – Rollingstone Magazine
Museum of Modern Art, New York.
Harper and Row Publishers – Randam House
Simon and Schuster Publishers.
Present Clients: Science 84 – Franklin Library
The Boston Glove – TWA Ambassador Magazine
Mother Jones Magazine – Pantheon Books
I also am a professor of illustration at the Rhode Island School of Design.

Bernard Fuchs 94–95

BERNARD FUCHS, has become a name almost legendary in the field of illustration. Educated at Washington University School of Fine Arts in St. Louis, Missouri, Fuchs met with fame immediately for his paintings done while working at the New Center Studio in Detroit.
Since that time his work has been published in all the major magazines, including Sports Illustrated, New Yorker, Ladies Home Journal, and TV Guide. His illustrations have accompanied great literature in books published by the Franklin Library.
He has received every honor and award bestowed by the New York Society of Illustrators, including the youngest illustrator ever elected to the Hall of Fame in 1975. He was named "Artist of the Year" by the Artists Guild in 1962.
Two portraits Fuchs painted of John F. Kennedy during his presidency hang at the Kennedy Library.
Fuchs now lives and works in Westport, Connecticut. He remains at the very top of the illustration field, continuing to produce the beautiful and powerful images he is so famous for.

G

Nicholas Gaetano 93

Nicholas Gaetano was born in Colorado Springs, Colorado on June 25, 1944. He moved with his family to Long Island, New York, where he spent his youth. He attended The Art Center in Los Angeles.
Mr. Gaetano's works have been exhibited in "Two Hundred Years of American Illustration" and "The Art of Time Magazine" as well as in numerous College, Gallery and Museum Shows throughout the United States. To date, he has received many awards from the Society of Illustrators, American Institute of Graphic Arts, Andy Awards, One Show and Creativity Show. Many United States corporations, including Young & Rubicam, Citibank and DataPoint Corp., own and exhibit his original work in their corporate collections. Nicholas Gaetano's expertise includes editorial (Time, Forbes, New York Magazine, Fortune), T.V. animation (Jello, Clairol, G.E.), illustration campaigns (Sony, Frontier Airlines, Eastern Airlines, Holland America), and poster design.
Mr. Gaetano presently lives with his wife and two children in a studio loft in New York City.

Stanley W. Galli 96–97

Born in San Francisco 1912
Scholarships at the California School of Fine Arts (now the San Francisco Art Institute) and studies at Art Center School in Los Angeles were the source of his formal art training. Worldwide attention was attracted to his many wildlife and forest conservation paintings for the Weyerhaeuser Company Collection. These paintings were produced over many years in national publications and in some encyclopedias. He also designed a series of 26 postage stamps for the United Postal Service. These stamps won him many important awards; the original designs now remain in the United States Postal Archives. For his distinguished contribution to the field illustration, Mr. Galli was installed in the New York Society of Illustrators Hall of Fame in 1982. Mr. Galli has been pursuing an awakened interest in early California history, in particular the period of Spanish colonization. Because of this interest, a large number of paintings has resulted. This work has been shown broadly and is in collections throughout the United States and Europe.

Nixon Galloway 98–99

"Nick" Galloway is a native Californian, and lives in Manhattan Beach in a house of his own design, with his wife of thirty years. After serving in the Aviation branch of the Navy during World War II he attended Art Center School, garduating in 1949.
He is a painter and illustrator who's work has won awards throughout the United States. His paintings have been exhibited at the L.A. County Museum of Art, the Air Force Museum, the Smithsonian Institution, and the White House. He is a founding partner of Group West, Inc. of Los Angeles and a past president of the L.A. Society of Illustrators.
When not slaving over a hot drawing board, Nick can usually be found on the ski slopes or avidly racing his sailboat in Southern California waters.

John Gamache 100

Place of Birth: Gardner, Massachusetts
Date of Birth: 2-11-45
Awards: New York Society of Illustrators Annual show (20 and

24)
Hatch Awards (3)
Andy Award (Advertising Club of New York)
Merit Award (Advertising Club of Western Massachusetts)
Member of Society of Illustrators of New York (7 yrs.)

Past Works: Magazine Editorial – Golf Digest Inc., Atlantic Monthly, Gallery Magazine.
Book Covers – Houghton Mifflin, Addison Wellsley, Mysterious Press.
Advertising – Polaroid Corp., Westinghouse, Raytheon Inc., Franmara Inc., General Electric, Etonic, ITT, Sanders Corp., Whiting and Davis, Ann Taylor, Colibri, Gant, Bay Bank Boston, Spiedel.

Present Clients: Spectrum Graphics (CA), Mysterious Press (NY), Jason Grant Assoc. (RI), Edward Western Graphics & Galleries (CA & NY), Dynamic Graphics (IL).
Boston Representative: Sharon Kurlansky (617) 872-4549.

John Gampert 101

Place of Birth, Year of Birth: New York 8-18-44
Clients: Random House, CBS, Dell, Doubleday, National Lampoon, New York Times, Psychology Today ......
Collections: Private Colloections

Joe Garnett 102

Education:
1958-59 Chicago Art Institute, Chicago, Illinois
1962-64 Texas Technological College, Lubbock, Texas
1965-67 Chouinard Art Institute BFA, Los Angeles, California
Experience:
1968 Illustration & design: L.G. Hughes Studio, Detroit
1969-70 Illustration & design: McNamara Studio, Detroit
1971-72 Illustration & design: Studio Artists, Los Angeles
1972-77 Freelance illustration & design
1975 Illustration instructor: California State University, Fullerton, California
Work includes television, magazine, newspaper, brochure, murals, posters, three-dimensional graphic design, illustration, design, lettering.
Shows, Publications, Awards
1970 Detroit Art Directers' Show
1972 Los Angeles Art Directors' Show
1972 Art Direction Magazine
1972 Graphis Magazine
1972 Photographis Annual
1973 Mental Image, New York
1973 San Diego Art Directors' Show
1973 CA Magazine
1973 Gaphis Record Album Book
1974 Los Angeles Illustrators' Show
1974 Edward Thorpe Gallery, Santa Barbara
1974 Long Beach Art Association, Long Beach
1975 Gold Medal: Detroit Art Directors' Show (Mural for Chevrolet TV commercial)
1976 CA Annual
1977 Album Cover Album
1977 ADI Gallery, San Francisco

Gerry Gersten 103

Born in New York City on Oct. 17, 1927. Attended the High School of Music & Art and then spent 3 years at the Cooper Union Art School. He has awards from the Art Directors Club in New York, the Society of Illustrators in New York and the A.I.G.A. (American Institute of Graphic Arts). He has also been published in 'Idea' and '200 Years of American Illustration' and 'Vision'. His clients include: Sports Illustrated magazine, Time, Newsweek, Money. City Bank (TV Commercial), Playboy, Esquire, Franklin Library (limited editions), book of the Month, Red Book, TV Guide, McCalls, Ladies Home Journal, United Artists, BOAC, Peoples Air... Galleries exhibiting his work are Spectrum and Diaz-Marcial, both are in New York City.

George Giusti 104–106

Born in Milan, Italy. Swiss Citizen.; now U.S.A. Citizenship.
Studied Fine Arts at the "Brera Academy of Fine Arts" in Milan, Italy.
Graphic Design in Milan.
Own Design Studio in Zurich, Switzerland.
Came to the U.S. in 1938.
Naturalized in 1946.
Free Lance Artist and Designer; Consultant to Industry, Communication Graphics for the U.S. Government.
Editorial Design for Publishers etc.
Ten years as Art Consultant to Geigy Pharmaceuticals and Chemicals (now Ciba-Geigy), U.S. and Basel, Switzerland.
Exhibitions, Installations, etc.
Magazine Covers: Fortune, Time, Holiday, Travel & Leisure, S.E.P., for most U.S.I.A. Publications (U.S. Information Agency).
Advertising and Graphic Work, Illustrations, Trademarks, Packageing Design for major Corporations.
Portfolios in: Graphis, Switzerland, Idea, Japan, Gebrauchsgraphik, Germany, Pagina, Italy, Communication Art, U.S.A.
Exhibitions in most Capitals of the World through the USIA.
Other Exhibitions in most large U.S. Cities.
Awards: more than ten Gold and Silver Medals and more than 80 other Awards and citations.
Elected Art Director of the Year in 1958 and awarded the Golden T Square. Elected to the AD Hall of Fame in 1979.
Member: Art Directors Club of New York,
The American Institute of Graphic Arts, N.Y.
Alliance Graphique Internationale, U.S. Chapter.
International Center for Graphic Art (Typographic Art).
Sculpture: Westinghouse Collection and other private collections. A major piece was recently exhibited at the Aldrich Museum of Contemporary Art in Ridgefield, Co.
For further information consult Who is Who in America, 1978.

Robert Giusti 107

Place of Birth: Zurich, Switzerland
Date of Birth: 11. 30. 1937
Awards: New York Society of Illustrators Annual Show, Society of Publication Design Awards, Graphic Design: U.S.A. awards, American Institute of Graphic Arts Awards, Art Directors Club Silver Awards, Andy Awards, Advertising Club of New York, Australian Writers and Art Directors Award
Past Works: Record Album covers for Atlantic Records and CBS Records
Magazine covers for Time, Inside Sports, TV Guide, Science Digest, Omni, Idea
Advertisements for Zerox, IBM, St. Regis, Champion International, Celestial Seasoning Teas, Thai Airlines
Annual Reports for H.J. Heinz Co., Eli Lilly & Co.
Magazine Editorial illustrations for Penthouse, Omni, Atlantic Monthly, McCalls, Redbook, Fortune.
Present Clients: Time Inc., Barklays Bank, Celestial Seasonings, Random House
Exhibitions: The New York Historical Society Museum, The Society of Illustrators, The American Institute of Graphic Arts, The Museum of The Surreal and Fantastique, Rizzoli Gallery, N.Y., Shibuya Parco Gallery, Tokyo
Collections: Time Inc., Eli Lilly & Co., Ethyl Corp.

Milton Glaser 108–111

1929 Born in New York City.
Awarded a Fulbright Scholarship to attend the Academy of Fine Arts in Bologna, Italy where he studied etching with the late George Morandi.
1974 Commissioned to do a 600-foot mural for the New Federal Office Building in Indianapolis.
Architectural and graphic commissions include the complete graphic and decorative programs for the restaurants at the World Trade Center in New York City and the design of the Observation Deck of the Twin Towers (1975).
1979 Elected to the Art Directors Club Hall of Fame in New York, and named Honorary Fellow by the Society of Arts in England. Also the recipient of the Society of Illustrators' Gold Medal.
1981 Exhibtion and lecture at Harvard University's Carpenter Center.
1983 Current magazine projects include design programs for several European as well as American publications.
Presently teaching at the School of Visual Arts and has conducted special programs in Ireland and Morocco under its auspices.

Alexander Gnidziejko 112

Since 1966, Alex Gnidziejko's art has been commissioned by major publications and corporations including NBC, Time Inc., Sports Illustrated, New York Magazine, McCall's Magazine, Mobile Oil Corporation, Holiday Inns, Penthouse, Good Housekeeping, Esquire, Boy's Life, National Geographic, Scott Foresman and Lenox China.
The Society of Illustrators awarded Alex Gnidziejko the prestigious Gold Medal in illustration in 1975. In 1979, he received a Creativity Certificate of Distinction from Art Direction Magazine. In 1980 he received advertising's Andy Award as well as an Award of Excellence from CA Magazine.
The New Jersey Watercolor Society awarded the painting "Thoughts of Home" the Pauline and Barnet Posner Award in their 39th annual open exhibition at the Morris Museum. The painting was chosen for Spectrum 1982 at Fairleigh Dickinson University.

Raphaelle Goetals 113

Place of Birth: Brussel, Belgium
Date of Birth: March 1, 1958
Awards: Society of Illustrator, Los Angeles Annual Show
Clients Include: KABC Channel & Television, Capitol Records, California magazine, Dyer Khan Design, Shape magazine, the Herald examiner, Los Angeles magazine
Exhibitions: Gallery 75, Brussel

Penelope Gottlieb 114

Education: Art Center College of Design: B.A. w/honors, 1976 Illustration
Immaculate Heart College: 1973
Chouinards: 1972
1976-1982 Freelance design and illustration
Sample list of clients and projects: Knott's Berry Farm, Magic Mountain, ABC, NBC, CBS, Passport Scotch, Sizzler Steak House, Laufer Publications, Playgirl Magazine, Emmy Magazine, L.A. Magazine, Manufacturers Bank, Paper Moon Graphics, New York West, B.D. Fox & Friends, Select TV
Brown & Gold Lighting (Belding Cup Award – 1978)
(Society of Illustrators – Illustration West Show, various awards 1976-1981)

James Graca 115

Born: Akron, Ohio, 10. 13. '48
Jim is an award-winning illustrator and graphic designer. His work has received "Certificates of Merit" for the last six years in the West Coast Illustrators' Show, and was requested and displayed in the Vision West Coast Artists Today show in Japan. Jim also has two posters that were requested and are on permanent display in the Fedier's Werbeagentur Poster Collection in Zurich, Switzerland. Jim is a graduate of The Art Center College of Design, where he became the first in the history of that school to receive a "Best" award in the prestigious "Art Center College of Design International Alumni Exhibition" within one year of graduation. He is also a listed biographee in the 1981-1982 edition of "Who's Who in California." Jim has done post-production artwork and sketches for over twenty-five motion picture campaigns. Hollywood reporter "Key Art" award for "Eating Raoul" 1983. Simpson paper "Award of Excellence" 1983, Pernod of France, client.
Partial Client List: ABC Motion Pictures, Billboard Magazine, The Burbank Studios, Carnation, Command Performance Hair Salons, Emmy Magazine, Fairchild Semi-Conductors, The Greek Theatre, Human Behavior Magazine, Jet America, Knott's Berry Farm, The Los Angeles County Fair, Litton Industries, Nat'l Lampoon Film Productions, NBC TV, New West Magazine, NISS, Pernod of France, Roth Greeting Cards, Score Internat'l Off-Road Racing, Subaru, Toyota, Taco Bell, 20th Century Fox, United California Bank, Universal Studios, Western Airlines

Alexa Grace 116

ALEXA GRACE's drawings have appeared in Time, Life, The New York Times, Town and Country, etc... in 1981 she collaborated with Colline Faure Poiree to make a French children's book, Une Journée de Chien. Her Porcelains are sometimes exhibited at the Graham Gallery, 1014 Madison Avenue, New York.

Daerick Gröss 117

Place of Birth: Dayton Ohio/United States
Date of Birth: 1/28/47
Awards: National Scholastic Asso. /1965
National Heart Fund/1977
International Poster Competition–France/1980 (P117 #3)
Past Works: Promotional Posters for Gold's Gym, Caesar's Palace, Mr. America & Olympic Gym.
Print illustrations for Cannon Films, MGM, Orion pictures, PKA
Internal editorial illustrations for Playgirl Magazine, After Dark Magazine, Muscle and Fitness Magazine, Flex Magazine, Hustler Magazine
Game Jackets for Sierra On-Line and Fun-Soft.
Present Clients: Data-Most, Gold's Gym Enterprises, Laugh Factory Magazine (Art Director), Flex Magazine, Santa Barbara Magazine, Otis Art Institute & Parson's School of Design
Exhibitions: Leslie-Lohman Gallery/New York
Collections: Private individuals

Bob Graham 118–119

He was born in Texas in 1947. He attended North Texas State University where he majored in Commerical Art. Mr. Graham's love of portraiture and his keen desire for knowledge led him to an artist's colony in Provincetown, Massachusetts, where he met the noted Impressionist Henry Hensche. After studying there for several years, Mr. Graham opened a studio on the prestigious Lombardy Way in Atlanta, Georgia. During his nine years there, he painted numerous portraits for some of the most respected families in Atlanta. He currently resides in New Orleans.
Q. How much time is required for you to paint a portrait?
A. For a large portrait my optimum working time is three weeks. A week of study sometimes precedes this.
Q. How long will I have to sit?
A. Perhaps only 1/2 hour if we work solely from photos that I take. Every project is different and we tailor it to meet both our needs. I can work from live sittings, photos, or a combination of both
Q. Do you like working with children?
A. I love to work with children.
Q. Do you teach?
A. Yes. Although I'm usually busy on a project I periodically teach workshops in pastel and give demonstrations in pastel and oil. I have taught in art clubs and private schools, and given demonstrations before clubs and organizations for many years.
Q. Should I commission a pastel or an oil?
A. Both mediums are very good and also very permanent. I use pastel not only for sketches but as a major medium as well. I can easily spend 80 hours on a head study in pastel, endlessly changing the way th subject projects. Pastel full-lengths have a softness to them, and the medium lends itself to the vignette. Pastel paintings are delightful to have in your home environment. The colors of oils have a wide range than pastels. The differences between colors are greater, allowing a greater range of harmonies and thus a greater variety of mood. Oil portraits have an important place in the march of art history. I

believe we are all influenced psychologically about participating in that march.

David Grove 120–121

Place of Brith and Date of Birth: Born in Washington D.C. U.S.A., February 27, 1940
Awards: Have received awards from both the Society of Illustrators in New York and the Society of Illustrators of Los Angeles including an Award of Excellence and a Gold Medal in advertising from the Society of Illustrators of Los Angeles.
Clients: Have done work for the following clients: Standard Oil, U.S. Navy, Bank of America, Dell Publishing Co., Atlantic Richfield Company, National Football League Properties Inc., Western Airlines, Gates Learjet, Bantam Books Inc. Universal Studios, Fawcett Books, Walt Disney Productions, Indianapolis Motor Speedway, Pendleton Woolen Mills, Deutche Bank, and many others.
Exhibitions: Have had several one-man shows – the most recent of which was at the Academy of Art Gallery in San Francisco in 1983. My work has appeared in the "200 years of American Illustration" exhibition in New York in 1976, The "Salon des Illustrateurs" in Paris in 1983, and the Annual Exhibit of the National Academy of Design in New York in 1984. In addition, my work appears regularly in the annual exhibitions of the Society of Illustrators in New York, The Society of Illustrators of Los angeles, and the San Francisco Society of Illustrators.
Collections: My work is part of several private collections.

Steven Guarnaccia 122

Place of Birth: Fairfield, Connecticut
Date of Birth: Oct. 23, 1953
Awards: New York Art Director's Club show 1980–1983
Society of Illustrators Annual Show 1980, 1982–1983
A.I.G.A. Mental Menagerie 1983
A.I.G.A. Cover Show 1984
American Illustration Annual 1982
Society of Newspaper Designers – Silver Award
Boston Art Director's Club Bronze Award
Best Comic Strip of the Year – Playboy 1982
Past Works: 6 bookcovers for the novels of P.G. Wodehouse published by Harper & Row
Logo, promotion, and album cover for Streetwise Records
Cover for Abitare magazine in Milan
Illustrations for book: Sin City Fables
Film poster in Milan "Nella Ciffá"
Present Clients: New York Times Book Review, Sports Illustrated, New York magazine Harper & Row, Altman & Manley Advertising Agency, Boston, Boston Globe Magazine

Helene Guetary 123

Born in Paris, 1957. Attended a artschool of Paris. After that, came to New York, studied etching and lithograph in School of Visual Arts. She has had one-woman shows in New York, Seatle, and in France every year. With a lot of applause and numerous collectors like Kennedy Museum of Art, her works has appeared in Ellé, Gap, and other major French magazines. Currnt clients include Penthouse, Interview, Camera Arts and many others. She got an award of Excellence of CEBA in 1981. She is represented by Jane Lander Associates, New York.

Abe Gurvin 128

Education: Otis Art Institute; Chouinard Art Institute; UCLA (B.A. June 1959 plus some course work toward M.A.)
Teaching: Art Center College of Design, Pasadena; California State University at Los Angeles; San Diego State University
Clients: Travel: Continental Airlines, western Airlines, PSA, Eastern Airlines, Hughes Air West, American Express, Carte Blanche, Westways, Caesar's Tahoe, Century Plaza Hotel, Universal Sheraton Hotel, Host Hotels, Motor Trend, Car & Driver
Entertainment: 20th Century Fox, Times-Mirror Dimension Cablevision, Warner Brothers, MGM, Goldwyn, Universal Pictures, Hanna-Barbara Productions, CBS-TV, NBC-TV, Westinghouse Broadcasting, San Diego Padres, Capitol Records, ABC Records, Atari, many others
Food: Jack-in-the-Box, Carl's Jr., Taco Bell, Burger King, Kentucky Fried Chicken, General Foods, Post Cereals, Armour Star, Ralph's Grocery Stores, Van de Kamps Bakery, Gallo Winery, Knudsen Dairy, Shakey's Pizza, Canada Dry, Foster's Freeze, Hunt-Wesson, Rosarita Mexican Foods, Van Kamps Sea Food, others
Financial: Home Federal Savings, Bank of America, Security-Pacific, E.F. Hutton, New York Stock Exchange, many others
Publishing: Harcourt-Brace-Jovanovitch, CRM Books – Psychology Today, American Heritage Press, Dell, Fairchild Publications, Ziff-Davis, McCalls – Rdbook, Parents Magazine Press, Wm. Morrow, Macmillan, Saturday Review Press, Los Angeles Herald-Examiner, San Diego Union – Tribune, others
Electronics: IBM, AT&T, Sanyo, Sony – Superscope, Marantz, Varian, Kenwood, Toshiba, Cable Net, New York Telephone Company, Fairchild, others
Advertising: Chiat-Day, Cochrane Chase – Livingston, Cole & Weber, Doyle Dane Bernbach, Grey, Benton & Bowles, Lane & Huff, J. Walter Thompson, Young & Rubicam, Wells Rich Green, McCan Erickson, SSC&B, Phillips – Ramsey, Della Femina Travisano, Dailey, Ketchum Communications others
Real Estate: Broadmoor Homes, Century 21, Larwin Development Co., Marina – Pacific Condominiums, Mission Viejo, Ponderosa Homes, Taylor Woodrow, University Square, Braemar Development Corp.
Industrial: Datsun, Toyota, Kawasaki, WD-40, Burlington Mills, Honda, Isuzu, Payless Shoes, McDonnell–Douglas, AMF-Voit, Olin Solar, Exxon, others
Public Sector: Orange County Transit District, Los Angeles County Fair, Phoenix Symphony, LA Philharmonic – Hollywood Bowl, Southern California Edison, LA City Performing Arts Festival
Miscellaneous: Blue Cross, Macy's, National Football League, Aurora, Pentil, Knotts Berry Farm, Bell Helmets, others
Community Service: Designed "Books for India Drive" poster (1959), designed theme poster for Peace Coalition march (1971), other poster designs and donations of thousands of dollars worth of paintings to worthy causes
Numerous awards including MAGGY Award for Best Publication (1977), 3 Golden Orange Awards (First Place) from Orange County Advertising Federation (1980), numerous certificates of merit and other awards, numerous publication credits

H

Kunio Hagio 124–125

Place of Birth: Chicago, Illinois U.S.A. October 11, 1947
Awards: Gold and Silver medals from The Society of Illustrators (New York), Communication Arts, Key Art Award, Print, Silver Medal from Art Directors Club (New York)
Past Works: Playboy, Penthouse, Twentieth Century Fox, Paramount, Universal, CBS, Tribune, Budweiser
Present Clients: same
Exhibitions: Society of Illustrators award exhibit
Collections: private only

H. Tom Hall 126–127

Place of Birth: Ridley Park, Pennsylvania.
Date of Birth: June 12, 1932.
Awards: New York Society of Illustrators Annual Shows. 1st recipient of Romance Convention's Illustrator of the year – 1982.
Past Works: In the beginning I illustrated children's books and magazines. My first job was illustrating a book I wrote while spending a pleasent year and a-half in Japan, called "The Golden Tombo", published by Alfred A. Knopf. After moving into the adult field I worked for Bantam Books, Avon Books, Warner Books, New American Library, Ballantine Books, Fawcett Books, Saturday Evening Post, Reader's Digest, National Geographic Books and others.
Present Clients: Ballantine and Fawcett Books.
Exhibitions: One man shows at The Art Alliance and Moore College of Art, Philadelphia, Pennsylvania. Group shows at the New York, Society of Illustrators.
Collections: Paintings owned by private collectors.

John Hamagami 129

Place of Birth: Nara, Japan (moved to the U.S. at the age of 2)
Date of Birth: November 27, 1955
Awards: None
Past Works/Present Clients: Carnation, Dancer Fitzgerald Sample, Inc., Dyer-Kahn, Inc., John Coulter Design, Reiser William-Deyong, Seiniger Advertising, Stan Evenson, Inc., Universal Pictures.

Cathy Heck 130

Borin in 1956 in San Antonio, Texas.
Attended college at the University of Texas at Austin and received her BFA in Advertising Design.
In 1978 married Jim Heck, also a Texan who is in oil and gas banking.
In 1979 Cathy Heck discontinued her masters program to accept an art directing position with Young and Rubicam in New York City. In 1981 Cathy Heck left Young and Rubicam to pursue a career in free lance illustration with Jane Lander Associates. Ms Heck has received awards of excellence in the "Art Directors Annual", "The One Show", and the "Clio Awards". Ms. Heck's interests include tennis, cooking, and Antiquing.
Cathy Heck works in Texas and New York.

Joe and Kathy Heiner 131

Joe Heiner, born in Aberdeen, Maryland October 1951 and Kathy Heiner, born in Salt Lake City, Utah July 1952 met at the age of eleven while sitting side by side in their 6th grade art class in Salt Lake City, Utah. Today they work side by side in their Utah mountain studio. They serve clients from across the United States including Levi Strauss, 7-Up, Paper Moon Graphics, Adidas, ABC Records and 20th Century Fox. They have contributed to many movie campaigns including "Star Wars" and "California Suite". Their work has appeared in magazines such as Time, Vogue, McCalls, and almour; on billboards, posters, package designs, greeting cards and product designs. They have received numerous awards including The One Show Gold Award. Their work is represented in the permanent collection of the New York Museum of Modern Art.

Albert Hirschfeld 132–133

Al Hirschfeld is as much a theatrical institution as the Actors' Studio, Hollywood and Vine and the Great White Way itself. For more than 50 years, his drawings in THE NEW YORK TIMES have been a Sunday tradition. They enliven our already Lively Arts and make their stars and personalities as familiar as his own signature.
One Hirschfeld trademark – "harmless insanity," as he describes it – is the appearance of his daughter's name, NINA, hidden in each drawing at least once. From an innocent beginning to herald her birth in 1945, the search for the concealed NINAs has become a passion for Hirschfeld fanciers.
Hirschfeld's first caricature appeared in the old WORLD in 1923, followed soon by one in the TRIBUNE and then the TIMES. Through the years his work has been reproduced in HOLIDAY, VOGUE, COLLIERS, SATURDAY EVENING POST, LIFE, LOOK and many other national periodicals. His work can be found in the collections of the Metropolitan Museum of Art, the Fogg Museum, Museum of Modern Art, Brooklyn Museum, New York Public Library and major museums throughout the United States.
Hirschfeld is represented exclusively by The Margo Feiden Galleries, New York, New York, where 50 years of his drawings are on permanent display.

Martin Hoffman 134

Born in Florida in 1935, Mr. Hoffman taught painting and drawing at the University of Miami from 1969 to 1971. During his career, he has held several one-man exhibitions. These include: Miami Museum of Modern Art, Florida (1960, 1964, and 1967) O.K. Harris gallery, New York City (1973, 1975 and 1979). His group exhibitions include: New York Cultural Center, New York City, "Realism Now" (1972); Skidmore College, Saratoga Springs, New York, "New Realism," (1974); Vassar College Art Gallery, Poughkeepsie, New York, "New American Landscapes," (1973); The Contemporary Art Center, Cincinnati, Ohio, "Painting and Sculpture Today," (1974); and many others. Past works include Nasa Space Shuttle Program, Blondie "Autoamerican" album, Basile International, Milano, New York Times, Ajinotomo, Tokyo. His illustrations were introduced in Japanese magazine, "Illustration" No. 18, Oct. issue of 1982. Current clients include Playboy, Fortune, L'UOMO, Hakuhodo Agency, Toyo Cinema, and so on.

Jamie Hogan 135

Place of Birth: Lincoln, New Hampshire
Date of Birth: October 12, 1958
Awards: New York Society of Illustrators 25th show, American Illustration vols. 1 & 2, Appeared in "Graphis" and "Print", Boston Art Directors Club show.
Past Works: Harvard Business Review
Present Clients: Digital Equipment Corporation, Boston Glove, Boston Magazine, New Age Journal, Ad Week, Fields Hosery, Philadelphia Inquirer, Texas Monthly Magazine
Exhibitions: Montserat School of Art, Drawings Exhibit, 1983; Society of Illustrators Show

Brad Holland 136–137

Born Fremont, Ohio
Self-taught as an artist.
Drawings and paintings appear regularly in major publications, including Time, Life, Playboy, Newsweek, The New York Times, The Atlantic Monthly, The Washington Post. Painted Time's Man-of-the-Year cover of the Ayatullah Khomeini, 1980.
Authored Human Scandals, T.Y. Crowell, 1977.
Work shown at numerous museums, including:
The Musee des Beaux-Arts, Brodeaux, France, 1973
The Louvre, 1974
The Amon Carter Museum, 1976
New York Historical Society, 1979
The Library of Congress, 1979
Work in permanent collection of the Library of Congress.
One-man show, Vontobel Gallery, Zurich, 1979.
Designed the 13¢ stamp of Crazy Horse for the U.S. Postal Service, 1982.
Did poster, program art and stage art for the American Book Awards, 1982.
10 foot × 30 foot wall drawing for the United Nations disarmanent Conference, 1983.
Gold Medals from the Society of Illustrators and the Art Directors Club of New York.
Twice awarded the Playboy Editorial Award.
Judges award, Los Angeles Society of Illustrators, 1983.
Illustrated several books, including collected works of Jack London, The Franklin Library, 1983.

Holly Hollington 138

Born 9th, May 1950. Attended West Sussex School of Art for pre. Dip. 1968–1969. Studied Fashion Design. Diploma in Art & Design at Birmingham College of Art. 1969–1972 B of Arts. Degre.
1972–1973 post Graduate year at Birmingham College of Art in Art History & Film. Started own clothing company for 2 years. moved to Majorca in drew trees & landscapes in 1975. Then Munich, West Germany, where she started commercial art. Took up airbrushing in 1978 in Munich and moved to America in 1979–1980. Worked for English Vogue, Tatler, Playgirl magazine Rod Dyer, Snyder Adv., Ahmanson Theatre, Paramount, MCA Records, A & M Records, MC Ann Erickson.

Katheryn Holt 139

Education: Art Center College of Design Los Angeles
 Bachelor of Fine Arts, 1975
 University of Southern California Fine Arts Major, 1969–1971
Experience: Freelance Illustrator
 Clients have included Rolling Stone, New York Magazine, The New York Times, GQ, Vogue, Fortune, Cue, Quest, Self, Scholastic Publications, Adamo Records, Album Graphics Inc., RCA Records, CBS Records, Scali, McCabe & Sloves Advertising, Ogilvy & Mather Advertising, Crabwalk Cards, Paper Moon Graphics, 1975–
 Samples of my work may be seen in the 1979, 1980, 1981, and 1982 issues of the Illustrator's Annual
 Teacher, 2nd year drawing and illustration, School of Visual Arts, New York, 1980–1983
 Staff Illustrator, Assistant Art Director, Sesame Street Magazine, Electric Company Magazine, 1975–1976
 Art Director, Fashion Coordinator May Co., Los Angeles, 1974
 Born Los Angeles, California, 5/2/51

Robert Hunt 140

Place of Birth: Berkeley, California
Date of Birth: November 5, 1952
Awards: Los Angeles Society of Illustrators; Western Art Directors Club
Present Clients: Levi Strauss; Bank of America; Atari; Texas Instruments; Gemco, Bantam Books; Dell Publishers; Design Ware; Lucasfilm
Exhibitions: Work exhibited in San Francisco, Los Angeles and New York Society of Illustrators shows

I

Bill Imhoff 141

Place of Birth: Los Angeles, Calif.
Date of Birth: Nov. 30, 1944
Past Works: Album covers, magazine covers and editorial art, book covers, posters, and studio art.

Glen Iwasaki 142

Born in Los Angeles. He began his freelance career in 1972, and worked for design studios, ad agencies, record companies, and magazines. From 1978–1981, he worked for Bowmar/Noble Publishers as art director and designer of educational materials. Sine 1981, he has been art director for National Football League Properties, producing work for the 28 NFL football clubs, the Super Bowl, and numerous collateral pieces for NFL clients. He recently has completed a set of four books for Architectural Digest and a series of illustrations for an elementary math book published by Addison-Wesley.

J

Barry Jackson 143

I'm from an Air Force family. I lived in many places as a child, but most of my life has been spent in California.
I discovered my talent as an artist at an early age, and decided to make it my major in college. I attended Long Beach State and Art Center College of Design. I graduated in 1977 and worked as a background painter for the Animated Films "American Pop" and "The Lord of the Rings".
I began freelancing in Los Angeles since 1980. I've worked for many movie campaigns and have been printed in many national campaigns.
I plan to move to New York.

Kathy Jacobi 144

Kathy Jacobi; born New York, N.Y., 1947
Drawings, Watercolors, Etchings, Oil Paintings Fine Book and Journal Illustration
Kathy graduated from California State University (Northridge) with a Master of Arts Degree. During her career she has held several solo exhibitions. Among these were: City Gallery, Agoura Hills, California (1984); Fowler Mills Gallery, Santa Monica, California (1981); C.S.U.N. Fine Arts Gallery 2, Nothridge, California (1980); Fowler MIlls Gallery, Santa Monica, California (1978) just to name a few. She has also participated in many group exhibitions. These include: 9th Annual Miniature International Art Show (1984), Clearwater, Florida; 5th Annual Paper in Particular (1984), Columbia College, Missouri; 27th National Print Exhibition, Hunterdon Art Center (1983), Clinton, New Jersey, etc. Some of Kathy's awards include National Watercolor Society Members' Cash Award, 63rd National Watercolor Society Annual Exhibition (1983); 9th Annual Minature International Art Show, 2nd place for graphics; national watercolor Society Cash Award, Los Angeles, California and many others. kathy belongs to such associations as the National Watercolor Society, Los Angeles Institution of Contemporary Art, Graphic Artists Guild, and others.

Jay 145

Occupation: Illustrator
Born 1949. Education: Bachelor's of Fine Arts in 1975 — Northern Illinois University. Master's of Fine Arts in 1977 — Northern Illionis University. Currently working as Free Lance Illustrator.

Lonnie Sue Johnson 148

Lonni Sue Johnson was born in 1950 and raised in Princeton, New Jersey. Her father is an electronics engineer and her mother is an artist, as her own mother had been. Interested in music as well as art, she studied piano, violin and viola, and played in her high school orchestra, the Princeton University Orchestra, and many chamber music ensembles.
After graduating from Princeton High School, Ms. Johnson attended the College of Wooster in Ohio for one year, and that summer studied French at the University of Strabourg. In 1972 she received a B.F.A. in printmaking & drawing from the University of Michigan's School of Architecture and Design.
Returning to Princeton, Ms. Johnson sold drawings and prints through local galleries while continuing to study the viola. She taught art at the Stuart Country Day School from 1974 until 1976 when she began to work full time as an illustrator. During 1977–78 she studied with R.O. Blechman and Charles B. Slackman at the School of Visual Arts in New York City.
Ms. Johnson's drawings and watercolors have appeared in many publications, such as The New Yorker, The New York Times, Time, Fortune, Business Week, Forbes, Good Housekeeping, Psychology Today, The Dial, Geo, and Womans's Day. She has worked for various design studios and advertising agencies, producing drawings for such companies as Exxon, General Motors, AT&T and IBM. She has just joined a new animation studio.
Ms. Johnson has also illustrated books for Random House, Harper and Row, Princeton University Press, and Simon and Schuster. A children's book, which she illustrated for Atheneum, will appear in the fall of 1983.
Her drawings are included in the Society of Illustrator's Annual, Vols. 24 and 25; Graphis Annuals 1981, 1982 and 1983; and the American Illustration Annuals Vols. 1 and 2. Her work can also be seen in the following public collections; the New Jersey State Museum at Trenton, the Princeton University Permanent Graphic Collection, The New Jersey Bicentennial Commission, Rockefeller University, the Newark Museum, and the Newark Public Library.
Ms. Johnson's other pursuits include cooking, reading, jogging and traveling in Europe and Japan. She lives on Manhattan's upper west side with her husband who is a composer.

K

Eugene Karlin 146–147

Eugene was born in Wisconsin.
He was awarded several scholarships for his field of study. These included: Chicago Professional School of Art (Chicago), Art Institute (Chicago), Art Students League (New York) and Colorado Springs Fine Art Center (Colorado). He has exhibited at galleries such as: Art Institute (Chicago), Pennsylvania Academy (Philadelphia), San Francisco Museum (San Francisco), Art Directors Club of New York (New York), Far Gallery (New York), Alonso Gallery (New York), and many others. Among his many awards are the Clyde M. Carr Prize, Art Institute (Chicago), Certificates of Excellence for three consecutive years; AIGA Exhibitions (New York), Award for Excellence, COMMUNICATION ARTS Magazine (New York), etc. Eugene has done illustrations for such magazines as: FORTUNE, ESQUIRE, SEVENTEEN, FAMILY CiRCLE, READERS DIGEST, and manay others. At present, he holds a teaching position at the School of Visual Arts. Eugene has also done books jackets for such publishers as: Knopf, Harcourt Brace, Bantam Books, John Wiley & Sons, Simon & Shuster and others.

John M. Kilroy 149

Place of Birth: Boston, Massachusetts
Data of Birth: March 20, 1957
Awards: New York Society of Illustrators Annual Show
Past and Present Clients Includes: Parker Brothers, Polaroid Corp. New England Telephone Co., Myashenia Gravis Foundation, Yankee Magazine, BASF, Accoustic Research, Howard Johnsons, Liberty Mutual Insurance Co., McDonald's Corp., Spaulding Corp.

Choel-Sa Kim 150

Born Fukuoka Pref., Japan, 1958. Moved Shiga Pref. and attended Nakanoshima Art School for two years. Then went to America, studied at Academy of Art in San Francisco for four years. Merit Scholarship (Academy of Art) in 1983, Illustrator's Society Annual Scholarship Competition (New York) in 1984. Present Clients are: Harcourt Brace Jovanovich, publishers, Bernad Hodes Advertising.

Thea Kliros 151

Born: New York City, New York
Awards: New York Society of Illustrators, Annual Show, Creativity II: A Photographic Review, California
Past Works: Good Housekeeping Magazine, Hudson's Department Store, Avon Cosmetics, Candies Shoes, Lady Manhatten Shirts
Present Clients: Hoeschst Fibers "Treveria", Pseudonyms, Ladies Home Journal
Exhibitions: Baltimore Museum 100 Years of American Illustration

Richard Kriegler 152

Richard Kriegler was born in St. Paul, Minnesota in 1946. He attended the University of Houston, where he recevied a BFA, and was awarded an MFA from Cranbrook Academy of Art in Michigan. He moved to Los Angeles, California in 1973, where he designed record album covers for London Records for two and one-half years. he later worked for Gallo Wineries for two years, then opened his own studio in 1979.
He has received three Los Angeles Art Director Awards and two New York Art Director Awards, and has had exhibits at the Los Angeles Art Directors in 1980, 1981 and 1982.
Current clients include: IT&T, ABC-TV, 20th Century Fox, Continental Airlines, Dynachem, Alpine Radio and Proton Radio.

John A. Kurtz 153

1942 Born in Chicago, Illionis
1962 Entered the Art Institute of Chicago on scholarship from the Park Ridge Art League.
1969 Organized first one-man show.
1977 "The 76th Chicago and Vicinity Show" Art Institute of Chicago
1981 One-man show: Drawings and Paintings Chicago
1982 One-man show: Recent Paintings Chicago
1984 80th Exhibition by Artists of Chicago and Vicinity Art Institute of Chicago
Publications:
1973 Paintings published as illustrations in OUI Magazine.
1982 February issue, PLAYBOY Magazine: illustration of short story by Robert Silverberg.
1983 Illustrations for Playboy Dec. 83 issue short story by Hunter S. Thomson
1984 Playboy to be published Apr. or May Story by Gary Taubes
Awards:
1981 Art Director Club, 60th Annual Exhibition (Merit Award). Society of Publication of Designers, (Award of Merit).

Bob Kurtz 154–155

Director, Writer, Designer, Producer
Born: Los Angeles, California, U.S.A.
Graduate: Chouinard Art Institute, Los Angeles El Camino, J.C., Los Angeles
Have worked as writer, designer, director on TV film-commercials as well entertainment filsm.
Various films included in the permanent collections of:
 Modern Museum of Art, New York
 San Francisco Museum of Art
 Los Angeles County Art Museum
Major award winner of the following film festivals:
 Los Angeles Society of Illustrators Show
 International Festival of Short Films-Cracow, Poland
 International Festival of Short Films-Mamia, Romania
 International Festival of Short Films-Annecy, France
 Atlanta Film Festival (both animation and live action)
 International Animation Tournee London Film Festival Locarno Film Festival — Uruguary
 Grenoble International Film Festival — France
 International Animation Film Festival (Childrens Educational Films)
 Oberhausen International Film Festival
 Philadelphia International Film Festival (Live Action)
 Landers Associates (Live Action)
 Cine Golden Eagle, American Representative to Foreign Film Festivals, Washington, D.C. (Live Action)
 New York International Film Festival
 International Russian Film Festival — Belding Award
 CLIO Awards
 International Film and Television Festivals New York
 OTTAWA
 Communication Arts
 The Art Directors of Los Angeles
 Chicago International Film Festival
 The 11th International Tournee of Animation
 Advertising Club of New York
 Society of Illustrators San Francisco
 Atlanta Film Festival

Am a recipient of the American Film Institute Grant
Member on the Board of Govenors of the Academy of Motion Pictures Arts and Sciences — Short Fiims Division
Member on the 1975 Executive Board of the Academy of Motion Pictures Arts and Sciences — Documentary Shorts Division
Member on Board of Directors, Asifa-West (International Animation Society)

L

Dave LaFleur 156

The Vintage '83 poster for the California Wine Festival was produced by Musgrave & Friends, an innovative advertising design group located in Monterey, California. The artist, Dave LaFleur, is the newest "Friend" in this multi-talented organizaton.

Dave graduated from Colorado Institute of Art in June, 1981. While still a student, he did his first professional artwork for Leo Burnett, the large advertising agency based in Chicago. It consisted of several portraits for 7-Up International.

Despite his youth (he's only twenty-two) and his brief career since graduating from college, Dave has worked on illustrations for an impressive list of clients including Doyle, Dane and Bernbach, Coors, Philip Morris, Denver Magazine, Los Angeles Magazine, Campus Life, Los Angeles Herald, California Today, Brentwood Publishing, American Bar Association, Atari, Tracey locke, Shaklee Corp., Hewlett-Packard, Jovan and American Oil & Gas Reporter.

LaFleur has received awards of excellence from the Art Directors Club of Denver, Colorado Institute of Art, Illustration West, Society of Illustrators (Illustrators 26), Print (Regional Annual), American Institute of Graphic Artists and Graphis. Musgrave & Friends is proud to include Dave LaFleur as one of its best "Friends."

Jim Lamb 157

Place of Birth: Hamilton, Montana
Date of Birth: September 5, 1946
Awards: Communication Arts Magazine's Award for Excellence (CA-79)
Orange County Ad Arts Award for Excellence 1980
Graphic Magazine's DESI Award 1980 (New York)
Tools of the Trade Show 5 1980
The West Coast Show 79
Nominated for Best Paperback Book Cover for American Book Awards 1982
Winner for Best Editorial Piece in Show, Society of Illustrator's Annual Show (Illustrator's West) 1982
Past Works: Illustrations for Fire of Life Published by Smithsonian Books
Seven Paintings for Western Christmas Story Told by Johnny Cash (Billy Graham Christmas Special) National TV
Covers for Pro! Magazine, National Football League
Books for Children's Press, Chicago
Word Records, Waco Texas
Light Records, California
Calendars (Football) for Pepsi Cola
Rose Bowl Posters, Adidas
Poster, Rain Bird Sprinkler Corp.
Football Plays Booklet, National Football League, Ford Motor Co.
Universal Studios Tours
Calendar, Allergan Pharmaceuticals
McCullough Chain Saws
Santa Anita Race Track
Hughes Airwest
Air California
Seattle Supersonics (Pro Basketball, Poster)
Montreal Expos (Pro Baseball, Poster)
California Surf (Pro Soccer)
Gray Stone Press (Limited Edition Print Art Publishers)
Universal Studios
United Artists Film Corp.
MGM
20th Century Fox
Warner Brothers Studios
Present Clients: Many of the Above
McDonald's Restaurants
Quaker Oats Company
Word Records
Collections: The White House (Painting an Easter Egg for Permanent Collection) Washington D.C.
Pentagon, Air Force Art Collection
Smithsonian Exhibition on the Sun
Jorgensen Steel Corp.
Exhibitions: Society of Illustrators of L.A. Annual Exhibitions 1976–1983
The 34th Annual Exhibition of the Communication Arts Society of L.A.
The 100 Yard Canvas Exhibit of National Football League Art
One Man Show, Biola University, LA Mirada, CA 1981

Saul Lambert 158

Born in Bronx, New York, 1928. Graduated the University of Brooklyn, then went to Florence, Italy and attended an artschool there. Moved to Israel and stayed there for two years. Back to U.S.A., became a freelance artist since 1960. He has gotten many awards from the Society of Illustrators, Artist Guild in Chicago, Communication Arts, AIGA, Art Directors Club in New York and in Chicago.

Joan Landis 159

Born: Cleveland, Ohio, October 7, 1928
Present Work: Illustration for United States Postage Stamp
Illustration For April, 1984 issue of Ladies' Home Journal Cover Illustration For James Beard Calendar — 1985
Painting for the Book of The Month included in the 1982 Society of Illustrator's Show.
Private portraits and paintings are included in many collections in the United States and Europe.
Client include the following: Exxon Corporation, Smith Kline Corporation, Swift, IBM, Olin Corporation and United States Historical Society.

Birney Lettick 160–162

Birney Lettick graduated with a B.F.A. from Yale University in 1942. While at Yale, he was awarded the Tiffany Scholarship, give to the ten most outstanding art students in the country. After four war years in Europe, Lettick began his career spannig nearly forty years as a commercial and easel painter.

Through the late 1940's, 50's and 60's the Artist became renowned for his cover paintings on the magazines of Collier's, Time, Scientific American and Readers Digest, for his historical paintings for National Geographic and his numerous paintings for advertising clients including General Electric, Coca Cola, Seagrams and General Motors. By the 1960's his still life painting had gained respect and notoriety through national magazines and reproductions of his work by R.R. Donnelley became internationally known and hung in the White House during the Kennedy years.

Birney Lettick's forte is painting realism; portraits, figures and still life. This versatility has helped in continuing to expand his success. Since the 1970's his movie posters have been recognized worldwide. He has created lasting images for such movies as "Heaven Can Wait," "Foul Play," "Escape from Alcatraz," "The Goodbye Girl," "Sharkey's Machine" and "Paternity." Among the personalities Lettick has painted are Bert Reynolds, Warren Beatty, Jack Nicholson, Richard Burton, Richard Dreyfus, Julie Andrews, John Belushi, Goldie Hawn and Clint Eastwood. Portraits by Lettick hang in the National Portrait Gallery, Yale University and other institutions here and abroad.

Among his advertising work of the 80's, Lettick's paintings of "Leaders of Achievement" for Cutty Sark has exposed the public to the likenesses of Ted Turner, Philip Glass, Maxi Anderson and Chuck Yeager.

Paintings, both illustration and fine art have been on exhibition at the Brooklyn Museum, The New York Historical Society, New Britain Museum of American Art, Albright-Knox Museum and a one man show at Graham Gallery, New York. An exhibition of Lettick's movie posters is currently in Japan.

Birney Lettick lives and works with his wife in their 19th Century townhouse in the middle of Manhattan.

Bette Levine 163

Born: Hollywood, Calif. Sep. 10, 1951. Graduated Art Center College of Design 1978. No awards worth mentioning. Only showing was being a part of the group show of Contemporary Illustrators at Calif. State University at Northridge in 1983.
Collections: Brian Zick, Dennis Mukai, Peggi Kroll

Tim Lewis 164

Place of Birth: Saginaw, Michigan
Date of Brith: June 9, 1937
Shows and publications of professional organizations where work has been exhibited or published: A.I.G.A., Society of Illustrators, N.Y. Art Director's Club, Chicago Art Director's Club, CA Annual, Print Annual, Graphis, Idea, American Illustration II. Clients are divided between advertising (agencies through U.S.A.) and publishing (books, magazines, newspapers). Regular magazines contributions: AT&T Long Lines (now called QUEST), Th Potlatch Story, ST. Regis' magazine, REACH — company journals. The Electric Company magazine, Glamour, Forbes — popular magazines.

Ed Lindlof 165

Born Long Beach, California, 6 November 1943
Illustrations have been exhibited and awards won in the leading national and international design publications and annual exhibitions sponsored by: New York Society of Illustrators, Gaphis Press, New York Art Directors Club, AIGA (American Institute of Graphic Arts), CA (Communication Arts) Magazine, Print Magazine, Art Direction Magazine, and American Illustration annual.
Member of AIGA, New York Society of Illustrators, and Graphic Artists Guild.
Past and present work has spanned a wide range of Advetising, Editorial (both book and magazine) and Institutional assignments with an emphasis in advertising and corporate institutional illustration. Have worked on commissions for major American and international corporations directly and through their advertising agencies.

Sue Llewellyn 166

Born: Sep. 3, 1946. Dayton, Ohio
Education: 1969 BFA — North Texas State University, Denton, Texas
Articles Published in: Dallas magazine (1976), Graphics U.S.A. (1980), Art Direction magazine (1980), Interior Design (1981)
Magazines in which Art has Appeared: Vogue, Interior Design, Science Digest, Town and Country, Sunday magazine (cover), American Way, Horchow, Texas Monthly, Dallas Life, Print magazine
Books Published in:
1975 THE ONE SHOW — New York
1979–1980 EUROPEAN ILLUSTRATORS — London
1979–1980 European Illustrators — Japan
1980 Illustrators XX — New York
1981 Illustrators XXI — New York (Award)
1981 C.A. Art Annual — California
1982 Illustrators XXII — New York
1982 Graphis Posters - Europe
1982 C.A. Art Annual — California
1982–1983 European Illustrators — London
1983 Illustrators XXIII — New York
1983 American Illustrators — New York
Traveling Exhibitions and Group Shows:
1975 THE ONE SHOW — New York
1978 Master Eagle Gallery — New York
1979 Forum de Halles — Paris
1979 Museum of Modern Art — Toronto, Canada
1979 Somerset House — London
1980 Museum of Modern Art — Sao Paulo, Brazil
1980 Preston Polytechnic Art Centre
1980 Master Eagle Gallery — New York
1981 Master Eagle Gallery — New York
1981 500 Exhibition Gallery — Dallas
1982 500 Exhibition Gallery — Dallas
1983 Square One — Houston, Texas
1983 The Alternative Museum — New York

John Lykes 167

Born in Long Beach, California, in 1952. Went to Cal. State, L.B. lived in Europe from 1979 to 1983. Painted all over Europe, now does illustration and Fine Art in Los Angeles. He is also a Film & TV actor.

M

Daniel Maffia 168

Place of Birth: France
Date of Brith: June 25, 1937 US Citizenship 1957
Awards: Silver Medal, N.Y. Society of Illustrators plus many others
Past Works: Time, Esquire, N.Y., Playboy, etc...
Present Clients: Time, Redbook, Fortune, etc...
Exhibition: One Man Shows
Trump Towers Jan. '84
West Broadway Gallery Oct., '83, etc...
Collections: Private

Greg Manchess 169

Born in Kentucky, 1955. Studied Western Minneapolis University of Art and Design, but he believes he has studied art mostly by himself. For a very short time, attended a Californian university of art and craft. After graduation, He worked for an illustration studio called Helman Design Associates as an illustrator. After two years, he resigned there and started as a freelance artist to control his overwork. About one and half years has passed since he met Mr. Dan Sell in Chicagl.
He is now represented by Sell Inc., Chicago.

Richard Mantel 170

Place of Birth: Cleveland, Ohio
Date of Birth: 10. 8. 1941
Awards: New York Society of Illustrators, American Institute of Graphic Arts, American Illustration, CA Magazine, New York Art Directors Club.
Past Works: Posters for Mobil Corp. sponsored PBS programs, Time Magazine Cover, Poster for U.S. Information Service, Album Covers for Elektra Records, Book Jackets for Simon & Schuster and Random House.
Present Clients: ⊐Living Anew Magazine, Pantheon Books, Simon & Schuster, Mobil Corp., Random House, St. Regis Paper, Holt Rinehart & Winston, Northrup King Seed Co.

Mark Marek 171

Place of Birth: Born in Dalls, Texas
Date of Birth: June 5, 1956
Awards: Awards of merit from the Society of Illustrators annual show in 1982 and 1983; American Illustration Annual 1 (1982), and American Illustration Annual 2 (1983)
Past Works: Comic strips for the National Lampoon; a humor book for Simon and Schuster entitled "The Patient's Revenge" (1983); illustrations for the New York Times Book Review; a book cover for Harper and Row

(1978)
Present Clients: National Lampoon, New York Times Book Review, Manhattan Design, The Progressive, The Rocket, The Mole.
Shows: Society of Illustrators Annual Exhibition, 1982 and 1983 (two pieces each year).

Cynthia Marsh 172

Birth: 1948, Boston, Massachusetts, U.S.A.
Awards:
1984 Distinguished Professor Nomination California State Uniersity, Northridge
1984 Awarded NEA Grant
1983 Elected to the Circle of Omicron Delta Kappa – an academic leadership society
1982 Vesta Award – for outstanding contributions in th areas of printing and design.
Past and Present Clients: (partial list)
A&M Records, CBS Records, Arts and Architecture Magazine, Chrysalis Reocrds, The Doors, Rod Dyer Inc., Elektra Asylum Records, Mike Doud Design, Heaven, IRS Records, MCA Records, MIT School of Architecture, Mismanagement (Supertramp), Mother Jones Magazine, Joni Mitchell, Playgirl Magazine, Ed Thrasher & Assoc., Michael Salisbury Design, Seineger & Assoc., Lily Tomlin, Warner Bros. Records, Capitol Records, Oglivy and Mather, DJMC Advertising
Exhibitions: (partial list)
1984 1984 Big Brother is Watching TRAVELLING EXHIBITION
1984 NEA Exhibition – The Woman's Building. Los Angeles
1983 The At Home Show, Artists' Books, Long Beach Museum of Art Long Beach, CA.
1983 One Hundred Unpublished Works by Fifty Published Artists (a look at West Coast Illustration). California State University, Northridge
1983 'Artists' Eggs, Easter Egg Show of one hundred American Artists, The Smithsonian Institute, Washington, D.C.
1982 The New Illustration Show, New York Society of Illustrators. NYC, NY
1982 The World Print Council, Prints and Typography. San Francisco Public Library, San Francisco
I have been in over forty shows since 1971 – These are the most recent. I have also shown at: The Whitney Museum of Art, NYC, NY, Rochester Memorial Art Gallery, Rochester, NY, Rochester Institute of Technology, Rochester, N.Y., The Pacific Design Center, Los Angeles, UC Berkeley Museum of Art, Scripts College, Claremont, CA., Los Angeles Institute of Contemporary Art, etc.
Collection: A&M Records, Joni Mitchell, Joanna Cassidy, the Woman's Building, Elektra Asylum Records, Otis Art Institute, California State University Nothridge.

John J. Martinez 173

Born: Miami, Florida, 1950
Shows/Annuals: The One Show, AIGA, New York Art Directors Club, American Illustration, Society of American Illustrators, etc.
Clients: Pantheon Books, Harper & Row, RCA, Seagram, Congdon Weed, GQ Magazine, New York Magazine, New York Times, Mirage Galleries, etc.

Marvin Mattelson 174

Born: Philadelphia, Pennsylvania Aug. 30, 1947
Awards: Society of Illustrators, New York Art Directors Club, Communication Arts Art Annual, American Illustration Annual, Graphis Annual
Clients: Time Inc., Newsweek, Playboy, Penthouse, Scietific American, The Atlantic, Dell Books, Bantom Books, Warner Books, Berkley Books, W.R. Grace, Merrill Lynch, Lincoln-Mercury, Cadbury, School fo Visual Arts, Society of Illustrators Annual Exhibition #26.

Bill Mayer 175

Bill Mayer is a native to the Southeast. He was born in Birmingham, Alabama, lived in Memphis, Tennessee, for four years, and then moved to New York for seven years before setting in Georgia in 1963. He attended Ringling School of Art, graduating in 1972. Upon graduation he landed a job at the Graphics Group in Atlanta, which acted as a four-year training ground for him. Further experience was gained through a two-year association with Whole Hog Studios. Since 1980 Bill has been doing free-lance work in Atlanta.

David B. Mattingly 176–177

David B. Mattingly was born on June 29, 1956 in Fort Collins, Colorado. His first interest in the fantastic started with looking at comic books as a small child. When he first began to read, he encountered Clarke, Asimov, and Heinlein and he was totally entranced with science fiction and fantasy. He started to draw and paint at the age of 8. A serious interest in becoming an illustrator developed in his early teens. Upon graduation from high school, he attended Colorado Institute of Art in Denver and then transferred to Art Center College of Design in Pasadena, California. After graduating from Art Center, he went to work for Howard Ziehm, the producer of the infamous "Flesh Gordon." He did production design on the sequel to "Flesh Gordon." Unfortunately, as of this date, the film has yet to be made. He was then hired by Walt disney Studios in Burbank, California as a matte artist. He married his wife, Barbara, in May, 1978. During the next three years, he assisted Harrison Ellenshaw and worked as a matte artist on such Disney's films as, "The Cat from Outer Space," "The Return of the Apple Dumpling Gang," and "The Black Hole." His work along with the rest of the special effects crew on "The Black Hole" was nominated for an Academy Award. At twnty-two, he became the youngest full union matte artist in the history of the motion picture industry. At twenty-four, he became the youngest department head in Walt Disney Studio's history. As head of the matte department, he supervised such movies as, "The Devil and Max Devlin," "The Watcher in the Woods," and "Condorman." He also started to do freelance work while at Disney Studios. His first published professional piece was an album cover for "The Commodores' Greatest Hits." His first professional book cover was "A Wizard in Bedlam" by Christopher Stasheff for DAW Books. At Disney Studios, he began to do pre-production work on "Tron." However, by that time, freelance work had become his consuming interest, so he resigned from Disney Studios. David moved to New York City in May, 1983 where he currently lives with his wife and their two cats.
Client List
Books: Ace Books, Berkley Books, Ballantine Books, DAW Books, Del Rey Books, Playboy Press, Tor Books, Signet Books.
Magazines: Amazing Science Fiction Magazine, Cinefantastique, Cycle News, Isaac Asimov's Science Fiction Magazine, The Magazine of Science Fiction and Fantasy, Mediascene Preview Magazine, Omni Magazine.
Motion Pictures Studios: Lucasfilm, New World Pictures, Paramount Pictures, 20th Century Fox, Universal Pictures, Walt Disney Studios.
Miscellaneous: Motown Records, Totco Oil Company, Galoob Toy Company.

Jerry McDonald 178

Jerry was born in Corvallis, Oregon in 1940.
He graduated from the University of Oregon (Eugene, Oregon) with a Master of Arts Degree in "Painting, Drawing, and Printmaking." He has held several teaching positions such as undergraduate teaching assistantship at the University of Oregon where he taught drawing, figure drawing and calligraphy. He has also worked as a freelance editorial and commercial illustrator. Some of his editorial clients have included such companies as: ROLLING STONE magazine, SATURDAY REVIEW magazine, PLAYBOY magainze, WALL STREET JOURNAL, SAN FRANCISCO EXAMINER, as well as many others. His commercial and corporate clients have included such companies as: Fantasy Records, CBS Records, Columbia Broadcasting System, Chevron Oil Company, Bank of Ameirca, Hewlett-Packard, Yamaha and others. He has participated in one-man shows such as: University of Oregon Museum of Art (1968), Waverly Art Center (1969), Fairbanks Gallery (1971) and several others. Jerry won the Western Art Directors Annual Awards in 1972, 1973, 1974, 1976 and 1980. He won the Society of Communication Arts Award in 1974, 1975, 1976, 1979 and 1981. Recent Professional distinctions include: Society of Illustrators Annual Exhibition in New York (1983), American Illustration Annual Publication (1983), GRAPHICS Magazine #224 (1983) just to name a few.

Karen Mercedes McDonald 179

Place of Birth: Raleigh, North Carolain
Date of Birth: January 11, 1956
Awards: Atlanta College of Art, BFA (1980), painting.
Ruth Mott Internship Award (1982–83), full tuition scholarship based on portfolio.
Florida Gulf Coast Art Center (1982), 3rd place award.
Illustrations: SAN FRANCISCO Magazine (full-page color illustration)
PC WORLD Magazine (full-page color illustration)
BERKELEY MONTHLY (full-color cover)
WEST Magazine (full-page color) and many others.
Exhibitions: UCSC-University of California/Berkeley, Studio Gallery; "Works on Paper," July 1983, one-man show.
California College of Arts & Crafts-Artists Gallery; "Dreams & Surrealism," March 1983.
McDonald Art Gallery; Charlotte, North Carolina, 1980.
Collections: Baltimore Gas & Electric Company, Baltimore, MD.
Heery & Heery Architects, Atlanta, GA.
IBM, Charlotte, North Carolina.

Mick McGinty 180

Mick McGinty is a Los Angeles based freelance illustrator who's diverse styles and techniques range from delicate graphite portraiture to high-tech color and chrome. Born in Sioux City, Iowa, December 7, 1952, Mick moved to Los Angeles in 1973, where he attended Art Center College of Design. After graduation, came a three year association with a west-coast design studio. Then Mick struck out on his own. McGinty has received awards of excellence from the Communication Arts Society and Print Magazine and has been nominated for a Clio for his work on accounts such as Dr. Pepper, Levi's, Union Carbide, C & H Sugar, Heublein's and MTV. In addition, Mick has illustrated album covers for Capitol, A & M and Warner Brothers, and motion picture campaigns for Universal, Twentieth Century Fox and MGM.

Mark McMahon 181

Mark McMahon is a Chicago-based artist and illustrator. His many works have appeared in galleries, magazines, books, corporate annual reports and brochures, and so forth. Among Mark's many clients have been such companies as: Sports Illustrated, Chicago Tribune, Lever Brothers Corporation, Coca Cola Company and Caterpillar Corporation just to name a few. Mark created a line of posters and prints on Chicago and Colorado. These prints are handled by Marshall Field and Company, Chicago Association of Commerce and Industry, Neville Sargent Gallery, and also many galleries in Colorado. Mark's work has appeaed in many international and national shows. For example: Society of Illustrators in New York, Communication Art Annual California, Art Directors Club of New York, Artists Guild of Chicago and Graphis Switzerland. Participation in these shows has won Mark many awards. Mark's permanent collections include: U.S. Gypsum, Hollister Corporation, Standard Oil Company of Indiana, The Union League Club of Chicago, NASA, U.S. Air Force, Lever Brothers, R.R. Donnelley Corporation, Kraft Incorporated, Joslins Department Stores, Carson Pirie Scott and Company and Commonwealth Edison.

Wilson McLean 182

Wilson McLean began work in a silk screen shop in Wembley, England at the age of fifteen and has worked as an illustrator since, with the exception of a two year stint in the R.A.F.
He came to New York in 1966, having worked on London's Fleet Street and in Copenhagen, Denmark.
He has worked for many prominent publications such as Time, Sports Illustrated, Playboy, New York, Penthouse, Esquire, etc., and numerous advertising agencies on major accounts, such as Perrier and Holland American Lines.
He has won three Society of Illustrator's gold medals and seven silver. In 1980 he won the "Hamilton King Award" for best single illustration that year. The New York Art Director's Show has honored him with gold and silver medals and the prestigous "CLEO" in 1974 for the Eastern Airlines Television Commercials.
He has had one-man shows at the Society of Illustrators in 1979 and in Zurich, Switzerland in 1982 which featured lithographs as well as illustrations.
He has taught at the School of Visual Arts in Manhattan and Workshop Courses at Syracuse and Kent State Universities.
He lives and works in a Manhattan Loft, in the shadow of the Flatiron Building, with his wife, Photographer, Rosemary Howard.

James McMullan 184

James McMullan was born in Tsingtao, North China, wher his grandparents founded an Anglican Mission and orphanage. He travelled and was educated in Darjeeling, India; Shanghai, China; Salt-Spring Island, Canada and Seattle, Washington. Afte serving in the United States Army he came to New York where he studied at Pratt Institute. Since that time, Mr. Mcmullan has produced illustrations for a wide range of uses including magazines, record jackets, book covers, posters, advertisements, and animated films. Although his work is distinguished by qualities of painterliness and craftsmanship, he is one of the few illustrators who also incorporates type and lettering into his images. He is also well known as a designer. His work has been honored by the American Institute of Graphic Arts, the Society of Illustrators, the Art Directors Club of New York, and Art Directors Clubs across the nation. In 1978 he created the acclaimed short film, "Christmas 1914" for the Public Broadcasting Network. This flm was shown as part of the Christmas program SIMPLE GIFTS. The film was painted entirely on paper in a complex watercolor style which had never been attempted before in animation. Mr. McMullan is currently working on a book on "drawing," as well as completing commissions for posters, book jackets, annual reports, and advertising work. His clients have included such companies as: Time, Life, New York Magazine, Schlumberger, Milton Glaser Incorporated, Hyatt Hotels, Town and Country, and American Express. He has had exhibitions at South Hampton College and Giraffics Gallery in Sag Harbor. Presently he is teaching his very popular evening course, "Finding Personal Style and Using it" at the Scool of Visual Arts. Later at this same school, he will inaugurate a Masters Program on "Journalistic Art in 1984."

Frank Mediate 185

Place of Birth: Pueblo Colorado
Awards: Awards of Merit, Illustration West Exhibitions, Print Case Book, Certificate of Design Excellence
Clients: Atlantic Richfield Company, Carnation Company, Home Savings of America, Mattel, Inc., Southern California Gas Company, Southern California Edison Company, Tomy Toys, Union Oil Company, Walt Disney Productions

Paul Meisel 186

Place of Birth: Freeport, New York
Date of Brith: April 14, 1955
Awards: Art Director's Club Valentine's Day Show
Featured: Mention in Print magazine article on "Spot Illustrators". Piece in American Illustration, volume 1
Past Works: "Shoelace Calendar for Kids", Workman Publishing Inc. 1982–1984

"Weight Training for Cats" (illustration for book) Ballantine Books
Present Clients: New York Magazine, The Boston Globe, The New York times, Adweek, Mademoiselle, Savvy, Geo, Racquet Quarterly
Exhibitions: Show of etchings at Rizzoli's, New York City

Gary Mele 187
Place of Birth: New York, New York
Date of Birth: June 10, 1960
Awards: New York 1981 Society of Illustrators Annual Scholarship Competition
Past Works: Album cover for AGI Record Company
Present Clients: TWA Ambassador Magazine, Northeast Magazine, Self Magazine, News Magazine, Esquire Magazine
Exhibitions: Master Eagle Gallery, New York, N.Y.

Paul Melia 188
Place of Birth: Dayton, Ohio
Date of Birth: December 4, 1929
Education: Bachelor of Fine Arts
Employment: Illustrator for H&H Art Studios, Dayton; freelance since 1976
Commercial Clients: Procter and Gamble, Baldwin Piano, Scotts, NCR, Marathon Oil, Frigidaire, Stewart Warner, Winters National Corporation, Wright State University, General Tire Company, Good Samaritan Hospital, True Magazine, Ashland Oil, Mead, General Electric, many others
Invitational exhibits: Wright State University (one man show); Victory Theater Gallery, Dayton (one man show); University of Dayton showcase, Ohio Watercolor Society traveling exhibits (1980–1983); Emery Galleries, Our Lady of Cincinnati College; Middletown Art Center, Middletown, Ohio
Awards: Western Ohio Watercolor Society Fall Exhibition, first prize 1975, 1979, 1981, 1982; Best of Show, Industrial Graphics International Exhibition, Washington D.C., 1978; first prize worth $1,000, Ohio Watercolor Society Fall Exhibit, 1983; many other awards mostly in Ohio
Juried Exhibits: Society of Illustrators, New York (10 different years); Industrial Graphics International Exhibition, 1975, 1976, 1978, 1979; Abercrombie and Fitch Sports in Illustration, New York; Society of Publication Designers, New York; Creativity '72, '75 and '81, New York; many others mostly in Ohio

Rick Meyerowitz 189
Rick Meyerowitz was born in New York City in November 1943. Rick has done thousands of illustrations in the 16 years he's been in the business. He's worked with clients all over the U.S.A., in Europe, and Australia. He has designed over 40 animated commercials for clients in the U.S., Britain, and France.
His well-known for his work in the National Lampoon and has exhibited that work in Japan. Rick is the author of "Nosemasks" (funny little masks you wear on your nose) and of "Dodosaurs" The Dinosaurs that didn't make it. His next book, a parody of Bird Buides, will be called "Birds of the World".

Gary Meyer 190–191
Place of Birth: Boonville, Missouri
Date of Birth: May 13, 1934
Present Clients: Seiniger Advertising, Universal Pictures, Columbia Studios, MGM, Walt Disney, 20th Century Fox, CBS Rcords, Levi Strauss, Ogilvy Mather, David Hirsch Admakers Inc., others
Past Works: Movie ads: "The Deep" (Columbia Studios); "Jaws 3-D" (Universal Pictures); "Endangered Species" (MGM); "Das Boot" (PSO); "Night Crossing" (Walt Disney Studios); "The Great Waldo Pepper" (Universal Pictures); "Shaft's Big Score" (MGM); others
Record album covers "Destiny" (The Jacksons, CBS Records); "LA" (The Beach Boys, CBS Records); "Chicago 13" (Chicago, CBS Records); others
Advertising art: "Olde English 800" Billboard Art; "Visicorp Poster; others
Editorial art: Cover for New West Magazine; story illustration for Westways Magazine; Illustration for a Ray Bradbury poem, "Ode to the Fast Computer"; others
Awards: Twelfth Annual Key Arts Awards First Place (European category); TIMA (Technical Illustration Management Association) X (Ten) First and third awards for color illustration; TIMA 11 first award color illustration; numerous other awards and Certificates of Merit

Wendell Minor 192
Place of Birth: Aurora, Illinois
Date of Birth: March 17, 1944
Awards: New York Art Directors Club
Society of Illustrators
American Institute of Graphic Arts
Art Direction Magazine
Print Magazine
Type Directors Club of New York
Glaphis
Communication Arts Magazine
Past Works: SULA, Alfred A. Knopf
LOOKING FOR MR. GOODBAR, Simon & Schuster
THE GREAT SANTINI, Houghton Mifflin Co.
THE LAST CONVERTIBLE, Putnam
A CRY IN THE NIGHT, Simon & Schuster
SUMMER GROSSING, Random House
Present Clients: Alfred A. Knopf
McCall's Magazine
The Atlantic Monthly
Simon & Schuster
Holt, Rinehart & Winston
Exhibitions: One Man Show — Wendell Minor —
15 Years of Cover Art
Society of Illustrators Museum of American Art, 1983
Silver Anniversary/Best Collection — American Exhibition travelling in Japan
200 Years of American Illustration Exhibition, New York, Historical Society Museum, 1976
Collections: Library of Congress
Arizona Historical Foundation
The Statue of Liberty Museum and numerous collections throughout the United States and Europe.

Paul Moch 193
Place of Birth: Chicago, Illinois
Date of Birth: 8. 12. 1959
Awards: The American Institute of Graphic Arts (AIGA) Cover Show. Certificate of Excellence. 1983.
Past Works: Chris Garland/XENO
Chicago Tribune
The Art Institute of Chicago
Downbeat Magazine
Advertising Age Magazine
R. Valicenti Design
N.W. Ayer Inc.
J. John Dzuryak Design
Marsteller Inc.
Diane Kavelaras Design
Present Clients: Playboy Magazine
Chicago Magazine
Scott, Foresman & Co.
Money Maker Magazine
Inside Sports Magazine
Success Magazine
No Exhibitions or Collections at this time.

Marilyn Montgomery 194
Graduated from Pepperdine University and Art Center College of Design. She has workd at Walt Disney Productions and Hanna Barbera as a background artist. Most recently she has done freelance illustration for a number of major accounts including MCA Records, and other advertising agencies. Teaching experience: Airbrush Fundamentals for Los Angeles City College. Member of Society of Illustrators (secretary). Awards: Special Judges Award 1981 for Society of Illustrators. Specializes in Airbrush Art.

David Montiel 195
Place of Birth: Cuernavaca, Morelos, Mexico.
Date of Birth: March 4, 1949.
Awards: New York Society of Illustrators Annual Show.
Communication Arts—The Art Annual.
American Illustration.
Graphis Annual.
Past Works: Ciba-Geigy Pharmaceuticals—Brochure Cover.
Random House Publishers—Book Covers.
Business Week—Magazine Cover.
Discover Magazine—Cover
Present Clients: Johnson, Pederson, Hinrichs & Shakery Design Studio.
13-30 Corporation
Harper & Row Publishers.

Jacqui Morgan 196
Education: B.F.A. Pratt Institute; New School, New York; M.A. Hunter College
One Person Exhibitions: Society of Illustrators, New York; Art Directors Club, New York; Gallery Nowe Miasto, Warsaw; Gallerie Baumeister, Munich; Hansen-Feuerman Gallery, New York
Group Exhibitions: Museum of Contemtporary Crafts, New York; Smithsonian Institution; Museum of Warsaw; Museum of Tokyo; Linden Gallery, New York; Arras Gallery, New York
Bibliography: Playboy; Print Magazine; American Artist Magazine; Teens & Boys Magazine; Advertising Techniques; Projekt Magazine (Warsaw, Poland); Kultura (Poland); Student (Krakow, Poland); Upper & Lower Case; Munchner Merkur (West Germany); Abendzeitung (West Germany); Novum Gebrauchs Graphik (West Germany); Graphis (Switzerland); Welt am Sonntag Magazine (West Germany); Art Speak (New York); Art/Work (West Germany); East Sider (New York)
Teaching: Pratt Institute, Parsons
Awards: Over fifty awards including Society of Illustrators, Federal Design Council, VI Warsaw International Poster Biennalle, Levi Design Center, others
Guest Lectures: Rhode Island School of Design, Universite du Quebec a Montreal, Syracuse University, Pratt Institute, New York University, Warsaw Television & Radio, Channel 9 News New York, others
Collections: Smithsonian Institute, Museum of Warsaw, Gallerie Nowe Miasto (Warsaw), many private collections

Frank K. Morris 197
Born in Memphis, Tennessee, in 1950. Studied there under Paul Penczner, Memphis' Academy of Art and Memphis State University. Originally a designer and a creative director in advertising, he formed a design studio before deciding to go to Art Center College of Design to study illustration. Presently freelancing in New York City since 1978. Clients include Newsweek, ABC Television, Bantam Books, New York magazine, Simon and Schuster, BBDO Grey Advertising, and AT&T. His work appears consistantly in Society of Illustrators, Communication Arts and American Illustration Annuals.

Dennis Mukai 198
Place of Birth: Hiroshima, Japan
Date of Birth: 7. 29. 1956
Education: Pasadena City College
Art Center College of Design (graduated in 1978)
Awards: Society of Illustrators Annual National Exhibition
Society of Publication Designers
Past Works: Program Cover for '83 Playboy Jazz Festival
Movie Posters for "Deathtrap" and "Merry Christmas, Mr. Lawrence"
Present Clients: Playboy Magazine, Sitmar Cruises, Paper Moon Graphics.

Tak Murakami 199
Place of Birth: Anaheim, California.
Date of Birth: March 13, 1933.
Awards/Shows: Art Directors Club of Chicago; Artists Guild of Chicago; New York Society of Illustrators Annual Show; other miscellaneous awards and shows.
Past Works: Illustrations for Wurlitzer; Chicago Magazine; Rotarian Magazine; Chicago Tribune Magazine; Scott, Foresman and Company; World Book Encyclopedia; Rand McNally; Laidlaw Brothers; Harper and Row; Encyclopedia Britannica; Georgia-Pacific Paper Company; etc.
Present Clients: Eagle Foods; Gould Inc.; Arthur J. Gallagher & Co.; Nalco International; McDonald's; Sieber & McIntyre; Leo Burnett; Campbell-Mithun; Foote, Cone & Belding; etc.
Exhibitions: Foot, Cone & Belding; Cambell-Mithun; Artists Guild of Chicago; etc.
Collections: private collection of Karl Wunderliche; private cllection of Woody Hayes; Heiwa Terrace (Chicago); Midwest Buddhist Temple (Chicago); etc.

N

Bill Nelson 200
Place and Date of Birth: Born Sep. 30, 1946, Richmond, VA.
Awards: Over 100, including ten gold medals from the Art Director's Club of New York and two silver medals from the Society of Illustrators.
Past Works: Eight Covers for Newsweek magazine. Eight covers for The Washington Post magazine. Six covers for New Times magazine. Five covers for Writers Digest magazine. Other editorial work includes cover for the following: Time, TV Guide, Cincinnati, Connecticut, Illustrators Quartely, New Jersey Monthly, New York Business, The Washingtonian, Family Weekly, Ms. The plain Dealer magazine. Editorial illustration for the following: Esquire, Playboy, Folio, The Runner, Texas Monthly. Advertising work for the following clients: AT&T, Allied Chemical, AMF, Best Products, The Beach Boxs, Borden, Inc. Bank America, Blue Cross/Blue Shield, CBS, Ethyl Corporation, Kelloggs, The Kennedy Center, McDonalds, Mobil Oil, National Public Radio, Parker Brothers, Reynolds Metals, Readers Digest, NBC.
Present Clinets: Time/Life Records, a series of record album cover for the band leaders of the big band era.
Rolf Werner Rosenthal, Inc. a series of brochures for Squibb Pharmaceutical.
Hill-Holiday. a poster for McDonalds, Washington D.C.
Exhibitions: Two one man shows in Richmond VA., 1980, 1981.
Group shows at the Virginia Museum of Fine Arts, Gallery 82, The Society of Illustrators, Art Director's Club of New York, Creativity (Art Direction)
Collections: National portrait Gallery, Washington D.C.

Will Nelson 201
Place and Date of Birth: Born 1932, Twin Falls, Idaho, USA.
Awards: Art Directors Club of Chicago, Academic Artists Association, Printers Guild, Communication Arts, Creative Arts Magazine.
Past Works: Allied Chemical, Beatrice Foods, Bucyrus Erie, Curtis Candy, Corning, Dow Chemical, G.E., General Mills, Jockey Int'l, Kellogg, Kraft, Proctor & Gamble,

Pillsbury, RCA, Upjohn, Zenith and other national accounts and publications.
Presnt Clients Include: Bank of America, Bumble Bee Foods, Early California Co., MGM, Frito-Lay, Mars Candy, Ortho, Potlatch, State of Alaska, Imagic, Playboy Int'l, Pacific Northwest Magazine and other national accounts.
Exhibitions Include: Kirsten Gallery and Stillwater Gallery, Seattle. Knickerbocker Club Annual, Northwest Watercolor Society, Academic Artists Association.
Collections: Corporate collections such as: Safeco Ins., Bucyrns Erie, Morrison Knudsen, Albertsons, Sunshine Mining, Field Enterprises and numerous private collections.

Meredith Nemirov 202

Born New York City, February 5, 1955
Past work sinclude Album Covers for RCA Records; Cosmetic Packaging for Avon Products, Revlon; Bookcovers for The Viking Press/Penguin Classics, Simon & Schuster; Advertising Campaigns for Money Magazine, Burger King; Editorial Illustration for Redbook Magazine, The New York Times.
Present Clients include Book of the Month Club, Ziff-Davis Publishing Co., Avon Products, Inc., Klemtner Advertising & William Douglas McAdams (both Pharmaceutical Agencies).
Exhibitions:
>The Society of Illustrators Annual Exhibition, New York 1983
>The Annual Watermedia Exhibition, National Arts Club, N.Y. 1983
>The Brooklyn Museum, New York 1983
>Zaner Gallery, Rochester, New York 1982
>A Place Apart Gallery, New York 1982
>The Tuscon Museum of Fine Arts, Arizona 1982
>The Palm Springs Desert Museum, California 1981
>The Rocky Mountain National Watercolor Exhibition, Colorado 1981
>Lincoln Center for The Performing Arts, New York 1980
>Custom House Gallery, World Trade Center, New York 1980
>Five Towns Music and Art Foundation, Woodmere, New York 1980
>The National Arts Club Annual Pastel Exhibition, 1980
>The Queens Museum Annual Exhibition, New York 1979
>Benton & Bowles International Gallery, New York 1977

Paintings in Private Collections
Work included in the First Edition of American Illustration.

Barbara Nessim 203

Place of Birth: New York, New York
Date of Birth: March 30, 1939
Education: B.F.A. Pratt Institute, 1960; Pratt Gaphic Art Center
Teaching: The School of Visual Arts, Fashion Institute of Technology, Pratt Institute
Faculty Exchange Scholar, State University of New York
Baord of Directors, Foundation for the Community of Artists
Design Work: Lady Van Heusen, designed clothes and fabric for special line called "Lady VanTastic"; Carber, designed "Barbara for Carber" special line of shoes
Books: Sketchbook (1975); illustrations for The Beach Book (Gloria Steinem, 1963); illustrations for Ti-Grace Atkinson, Amazon Odyssey (1974); Stories Mother Never Told Me (1981); others
Awards: Special Mention Award, The Society of Illustrators, and over 100 awards since 1961 from the Society of Illustrators, Art Director Club, Andy Awards, Illustrator West and many others
Participation in Art Juries: Society of Illustrators Show, Philadelphia Art Directors Show, American Institute of Graphic Arts, Mead Library of Ideas, "Chicago 4", others
One-woman Shows: Rhode Island School of Design, Triangle Gallery (New York), Corridor Gallery (New York), Benson Gallery (Bridgehampton, Long Island), Hampshire College Gallery (Amherst, Massachusetts)
Group Shows: American Institute of Graphic Arts Gallery; Lunds Konsthall (Museum of Modern Art, Lund, Sweden) "The First International Exhibition of Erotic Art, traveled throughout Europe and presently in San Francisco; Mead Gallery (New York); The Louvre (Paris), "The Push Pin Graphic Exhibit", traveled to Milano, Tokyo, elsewhere; many others mostly in New York
Invited to do 3 lithographs in Zurich, Switzerland (Printer "Mattieu") on stone
Theater: Big and Little by Botho Strauss, 1979, directed by Daniel Freudenberger, starring Barbara Barrie. Presented by the Phoenix Theater at Marymount Manhattan. Produced over 40 drawings that wer rear projected on screens and made up a major part of the sets.
Magazine Articles: New York Magazine, Ameryka (by U.S.I.A. in Polish and Russian), Fujin Gahosha, Interpresgrafik (Polish), Vision — American Artists Today (Japanese), Graphis (German), Interpressgrafik (Hungarian), From 4 (Korean), Illustration (Japanese), others; work has appeared in Esquire, New York Magazine, Playboy, New York Times Sunday Magazine, many others
Collections: Shearson, Hammill & Co., Westinghouse Inc., Warren Communications, Inc., many private collections

Susan Nethery 204

Place of Brith: Coviana, California USA
Date of Birth: 20 December 1939
Awards: American Institute of Graphic Arts Los Angeles Advertising Women, Inc.
Past Works: Packaging illustrations for Carnation Foods, Tomy Toys; letter-head design & illustration for Xerox; advertising illustrations for Max Factor, Teleflora, Union Oil; children's book illustration for Harcourt Brace Jovanovich Publishing and Macmillan Publishing.
Present Clinents: Xerox, NBC (National Broadcasting Co.) Holy Land Tree Foundation, Travelodge Hotels, Price Stern Sloan Publishers.
Exhibitions: Los Angeles Art Directors Club
Collections: None

O

Mel Odom 205

Mel Odom was born in 1950 in Richmond, Virginia, and spent the first seventeen years of his life growing up in the small town of Ahoskie, North Carolina, (population approximately 5,000). He was a product of Walt Disney, TV, and science fiction; his chief interest was drawing. Induced by his parents childhood worries were nuclear war, and accidnetally walking into another dimension. His chief interest was drawing. Indulged by his parents, he startedtaking lessons once a week after school. His art teacher found htat he worked best when angry. Drawing became the means he used throughout school to acquire decent grades in the subjects that bored or eluded him. He returned to Richmond to attend Virginia Commonwealth University, where he majored in fashion illustration. He then attended Leeds Polytechnic Institute of Art and Design in England. He stayed in London for six months, studying music, went back to Richmond, where he waited tables and worked on a portfolio for nine months, and then moved to New York City in 1975. Since that time he was worked for many magazines, book publishers, and commercial clients. Mr. Odom has exhibited his work in group shows in New York City at the Cooper-Hewitt Museum and the Society of Illustrators. The recipient of two awards of excellence from the Society of Illustrators, he was named illustrator of the Year in 1980 by Playboy magazine.

J. Rafal Olbinski 206

Place of Birth: Kielce, Poland
Date of Birth: Feb. 21, 1945
>in U.S.A. From Nov. 1981
Awards: Over 25 different prizes in Europe, including:
>First Prize in the International Poster Competition for Human Rights Institute in Strasburg France, 1975
>First Prize in the International Trademarks Competition for the International Jazz Federation — Vienna, Austria, 1976.
>Best Designed Stand in the International Fair — Midem 1975, Cannes, France.
Past Works: International Jazz Federation — posters for Jazz Festivals. Jazz Jamboree — Warsaw, Jazz Yatra—India, Pori Jazz — Finland, Northsea Jazz Festival—Holland, Skane Jazz — Sweden.
>Unesco — Paris, Polish Film — Warsaw, CBS Records.
Present Clients: New York Times, Time magazine,RCA Records, Viking Press, etc.
Exhibitions: Nine one man shows, over thirty group exhibitions around the world.
Collections: Poster Museum Lahti — Finland, Poster Museum Warsaw Poland, Poster Museum — Paris, Carnagie Foundation New York and others.

Jim Owens 207

Jim Owens — 35; Illustrator joining Eucalyptus Tree in 1981; attended the Art Students League and received BFA in illustration from Syracuse University; 1978-1981 partner in design and illustration studio in Virginia Beach called "Stuff Studio". Recognition in Graphis Poster Annual, Washington Art Direcotr's Show, Gold and Silver Awards in Syracuse Society in Communicating Arts.
Clients: AT&T
>Video Games Magazine
>Home Computing
>American Film Magazine
>USF&G
>McDonald's
>U.S. Dept. of Transportation
>Scholastic Book Services
>DuPont

P

Jack Pardue 208

Jack Pardue is a 38 year old illustrator who has been working and painting in the Washington, D.C. area for the past eighteen years. He was born in Raleigh, North Carolina, but spent the majority of his youth in Jacksonville,Florida. His artistic abilities were revealed in his early portraits of family members and his passion for drawing antique cars. He has been painting and freelancing for many years since graduating fromthe Ringling School of Art in Sarasota, Florida.
Today Pardue paintings hang in the White House; His portrait of George Washington in a cowboy hat, done for an Alexandria-based country western radio station, was selected by the American History Museum of the Smithsonian Institution to hang in their current show commerating the 250th birthday of George Washington; Pardue protraits have appeared on he covers of many magazines, including U.S. News & World Report, The New Republic, Liberty, Air Force Magazine and FDA Consumer. He has done portraits of great jazz musicians for the Time-Life Jazz Album Series and portraits for inumerable editorial illustrations for other publications; His work has been selected by the New York Society of Illustrators and the Art Director's Club of Metropolitan Washington to hang in their juried shows.
Mr. Pardue has been able to combine his natural talent for figurative painting with his work as an illustrator. He uses his strong sense of design and color to create a variety of styles. He feels at ease working in just about any medium and often mixes media to obtain a unique effect.
His most recent interests include a one-man show of the American Indian and American Cowboy of the 1800's, which recently hung in the Watergate Gallery, Ltd. In Washington, D.C. He has also started a print company called Tuxedo Prints. His goal is to make reproductions of his work more readily available to a broader spectrum of collectors.
Mr. Pardue lives with his wife Judy in Alexandria, Virginia. He is represented by Jane Lander Associates.
Awards: The Art Directors Club of Metropolitan Washington, 1977, 1981, 1982 Society of Illustrators, New York, 1980, 1981
>Society of Technical Communication, Washington, D.C. Chapter, 1981
>DESI Award, Graphic Design: U.S.A., 1981
>Graphis Annual, 1981, 1982
>Print Magazine Eastern Regional Annual, 1982

Al Parker 209-211

Born in Norfork, Virginia, 1927. Attended the Art Institute of Chicago from 1948 to 1952. After graduation in 1952, he joined Atelier Seventeen in New York and started as an illustrator. In that year, he sent his artworks to the Exhibtion of Metropolitan Museum of Art.
Since then, he has held one-man shows and group-shows almost every year, and his numerous clients which are the top-ranking companies of America, believe he is the one of the best illustrators.
With such a lot of applause, he joined the Bicentennial Anniversary Posters Biennale by Contemporary American Illustrators, and has done numerous creative works for children's books.

Gary Patterson 212-213

Date of Birth: November 16, 1941
Place of Birth: Los Angeles, California
Present Clients: American Broadcasting Corporation (1984 Winter Olympic poster); Sony; Editions Agep. (France); Arte Y Hobby (Colombia); Sport Joaan A.B. (Sweden); Ink Corp. (Australia); James River – Dixie Northern Corp. (illustrations for 1984 winter and summer olympics); Anglo American Prints (England); European Sports Distributors (Germany); Campus Craft (Canada)
Past Works: Golf Magazine; National Racquetball Magzine; Los Angeles Times; Ski Magazine; Chicago Tribune; NBC Television; Graphics To day; P.G.A. Tour Magazine; KTTV World Series television coverage; Lincoln Journal; United States Ski News; United States Air Force; Sony; Wrangler; CBS Television; Wilson Sports Products; others
Awards: United States Sports Artist of the Year; Art Director for Academy Award winning film; several other excellence awards and Certificates of Merit
Exhibitions: Mark Twain Museum; United States Air Force; other art galleries throughout America
Collections: Los Angeles County Museum of Art; private collections including ex-President Richard Nixon, Producer Steven Spielberg, Bob Hope, Lucille Ball, Johnny Carson and many other individuals

Bob Peak 214-217

Born: Denver, Colorado
Education: Wichita State University 44-45, 46-49
>Art Center College of Design, Los Angeles, CA 50-52 BPA
Service: United States Navy
Teaching Experience: Art Center College of Design, Los Angeles, CA.
>Art Students League, new York, New York.
>Famous Artists Schools

Individual Articles: Annual of Advertising Art in Japan 1959.
American Artist September 1962
Gezeichnete reportagen aus den USA arbeitem von Robert Peak with English, French, Spanish texts H. Kuh Gebrauch April 1963
Graphics: New York October 1977
Print: Illustrators Workshop: an original approach to teaching tommorrow's artists November 1977
Art News April 1978
American Artist March 1979
Communication Arts March 1979
Communication Arts cover and article September 1979
American Artist: Bob Peak: images that work February 1982
Communication Arts May/June 1982
Los Angeles Magazine: Hollywood's Real Unsung Heros/Meet Artists Who Make the Posters February 1983
Enginneerng New Record May 19, 1983
Scottsdale Magazine Fall 1983
The Art Institutes: A Pictorial Journal Fall 1983
The Scottsdale Daily Progress: Artist Licks Stamp Project, January 26, 1984
Publications: Famous Artist School
Illustrators in America 1900-1960's by Walter Reed
The Great Illustrators by Walter Reed
Awards: Awards from the Society of Illustators New York, New York Since 1959 to the present over 100 awards including:
Hamilton King Award 1968
Hall f Fame 1977
Gold Medals 1971, 1972, 1975, 1977, 1981, 1982
Siver Medals 1962, 1964, 1966, 1969, 1971, 1972
1974, 1975, 1976, 1977, 1978, 1979
Artist of the Year 1961 by the Artist Guild of New York
Bob Peak has won over 150 awards from the following organizations:
Art Directors Club of New York, Philadelphia, Chicago, Denver, New Jersey, Tulsa
Art Directors Annual, Art Drection Magazine
Communication Arts
Advertising Club of Boston, New York
ORAD
Mead Library of Design
Motion Picture Advertising Exhibition
The Artist Guild of Delaware, Chicago
Communigraphics Exhibition
Printing Industries of Metropolitan New York Inc.
Chicago Society of Communication Arts and so on.
Shows: New York Historical Society: 200 Years of American Illustration
Brooklyn Museum: 100 Years of American illustration
The Greenwich Workshop Gallery, National Art Museum of Sport
McCulley Fine Arts Gallery, Dallas, Texas July 1974, November 1974, December 1983
Rizzoli Gallery, New York, New York: Great Illustrators of Our Time
O'Grady Galleries, Scottsdale, Arizona 1983
One Man Shows: Art Center College of Design, Los Angeles, California
Art Students League, New York, New York
Famous Artist Schools
Society of Illustrators, New York, New York
Oklahoma Christian College, Oklahoma City, Oklahoma
Wichita State University 1972, 1982
Ringling Museum of Art, Sarasota, Florida
O'Grady Galleries, Chicago, Illinois: People, Places and Things April 1978
Academy of Art and Design, Denver, Colorado 1983
The Academy of Art College, San Francisco, California
Permanent Collections: American Express, New York, New York
Special Olympics, Washington, DC
Playboy
Phillip Morris, New York, New York
20th Century Fox
Society of Illustrators, New York, New York
Academy of Motion Picture Arts and Science, Beverly Hills, California
Clint Eastwood, Audrey Hepburn, Sidney Pointier, Lucille Ball, Hugh O'brien, Tony Bennett
Special Assignments: Sports Illustrated: On Safari with the Shah of Iran, hunting Ibex, 1964
Sports Illustrated: Grand Prix Tour with Jackie Stewart, 1967
Ford Motor Company: Car Design 1968-1970
Special Olympics: 15th Anniversary of the Special Olympics. Eunice Kennedy Shriver and the Special Olympic Committee commissioned six paintings on "The Spirit of Sport". The imagery of the paintings was the aritist's interpretation of quotations from six famous athletes: Frank Gifford, Chris Evert Lloyd, Joe DiMaggio, jack Nicklaus, Pele, and WiltChamberlain. 1982-1983
United States Postal Service: The largest commission ever given to an individual artist: designed 30 stamps for the 1984 Olympics.
United States Postal service: Commissioned to paint 31 watercolors depicting various sport events in the history of the Olympics, for the book entitled "Golden Moments" published by the United States government.
Clients: Bob Peak has worked with various clients, a selected few include: Old Hickory Whiskey, Life, Look, Esquire, American, Cosmopolitan, Red Book, Playboy, Sports Illustrated, McCalls, Good Housekeeping, TV Guide, Puritian Sportswear, TWA, Coca-Cola, Owens-Illinois, Schaefer Beer, 7-Up, Paramount Pictures, Universal, United Artists, Orion, Zoetrop, Walt Disney, 20th Century Fox, MGM, Henson and Associates, Western Bell, New York Racing Association, Phillip Morris, Speical Olympics, and the United States Postal Service, and many others.

Jim Pearson 218
Place of Birth: San Mateo, California
Date of Birth: July, 23, 1956
Awards: None
Past Works: Magazine covers for Pacific Press Publishing; San Jose Mercury-News
Present Clients: Learning Magazine; Sunshine magazine
Exhibitions: None
Collections: Michael McCambrige Private Collection

Everett Peck 219
Place of Birth: San Diego, California
Date of Birth: October 9, 1950
Awards: Los Angeles Society of Illustrators Annual Show, Communication Arts Group of San Diego Annual Show, Phillladelphia Art Directors Club Anuual Show, Art Directors Club of Los Angeles Annual Show.
Past Works: Album Cover: CBS records, Animation Design: Levis strauss Co., Animation Design: Mobil Oil Inc., Flm Poster: 20th Century Fox, Fabric Design: Heaven Contemporary Retail Stores. Editorial Illustration: Playboy enterprises, Psychology Today, New York Times, California Magazine, New York Magazine.
Present Clients: National Football League, Heaven Retail Stores, Kaypro Computers Inc., Hartcort, Brace, and Jovananvich Publishing, PSA Airlines.
Exhibitions: Smithsonian Institution, Washington D.C., "The New Illustration Show" New York Society of Illustrators, New York, N.Y., "100 Unpublished Works by Fifty Published Illustrators", Fullerton State College, Fullerton, California.
Collections: Smithsonian Institution, Washington D.C.

Judy Pederson 220
Place of Birth: Brookly, New York
Date of Bitrh: Oct. 15, 1957
Awards: None
Past Works: Book jackets for various publishers. Greeting cards, editorial works.
Present Clients: Random House, Simon & Schuster, Pantheon, Sunrise Publications Inc., Time-Life Inc., Playboy, The New York Times
Exhibitions: None
Collections: None

Robert Peluce 221
Place of Birth: New York City
Date of Birth: December 21, 1937
Awards: Gold and Silver Medals from Society of Illustrators
Award of Excellence from CA Magazine
Merit Award fromArt Directors Club
Certificate of Merit from Society of Illustrators of Los Angeles
Works: Animation Film Designer at Kurtz & Friends since 1973. Designed packages and ads for Rachel Perry Cosmetics. Card illustrations for Hallmark Cards.

Julie Peterson 222
Place of Birth: Palo Alto, California, U.S.A.
Date of Birth: November 22, 1954
Awards: 18th Annual Los Angeles Society of Illustrators San Francisco Cable Car Awards
Past Works: Greeting cards for Paper Moon Graphics and Portal Publications
Billboard for San Diego Convention Center
Advertisement for Post Cereals
Poster for Avco Financial Corporation
Christmas canister for Shaklee Corporation
Christmas canister for Shaklee Corporation
Christmas card for San Francisco Forty Niners Football team
Advertisement for Activision
Exhibitions: Los Angeles Society of Illustrators Show
J. Walter Thompson Advertising Agency
Private Exhibition
San Francisco Society of Illustrators
Annual Exibition

Clive Piercy 223
Place of Birth: Cheltenham, England
Date of Birth: 29th May 1955
Awards: British Association of Illustrators Show, The New American Illustration Show
Past Works: BBC Television England 1977-81
Present Client: Dyer Kahn Inc., Los Angeles, CA

Jerry Pinkney 224-225
Date of Birth: 1939
Place of Birth: Philadelphia, Pennsylvania
Education: Philadelphia Museum of Art
Employment: Rustcraft Greeting Card Company, Dedham, Massachusetts; Barker – Black Studio; co-founder of Kaleidoscope Studio; Jeery Pinkney Studio, Croton-on-Hudson, New York Boston National Center of Afro-American Artists; Visiting Critic and Adjunct Professor at Rhode Island School of Design
Clients: Strathmore Paper; General Foods; General Electric; RCA; Seagram; Canada Dry; Warren Paper; Dell Publishing; Harper & Row; Houghton Mifflin; ITT; Kraft; Franklin Library; Franklin Mint; Negro Ensemble Company; Macy's; NASA Artist Team Space Shuttle Columiba STS 3 Kennedy Space Center, Florida; others
Past Works: Illustrated Seagrams Black History Calendar; designed Harriet Tubman, Martin Luther King Jr., Benjamin Banneker and Whitney Moore Young Jr. Commemorative Stamps for United States Postal Service Black Heritage Series; designed Honey Bee Commemorative Envelope for Postal Service; United States Postal Service Stamp Advisory Committee; Jackie Robinson and Scott Joplin stamps
Awards: National Conference of Christians and Jews: The Human Family; National Council for Social Studies: Carter G. Woodson Book Award; runner-up book, Coretta Scott King Award 1981; Outstanding Science Trade Book for Children, 1981; many others
Exhibitions: Boston Museum of Fine Arts; Brooklyn Museum; Rhode Island Black Heritage Society; Towson State College, Baltimore; Miami Dade Public Library System; National Center of Afro-American Artists, Boston; Studia Museum, Harlem; others
Featured: Communication Art Magazine U.S.; American Artist Magazine; Idea Magazine, Japan; Graphic World, England

Paola Piglia 226
Place of Birth: Turin, Italy.
Date of Birth: May 5, 1955
Awards: American Illustration and Graphis Shows
Past Works: Editorial Illustration for Esquire, Rolling Stone, Self, New York, Book Digest, Ms., Savvy, Seventeen, etc. Poster for Estee Lauder in Prmotional pieces for Conran's, Covers for Trilateral Commission publications. Covers for food section of the Daily News, etc.
Present Works: Esquire, Ms., Redbook, Home, Northeast, and Savvy magazines; and Hetherington Seelig (London).

Scott Pollack 227
Place of Birth: New York
Date of Birth: June 1, 1958
Clients: Runner Magazine, Barron's newspaper, Business Week magazine, Wall Street Journal, Ski Magazine, Outdoor Life magazine, Inquiry Magazine, Doyle Dane Bernbach Advertising, Whitney Communications, Peat, Marwick & Mitchell management focus magazine, Grey advertising, Suddler & Hennesy Advertising, Institutional Investor Magazine, 1330 Corporation, Scali, McCabe Sloves Advertising, Larson Bateman McAlister Advertising, Backer & Spielvogel Advertising, Mingo Jones Advertising, Games Magazine, Rumrill Hoyt Advertising.

Ivan Powell 228
Place of Birth: Miami, Florida
Date of Birth: December 3, 1936
Teaching: Syracuse University; Parsons School of Design
Present Clients: PC Magazine; Atlantic Records; Book-of-the Month Club; Boys Life Magazine; IBM; AT&T; American Express Company; Working Woman Magazine; Geo Magazine; Datamation Magazine; Chief Executive Magazine; Emergency Medicine Magazine
Past Works: Fortune Magazine; Salt City Playhouse; General Electric; Carrier Air Conditioning; Everson Museum of Art; Syracuse University; The New York Times; Sports Illustrated Magazine
Awards: New York Society of Illustrators; New York Art Directors Club;Syracuse Society of Communication Artists
Exhibitions: Everson Musem of Art, Syracuse; Butler Institute of American Art, Youngstown, Ohio; Art Directors Club of New York; Society of Illustrators; Shibuya Parco Gallery, Tokyo; The One Show, Hamilton College; Syracuse University; Associated Artists of Syracuse
Advice to Students:
I think it is helpful to divide the making of an illustration into two parts: 1) The concept or plan. Deciding what image to produce. This is the creative process. 2) Using acquired skills to produce an illustration, turning the concept into an illustration.
We learn best when we have a need to know. Not simply because we are told we should know. If a student has something he or she wishes to communicate, they will be motivated to master those skills needed to express their thoughts (concepts) clearly and effectively. The stronger the students desire to

express themselves, the greater will be their efforts to achieve. I urge students to explore how they "see" and feel. I encourage them to develop their skills and understandings so they can create meaningful illustrations, not just "pretty" illustrations. They must develop their own personal vision, not simply study technique.

Those students who get their technique first, without personal insight, end up with a very ready-made technique, lacking life and excitement. The more personal we become, the larger the audience that will respond to the images we create.

Since it is necessary for the artist to sell his or her illustrations, it is important to understand and respect the needs of the person or publication commissioning the artwork. To understand the function of illustration as a means of communication and how it communicates, the student should not simply study illustration and related skills, but, also life around them and how they can, through their art, make a contribution.

Don Ivan Punchatz 230–231
Date of Birth: September 8, 1936
Education: School of Visual Arts, New York; Cooper Union School of Fine Arts
Military: U.S. Army; worked as medical illustrator and produced training films
Employment: Warwick & Legler Advertising; Animatic Inc.; Ketchum macLeod and Grove Advertising, Pittsburgh; freelance from 1966; opened own studio, The Sketch Pad, in June 1970
Clients: Alcoa; IBM; RCA; Chrysler Mine Safety Applicances; Martin-Marietta; GE; Stouffers; Koppers; Seagrams; Exxon; Pittsburgh Corning; Talon; Calgon; Ciba; Remington; Blue Cross; Macmillan Publishing; Hearst Publishing; U.S. Steel; Berkley Publishing; Atlantic Records; Mercury Records; General Telephone & Telegraph; Dell Publishing; Smith Kline & French; Bell Helicopter; Indiana General Magnetics; Hallmark Electronics; Texas Instruments; Allied Radio Shack; Esquire; Playboy; True; Look; Time; First National Bank of Chicago; Hanover Bank and Trust; Boston Globe; Chemical Bank of New York; Braniff; LTV Aerospace; Science Digest; others
Awards: Art Directors Clubs of New York, Los Angeles, Chicago, Philadelphia, Pittsburgh, The Society of Illustrators, CA Magazine; Houston Art Directors Society; Tuscon Art Directors Society; Brno (Czechoslovakia) Design Biennale; Society of Publication Designers, 'Golden Egg' Award from the Dallas Society of Visual Communications (1983)
Article about work in Graphis Magazine
Covers for Time Magazine part of permanent collection at Smithsonian Institution
Exhibitions: Witte Museum (San Antonio); Palace of Fine Art (Mexico City); Men of Art Guild (San Antonio); Pittsburgh Gallery of Fine Art; Ellsworth Gallery; MPO Gallery (New York); others.
Collections: Dallas Museum; George Eastman House, Rochester; many private collections
Teaching: East Texas State University; Texas Christian University

Bill Prochnow 232
Born: May 27, 1943 in Holbrook, Arizona
Awards: American Institute of Graphic Arts. The Mental Menagerie 1983
AIGA, CAlifornia Design, 1980–1982
Society of Publication Designers, 1982
Print Casebooks, The Best in Posters & Bookcovers, 1982–1983
New York Society of Illustrators, Illustration 23, 1981
San Francisco Society of Communicating Arts, 1980 (Gold Medal)
Society of Illustrators, Los Angeles, Illustration West 17, 1978
Society of Illustrators, L.A., Illustration West 16, 1977
Art Direction Annual, Creativity 4, 1974
Past Works: Illustrations for book, "The Living Kitchen", Sierra Club Books, Publiser
Series of illustrations for the newsletter department of Adventure Travel Magazine (2 years)
Map of Alaska for Foote Cone Belding/Honig, San Francisco Contributing illustrator to: Flowers & Magazine, Los Angeles, (2 years). Learning Magazine, Palo Alto, California (3 years). Oceans Magazine, San Francisco, California (5 years). California Living Magazine, San Francisco, California (2-1/2 years).
Series of illustration & article for Communication Arts Magazine, Palo Alto, California, "The Endangered Species of the Communicating Arts".
Present Clients Include: Sports Illustrated Magazine, Sierra Club, West Magazine, California Academy of Sciences, Oceans Magazine, Mother Jones Magazine, National Semiconductor

Q

Dan Quarnstrom 233
Place of Birth: Willits, California
Date of Brith: Jan. 26, 1951
Awards: None
Past Works: Editorial illustrations:
Playboy, Rolling Stone, Oui, New West/California, Saturday Night, Surfer (magazine). Paper Moon, Lookout (cards/graphics)
Advertising illustrations:
Levi Strauss, Xerox Co., Yamaha, Suzuki, A&M, Warner Bros., United Artists, Elektra/Asylum, Amtrak, Unon Carbide, American Airlines, Pioneer, KNBC-TV, McDonalds, Home Box Office
Film Work Graphics/Advertising:
Pacific Electric Pictures (Production Design), Robert Abel & Co., Gehring Aviation
Present Clients: Universal Pictures (Film Title Design), CBS Video, CBS Records, Walt Disney Productions, Sega Video Games, Mattel Electronics, Motown Records
Exhibitions: None
Collections: None

Mike Quon 234–235
Place of Birth: Los Angeles, California
Date of Birth: August 3, 1947
Awards: Art Directors Clubs of Los Angeles and New York, STA 100, AIGA, Print Magazine, Art Direction Creativity Show, Society of Illustrators of Los Angeles, and American Illustration, and Graphis Magazine.
Past Works: Businessweek Magazine Covers, and Album Covers for CBS Records.
Present Clients: Merrill Lynch, Time, Inc., Newsweek, ITT and Fred S. James.
Exhibitions: Society of Illustrators, Art Directors Club of New York.
Collections: Library of Congress

R

Scott Reynolds 236
Place of Birth: Lansing, Michigan
Date of Birth: April, 23, 1956
Awards: Society of Illustrators Annuals Nos. 22, 25, 26. American Illustration Annuals 82–83, 83–84. Society of Publication Designers Annual, 1982. Print Case Books 1983. New York Art Directors Club 1983. Dallas Art Directors Club 1983
Past Works: American Express Annual Report, 1982. Album covers for Time-Life Records (Metropolitan Opera Centennial). Promotion portraits of authors for the Franklin Library
Present Clients: Texas Monthly, Postgraduate Medicine Magazine, The New York Times, The Dallas Times Herald, Landor Associates (Guy LaRoche Parfum), etc.
Exhibitions: Society of Illustrators, New York. Master Eagle Gallery, New York. Port Washington Public Library, Port Washington, New York. Fashion Institute of Technology, New York.

William Reynolds 237
Place of Birth: Greensboro, North Carolina
Date of Brith: Sep. 15, 1952
Awards: New York Society of Illustrators Show "Illustrators 24"
Best Poster 1980 — Dayton's Advertising, Minneapolis
Award of Achievement — Minnesota Art Directors Club — 1979
First Place Poster Design — Canadian Dept., of Toursim — 1978
Past Works: Posters for Republic Airlines commissioned painting for Control Data Corp.
Present Clients: Control Data Corp., Dayton's, IBM, Cargill Inc., General Mills
Exhibitions: Society of Illustrators Gallery — New York
Collections: Control Data Corp., Cargill Inc.

William Rieser 238
Place of Birth: Madison, Wisconsin
Date of Birth: Sept. 22, 1954
Awards: None
Past Works: Ad Campaign: Lois Jeans, Levi's
Album Covers for RCA Records, MCA Records, Playboy magazine
Present Clients: Levi's, RCA Records, MCA Records, Lois, Bloomingdales, Playboy magazine, Nordstroms, Atari, Foote Cone Belding

Frank Riley 239
Frank Riley was born on October 7, 1949 in Paterson, N.J. He attended the Newark School of Fine and Industrial Art where he studied industrial design. After completing his studies there, he decided to study art and attended the Scool of Visual Arts in New York City.

After receiving his certification from SVA, he became a freelance illustrator. He is a recipient of an "ANDY" Award from the Art Directors Club of New York; Society of Illustrators; The Society of Publication Designers.

He lives in Hawthorne, N.J. with his wife Phyllis and son Frank.

Frank is represented by Jane Lander Associates.

Robert Risko 240
Place of Birth: Ellwood City, Pennsylvania
Date of Birth: Nov. 11, 1956
Books in which work has appeared: Brad Benedict's "FAME". Brad Benedict's "LOVE". Brad Benedict's "COOL CATS". AMERICAN ILLUSTRATION 2
Magazines in which work has appeared: Andy Warhol's "INTERVIEW". VANITY FAIR. TIME. VOGUE. PLAYBOY. DAILY NEWS. NEW YORK TIMES. MADISON AVENUE
These are also present clients
Exhibitions: New York Society of Illustrators Annual Show. New York Society of Illustrators NEW ILLUSTRATION Show

Stanley Roberts 241
Place of Birth: Cambridge, Masachusetts
Date of Birth: Nov. 30, 1956
Awards: New York Society of Illustrators Annual Show, Graphic Design USA
Past Works: Cover illustration for Prentice Assoc. for Software Co.
Present Clients: Digital Equipment Corp., Gauchat Architects, Prentice Assoc., LTX Corp.
Exhibitions: Woods Gerry Gallery, Providence R.I.

Bryan Robley 242
Bryan Robley was born March 20, 1949 in Los Angeles, California, and began his career as a courtroom sketch artist for the Los Angeles Herald Examiner, covering the Robert Kennedy assassination trial. In addition to working as a freelance illustrator and designer, Bryan has also toured as a factory ski team member and now resides ouside the ski resort city of Sun Valley, Idaho. Robley draws upon his athletic background to bring an intimate understanding of motion, anatomy and color to his paintings. A member of the New York Society of Illustrators, Bryan has won over 20 awards for illustration and design since 1981. Recent projects for U.S. and international clients include posters for the 1983 US Festival and Maxel Recording Tape, the 1984 Olympics and ABC Television, NFL Football, and limited edition prints for Salomon Ski Equipment of France.

Robert Rodoriguez 243
Place of Birth: New Orleans, Louisiana
Date of Birth: May 3, 1947
Awards: Awards of Merit (New York Society of illustrators Anual Show)
First Prize for Color Newspaper Advertisement (Newspaper Advertisers Show)
Finalist in Grammy Awards/Album Cover (Nat'l Academy of Recording Arts & Sciences)
Past Works: Posters, Calendars, Advertisements, Greeting Cards, Editorial Illustrations, etc.
Present Clients: Oui magazine, Budweiser Beer, Coors Beer, Almaden Wine, Kaluhá, Ringling Bros. and Barnum & Circus, Merrill-Lynchi, Paper Moon Graphics, Walt Disney Productions, Atari Video Games
Exhibitions: Pasadena City College of Art Gallery/S So. Cal. Artists, Cal. State Northridge/100 Unpublished Works by 50 Published Artists
Collections: Ringling Bros. And Barnum & Bailey Circus Collection
Vivan Santibáñez Collection

Mario Rossetti 244
Place of Birth: Allentown, Pennsylvania
Date of Birth: October 9, 1951
Awards: New York Society of Illustrators Annual Show
Past Works: Album cover for Robert Andresen & Banjar Records, New York Times Magazine, Scholastic Magazine, etc.
Present Clients: Harcourt Brace Jovanovich Publications, Image Masters
Exhibitions: New York Society of Illustrators Annual Show, Bethlehem Bicentenial Competition

John Rush 245
Place of Birth: Indianapolis Indiana
Date of Birth: June 27, 1948
Awards: Awards from the Society of Illustrators (Gold Medal) and the Society of Publication Designers
Past and Present Work:
Editorial:
Psychology Today, 'Esquire, Playboy, Penthouse, Science Digest, Advertising Age
Book Work:
Random House, Bantam Books, Ballantine Books, Berkley Books
Advertising:
IBM, Standard Oil, Texico, Dupont, Upjohn, American Airlines, NBC, etc. Also album covers for RCA Records

S

Tracy Sabin 246

Place of Birth: Eugene, Oregon
Date of Birth: January 10, 1948
Education: University of Oregon (under LaVerne Krause); individual study in Milan and Florence; Brigham Young University (B.F.A., 1973)
Present Clients: Japanese Village Plaza; Bill Gamble's Mens Wear; Mirage Editions; UCSD Music Department; Tuned-In Magazine and many others
Past Works: Ernest Hahn Shopping Centers; Bell & Howell; Portal Publications; Courseware, Inc.; animated films for TICCIT project (NSF – funded computer education project) and many others
Exhibitions: House of Lords Gallery, Provo, Utah; others throughout western United States; serigraph "Tanabata" accepted in New York Society of Illustrtors annual show (1981)
Awards: Communicating Arts Group of San Diego Silver Medal; Art Directors Club of Los Angeles Annual Show; New York Society of Illustrators Annual Show

Jim Salvati 247

Born 5-5-57 in Los Angeles, CA.
Pastt Clients: Bell Telephone, Foote-Cone Belding, Buick, MCA Records, A&M Records, Atlantic Records, Sherwood Films, Metro Graphics.
Present Clients: Klein & Co., 20th Century Fox, Paper Moon Graphics, Gotcha Sportswear, Concerts West, AT&T, Republic Airlines, Continental Airlines.
Exhibitions: A Look at West Coast Illustration

Emanuel Schongut 248

Born in Monticello, New York, 1938. Attended Pratt Institute – BFA – MFA. Shows and awards from New York Society of Ilustrators, AIGA, etc. Works includes – Mobil Masterpiece Theatre Posters, children's books, book covers, illustrations for New York magazine, Esquire, Cosmopolitan, Red Book, New York Times, CBS Records.

Daniel B. Schwartz 249

Place of Birth: New York City
Date of Birth: Feb. 16, 1929
Awards: Eight Gold Medals, Society of Illustrators. Two Louis Comfort Tiffany Grants in Painting Purchase Prize Childe Hassam Fund, American Academy of Arts & Letters
Past Works: Work commissioned by all major magazines, including LIFE, LOOK FORTUNE, SPORTS ILLUSTRATED, MCCALL's, REDBOOK, TIME, NEWSWEEK, Oil, Equitable Life, Merrill Lynch, H.J. Heinz, AMFAC, etc.
Exhibitions: Eight one-man shows, many group exhibitions Work included in many private collections

Jeffery Seaver 250

Born Omaha, Nebraska November 25, 1952
Awards received for: New York Society of Illustrators Shows 1977, 1978 (2), 1981 (2), 1982, 1983 (2); Communication Arts Annual; Art Direction magazine; National Lampoon Art Poster Book and Exhibition; Western Art Directors Club; Citaion for Merit, New York Art Directors Club; American Humorous Illustration Exhibit, Tokyo, Japan.
Works exhibited Museum of Art & Science, Chicago, Illinois
Extensive commissioned work done for most major publications, and advertising for many Fortune 500 companies, including The New York Times, Fortune magazine, J.W. Thompson, American Express, Business Week and others.

Isadore Seltzer 251

Place of Birth: St. Louis, Missouri
Date of Birth: 1930
Education: Los Angeles City College; Chouinard Institute; Art Center (Los Angeles)
Military: United States Air Force
Teaching: School of Visual Arts; Syracuse University; Parsons
Clinets: Copco; du Pont; N.W. Ayer; many others
"Over fifty percent of my work is advertising," Isadore Seltzer says. "I like advertising and find it interesting. Art directors will give me a concept and frequently a sketch, but they usually say 'you don't have to go by this too much' and I have a chance to put my own thinking into the assignment. I rarely do comps or even tight sketches.
"I enjoy the painting, where things can just kind of happen, and one thing suggests another. Sometimes I'm not even sure what media or tools I'm going to use when I start, so I don't like to resolve everything in the concept and sketch. If you work too tightly, you can get bored, and I like to enjoy my work."
"A number of my former students are art directors, now" smiles Isadore, "and it's fun to work with them."
"I wasn't getting anywhere free lancing in New York and decided I'd better get a job or get out, so I put together a portfolio and Push Pin hired me, just two months after they hired Paul Davis. I worked there for five years and I'm grateful for the experience, particularly the work habits I learned."
(review by Jean A. Coyne, Communicatiion Arts Jan/Feb 1979)

R.J. Shay 252

Born in 1950. Attended the University of South Illinoi and studied art. Started as an illustrator since 1972. He lives in St. Louis now and has continued to offer his powerful works to his cliants. He is represented by Sell Inc., Chicago.

Mamoru Shimokochi 253

Born in Japan, 1942
1963 Came to U.S.A. as a student
1966 Graduated from Berkley Unified School.
1967–1970 Attended the Art Center College of Design on a scholarship and was graduated with honor (B.F.A.)
1970–1974 Joined Saul Bass & Associates, as a graphic designer.
1976 Rejoined Saul Bass & Associates as a senior designer.
Contributed to the following assignment: Ajinomoto Co. (Japan), Laura Scudder's, Lawry's Foods Co., Quaker Oats Co., Ticor, United Airlines and United Way of America etc.
1974–1975 Set up own office as a freelance artist, creating illustration, fine art, and graphic design.
1977–1978 Opened a design office, Carra, flynn & Shimokochi in Los Angeles.
1978 to present: Set up own office, Mamoru Shimokochi/ Design-Illustration.
1980–1981 TAught design classes at the Art Center College of Design, Pasadena.
Design awards and exhibitions: AIGA Show, CA Magazine Annual, Los Angeles Art Directors Exhibitions, Graphis, Graphis Packaging 3, Poster U.S.A., Creativity Annuals, New York Art Directors Exhibitions, New York Type Directors Show etc.
Painting awards and exhibitions: All California Juried "National Orange Show"
The Downey Museum of Art
Mt. San Antonio College, CA (purchase award)
The Gallery, Painting Show-Barnegat Light, New Jersey
The Los Angeles Art Association Gallery
The McKenthaler Cultural Center Juried Exhibition, Fullerton, CA
The First Biennial Juried Exhibition, L.A. Municipal Gallery

William A. Sloan 254

Place of Birth: Philadelphia, Pennsylvania
Date of Birth: Feb. 27, 1954
Awards: New York Society of Illustrators Annual Show
American Illustration 1982/83
Creativity Annual Show
New York Art Directors Show
Past Works: Travel poster and brochure covers for Cunard Lines Queen Elizabeth 2
Magazine illustration for Redbook, New Body, and Children's Television Workshop
Poster for Art Expo New York
Promotion poster for Dupon Quallofil
Present Clients: Ash LeDonne, Inc.; Avon Products, Inc.; Broadway Play Publishing, Inc.; Dow Jones & Co., Inc.; Millennium Design Comm.; New York Times; Revlon, Inc.; Tamotsu, Inc.; Viking Penguin Publishing; Vogue
Exhibitions: "57th and 59th Annual Exhibitions" Art Directors Club of New York
Ten at Sugarloaf, Philadelphia, Pennsylvania.

Doug Smith 255

Place of Birth: New York, NY
Date of Birth: Mar. 1, 1952
Awards: (twice in) NY Society of Illustrators Show, selected for American Illustration – vols. 1 & 2, pieces have appeared in Print, Graphis, NY Art Directors Club Show, Boston Art Directors Club Show, AD Club, Hatch.
Present Clients: Boston Globe, Boston Magazine, Rolling Stone, Greenpeace, Outside Magazine, Cross Country Skier, High Technology, Wang Corporation.

Jes Smithback 256

Place of Birth: Wellington, Kansas, USA
Date of Birth: January 19, 1948
Awards: Wichita Advertising Club Addy Awards
Wichita Art Directors Awards
Past Works: Illustrations for: Kill Devil Hill, by Harry Combs, The Wichitan magazine, Cessna Citation Division, Gates Lear Jet, Pizza Hut, Goldsmiths, First National Bank, Lee Company, Union National Bank, Continental Theatre Company, First Edition Restaurants, Fuller Brush Company, Regional Department of Labor, Jeppesen-Sanderson, National Women's Political Caucus, and others
Present Clients: Sedgwick County Zoo (Wichita, Kansas), Kansas Elks Training Center (Wichita, Kansas), Health Care Plus (Wichita, Kansas), Harvey Hutter and Company (New York, New York), John T. Stewart (Wellington, Kansas), First National Bank (Medford, Oklahoma), St. Lukes Hospital (Wellington, Kansas), Chromatech Lab and Graphics Corporations (Wichita, Kansas), Renn & Company (Wellington, Kansas), and additional clients.
Exhibitions: Local Only
Collections: Private Only

Greg Spalenka 257

Born: March 13, 1958 in Arcadia, California
Awards: New York Society of Illustrators Annual Show
American Illustration Annual 1983
Past Works: Playbill Poster for the Ahmanson Theatre Neil Simons' Brighton Beach Memoirs
Rolling Stone Magazine
P.C. World Magazine
Atari
Syntex Corp.
California Magazine
Present: Fortune Magazine
Los Angeles Magazine
P.C. Magazine
Exhibitions: Saddleback College – 1983

Randy Spear 258

Place of Birth: Los Angeles, California
Date of Birth: Jan. 1st, 1958 (American New Years)
Awards: None
Past Works: Designed and created Huggy Chuggy Character and Mural. Ray Bradbury cover Intro magazine. Double page spreads Joe Wiedner's magazine. Sergio Tacchini label. magazine cover California Living
Present Clients: Warner Bros. Inc., Michael Mania Productions, the Coordinator magazine, Joe Wiedner's Muscle and Fitness magazine, Flex magazine, Celestial Mechanics Inc., Cartoon Junction, Tishkoff, Wentworth and Associates, Miura Design, Herald Examiner, Frand Hubbard and Associates, JMR Advertising, Nelson and Gilmore Advertising, Bramson and Associates, Intro magazine, Total Health magazine, Tomy Toys

Barron Storey 259

Barron Storey was born April 6, 1940, in Dallas Texas. He attended Art Center School in Los Angeles, CA., and the School of Visual Arts, New York City.
Mr. Storey is represented in the collection of the National Portrait Gallery in Washington D.C. as well as the National Air and Space Museum. His paintings have been exhibited in the U.S. Information Agnecy Show, Moscow and Washington. In 1976 he received the Gold Medal award for his poster of Lotte Lenya, from the Society of Illustrators. Other awards include: Merit Award from the Art Directors Club, N.Y. in 1977; certificates of distinction from Art Directions Magazine, Art Directors Club in Los Angeles, and the Society of Publication Designers Show.
Mr. Storey has worked for most national publications and his clients have included a wide variey of major companies and agencies.
In addition to being a well respected illustrator, he is a print maker, an accomplished musician, and a teacher.
In 1976 and 1977 he was chairman of the Illustration department at Art Center College of Design where he taught. In 1981 he taught at Syracuse University and at Pratt Institute in New York.
Mr. Storey is married and has 3 children. He lives and works in San Francisco, California.
He is represented by Jane Lander Associates.

George Stavrinos 260–261

Place of Birth: Boston, Massachusetts
Date of Birth: Mar. 13, 1948
Awards: New York Society of Illustrators Annual Show 1984
Past Works: Bergdorf Goodman Department Store – New York City. Barney's Department Store – New York City. New York Times Sunday Magazine, Book Reviw, and Travel Section. New York Magazine. Gentlemen's Quarterly. Random House Publishers
Present Clients: New York City Opera. Keio Department Store – Japan. Mauricius Department Store – West Germany
Exhibitions: Tatistcheff Gallery – New York City 1981
Collections: Philip Morris Corp.. Metropolitan Museum of Art

Dugald Stermer 262–263

Born in Los Angeles, California, on December 17, 1936
Awards: CA Art Annuals; AIGA Exhibits; Society of Illustrators; American Illustration 1 and 2; CA Design and Advertising Annuals; NYADC Annual Exhibitions.
Past Works: Levi Strauss, Time covers, Ramparts magazine, California Living magazine, Flowers & magazine, Oceans magazine, Communication Arts magazine, Bank of America, Mother Jones magazine, Sierra magazine, Pacific Telephone, Henry Winhard's Beer, Gallo, etc.
Author of The Art of Revolution (McGraw-Hill), Vanishing Creatures (Lancaster-Miller), and the forthcoming Vanishing Plants & Flowers (Overlook Press).
Currently working as freelance illustrator with Ogilvy & Mather, Johnson Pederson Hinrichs & Shakery, Goodby Berlin & Silverstein, The Los Angeles Olympic Games, Dancer Fitzgerald & Sample, and Communication Arts magazine as Associate Editor; also completing work on my book, Vanishing Plants & Flowers

Susan Sumichrast 264
Place of Birth: Minneapolis, Minnesota
Date of Birth: July 1, 1946
Awards: New York Society of Illustrators #22, 23, 24, 25, 26
Chicago Book Clinic 1980, 1981
Chicago Artist Guild 1981, 1982
Chicago Show 1981
Women in Design 1981
Books: Women in Design Compendium
"American Artists"
Clinets: Reader's Digest Magazine
Skiing Magazine
Apple Computer Magazine
Vantage Point Magazine
New Realities Magazine
Meeting and Conventions Magazine
Random House Publishing House
Ginn Publishers
Scott Foresman Publishing Co.
Portal Publications
California Dreamers
McDougal Littel Publishing Co.
Other: lecture given to Milwaukee Art Directors Club.
lecture given to Phoenix Art Directors Club
taught class in soft sculpture
School: Received B.F.A. degree from Bradley University, Peoria Illinois
1 year at American Academy of Art – Chicago

George Suyeoka 265
Place of Birth: Honolulu, Hawaii
Date of Birth: Feb. 3, 1926
Awards: New York Society of Illustrators Annual Show, Artist Guild of Chicago, A.I.G.A., Society of Typographic Arts (Chicago), C.S.C.A.
Past Works and Clients: Playboy, Abbott; Scott Foresman and Company, Container Corp. of America, World Book, Rotarian, Various publishers and agencies
Exhibitions: Evanston Art Center, Art Institute of Chicago Sales and Rental Gallery, Chicago Public Library, Playboy International Travelling Show, National College, Old Orhard and other Chicago area artfairs
Collections: Oak Park, Playboy, and private

Brock Swanson 266
Place of Birth: Spokane, Washington
Date of Birth: Oct. 13, 1948
Live and Work: New Orleans, Louisiana
Awards: B.F.A. Univ. of Arizona
Past Works: Over 6,000 original portraits and paintings in private collections world wide.
Studio: Nairobi, Kenya 1971; Kabul, Afganistan, 1972; La Paz, Bolivia 1974; Paris, France 1975–77; Lihue Hawaii 1979–1980; New Orleans, LA 1980 to present
Present Clients: Adler Film & Video Production, N.O. LA. Committee member, Jackson Square Artist Assoc.
Exhibitions: Coos County Museum, Coos Bay, Oregon, 1979
Kuaui County Museum Lihue, Hawaii, 1981

T

Nick Taggart 267
Born 19 December, Cheshire, England, 1954.
Graduated Cambridge Art College 1975.
1975–1977 Worked in London.
1977 moved to Los Angeles.
Past Works and Clients:
Posters:
Los Angeles music center
Mark Taper Forum
Ahmanson Theatre
Warner Brothers Records
Magazine Illustrations:
Cuisine magazine
California magazine/New West
Esquire magazine
London Illustrated News
B.B.C. Radio Times
Steet Life magazine
Oui magazine
Montreal Standard Weekend magazine
Wet magazine
Book Covers:
Penguin Books
Macmillan Books
W.H. Allen Books
Record Covers:
Warner Brothers Records
Capitol Records
CBS Records
MCA Records
EMI Records
Fabric designs for swimsuits, clothing, T-shirts etc. Designers Novelli/Barely Legal "Heaven"
Exhibitions:
Group shows
Jan. 1984 Bernard Jacobson Gallery, Los Angeles
Oct. 1983 California state University, Northridge
Sept. 1980 Aztlan Gallery, Los Angeles
One man shows
Oct. 1982 Warner Brothers records, Burbank
Sept. 1981 Steve Samiof Gallery, Los Angeles
Jan. 1981 California Institute of the Arts, Valencia
Collections: Various private collections in Great Britain and the U.S.A.
Selected Reading: American Art Review, November 1978 "The Los Angeles work of Nick Taggart"

Yuriko Takata 268
Place of Birth: Los Angeles, California
Date of Birth: August 27, 1957
Past Works: Magazine covers for Flowers & magazine
Greeting Card illustration
Posters for the Conservatery of Flowers and Japanese Tea Garden of S.F.
Jewelry design for Shashi Inc., S.F.
Present Clients: China designs for Noritake China Co., Chicago
Posters published by Bruce McGaw Graphics, N.Y.
Foote, Cone, Belding & Honig Ad Agency Ketchum Advertising
Exhibitions: Shoshanna Mayne Gallery, Los Angeles
Galleries: Jayne Baum Gallery, New York
Transworld Gallery, New York
Haller Gallery, New York
Neville Sargent Gallery, Chicago, Illinois
Christie Sahara Gallery, Newport Beach, CA
Art Collector Gallery, San Diego
Clark & Wade Gallery, San Francisco
Collections: Bank of America
AT&T
Cannell and Chafin
Cooper, Carry and Associates
Crocker Bank
Dean Witter & Co.
Foremost & McKesson, Inc.
GT&T
IBM
Transamerica Corporation
VISA
Western Electric
Wells Fargo Bank

Robert Tanenbaum 269
Place of Birth: Chillicothe, Mo.
Date of Birth: July 31, 1936
Awards: Los Angeles Society of Illustrators, New York Society of Illustrators
Past Works: Life size portrait of Howard Huges for Huges Aircraft. 1.5 foot × 8 feet painting for ROOTS, TV. 22 portraits for Miehner's CENTENNIEL, Universal TV
Present Clients: Hitachi, MGM Pictures, 20th Century Fox, Warner Brothers, Universal Pictures, Levi's, Coerpeal Food, Denny's Restaurants, ABC TV, CBS TV, Delmonte Foods, Desert Inn, Triad, Warner Brothers Records
Exhibitions: Elprado Gallery, Sedona Arizona
Collections: Numerous private collections

C. Winston Taylor 270–271
Place of Birth: Oklahoma City, Oklahoma
Date of Birth: Feb. 16, 1943
Awards: Award of Merit, Society of Illustrators of Los Angeles
The Society of Art Center Alumni
Western Publications Association: Maggies
Clients: Warner Brothers, Orion Pictures Release, MGM/UA, Universal Pictures, 20th Century Fox, CBS TV, Walt Disney Studios, Kcop Ch. 13, Telepictures Corp., Ambassador Television Production
Past Works: Publisher of The "Catalog of Illustrators" for the past ten years.

Aki Tomita 272
Place of Birth: Tokyo Japan
Date of Birth: Jan. 1, 1944
Awards: "SILA" Annual Show
Past Works: Paperbacks Cover for Pinnacle Books, Poster for Movie
Present Clients: Plus Products, etc.
Exhibitions: None
Collections: None

Tom T. Tomita 273
Place of Birth: Fujisawa-Shi, Kanagawa, Japan
Date of Birth: October 16, 1952
Awards: Society of Illustrators of Los Angeles Award of Merit
Past Works: Movie posters, greeting cards, magazine covers, billboards
Present Clients: NBC (TV), Computer Magazine Publication, 20th Century Fox, CBS (TV)

V

Dale C. Verzaal 274
Born: May 28, 1952
Education: B.F.A., 1973 East Carolina University
M.F.A., 1977, East Carolina University
Major Area: Graphic Design
Minor Area: Painting
Teaching: 1977–1979 Assistant Professor of Art, Indiana State University
1979–1984 Assistant Professor of Art, Arizona State University
Professional Experience: 1973–1974 Illustrator for Graphics Group, Inc.
1975 to present Freelance illustration and design
Clients Include: Arrow Shirts, Dr. Pepper, Union 76, Indiana State University, First Interstate Bank, Doubletree Resorts, Arizona Highways magazine

Fran Vuksanovich 275
Born in Chicago in 1941 and have lived and worked there ever sine. Attended the American Academy of Art and studied figure drawing and oil painting for three years. Her present work is done with pencil and dyes.

William Vuksanovich 276–277
I was born in Belgrade, Yugoslavia in 1938, came to the U.S. 13 years later and made Chicago my home. I apprenticed at S.B.D., attended the American Academy of Art for 3 years, night school at the School of Professional Art for 2 years and then went into illustration.
All My energies are channeled into my work and I am at all times striving for growth and new visions.
I believe that today's illustration is of the highest quality and need not take a back seat to any other art form.
Clients Include: McDonald's, GATX, Illinois Bell, Playboy Magazine, Penthouse, John Deere, Kraft, O.A.G., Busch Beer, State of Illinois, Illinois State Lottery, Old Style, Kellogg's, etc...

W

Jeff Wack 278
Born Jan. 24, 1956, Orange, California. Various awards as Art Center Alumni. Clients include motion picture, magazine, record companies, TV animation, corporate.

Robert L. Wade 279
Place of Birth: Chattanooga, Tennessee
Date of Birth: December 14, 1955
Awards: Received a purchase award from National Art on Paper Exhibition (drawings & prints) at the University of Southern Illinois in 1976. Accepted in several other national print shows during the same year.
In 1983, was included in American Illustration 1983–84 (volume II).
Past Works: Editorial illustration for regional as well as nationally distributed magazines and newspapers. Album cover for Smash Records.
Present Clients: Texas Monthly, D. Magazine, The Denver Post, Empire Magazine, Oil & Gas Investor (Hart Publications), Bloomsbury Book Review, New Age Journal, Westword, New York Times Magazine
Exhibitions: Editorial illustration show at Goodfriend's Gallery; Denver, Colorado.
Collections: University of Southern Illinois Art Museum; Carbondale, Illinois

Richard Waldrep 280
Richard Waldrep – 41; Vice President joined Eucalyptus Tree in 1976; illustrator; received BFA in graphic design and MFA in illustration from the University of Georgia. Recognition in New York Art Director's Show, U&lc, Illustrator's Annual, Graphis Annual, CA Art Annual, Best in Baltimore, Washington Art Director's Show, Philadelphia Art Director's Show.
Clients: U.S. News & World Report, Ohio Magazine, Wahington Post Magazine, National Geographic, McDonald's, Roy Rogers, Parker Brothers, Coor's, Colt 45, Baltimore Orioles, USF&G, Penthouse, Quest, Time-Life

Stan Watts 281–283
Place of Birth: Ponca City, Oklahoma
Date of Birth: Dec. 30, 1952
Awards: Soc. of Illustrators, N.Y., L.A., San Francisco, etc.
The Key Art Award 1982, 1st prize for the "Howling". Grammy 1983. 1984 Grammy nomination for Best Album Art
Past & Present Works: Levi's CBS Records, Carnation, Paper Moon, Mattel, 20th Century Fox, Playboy, Flying Tiger, Sunkist, Belltel, etc.
Exhibitions: Soc. of Ill., New York, L.A. San Francisco, etc.
Collections: Private collections.
Began as a cartoonist, for school newspapers and yearbooks until an instructor of watercolor, Gene Dougherty, moved his interest into painting. He trained for two year under a well-known

illustrator, Don Ivan Punchatz, and then began freelancing. Relocated in L.A. under the representation of Paul Cormany, Jim Lilie in San Francisco, Joel Harlib in Chicago, and Marilyn Murray in the South.

Robert Weaver 284–286

Born: 1924, Pittsburgh, Pennsylvania
Education: Carnegie Institute of Technology, Pittsburgh, Pennsylvania
Art Students League, New York City
Academia Delle Belle Arti, Venice, Italy
Published Work in: Life, Look, Newsweek, Esquire, Playboy, New York, The New York Times, Sports Illustrated, Fortune, Graphis, Audience, Show, American Artist, Psychology Today
Articles About Mr. Weaver:
1957 "Robert Weaver: Objective," Esquire, December
1959 "The Realism of Robert Weaver," American Artist, September
1970 "Sketching from Life," American Artist, May
1971 "Images, Illusions: A Portfolio of Illustrations by Robert Weaver," Audience, January
1976 "Realism in Illustration," Print, January; "Weaver's Way," New York Magazine, January
1978 "Robert Weaver," Communication Arts, May
1979 "Robert Weaver's Illustration Issue," Print, November/ December
1980 "Robert Weaver," Illustrators 39, London
1982 "Robert Weaver," Graphis #218
Books:
1966 "The Illustrators in America 1900–1960's," Walt Reed, Reinhold Publishing, New York
1969 "One the Spot Drawing," Watson Guptill, New York
1970 "Shark Bites Back," McGraw Hill, New York
1971 "Me Day," Dial, New York; "Around the Corner," Harcourt, New York
1972 "Comics," Graphis Press Corp., Zurich, Switzerland
1979 "My House is Your House," Courtes, New York; "Great American Illustrators," Abbeville Press, New York
1983 "New York in Art," Edited by Seymour Chwast & Steven Heller, Harry N. Abrams, New York
Awards:
1963 Gold Medal, Society of Illustrators
1975 Gold Medal, Society of Illustrators; Silver Medal, One Show, Art Directors Club of New York
1976 Gold Medal, Art Directors Club of Philadelphia
Selected Exhibitions:
Numerous Exhibitions including:
The New York Historical Society, New York City
Society of Illustrators, New York City
Art Directors Club of New York
Art Directors Club of Philadelphia
Art Directors Club of Washington, D.C.
1977 Retrospective, Visual Arts Museum, New York City
Exhibitions:
1966 New Talent Show, Rochester University, Guest Curator, Ivan Karp, Castelli Gallery, New York City
1968 Listening to Pictures Exhibition, Brooklyn Museum, Brooklyn, New York
1969 Annual Print Show, Brooklyn Museum, Brooklyn, New York
1975 Political drawings from The New York Times, Musée des Arts Decoratifs, the Louvre, Paris, France
1977 One-Man Show, Corridor Gallery, New York City
1978 7th International Poster Biennale, Poland
1979 One-Man Show, Sindin Galleries, New York City
1980 One-Man Show, Kutztown Museum, Kutztown, Pennsylvania
1981 One-Man Show, Sindin Galleries, New York City; Images of Labor, District 1199, New York, Traveling Exhibition, Smithsonian Institution, Washington, D.C.
1982 One-Man Show, Galerie Philippe Guimiot, Belgium; One-Man Show, Harcourts Gallery, San Francisco, California
1983 One-Man Show, Sindin Galleries, New York City

Don Weller 287–289

He was born and raised in eastern Washington State, and received a Bachelor of Arts in Fine Arts at Washington State University.
He worked in various design studios in Los Angeles until 1965 when he began to freelance Graphic Design and Illustration, and to teach Design at the University of California at Los Angeles. In 1970 he formed a design studio with Dennis Juett, Weller & Juett, Inc. In 1973 he formed the Weller Institute for the Cure of Design, Inc. where he works at present in the capacity of "founder". He also taught design and illustration at Art Center College of Design.
Currently, projects of the Weller Institute include: Trademarks, Packaging, Annual Reports, Collateral Material, Industrial Film, Advertising and Editorial Illustrations, and limited publishing ventures.
Don Weller's work has appeared in all major Design Shows including The Art Director's Club of New York, Art Director's Club of Los Angeles, The One Show, Creativity, Communication Arts, Andy Awards, Graphis, Photo Graphis, Graphis Posters, Modern Publicity, The Society of Illustrators Exhibit, Illustration West, Bienale Uzile Grafiky Bruno, The American Institute of Graphic Arts, The Society of Publication Designers, The Type Directors Club, and more.
His awards include Gold Medals from The New York Art Directors Show, The One Show, The Los Angeles Art Directors Show, The West Coast Show and others including the famous Hugo Hammer Memorial Trophy.
His work has appeared in many publications including: CA, Idea, Graphics Today, Design, Print, Art Direction, Trade Marks and Symbols, The Book of American Trademarks, Signet Signal Symbol, and others.

Jim White 290

Place of Birth: Wyatt, Missouri
Date of Birth: Aug. 21, 1947
Awards: New York Society of Illustrators, Midwest Regional Shows and Awards Chicago Design & illustrators shows.
Past Works: Illustrations for Playboy and Penthouse magazines. Various calendars and posters. National & regional ads.
Present Clients: Palyboy. Foote, Cone & Belding. J. Walter Thompson. Leo Burnett. International Harvester. Cummins Diesel. Swift Foods. Nalco Chemical Co.
Collections: Work in business and private collections

Kim Whitesides 292

Place of Birth: Logan, Utah
Date of Birth: May 25, 1941
Awards: New York Art Directors Club – several awards of Merit – 1969–1981
Society of Illustrators – several awards – 1969–1975
Past Works: 8 covers for Rolling Stone, cover for Time magazine, posters and albums for Atlantic Records, Playboy magazine, United Airlines, Levi's, Paper Moon Graphics
Present Clients: Holland America Cruise Ships, Royale Cruise Lines, album cover for Steve Perry, catalog cover for Pottery Barn, Levi's, Paper Moon Graphics
Exhibitions: 1974 Greengrass Galley N.Y.C.
1975 University of Utah, Fine Arts Museum
1976 Good Company Gallery N.Y.C.
1981 Kimbau Art Center, Utah
1983 Old Town Gallery, Utah
1984 Tivoli Gallery, Utah

Terry Widener 293

Place of Birth: Tulsa, Oklahoma
Date of Birth: Dec. 15, 1950
Awards: American Illustration
Society of Illustrators
Graphis Annual
Art Directors Club of New York
print Magazine
Art Directors Club of Houston
Dallas Society of Visual Communications
Past Works: Northern Telecommunications Quarterly Report
Pepsi Cola-Various advertising illustrations
The Rouse Company-Illustrations for shopping mall campaigns
Paul Broadhead & Assoc.-Illustrations for shopping mall campaigns
Dallas Jazz Orchestra Poster
Present Clients: American Airlines
13–30 Corporation
Texas Monthly Magazine
Boston Magazine
D Magazine
American Way Magazine
Westward Magazine
Continental Trailways
Exhibitions: Society of Illustrators 26th Annual Exhibition
100 of Tomorrows Great Illustrators, Master Eagle Gallery, New York

Larry C. Winborg 294

He was born in Idaho Falls, Idaho, March 12, 1942.
Received BFA 1964 and MFA 1967 at Utah State University, Logan, Utah. Larry's work has been consistently exhibited and published in the New York Society of Illustrators Annual Show and publication. He has also exhibited his work in the Utah Watercolor Society, Graphis Annual, and Los Angeles Society of Illustrators.
Larry's clients have included: Proctor & Gamble, Warner Publications, Owen-Illinois, Audubon Society, Franklin Mint, Coca Cola, Helene Curtis, Latter Day Saints Church, Money Magazine, IBM, Mead Paper Company, Quaker Oats, Terracor, Standard Energy Company, Bonneville International, Catepillar Tractor, Jewel Tea Company, Sports Illustrated Magazine, Marriott Corp., ITT
His work is owned by many private collectors.

Ron Wolin 295

Place of Birth: Brooklyn, New York
Date of Birth: November 11, 1942
Awards: Graphis Annual, AIGA, Creativity, New York Society of Illustrators, Los Angeles Society of Illustrators, Belding Awards
Past Works: Mural for UCLA, cover for Getty Oil Co. Annual Report, poster for the movie "Greystone"
Present Clients: UA, MGM, Honda, Vivitar, UCLA, N.F.L., Doubleday Books, RCA Records, T.W.A., Toyota, Boys Life Magazine, PSA Airlines

Bruce Wolfe 296–297

Bruce Wolfe was born in Los Angeles, California, March 29, 1941. He had a show of his portraits in San Francisco and completed a bronze sculpture for the S.F. Opera House. He has shown his work in many graphic exhibitions including a show of his work in Paris, France. He has been the recipient of awards from many shows including the Art Directors Club of LA, Best of Show-Illustration West, Outdoor Advertising award, Foster & Kleiser Award, S.F. Society of Communication Arts Award of Excellence, Zellerbach Award, West Coast Show Award, The Show and Communication Arts magazine awards, also Society of Illustrators citation for Merit, and the S.F. Cable Car awards. His present clients Are: Celestial Seasonings, Henry Weinhard, Levi-Strauss, Lucas Films, Paper Moon, Playboy Magazine, San Miguel International, Southern Pacific, Volvo, Gallo Wine, Oroweat, Mastercraft Press, Bank of America and General Cigar.

Teresa Woodward 298

Teresa Woodward was born in San Diego, Califronia. She grew up in Northern California, Sacramento, where she attended and graduated from Sacramento Junior (City) College where she studied painting under Wayne Thiebaud.
She later attended Chouinard Art Institute, The Art Center College of Design, U.C.L.A. and USC, The University of Southern California.
Her illustration and design work has been utilized for television, packaging, posters, books, advertising, brochures, products and environmental graphics. It has been represented in The American Institute of Graphic Arts, Communication Arts Magazine, Graphis Magazine, The Art Directors Clubs and The Societies of Illustrators of both New York and Los Angeles. She has made numerous presentations of her work in various cities and has been a judge in many illustration and design shows.
She is past president of The Los Angeles Society of Illustrators and the initiator of The Los angeles Chapter of The Graphic Artists Guild.
As a freelance illustrator-designer, she has also taught illustration, design and drawing at The California State Universities in Long Beach, Northridge, University of Southern California and The Art Center College of Design.
Teresa is also a painter and is presently working towards a show regarding The Mexican Revolution in which her father participated as a Colonel under President Madero. She is painting the involvement of the women's role as soldiers.
Shie resides in Pacific Palisades, the coastal area of Los Angeles.

Y

Gary Yealdhall 299

Gary Yealdhall – 26; Illustrator joining Eucalyptus Tree in 1980; attended the Maryland Institute of Art. Recognition in 1981 and 1982 Print Regional Issue, Upper and Lower Case Magazine, Graphis Annual and Graphis Poster Annual, Best in Baltimore, Washington Art Director's Show. Lectured at the Maryland Institiue of Art and George Washington University (Washington Art Director's Career Day). Teaching illustration at the Maryland Institute of Art.
Clients: McDonald's
Visa Fabrics
Choice
U.S. News & World Report
Video Games Magazine
National Geographic
Letraset
AT&T
American Film Magazine

Z

James Courtney Zar 300

I am an aritst whose love of realism in subject matter has determined the course of direction I have sought in accumulating information from post masters and present giants to form a working teachnique that has proven reliable over the past fifteen years.
In my formative years as a student, I studied at the Art Institute of San Francisco. For five years I studied privately, off and on, with the great Keith Finch, and was greatly influenced by Joe Hales and Raymond Escar or San Jose Junior College. Despire the aid of these talented men and resourceful institutions, I was to a great extent lost as to a deep conviction of where and in what mode of expression my energies should be best channeled.
For me, art has been an obsession and an enigma that stubbornly given up her secrets only to the extent that I have been willing to go to any extreme of time and investigation to acquire the technical knowledge in order to experience any degree of freedom in performance.
I am a fanatic worshipper of excellence in life's drama of performers, be they football players, body builders, actors, singers, musicians, writers, philosophers, businessmen — you name it. If someone excels, I want to know what they do and why it works.
This summation documents a personal Dream-Come-True. It also reaffirms the conviction of such success-philosophers as Napoleon Hill, that only through the emulation of excellence

can a person hope to achieve his or her desired result in their chosen field of endeavor.

My Dream-Come-True is the actual face-to-face meeting with my contemporary artist-heroes who, through their published works in paperback covers, posters and art books, have been my silent and hitherto distant reachers.

Slowly but surely, by breaking down, analyzing and reconstructing my hero-artist's words—time and time again in pencil drawings and oil sketches, I was able to incorporate some of their strong points into a personal and comfortable approach to as workable technique that to this day, thogh subject to variation as needs arise, remains solid and workable. Today I double as a commercial artist and fine arts painter, a line of demarcation that is ever less visible in the field of painting in this present era.

Place of Birth: San Pedro, Clifornia
Date of Birth: July 3, 1941
Education: San Pedro High School — footabll team captain and Marine League Player of the Year in 1959; Valley College football team 1961
Present Clients: Los Angeles Dodgers; Entertainment Marketing Corp.: Los Angeles Raiders; Muscle & Fitness Magzine; Pro Mangazine
Past Work: Desert Magazine; New Mexico Magazine; Lincoln Mercury; Rendezvous Magazine; many team posters of leading professional sports teams including Minnesota Vikings, Baltimore Colts, Los Angeles Rams, Los Angeles Dodgers, California Angels, San Francisco Giants, Oakland Raiders, Stanford University, Pittsburgh Pirates, and others; Heroic Bodybuilder paintings of Joe Weiders Superstars, Mike Boyer and Valerie Coe, Chris Dickerson, Lou Ferrigno and Richelle Sepeda, Franco Columbu; portraits of Arnold Schwartzeneegger, Steve Garvey Frank Sinatra, Tom Fears, Merlin Olsen, Terry Donahue and others, most in private collections
Awards: First Place Port of Los Angeles Bicentennial Art Show 1976; Peoples Choice Award Los Angeles City Bicennial Art Show 1976; Peoples choce Award Los Angelle City Bicentennial Art Show 1976; Gold Medal from American cowboy Association

Brian Zick 301

Place of Birth: Los Angeles, California
Date of Birth: 1949
Past Works: Lots and lots of work for several major airlines, department stores and movie studios. Soft drink, dairy product, coffee, banking, feminine hygiene, panty hose and blue jean advertisers as well as assignments from a number of magazines and record companies
Present Works: Lots more of the same
Exhibitions: Only a few small, intimate, almost private showings for a very special (one might even say elite) clientele
Collections: personal collections of many famous artists, publishers, personalities and bon vivants

John Zielinski 302

Born in Chicago, Il., 1945. Graduated Chicago Academy of Fine Arts, and worked for Illustrator's Workshop and Milton Glaser Workshop. He has various clients like World Book Encyclopedia, Playboy magazine, Tribune magazine, Encyclopedia Britanica, and so on.

My influences include those artists who sometimes depict in a straightforward manner, quite ordinary subjects in strange and unusual circumstances. Magritte, Hopper, Diane Arbus are among those whose work I greatly admire.

Andy Zito 303

Andy Zito attended Art Center College of Design from 1964 to 1967. He is a freelance illustrator in Los Angeles where he has had a studio for the last 13 years.

His work has appeared in the New York Art Directors Club Show, AIGA Show and Permanent Collection, Los Angeles and New York Illustrators Shows and numerous other commercial art publications.

Some of his current clients are listed below:
CBS Records, Atalantic Records, California Magazine, Paper Moon Graphics, Texas Instruments, McCann-Erickson, Young and Rubicam, J. Walter Thompson, Chiat/Day Advertising, Grey Advertising, National Football League Properties

COLLABORATORS LIST

Harvey Kahn
Address & Telephone: 50 E. 50th St., N.Y. N.Y. 10022 (212) 752-8490
Represents: Bob Peak, Gerry Gersten, Wilson McLean, Alan E. Cober, Nicholas Gaetano, Bernard Fuchs

Vicki Morgan
Address & Telephone: 194 3rd Ave, N.Y. N.Y. (212) 475-0440
Represents: Tim Lewis, Richard Mantel, Brian Zick, Ray Cruz, Joe and Kathy Heiner Emanuel Schongut

Darwin Bahm
Address & Telephone: 6 Jane St., N.Y. N.Y. (212) 989-7074
Represents: Jullien Allen, Robert Weaver, Joan Landis, Rick Meyerowitz, Don Ivan Punchatz

Jane Lander Associates
Address & Telephone: 333 E 30th St., N.Y. N.Y. (212) 355-0910
Represents: Tom Ballenger, Francois Cloteaux, Phil Franké, Helene Guetary, Cathy Heck, Saul Lambert, Jack Pardue, Frank Riley, Barron Storey

Margo Feiden Galleries
Address & Telephone: 51 E. 10th St., N.Y. N.Y. 10003 (212) 677-5330
Represents: Albert Hirschfeld

Alex Ducane
Represents: Cynthia Marsh, Jim Salvati, Holly Hollington

Kathy Brown Represents
Address & Telephone: 425A Bryant St., San Francisco, CA. 94107 (415) 543-7377
Represents: Anka Ente

Sell, Inc. (Dan Sell)
Address & Telephone: 233 E. Wacker, Chicago Il. (312) 565-2701
Represents: Justin Carroll, Bobbye Cochran, Jerry Dadds, Bill Ersland, Dick Flood, Dave LaFleur, Greg Manchess, Bill Mayer, Jim Owens, Richard Waldrep, Gary Yealdhall, Jay, R.J. Shay, Frank K. Morris. Dale C. Vezaal, John Zielinski

Jacqueline Dedell
Address & Telephone: 58 W 15th St., N.Y. N.Y. (212) 741-2539
Represents: Teresa Fasolino, Ivan Powel

あとがきに代えて————藤井 聖

「アメリカがくしゃみをすると、日本が風邪をひく」などと、よくいわれます。これは、両者が密接な関係にあって、アメリカの影響を受けやすい日本のことを、端的に皮肉ったことばですが、いま日本のイラストレーションについて考えてみても、このたとえ話を否定することはできません。日本のイラストレーターたちは、何らかの形でアメリカのイラストレーションに影響を受けてきました。

外国の美術館を見て歩くと経験することですが、日本の著名な画家たちのスタイルのオリジンともいえるものによくぶつかります。誰それはこの人の影響を受けていたのかと、初めてわかったりするのですが、イラストレーションの場合も同じで、日本のイラストレーターたちは多かれ少なかれ、アメリカのイラストレーションに啓発されてきました。第2次大戦後、とくに1960年代中頃からは、アメリカン・イラストレーションを模倣してきたといっても過言ではないでしょう。ポップアートしかり、エアブラシ・テクニックしかり、スーパー・レアリズム、ナイーブイズム等々、みなアメリカのあとを追うようにして流行を見てきました。イラストレーションを含む日本のデザイン界そのものが、アメリカに学び、アメリカを手本としてやってきました。

いまや日米の間はきわめて近くなり、電波回線の発達によって、ロサンゼルス・オリンピックのニュースが同時中継で日本のテレビに映る時代ですから、両国間の情報伝達の早さには驚かされます。きょうニューヨークで見かけたものが、あすはもう銀座にも現われるといったスピードです。アメリカの影響を日本がすぐ受けるというのも、当然といえなくもありません。

とはいっても、アメリカのイラストレーションなるものは、せいぜい60～70年の歴史しかなく、そのうち日本がもっとも影響を受けているのは1960年代からで、わずか20年間ということになりますが、しかしこの20年間は、アメリカのイラストレーションが著しい変化をとげた時代でした。ここで、簡単に、アメリカのイラストレーションの流れを追ってみたいと思います。

その前に、イラストレーションなるものについてちょっと触れますと、これはもともと、目に見えないものを視覚化(Visualize)することからきているといわれています。たとえば、実際に見ることの出来ない宇宙の構造が、"想像の創造"(Creative imagination)で天体図のように見ることができますし、あるいは、実際に行ったことのないところでも、地図の上では具体的に地形や位置などを知ることが出来ます。この天体図化や地図化が、イラストレーションの発生にかかわっているといってよいでしょう。そして、これが絵画的な意味で使われるようになったのは、ビアズレーがオスカー・ワイルドの「サロメ」の文章を視覚化し、イギリスの詩人ウィリアム・ブレイクが、自らの文章に挿絵をつけた頃からだと思います。

ところで、アメリカのイラストレーションですが、その始まりというと1910年代でした。アメリカのイラストレーション史上のパイオニアともいえるハーワード・パイルやフレデリック・レミントンが出、1920年代ではN.C.ワイエス、マックスフィールド・パリッシュなどが輩出しました。彼らは、西部開拓史や南北戦争の歴史、日常の生活などを、理想化された美しいものとして、ロマンチックに描いていました。いわば、当時は、報道的イラスト、日記風イラストともいえる時代でした。

1930年代になると、ノーマン・ロックウェル、ジョン・ヘラルド・ジュニア、ロックウェル・ケントなどが活躍します。いまやアメリカイラスト界の巨匠とも呼ばれるノーマン・ロックウェルが、「ザ・サタデー・イヴニング・ポスト」などにロックウェル調とも呼ばれる甘いロマンスとファンタジーに満ち満ちた作品を発表しました。

1940年代から50年代中頃にかけて、アメリカのイラストレーションに新しい表現形式が加わります。オースチン・ブリッグス、ローレン・フォックス、ロバート・ウィーバー、アルフレッド・パーカー、デイヴィッド・ストーン・マーチン、フランクリン・マクマホン、ミルトン・グレーサー、シーモア・クワストなどがこの頃に抬頭してきます。今世紀の偉大な作家の一人であるロバート・ウィーバーは、雑誌「フォーチュン」や「ライフ」「タイム」などを舞台に、作品を次々と発表しました。

いま、プレイボーイ・エンタープライズの副社長であるアーサー・ポールが、「プレイボーイ」誌のアート・ディレクターに就任したのは1953年でした。彼は「プレイボーイ」誌によってシカゴ派と呼ばれるアーティストたちを育成し、いまもまだ世界各地の若いアーティストたちに影響を与え続けています。若い人たちにとって、「プレイボーイ」誌に載るということは、アーティストへの一種の登竜門であり、いまだに投稿のやむ日がありません。同誌のアート・デパートメント・ディレクターの机の上や横には、世界中の若いアーティストから送られてきた作品が山積みされています。ミッドウェストを代表する作家としては、ロジャー・ブラウン、エド・パシフ、シーモア・ソロコフスキー、F.A.シェラーなどを挙げることが出来ます。

ミルトン・グレイサーとシーモア・クワストが"プッシュピン・スタジオ"を設立したのも、1954年でした。ここのスタジオからも多くの有能な人材が輩出しています。その主なるアーティストとしては、いまは亡きJ・シンダー、エド・ソレル、イサドラ・セルツァー、D・パラディーニ、J・コリナー、そしてただ一人の日本人ハルオ宮内などがいます。宮内は1971年から9年間、このスタジオに在籍しました。プッシュピンの活動が、世界中の人々にグラフィック・イラストというものを浸透させ、刺激を与えたといっても過言ではないでしょう。

さて、1960年代になると、ロバート・ウィーバー、N・ボイル、G・ガースティンなどが活躍しますし、60年代の後半には、R・フォックス、バーナード・フックス、ダニエル・シュワルツ、クリフォード・A・コンダック、ロバート・ピーク、ロバート・A・パーカーなどの活躍が特筆されます。また、ビクター・モスコーソー、マウス＆ケリー、ミック・グリフィンなど、ルミカラー(蛍光色)、サイケデリック・アート等の流行の波となったサンフランシスコのヒッピー・アーティストたちが抬頭したのもこの頃でした。彼らが日本の横尾忠則などのアーティストたちに与えた影響は大きかったと思います。

やはり同じ頃、チャールス・ホワイト3世やキム・ホワイトサイズ、デイディッド・ウィルダーソンなどによって、エアブラシ・テクニックが確立されました。それまでのエアブラシというと、写真等を修正するための一技法にしかすぎなかったものが、彼らによって初めて、絵画やイラストレーションの世界に市民権を獲得したのでした。そして、そのあとを受け継いで、エアブラシ・イラストレーションをより一段と向上・発展させたのがピーター・ロイド、ピーター・パロンビー、長岡秀星たちです。いま日本でも、山口はるみ、空山基、斎藤雅緒、大西洋介など、エアブラシを使っている人たちは少なくありません。

1970年代に入ると、アメリカのイラストレーションは、二つの大きな流れに分かれます。一つはニューヨークを中心とする東海岸、もう一つはロサンゼルスとサンフランシスコを中心とした西海岸のイラストレーションです。

ニューヨークは、いうまでもなく、書籍・雑誌等の出版、演劇、広告、金融、コミュニケーション・メディアの中心地であり、ロサンゼルスとサンフランシスコは、映画、テレビ、レコード産業の中心地です。それで、イラストレーションのほうも、それぞれの土地柄に合ったものが盛んになりました。たとえば、ニューヨークのイラストレーターは、「ニューヨーカー」「エスクワイア」「MS」「サイコロジー・ツゥデイ」「ニューヨーク・タイムス」「スポーツ・イラストレイテッド」などの雑誌を舞台に創作活動をしています。マーシャル・アリスマンやスー・コーなど、それまではタブーとされていた暴力、セックス、社会の裏面をテーマにした強烈な個性のイラストレーションが世に出たのも、ニューヨークならではのことでした。同様に、エドワード・ソレル、デイヴィド・レバイン、ブラッド・ホーランド、ラーナン・ルリーといった人たちの風刺作品も、いろいろな雑誌や新聞に登場しています。雑誌のカバー・イラスト、挿絵…、氾濫するほどに出ているおびただしい数の雑誌が、アメリカのイラストレーションの隆盛に貢献していることは確かです。ロサンゼルスのほうでいえば、先に挙げたエアブラシのアーティスト——ピーター・ロイドやピーター・パロンビー、ジェフ・ワックなどは、レコード・ジャケットの仕事で世に出た人たちです。

ところで、現代アメリカのイラストレーションには、これら東海岸、西海岸のどちらにも属さないものがあります。一つは、中部イリノイ州シカゴを中心としたアーティストのグループで、これには今世紀の偉大な作家F・マクマホンや、先にも触れましたが「プレイボーイ」誌で活躍した人たちです。また、ほかには、「レージング・ブル」「インディ・ジョーンズ」などの映画ポスターや「プレイボーイ」の仕事で第一線に躍り出たクニオ・ハギオ、レアリスティック・イラストレーターのビル・ビックサノビックやキヌコ・クラフト、漫画的イラストのチャック・スラックなどがいます（キヌコ・クラストは現在コネチカット州在住）。

南部へ行くと、ジョージア州のアトランタやテキサス州のダラス、ルイジアナ州のニューオーリアンズなど、かつては"不毛の南部"といわれたところにも、新しいアーティストが抬頭してきています。アトランタではルイス・メイヤー、R・マクドナルド（現在はカリフォルニア州在住）、テキサスではB・フォーブス、アイバン・パンチェス、アレックス・ムロスキーなどを挙げることが出来、大都会から地方への分散が見られるようになってきています。大都市で成功したアーティストたちが故郷へUターンしたり、田舎へ安らぎの地を求めて都会を去る傾向もあります。キム・ホワイトサイズ、ボブ・ピーク、マーク・イングリッシュ、ジョン・コナリーなどがその例です。

また、最近の傾向として、ナンセンスやパロディ風のイラストがうけ、ルー・ブルックスやボブ・ゾレル、G・パンター、ミック・ハガティーなどが新しい分野へ野心的なチャレンジをしていますし、SFのリチャード・クリューガー、ファンタジーのロバート・エベル、フランク・フラゼッタ、ロエーナ・モリエール、ボリヤス・バレーホ等なども活躍しています。

日本からアメリカへ渡ったイラストレーターたちの活躍も忘れてはならないでしょう。昨今ではロサンゼルスの長岡秀星、マモル・シモコウチ、トム・トミタ、「スター・ウォーズ」の映画ポスター・イラストで知られるサンフランシスコ在住の佐野一彦、シカゴのキヌコ・クラフト、ニューヨークの三橋陽子、津上久三など、アメリカで成功し、逆に影響を与えている人たちです。まだここ10年のことではありますが、特筆してもよいだろうと思います。

以上、駆け足でアメリカのイラストレーションの流れを述べました。わずか60～70年の間にどのような人たちが活躍して今日に至っているかがわかると思います。そして、それは、彼らアメリカのイラストレーターたちの、つねに未来へ向ったあくなき探求と努力の結果であることを知るべきであります。

アメリカのアーティストたちの作品を集成した本は、「ニューヨーク・イラストレーターズ・アニュアル」「ニューヨーク・アート・ディレクターズ・アニュアル」「AIGA・アニュアル」「パブリケーショーン・デザイナース」などのほか、「アート・ディレクターズ・インデックス」や「アメリカン・ショーケース」など、アーティストたちが仕事を得るための本まで数多く出版されています。しかし、そのいずれもが、東海岸や西海岸、シカゴなどの限られた人々のものばかりです。その点、本書は、東西中南部全般にわたるアーティストを収録しているところに特色があると思います。

また、既存の大家たちから新人までを紹介して、新旧アーティストの作風が一見してわかるようにしたことも、本書の特徴といえるでしょう。いまは、大家と呼ばれる人たちの多くが、若手を育てる側にまわっていますし、新人ではあっても、現代アメリカのイラストレーションを代表する力量を十分にそなえているからです。

広い広いアメリカには、ほかにも優れたアーティストがたくさんいます。本書に収録出来なかった人たちの作品は、またの機会にまとめたいと考えています。本書が、アメリカのイラストレーションに関心を持つ多くの方々に受け入れられるなら、望外のよろこびであります。

コーディネーター	藤井 聖／マーシャル・アリスマン
カバー・扉イラストレーション	武田育雄
デザイン・レイアウト	柳川研一
写植印字	株式会社 萩原印刷所
版下製作	株式会社 萩原印刷所

イラストレーションU.S.A.

1984年10月25日　初版第1刷発行

定　価	13,500円
編集者	藤井 聖
発行者	久世利郎
印刷所	凸版印刷株式会社
製本所	凸版製本株式会社
発行所	株式会社グラフィック社
	〒102 東京都千代田区九段北1-9-12
	電話03(263)4318 振替 東京3-114345

乱丁・落丁本はお取替えいたします。

ISBN4-7661-0321-1 C3071 ¥13500E